JAG
18.99

GN
TR⊘

APR   2012

Lewis Trondheim

Approximate Continuum Comics

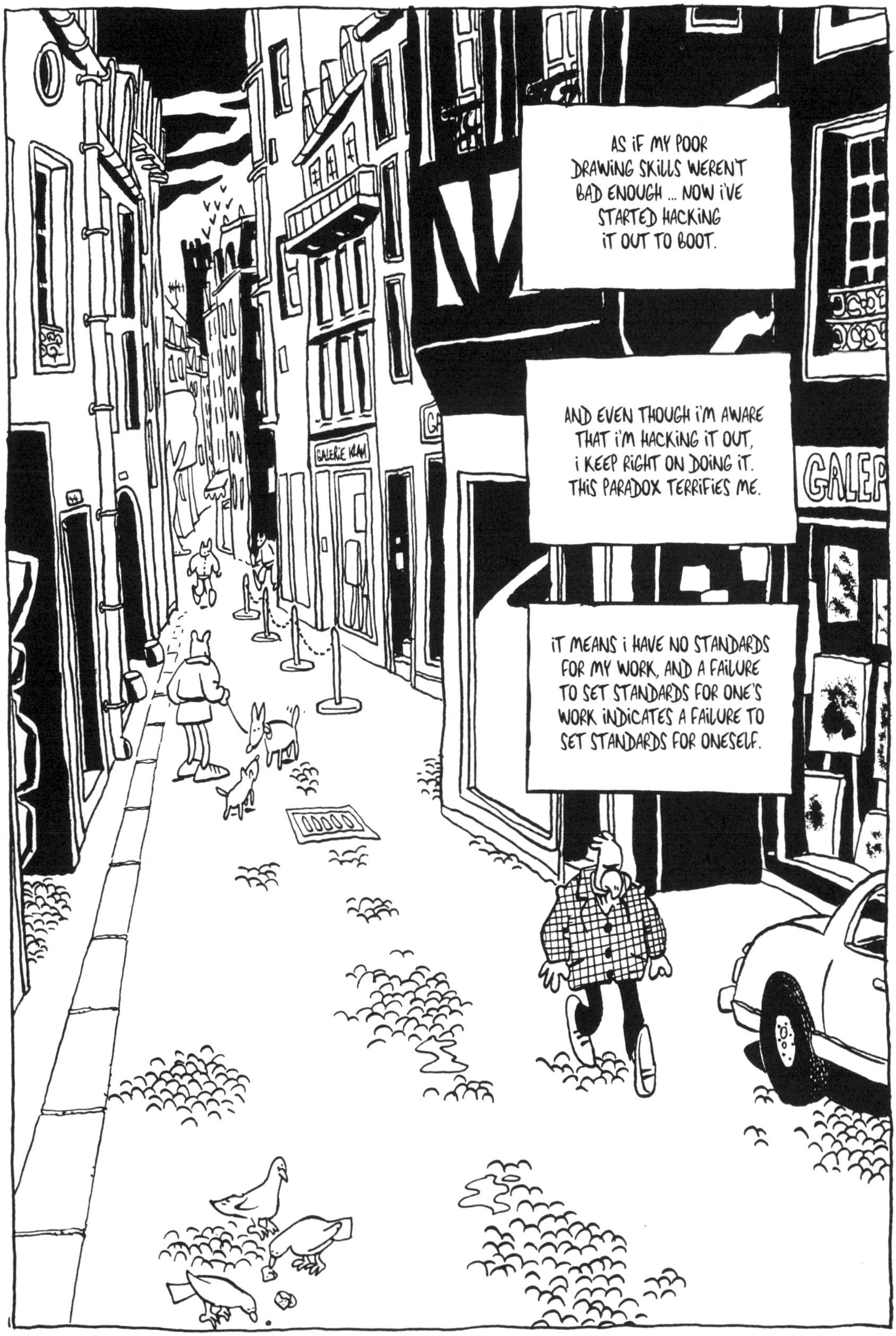
AS iF MY POOR DRAWiNG SKiLLS WEREN'T BAD ENOUGH ... NOW i'VE STARTED HACKiNG iT OUT TO BOOT.
AND EVEN THOUGH i'M AWARE THAT i'M HACKiNG iT OUT, i KEEP RiGHT ON DOiNG iT. THiS PARADOX TERRiFiES ME.
iT MEANS i HAVE NO STANDARDS FOR MY WORK, AND A FAiLURE TO SET STANDARDS FOR ONE'S WORK iNDiCATES A FAiLURE TO SET STANDARDS FOR ONESELF.
GALERiE

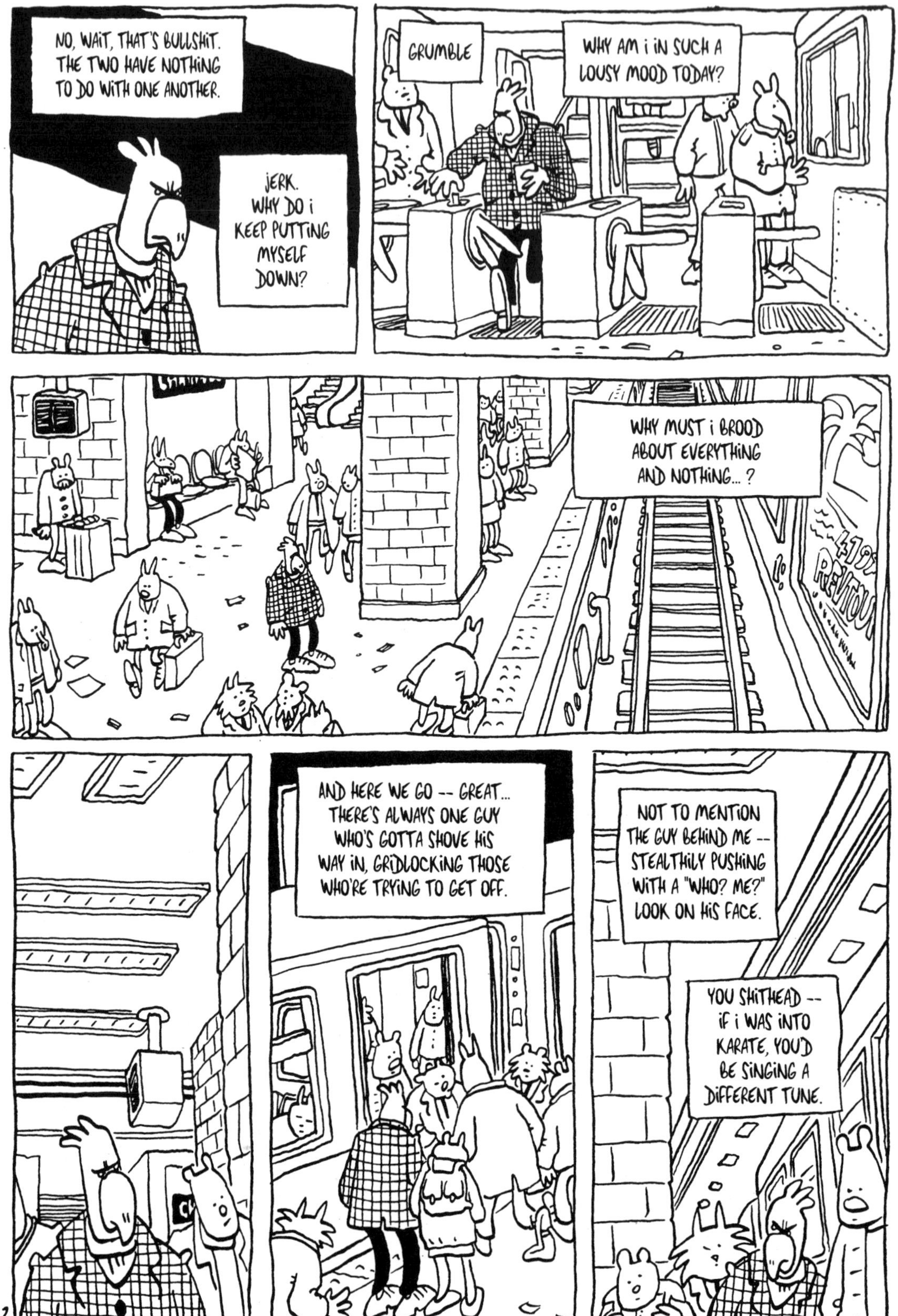
NO, WAIT, THAT'S BULLSHIT. THE TWO HAVE NOTHING TO DO WITH ONE ANOTHER.
JERK. WHY DO i KEEP PUTTING MYSELF DOWN?
GRUMBLE
WHY AM i iN SUCH A LOUSY MOOD TODAY?
WHY MUST i BROOD ABOUT EVERYTHING AND NOTHING... ?
AND HERE WE GO -- GREAT... THERE'S ALWAYS ONE GUY WHO'S GOTTA SHOVE HIS WAY IN, GRIDLOCKING THOSE WHO'RE TRYING TO GET OFF.
NOT TO MENTION THE GUY BEHIND ME -- STEALTHILY PUSHING WITH A "WHO? ME?" LOOK ON HIS FACE.
YOU SHITHEAD -- iF i WAS INTO KARATE, YOU'D BE SINGING A DIFFERENT TUNE.

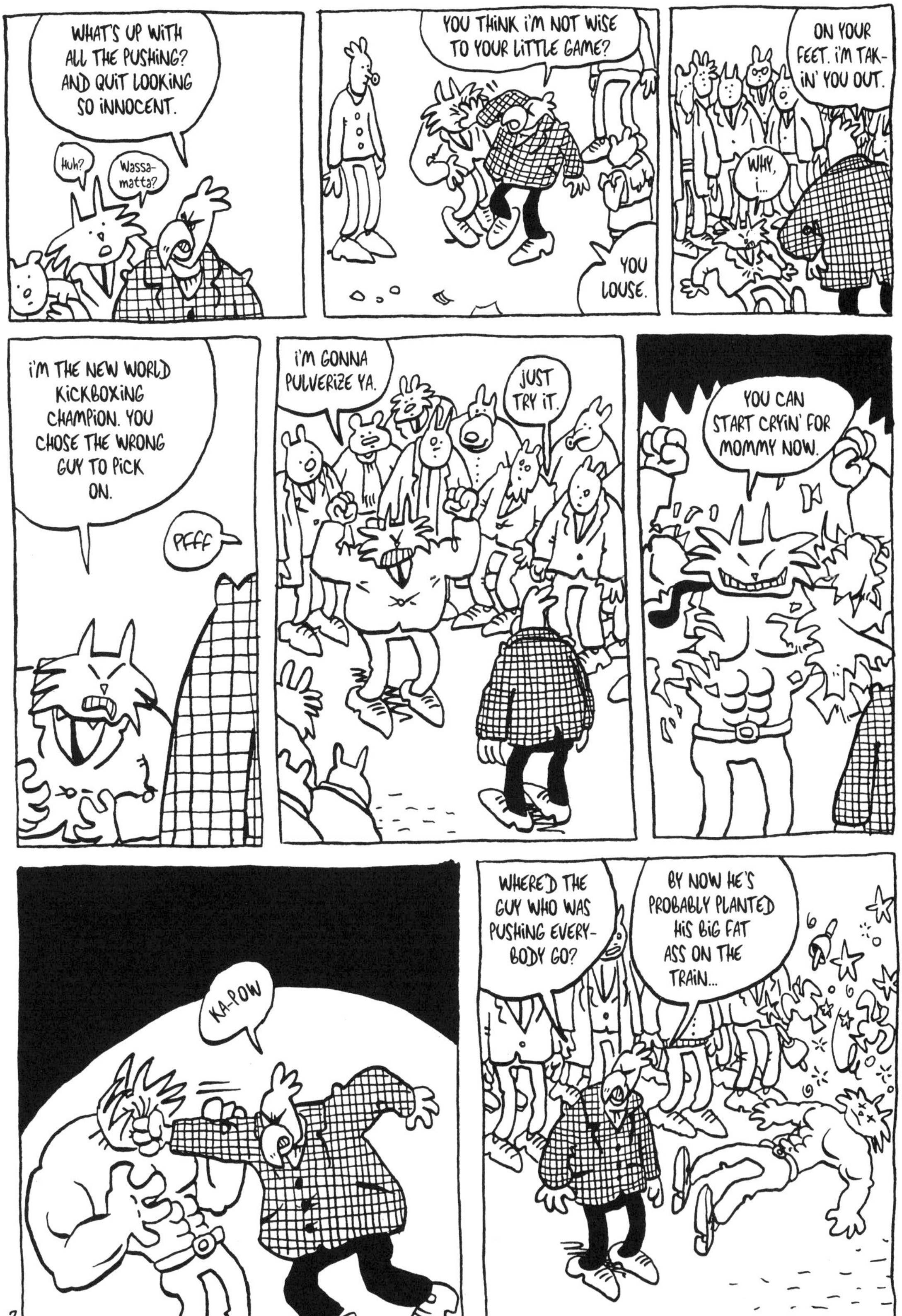
WHAT'S UP WITH ALL THE PUSHING? AND QUIT LOOKING SO INNOCENT.
Huh?
Wassa-matta?
YOU THINK I'M NOT WISE TO YOUR LITTLE GAME?
YOU LOUSE.
ON YOUR FEET. I'M TAK-IN' YOU OUT.
WHY, I...
I'M THE NEW WORLD KICKBOXING CHAMPION. YOU CHOSE THE WRONG GUY TO PICK ON.
PFFF
I'M GONNA PULVERIZE YA.
JUST TRY IT.
YOU CAN START CRYIN' FOR MOMMY NOW.
KA-POW
WHERE'D THE GUY WHO WAS PUSHING EVERY-BODY GO?
BY NOW HE'S PROBABLY PLANTED HIS BIG FAT ASS ON THE TRAIN...

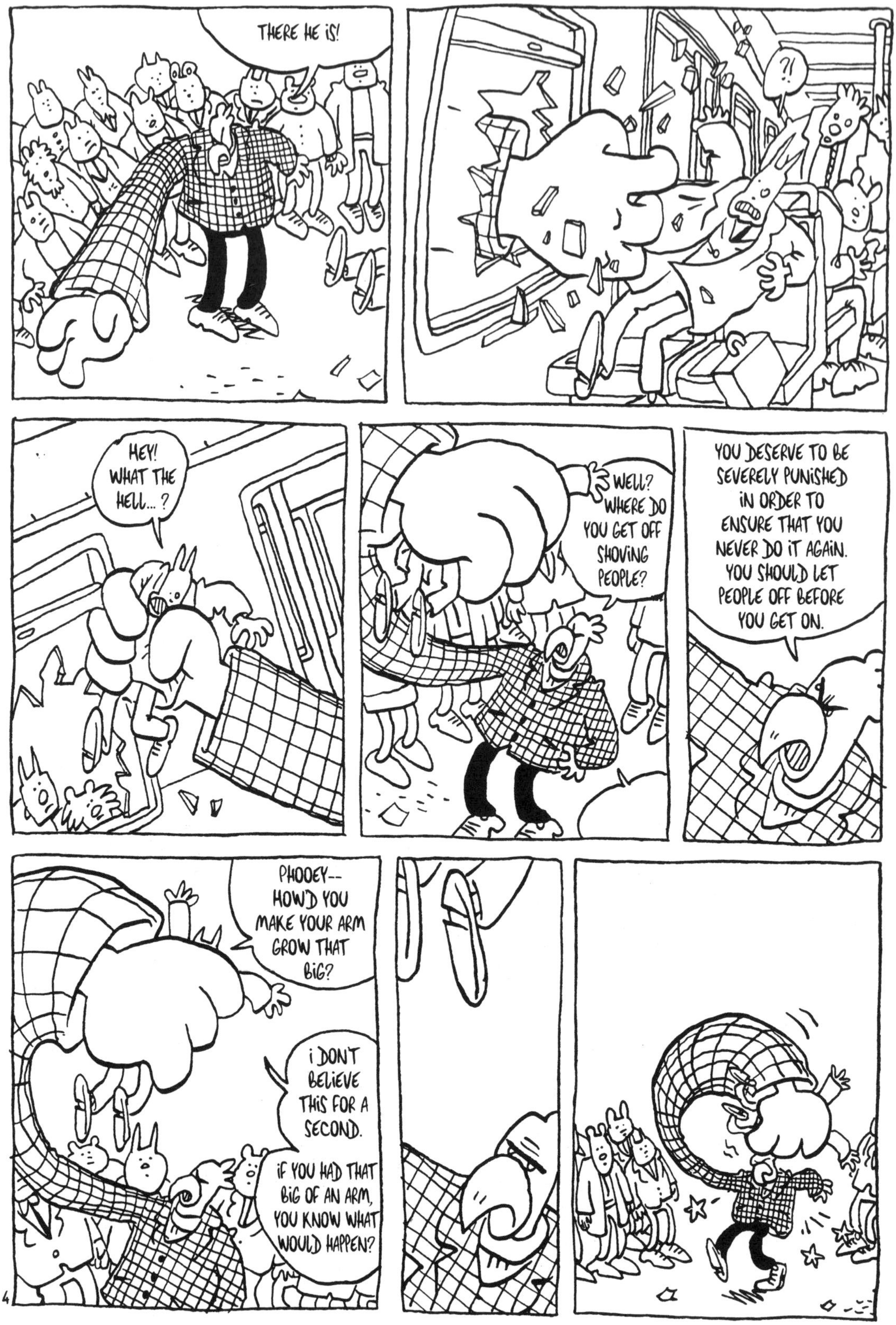
THERE HE iS!
?!
HEY! WHAT THE HELL...?
WELL? WHERE DO YOU GET OFF SHOViNG PEOPLE?
YOU DESERVE TO BE SEVERELY PUNiSHED iN ORDER TO ENSURE THAT YOU NEVER DO iT AGAiN. YOU SHOULD LET PEOPLE OFF BEFORE YOU GET ON.
PHOOEY-- HOW'D YOU MAKE YOUR ARM GROW THAT BiG?
i DON'T BELiEVE THiS FOR A SECOND.
iF YOU HAD THAT BiG OF AN ARM, YOU KNOW WHAT WOULD HAPPEN?

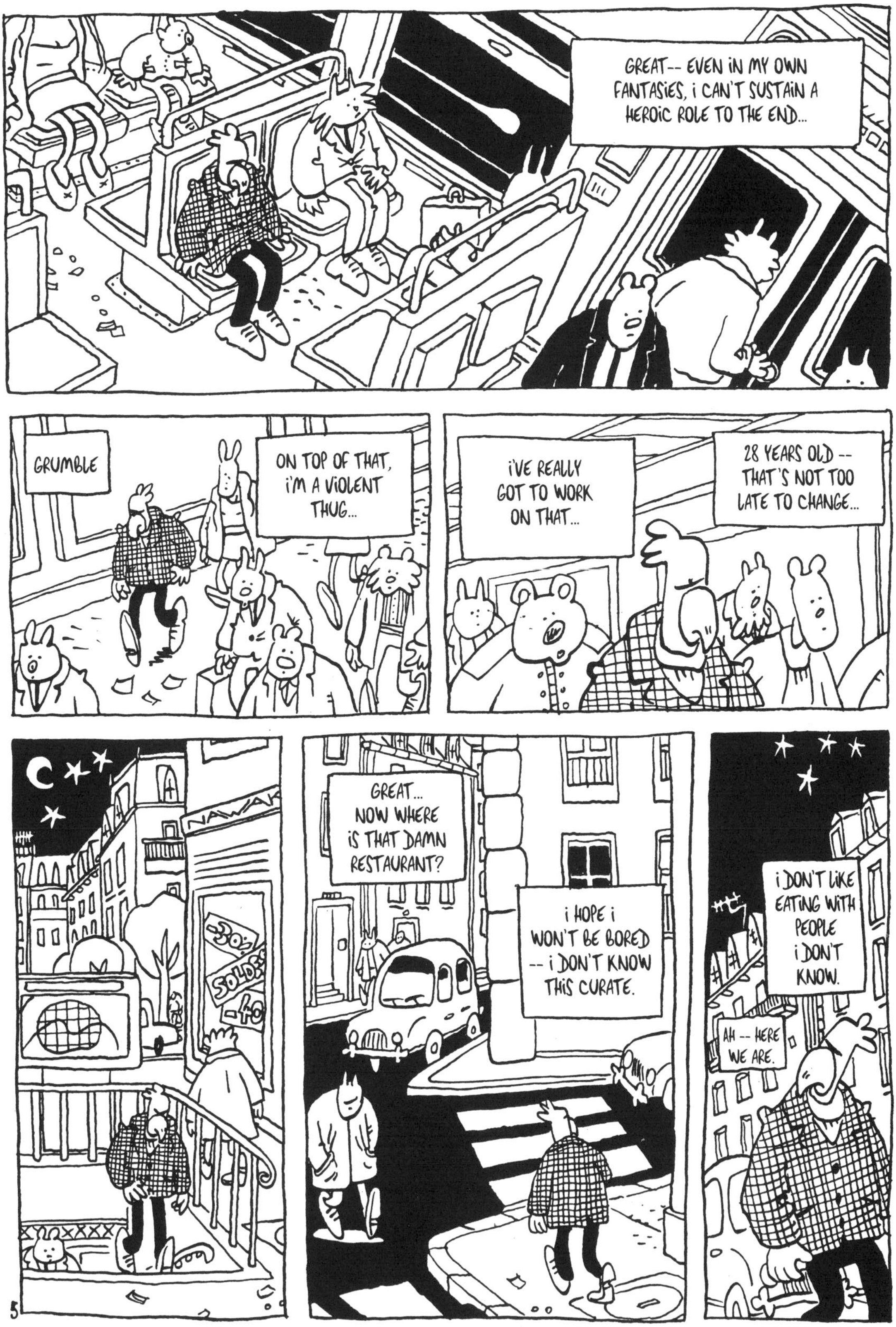
GREAT-- EVEN IN MY OWN FANTASIES, I CAN'T SUSTAIN A HEROIC ROLE TO THE END...
GRUMBLE
ON TOP OF THAT, I'M A VIOLENT THUG...
I'VE REALLY GOT TO WORK ON THAT...
28 YEARS OLD -- THAT'S NOT TOO LATE TO CHANGE...
NAWAK
-30%
SOLDES
-40
GREAT... NOW WHERE IS THAT DAMN RESTAURANT?
I HOPE I WON'T BE BORED -- I DON'T KNOW THIS CURATE.
I DON'T LIKE EATING WITH PEOPLE I DON'T KNOW.
AH -- HERE WE ARE.

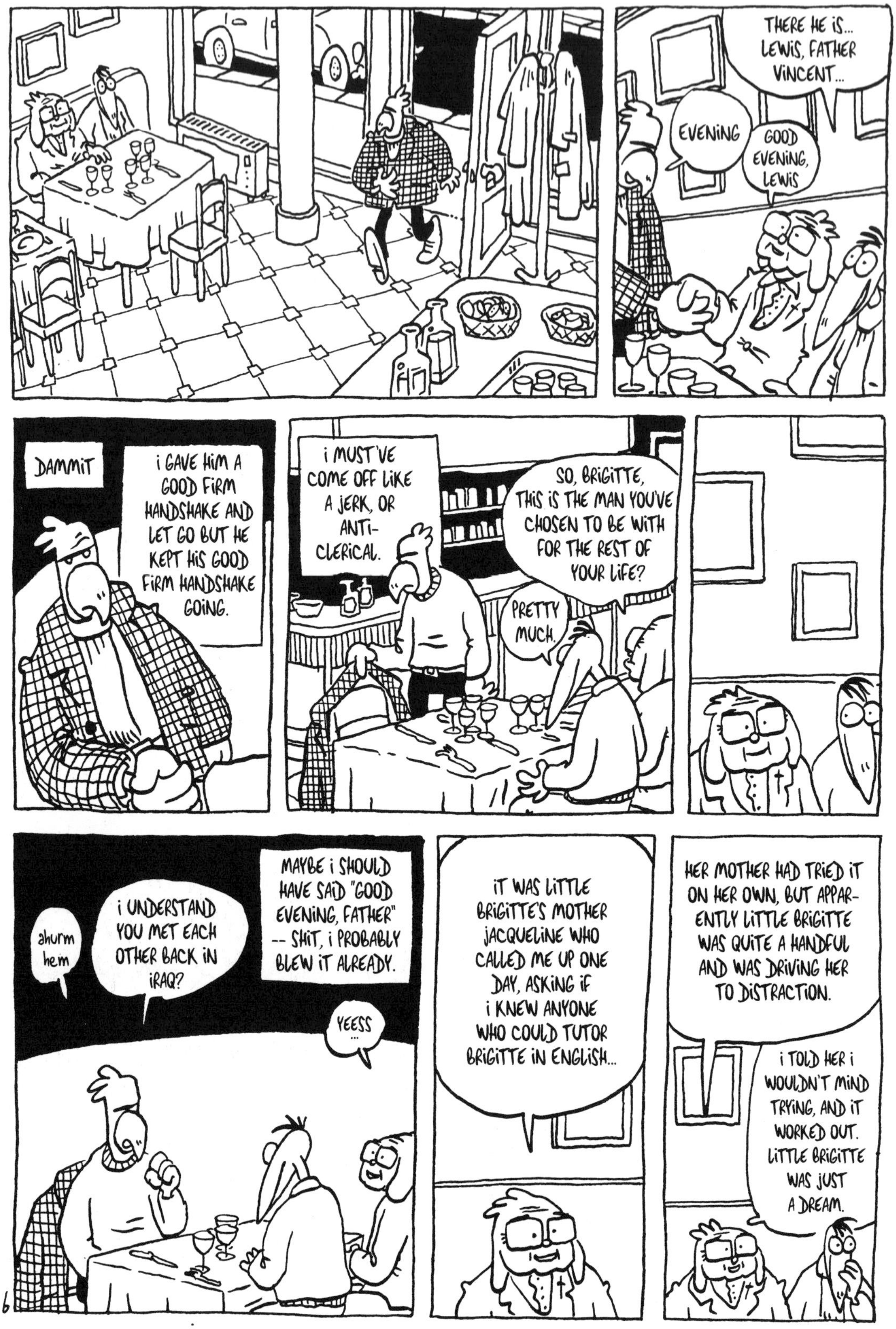
THERE HE IS... LEWIS, FATHER VINCENT...
EVENING
GOOD EVENING, LEWIS
DAMMIT
I GAVE HIM A GOOD FIRM HANDSHAKE AND LET GO BUT HE KEPT HIS GOOD FIRM HANDSHAKE GOING.
I MUST'VE COME OFF LIKE A JERK, OR ANTI-CLERICAL.
SO, BRIGITTE, THIS IS THE MAN YOU'VE CHOSEN TO BE WITH FOR THE REST OF YOUR LIFE?
PRETTY MUCH.
ahurm hem
I UNDERSTAND YOU MET EACH OTHER BACK IN IRAQ?
MAYBE I SHOULD HAVE SAID "GOOD EVENING, FATHER" -- SHIT, I PROBABLY BLEW IT ALREADY.
YEESS ...
IT WAS LITTLE BRIGITTE'S MOTHER JACQUELINE WHO CALLED ME UP ONE DAY, ASKING IF I KNEW ANYONE WHO COULD TUTOR BRIGITTE IN ENGLISH...
HER MOTHER HAD TRIED IT ON HER OWN, BUT APPARENTLY LITTLE BRIGITTE WAS QUITE A HANDFUL AND WAS DRIVING HER TO DISTRACTION.
I TOLD HER I WOULDN'T MIND TRYING, AND IT WORKED OUT. LITTLE BRIGITTE WAS JUST A DREAM.

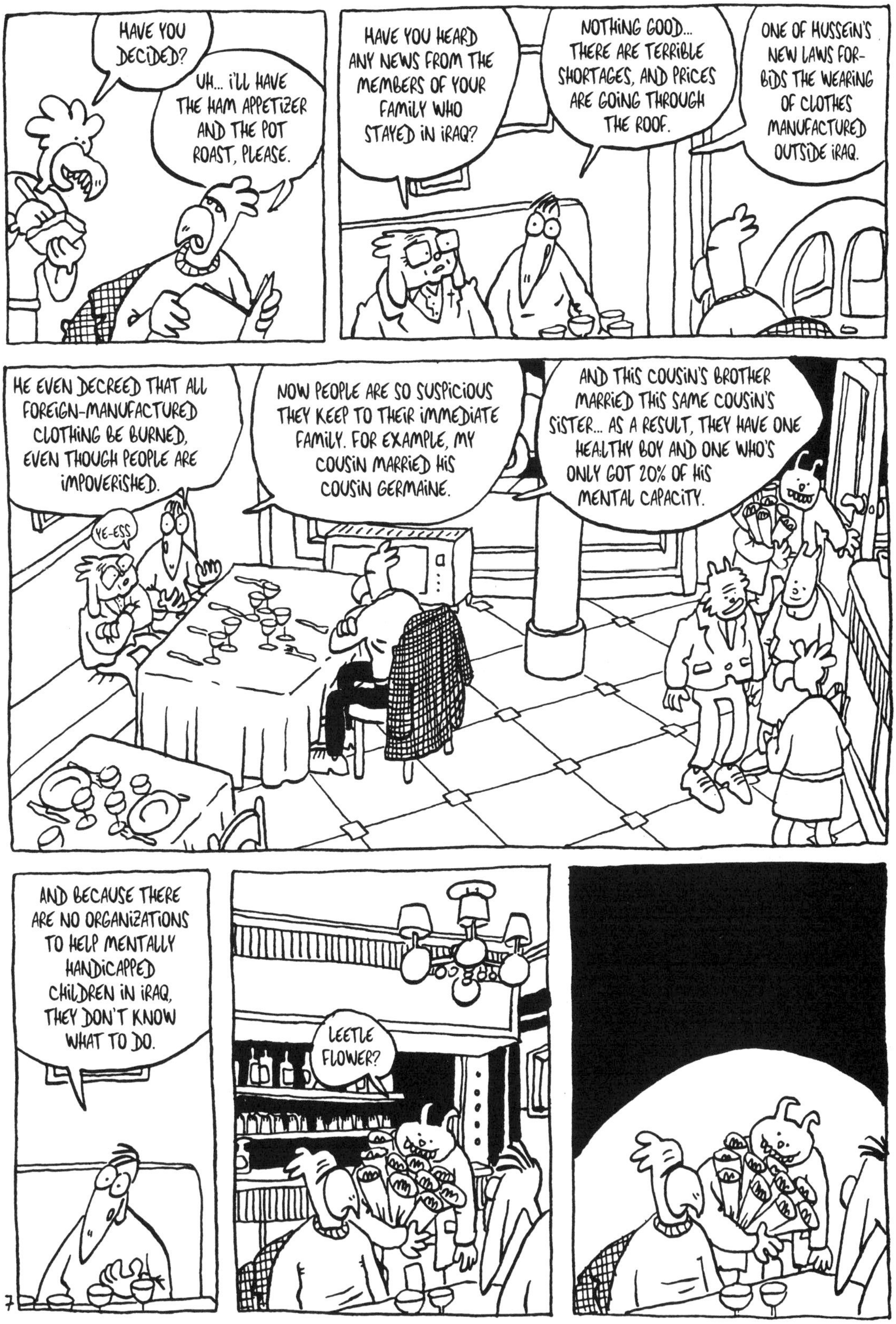
HAVE YOU DECIDED?
UH... I'LL HAVE THE HAM APPETIZER AND THE POT ROAST, PLEASE.
HAVE YOU HEARD ANY NEWS FROM THE MEMBERS OF YOUR FAMILY WHO STAYED IN IRAQ?
NOTHING GOOD... THERE ARE TERRIBLE SHORTAGES, AND PRICES ARE GOING THROUGH THE ROOF.
ONE OF HUSSEIN'S NEW LAWS FORBIDS THE WEARING OF CLOTHES MANUFACTURED OUTSIDE IRAQ.
HE EVEN DECREED THAT ALL FOREIGN-MANUFACTURED CLOTHING BE BURNED, EVEN THOUGH PEOPLE ARE IMPOVERISHED.
YE-ESS
NOW PEOPLE ARE SO SUSPICIOUS THEY KEEP TO THEIR IMMEDIATE FAMILY. FOR EXAMPLE, MY COUSIN MARRIED HIS COUSIN GERMAINE.
AND THIS COUSIN'S BROTHER MARRIED THIS SAME COUSIN'S SISTER... AS A RESULT, THEY HAVE ONE HEALTHY BOY AND ONE WHO'S ONLY GOT 20% OF HIS MENTAL CAPACITY.
AND BECAUSE THERE ARE NO ORGANIZATIONS TO HELP MENTALLY HANDICAPPED CHILDREN IN IRAQ, THEY DON'T KNOW WHAT TO DO.
LEETLE FLOWER?

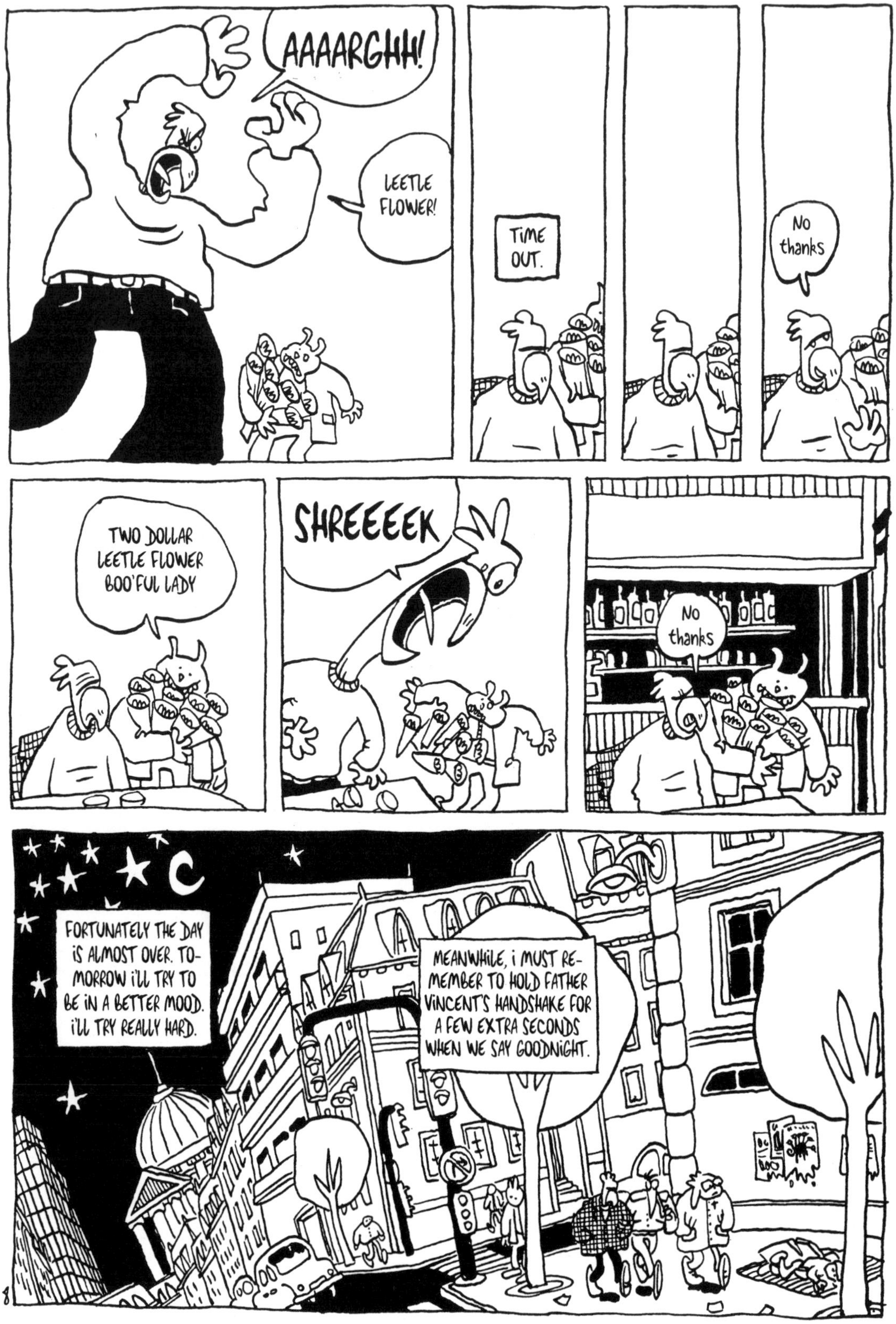
AAAARGHH!
LEETLE FLOWER!
TIME OUT.
No thanks
TWO DOLLAR LEETLE FLOWER BOO'FUL LADY
SHREEEEK
No thanks
FORTUNATELY THE DAY IS ALMOST OVER. TO-MORROW I'LL TRY TO BE IN A BETTER MOOD. I'LL TRY REALLY HARD.
MEANWHILE, I MUST RE-MEMBER TO HOLD FATHER VINCENT'S HANDSHAKE FOR A FEW EXTRA SECONDS WHEN WE SAY GOODNIGHT.

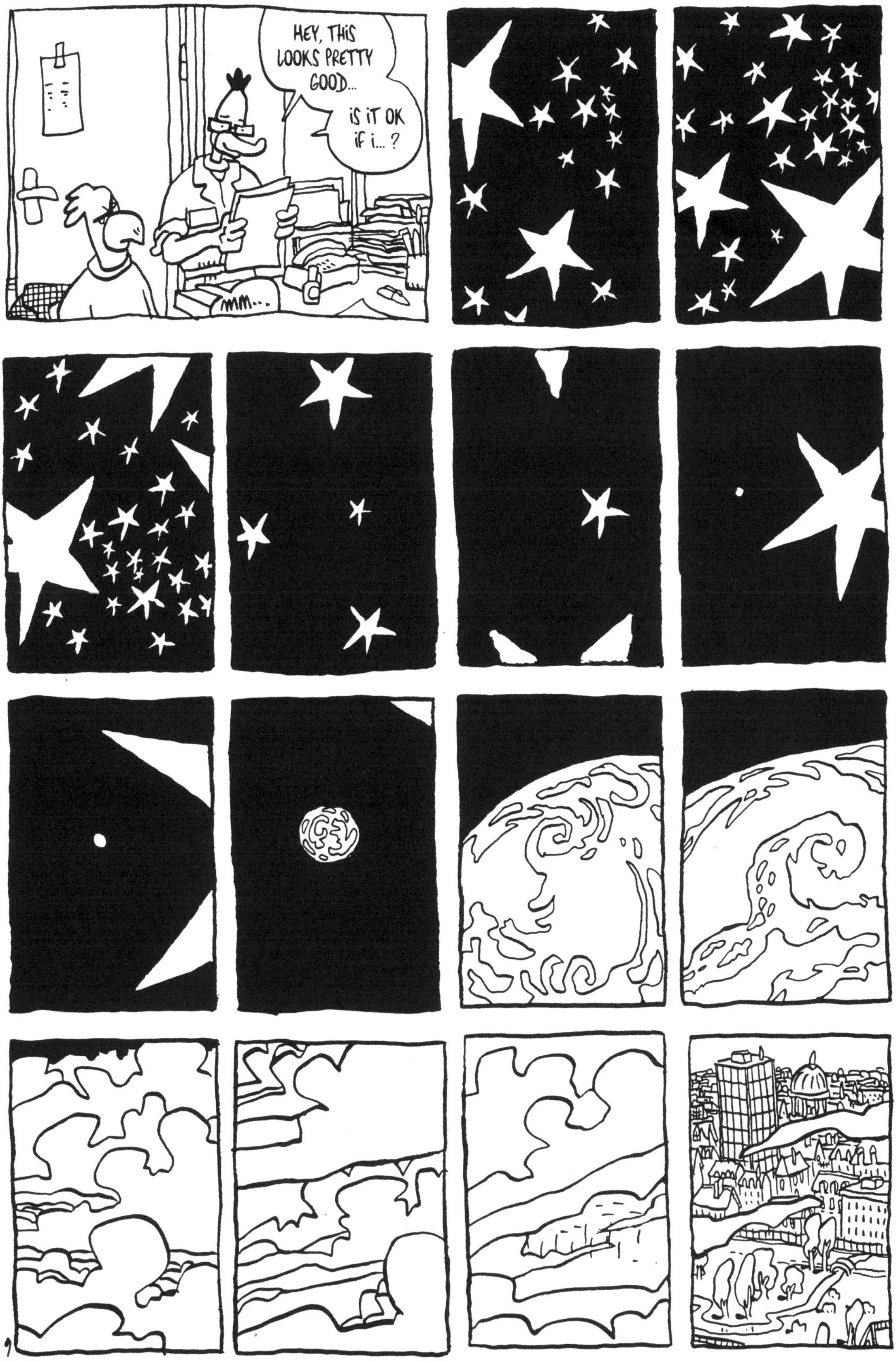
HEY, THIS LOOKS PRETTY GOOD...
IS IT OK IF I... ?
MM...

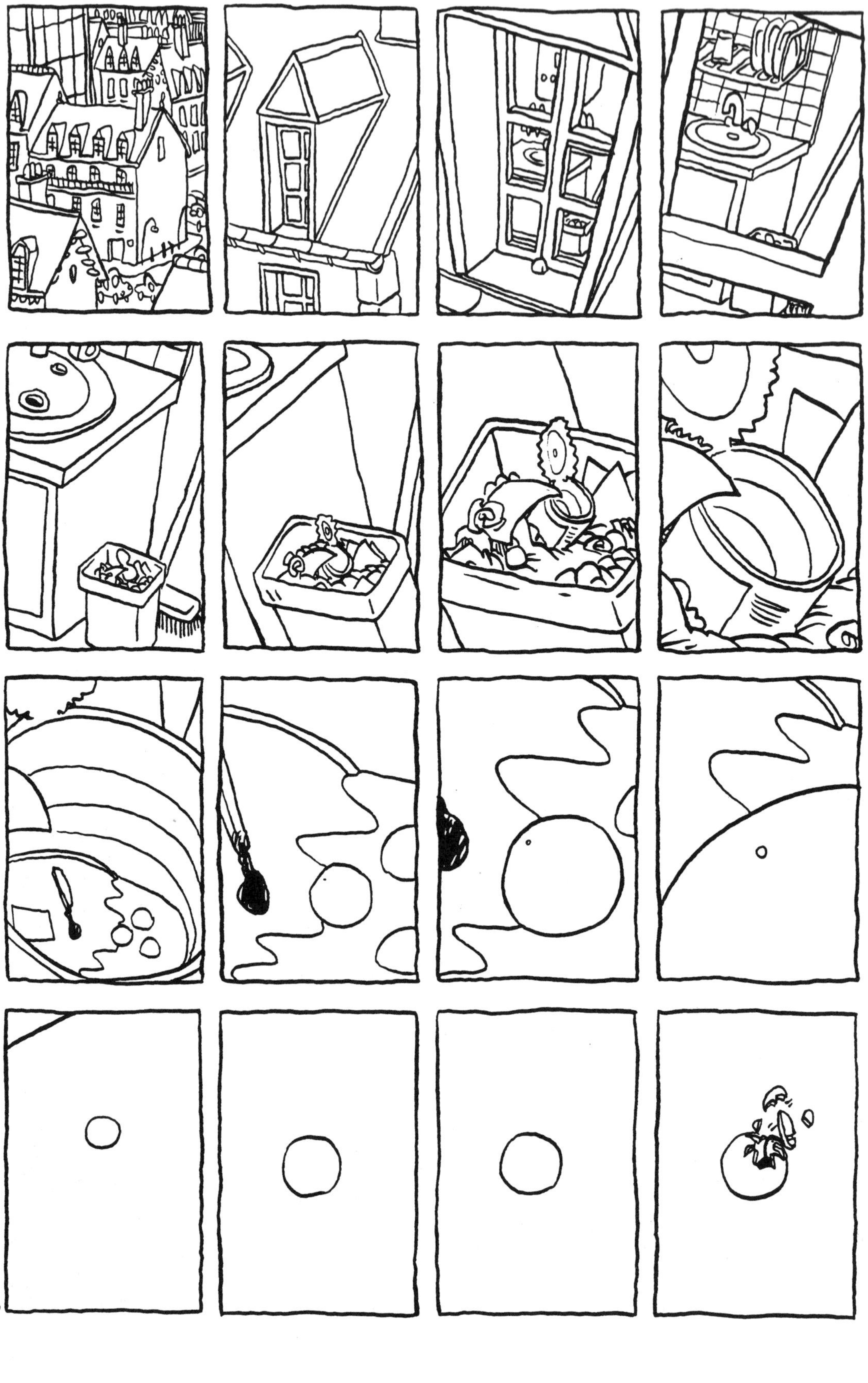

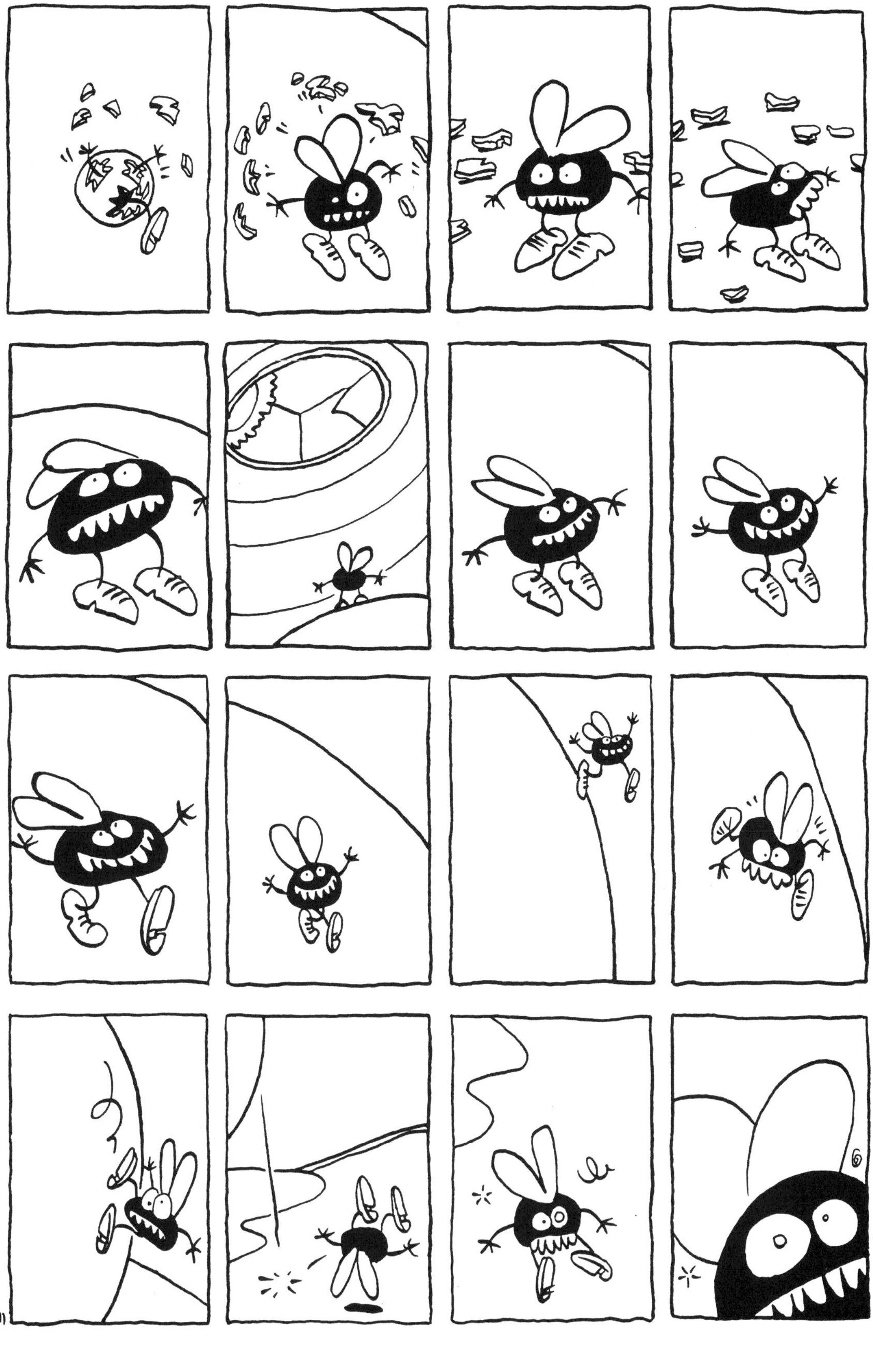

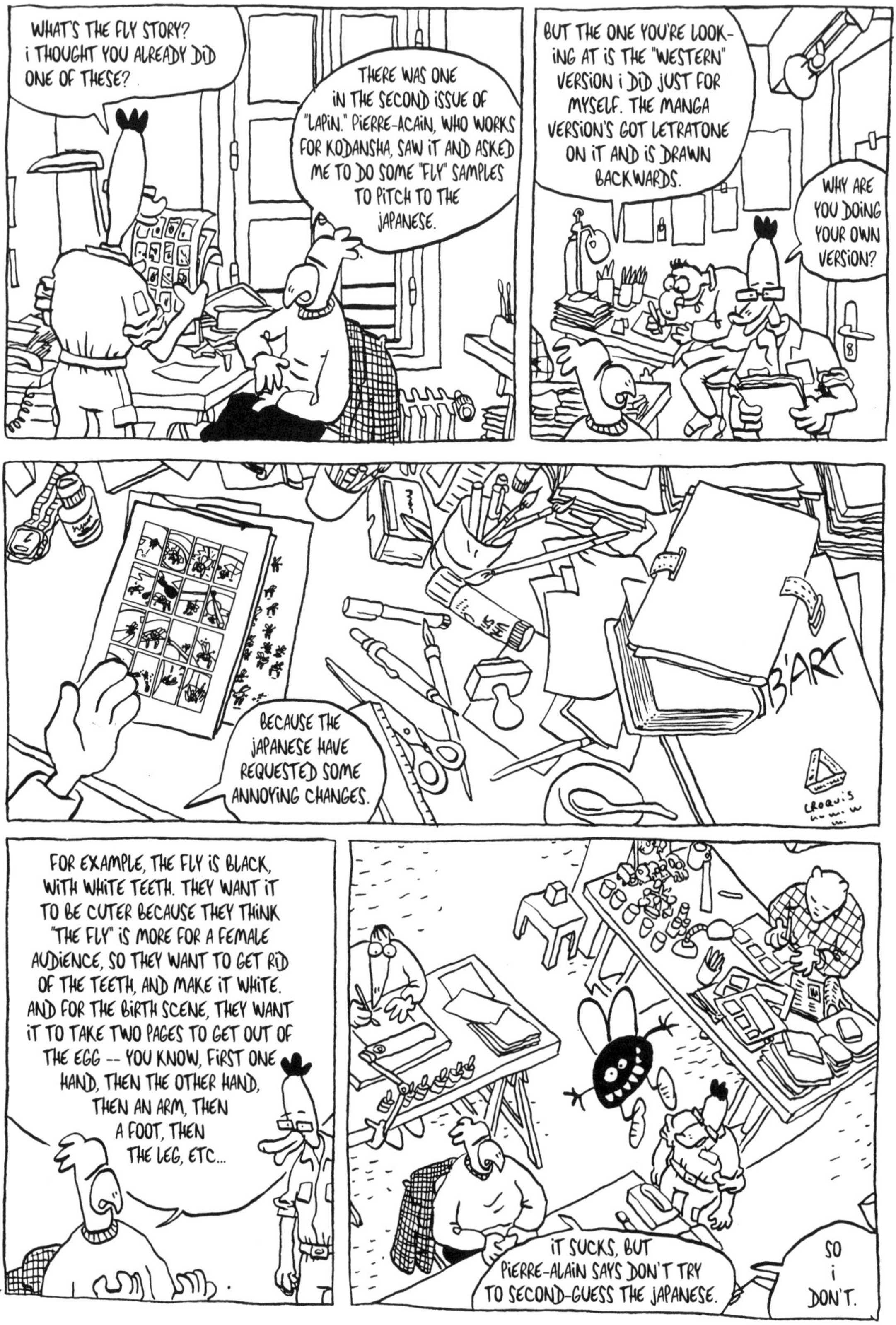
WHAT'S THE FLY STORY? I THOUGHT YOU ALREADY DID ONE OF THESE?
THERE WAS ONE IN THE SECOND ISSUE OF "LAPIN." PIERRE-ACAIN, WHO WORKS FOR KODANSHA, SAW IT AND ASKED ME TO DO SOME "FLY" SAMPLES TO PITCH TO THE JAPANESE.
BUT THE ONE YOU'RE LOOKING AT IS THE "WESTERN" VERSION I DID JUST FOR MYSELF. THE MANGA VERSION'S GOT LETRATONE ON IT AND IS DRAWN BACKWARDS.
WHY ARE YOU DOING YOUR OWN VERSION?
BECAUSE THE JAPANESE HAVE REQUESTED SOME ANNOYING CHANGES.
B'ART
CROQUIS
FOR EXAMPLE, THE FLY IS BLACK, WITH WHITE TEETH. THEY WANT IT TO BE CUTER BECAUSE THEY THINK "THE FLY" IS MORE FOR A FEMALE AUDIENCE, SO THEY WANT TO GET RID OF THE TEETH, AND MAKE IT WHITE. AND FOR THE BIRTH SCENE, THEY WANT IT TO TAKE TWO PAGES TO GET OUT OF THE EGG -- YOU KNOW, FIRST ONE HAND, THEN THE OTHER HAND, THEN AN ARM, THEN A FOOT, THEN THE LEG, ETC...
IT SUCKS, BUT PIERRE-ALAIN SAYS DON'T TRY TO SECOND-GUESS THE JAPANESE.
SO I DON'T.

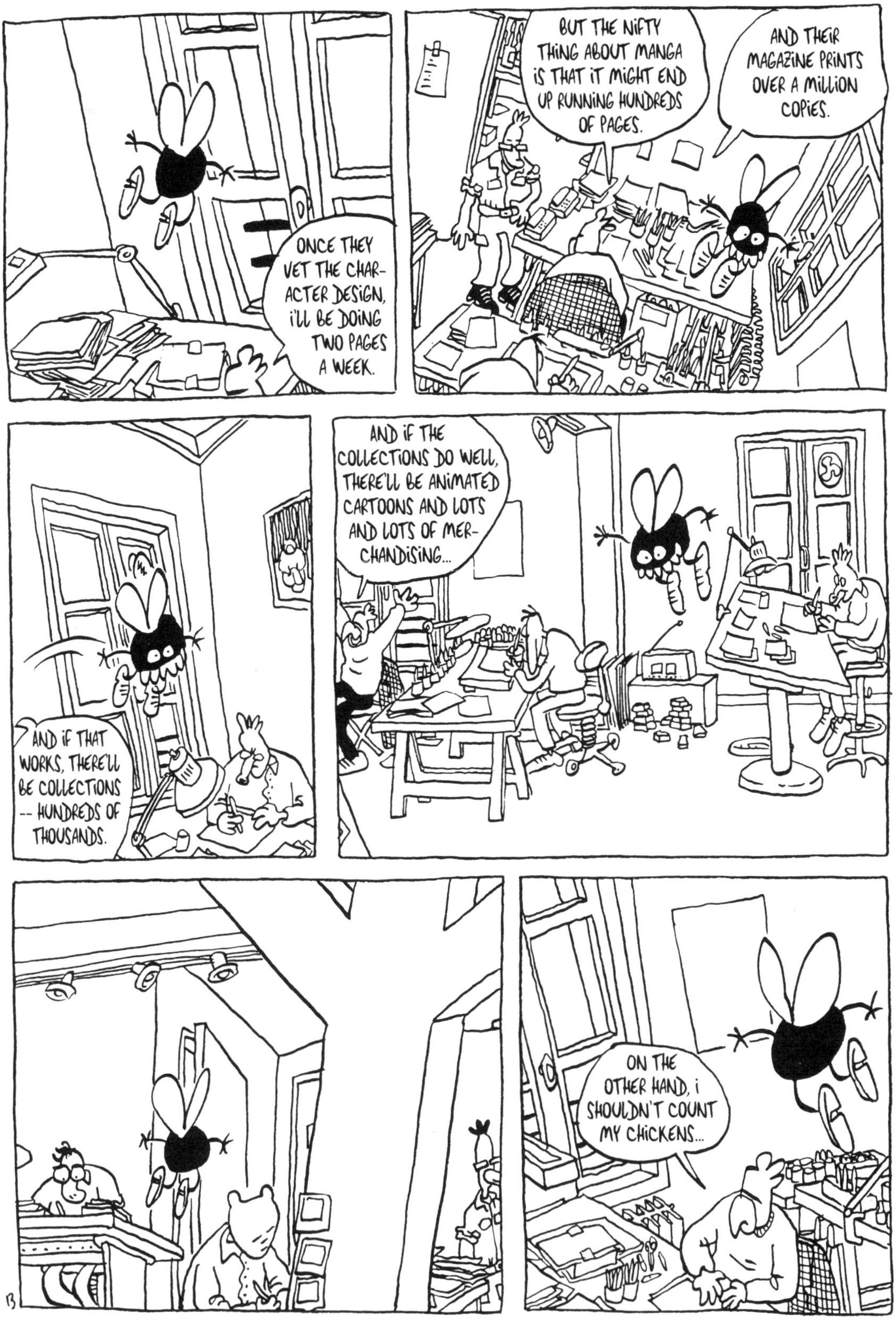
ONCE THEY VET THE CHARACTER DESIGN, i'LL BE DOING TWO PAGES A WEEK.
BUT THE NiFTY THiNG ABOUT MANGA iS THAT iT MiGHT END UP RUNNiNG HUNDREDS OF PAGES.
AND THEiR MAGAZiNE PRiNTS OVER A MiLLiON COPiES.
AND iF THAT WORKS, THERE'LL BE COLLECTiONS -- HUNDREDS OF THOUSANDS.
AND iF THE COLLECTiONS DO WELL, THERE'LL BE ANiMATED CARTOONS AND LOTS AND LOTS OF MERCHANDiSiNG...
ON THE OTHER HAND, i SHOULDN'T COUNT MY CHiCKENS...

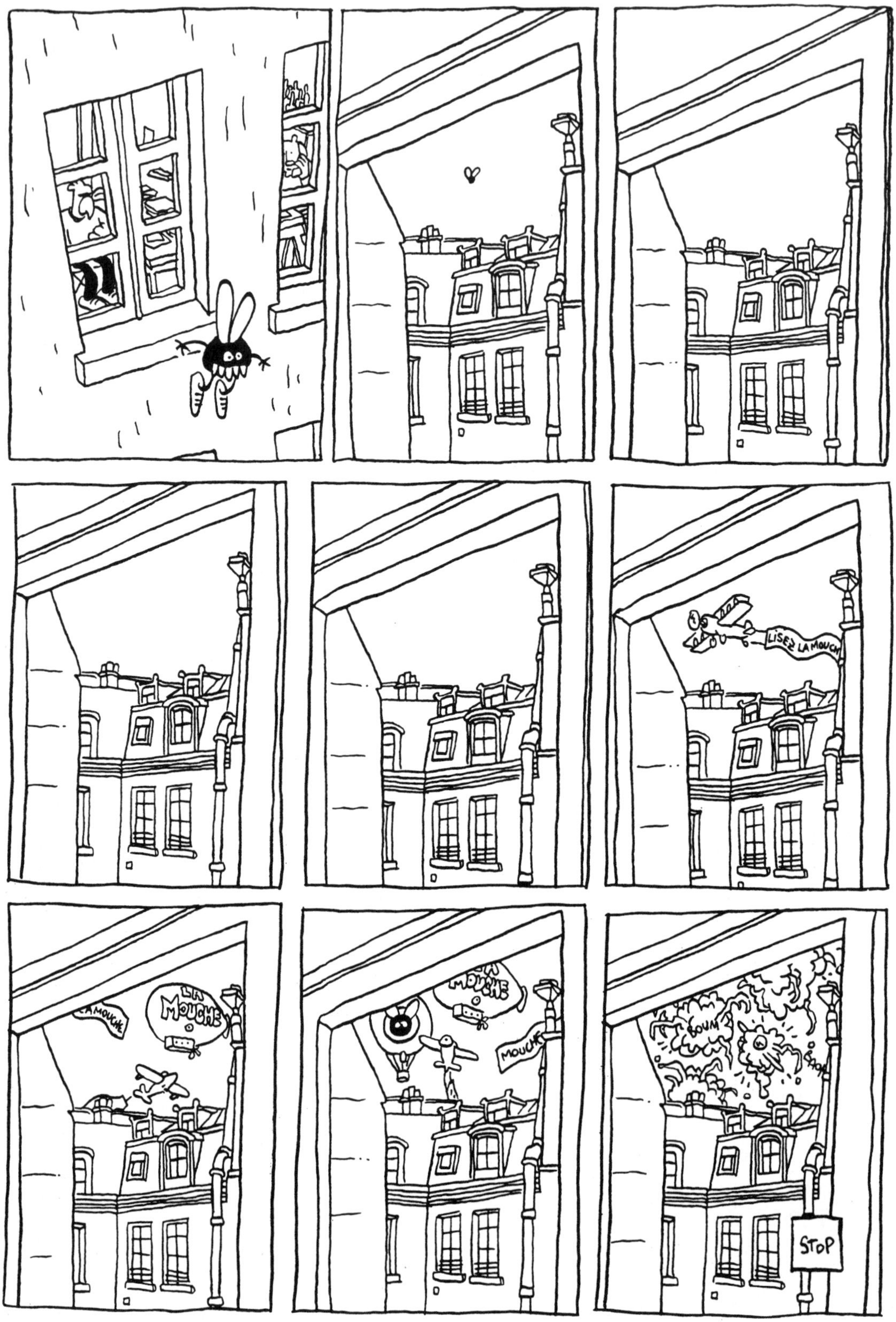
LISEZ LA MOUCH
LA MOUCHE
LA MOUCHE
MOUCHE
BOUM
STOP

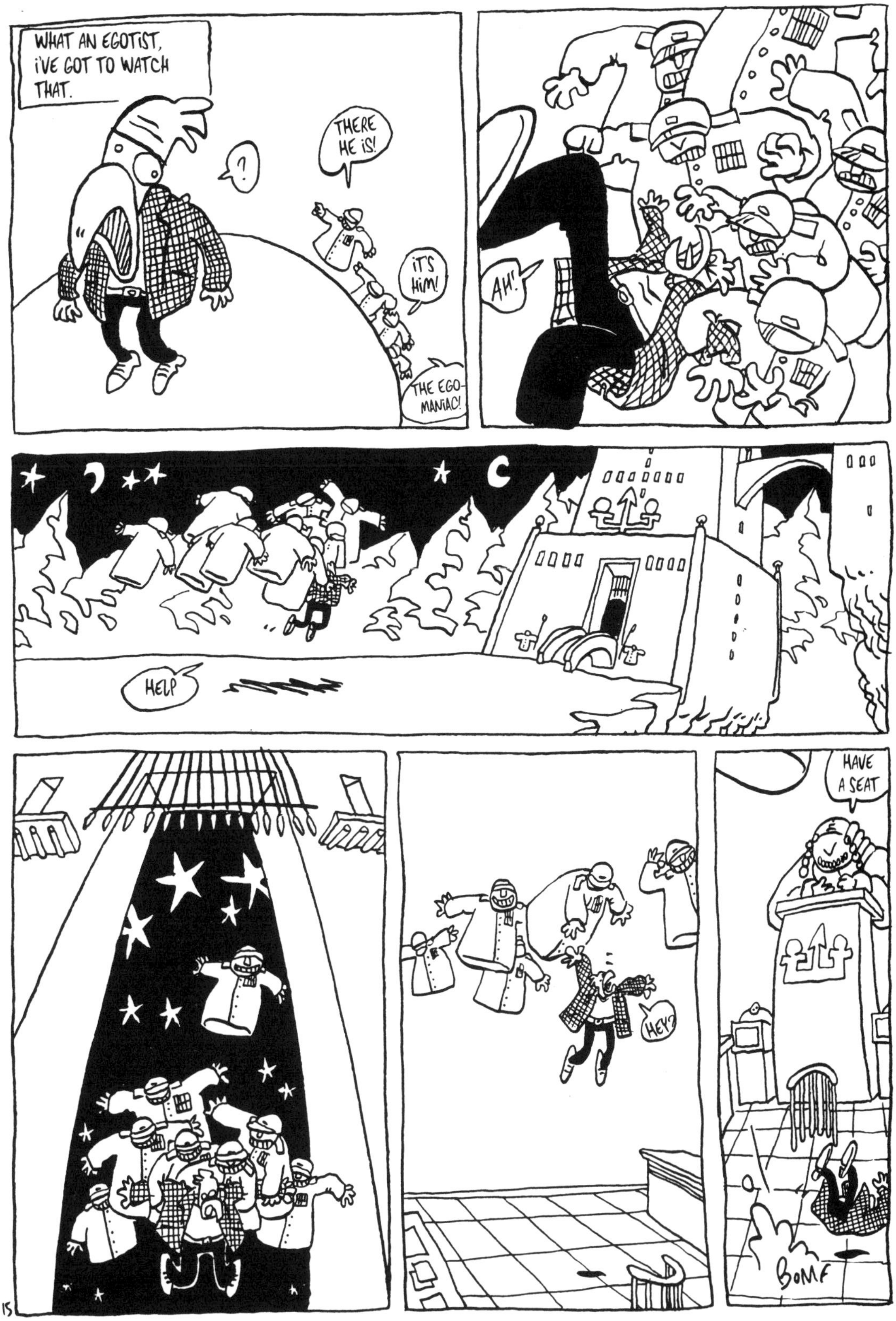
WHAT AN EGOTIST,
I'VE GOT TO WATCH
THAT.
?
THERE HE IS!
IT'S HIM!
THE EGO-MANIAC!
AH!
HELP
HEY?
HAVE A SEAT
BOMF

YOU ARE HEREBY ACCUSED OF RECIDIVIST MEGALOMANIA. THE JUDGEMENT HAS ALREADY BEEN HANDED DOWN.

YOU ARE HEREBY SENTENCED NOT TO SPEAK ABOUT YOURSELF OR YOUR WORK FOR THE DURATION OF ONE WEEK.

WHAT?! ...

i... i CAN'T DO THAT.

FOR THAT MATTER -- iT'S NOT FAIR. i ONLY TALKED A LiTTLE BiT ABOUT ME AND WHEN i STARTED DAYDREAMING i QUIT ALL BY MYSELF.

BAiLiFF.

HAND OVER THAT PAPER. DON'T YOU THINK i SAW YOU?

WHY, YOU...

YADDA YADDA YADDA YADDA

?

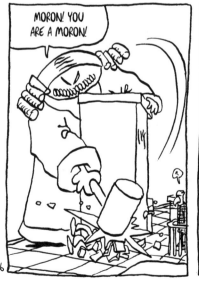

MORON! YOU ARE A MORON!

AS FOR YOU, iF i CATCH YOU BEiNG A MEGALOMANiAC...

i'LL MAKE SURE YOU GET PARKiNSON'S DISEASE AND ARE NEVER ABLE TO DRAW AGAIN.

B-BUT... THAT'S MEAN...

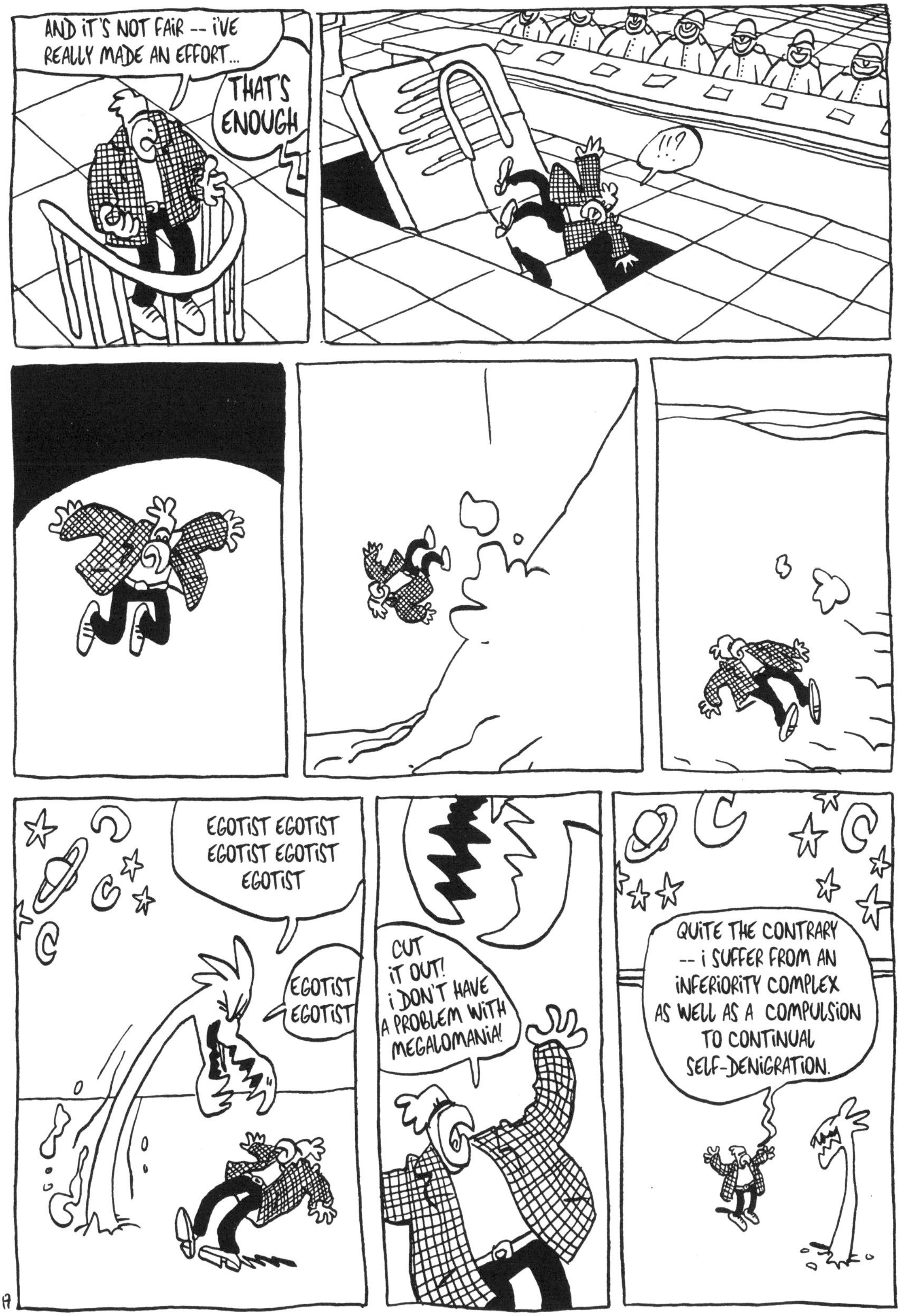
AND iT'S NOT FAiR -- i'VE REALLY MADE AN EFFORT...
THAT'S ENOUGH
!!?
EGOTiST EGOTiST EGOTiST EGOTiST EGOTiST
EGOTiST EGOTiST
CUT iT OUT! i DON'T HAVE A PROBLEM WiTH MEGALOMANiA!
QUiTE THE CONTRARY -- i SUFFER FROM AN iNFERiORiTY COMPLEX AS WELL AS A COMPULSiON TO CONTiNUAL SELF-DENiGRATiON.

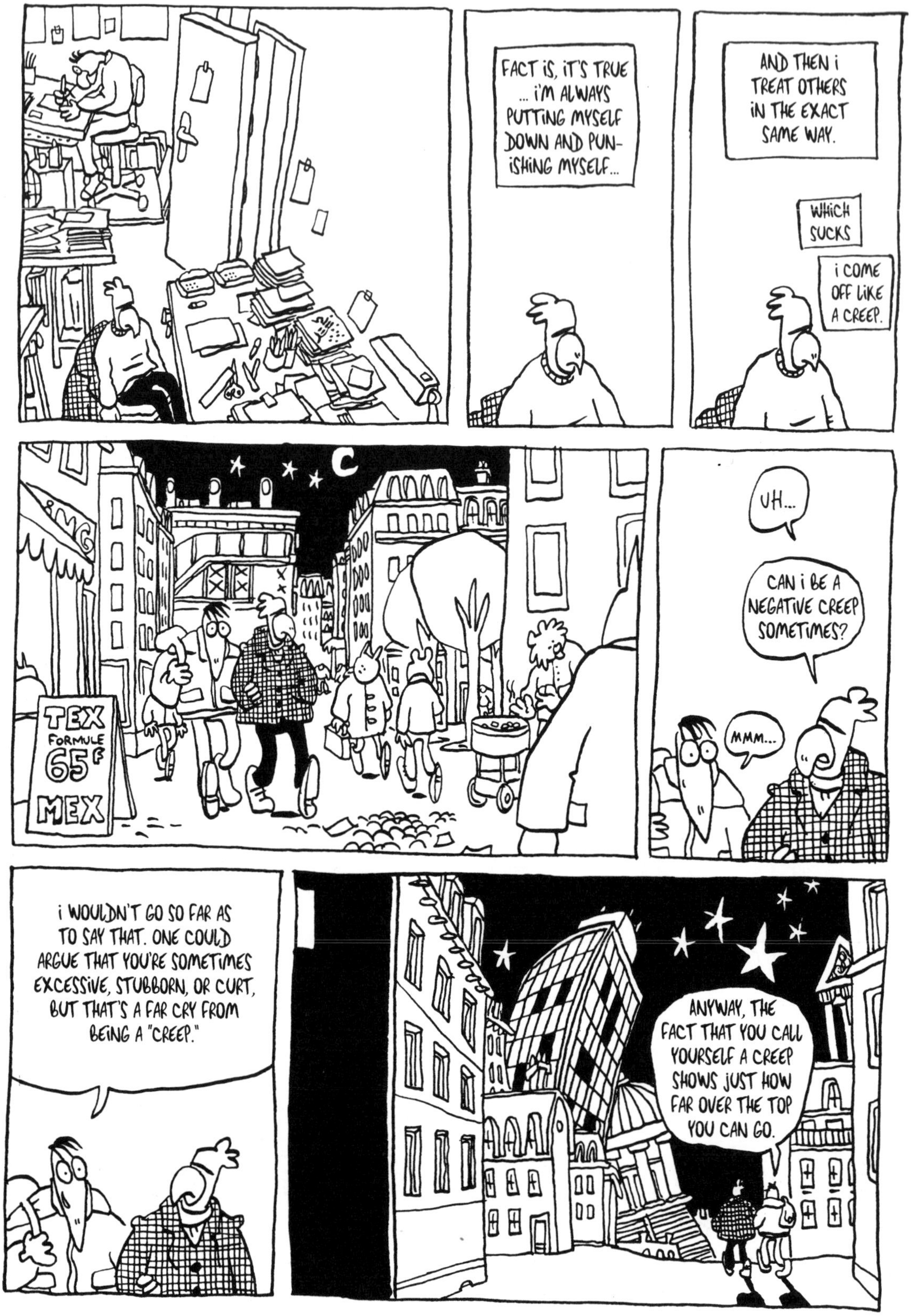
FACT IS, IT'S TRUE ... I'M ALWAYS PUTTING MYSELF DOWN AND PUN-ISHING MYSELF...
AND THEN I TREAT OTHERS IN THE EXACT SAME WAY.
WHICH SUCKS
I COME OFF LIKE A CREEP.
TEX FORMULE 65F MEX
UH...
CAN I BE A NEGATIVE CREEP SOMETIMES?
MMM...
I WOULDN'T GO SO FAR AS TO SAY THAT. ONE COULD ARGUE THAT YOU'RE SOMETIMES EXCESSIVE, STUBBORN, OR CURT, BUT THAT'S A FAR CRY FROM BEING A "CREEP."
ANYWAY, THE FACT THAT YOU CALL YOURSELF A CREEP SHOWS JUST HOW FAR OVER THE TOP YOU CAN GO.

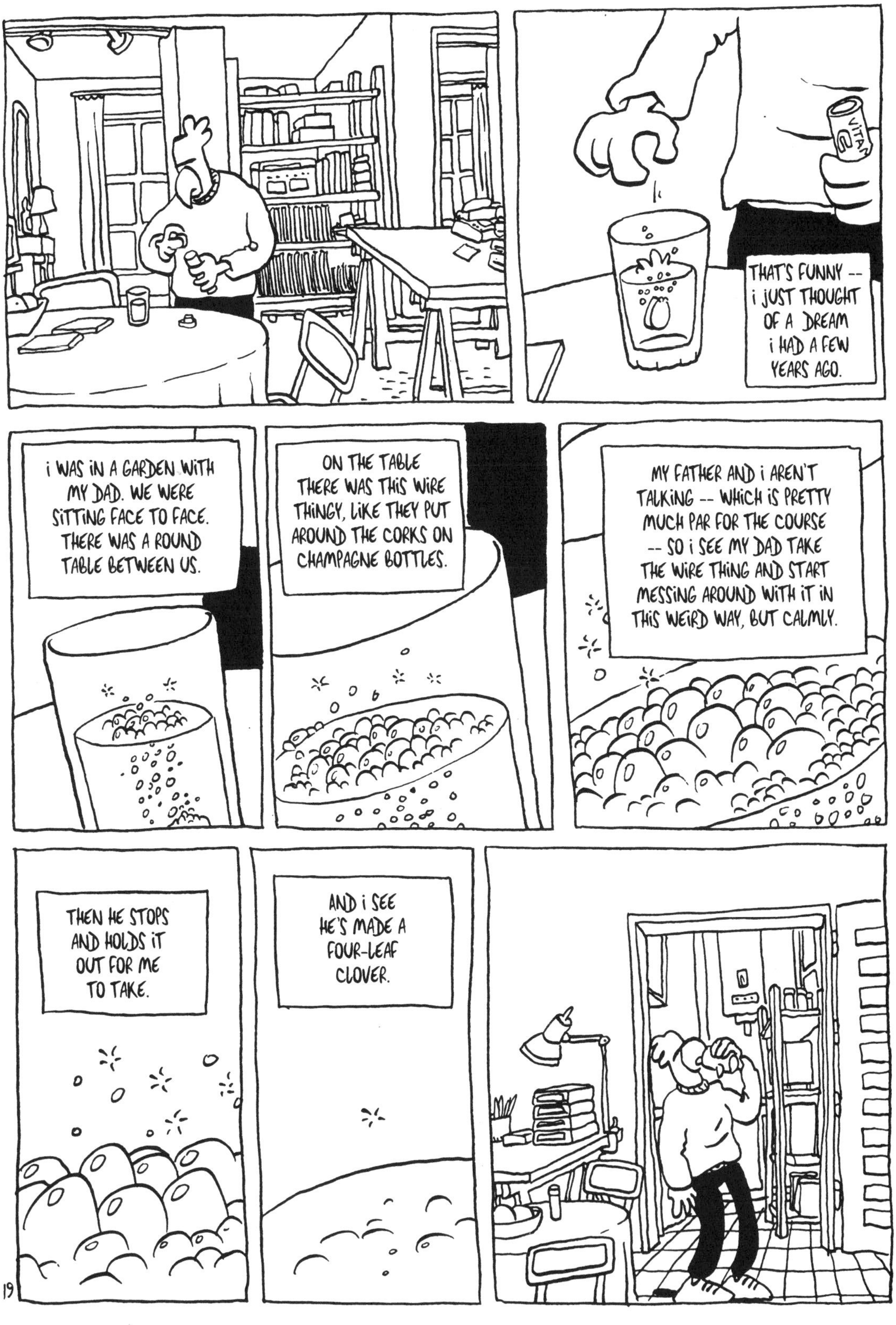
VITAM
THAT'S FUNNY -- i JUST THOUGHT OF A DREAM i HAD A FEW YEARS AGO.
i WAS IN A GARDEN WITH MY DAD. WE WERE SITTING FACE TO FACE. THERE WAS A ROUND TABLE BETWEEN US.
ON THE TABLE THERE WAS THIS WIRE THINGY, LIKE THEY PUT AROUND THE CORKS ON CHAMPAGNE BOTTLES.
MY FATHER AND i AREN'T TALKING -- WHICH IS PRETTY MUCH PAR FOR THE COURSE -- SO i SEE MY DAD TAKE THE WIRE THING AND START MESSING AROUND WITH IT IN THIS WEIRD WAY, BUT CALMLY.
THEN HE STOPS AND HOLDS IT OUT FOR ME TO TAKE.
AND i SEE HE'S MADE A FOUR-LEAF CLOVER.

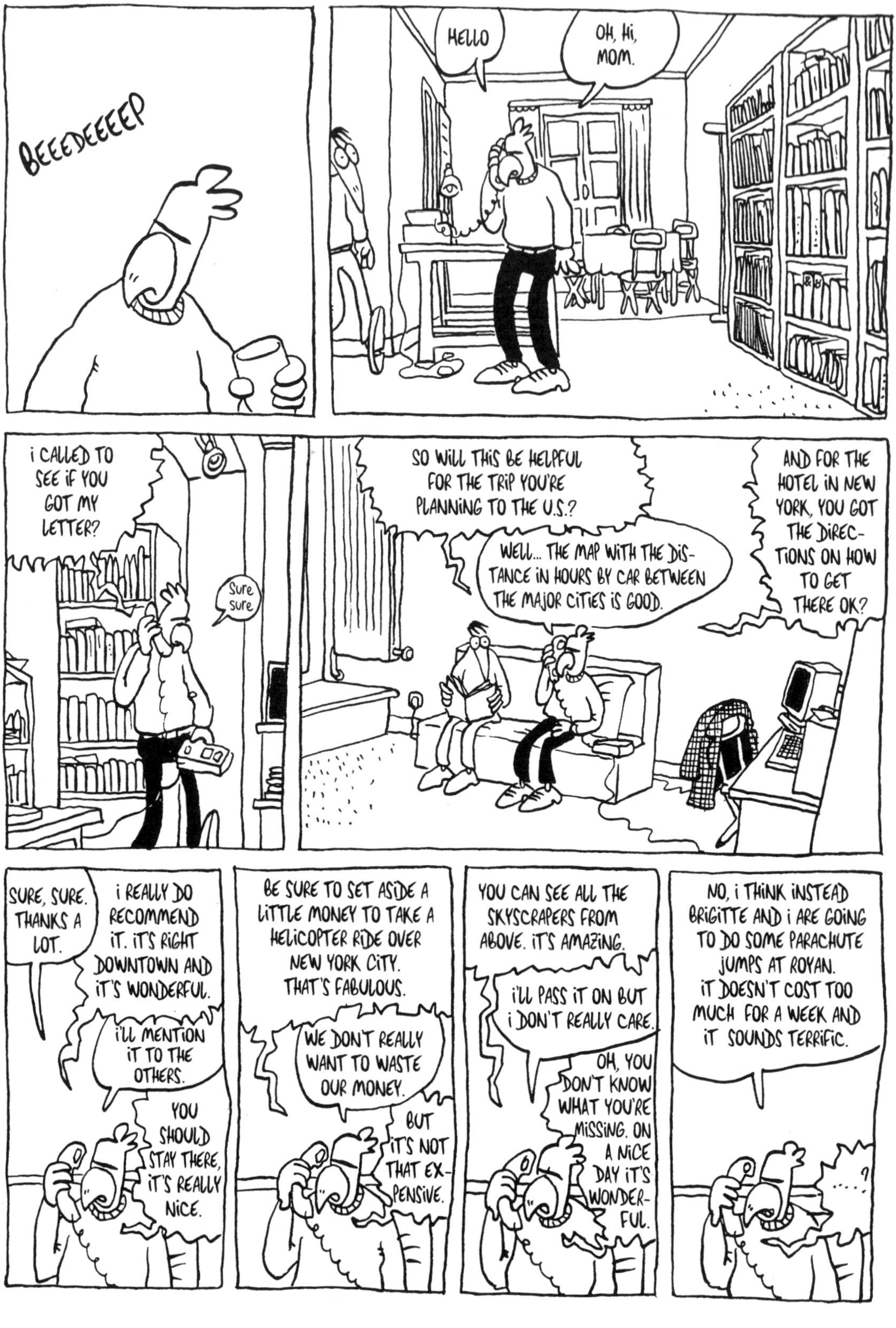
BEEEDEEEEP
HELLO
OH, Hi, MOM.
i CALLED TO SEE iF YOU GOT MY LETTER?
Sure sure
SO WiLL THiS BE HELPFUL FOR THE TRiP YOU'RE PLANNiNG TO THE U.S.?
WELL... THE MAP WiTH THE DiS-TANCE iN HOURS BY CAR BETWEEN THE MAJOR CiTiES iS GOOD.
AND FOR THE HOTEL iN NEW YORK, YOU GOT THE DiREC-TiONS ON HOW TO GET THERE OK?
SURE, SURE. THANKS A LOT.
i REALLY DO RECOMMEND iT. iT'S RiGHT DOWNTOWN AND iT'S WONDERFUL.
i'LL MENTiON iT TO THE OTHERS.
YOU SHOULD STAY THERE, iT'S REALLY NiCE.
BE SURE TO SET ASiDE A LiTTLE MONEY TO TAKE A HELiCOPTER RiDE OVER NEW YORK CiTY. THAT'S FABULOUS.
WE DON'T REALLY WANT TO WASTE OUR MONEY.
BUT iT'S NOT THAT EX-PENSiVE.
YOU CAN SEE ALL THE SKYSCRAPERS FROM ABOVE. iT'S AMAZiNG.
i'LL PASS iT ON BUT i DON'T REALLY CARE.
OH, YOU DON'T KNOW WHAT YOU'RE MiSSiNG. ON A NiCE DAY iT'S WONDER-FUL.
NO, i THiNK iNSTEAD BRiGiTTE AND i ARE GOiNG TO DO SOME PARACHUTE JUMPS AT ROYAN. iT DOESN'T COST TOO MUCH FOR A WEEK AND iT SOUNDS TERRiFiC.
...?

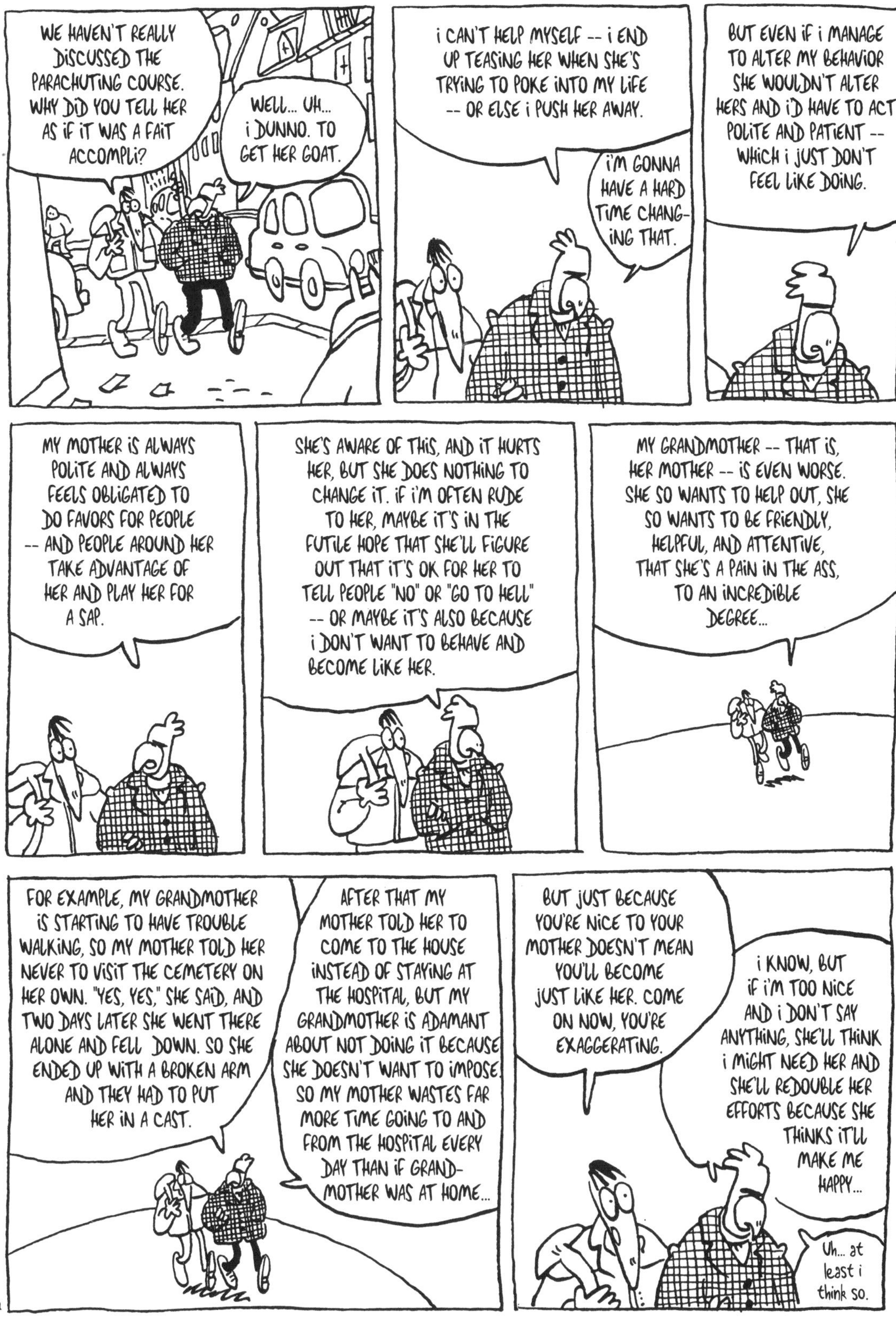
WE HAVEN'T REALLY DISCUSSED THE PARACHUTING COURSE. WHY DID YOU TELL HER AS IF IT WAS A FAIT ACCOMPLI?
WELL... UH... I DUNNO. TO GET HER GOAT.
I CAN'T HELP MYSELF -- I END UP TEASING HER WHEN SHE'S TRYING TO POKE INTO MY LIFE -- OR ELSE I PUSH HER AWAY.
I'M GONNA HAVE A HARD TIME CHANGING THAT.
BUT EVEN IF I MANAGE TO ALTER MY BEHAVIOR SHE WOULDN'T ALTER HERS AND I'D HAVE TO ACT POLITE AND PATIENT -- WHICH I JUST DON'T FEEL LIKE DOING.
MY MOTHER IS ALWAYS POLITE AND ALWAYS FEELS OBLIGATED TO DO FAVORS FOR PEOPLE -- AND PEOPLE AROUND HER TAKE ADVANTAGE OF HER AND PLAY HER FOR A SAP.
SHE'S AWARE OF THIS, AND IT HURTS HER, BUT SHE DOES NOTHING TO CHANGE IT. IF I'M OFTEN RUDE TO HER, MAYBE IT'S IN THE FUTILE HOPE THAT SHE'LL FIGURE OUT THAT IT'S OK FOR HER TO TELL PEOPLE "NO" OR "GO TO HELL" -- OR MAYBE IT'S ALSO BECAUSE I DON'T WANT TO BEHAVE AND BECOME LIKE HER.
MY GRANDMOTHER -- THAT IS, HER MOTHER -- IS EVEN WORSE. SHE SO WANTS TO HELP OUT, SHE SO WANTS TO BE FRIENDLY, HELPFUL, AND ATTENTIVE, THAT SHE'S A PAIN IN THE ASS, TO AN INCREDIBLE DEGREE...
FOR EXAMPLE, MY GRANDMOTHER IS STARTING TO HAVE TROUBLE WALKING, SO MY MOTHER TOLD HER NEVER TO VISIT THE CEMETERY ON HER OWN. "YES, YES," SHE SAID, AND TWO DAYS LATER SHE WENT THERE ALONE AND FELL DOWN. SO SHE ENDED UP WITH A BROKEN ARM AND THEY HAD TO PUT HER IN A CAST.
AFTER THAT MY MOTHER TOLD HER TO COME TO THE HOUSE INSTEAD OF STAYING AT THE HOSPITAL, BUT MY GRANDMOTHER IS ADAMANT ABOUT NOT DOING IT BECAUSE SHE DOESN'T WANT TO IMPOSE. SO MY MOTHER WASTES FAR MORE TIME GOING TO AND FROM THE HOSPITAL EVERY DAY THAN IF GRANDMOTHER WAS AT HOME...
BUT JUST BECAUSE YOU'RE NICE TO YOUR MOTHER DOESN'T MEAN YOU'LL BECOME JUST LIKE HER. COME ON NOW, YOU'RE EXAGGERATING.
I KNOW, BUT IF I'M TOO NICE AND I DON'T SAY ANYTHING, SHE'LL THINK I MIGHT NEED HER AND SHE'LL REDOUBLE HER EFFORTS BECAUSE SHE THINKS IT'LL MAKE ME HAPPY...
Uh... at least i think so.

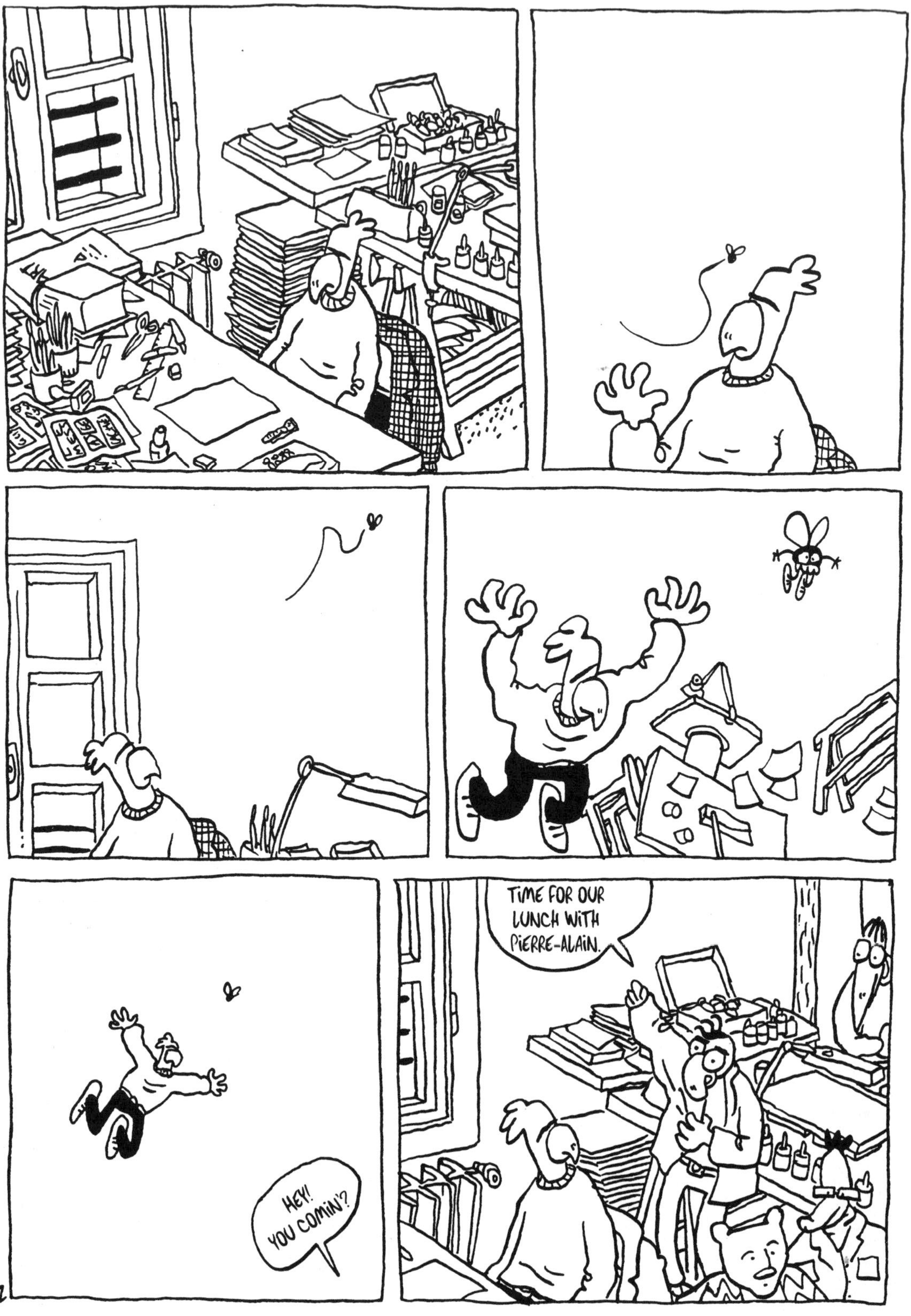
HEY! YOU COMIN'?
TIME FOR OUR LUNCH WITH PIERRE-ALAIN.

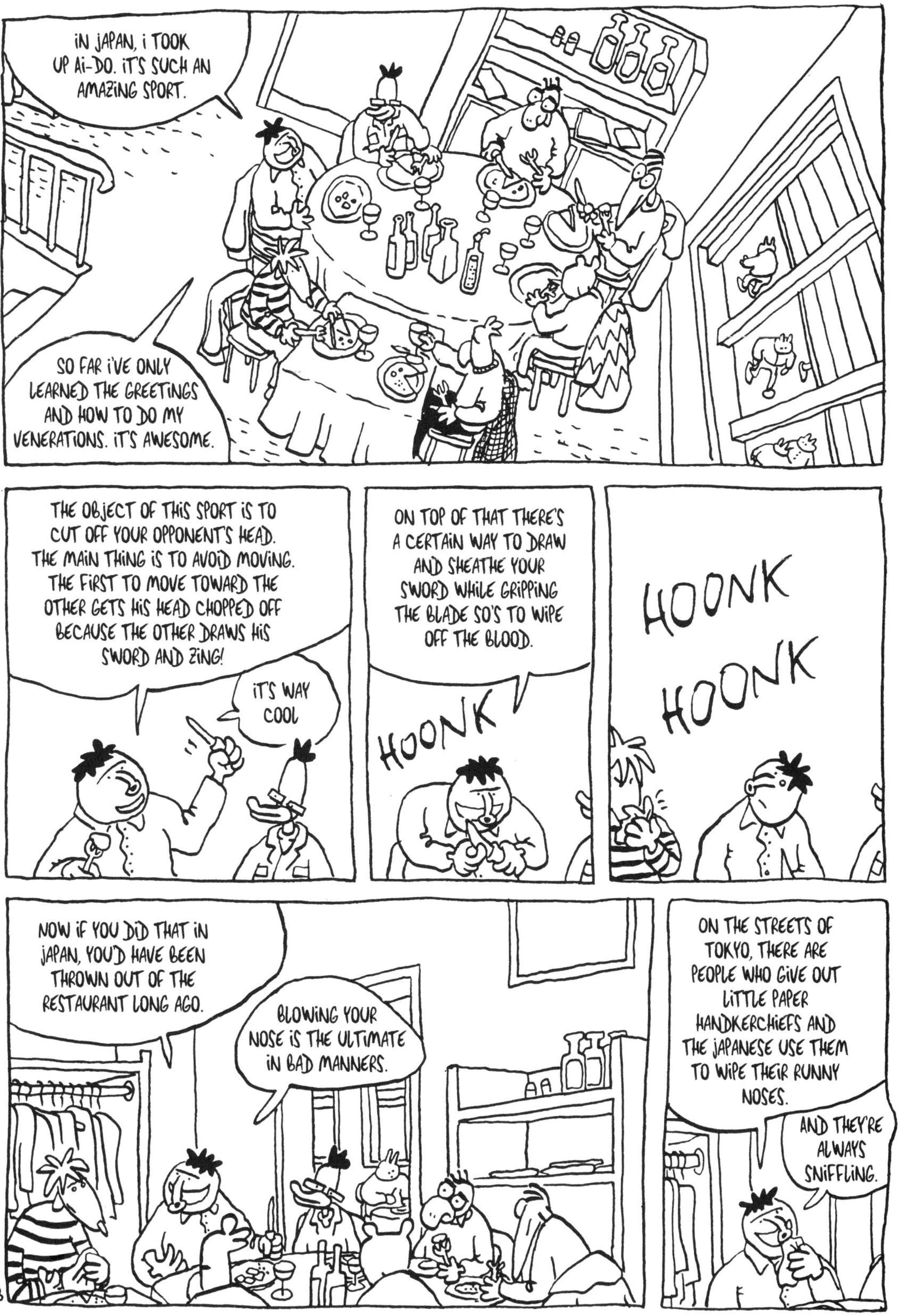

IN JAPAN, I TOOK UP AI-DO. IT'S SUCH AN AMAZING SPORT.
SO FAR I'VE ONLY LEARNED THE GREETINGS AND HOW TO DO MY VENERATIONS. IT'S AWESOME.
THE OBJECT OF THIS SPORT IS TO CUT OFF YOUR OPPONENT'S HEAD. THE MAIN THING IS TO AVOID MOVING. THE FIRST TO MOVE TOWARD THE OTHER GETS HIS HEAD CHOPPED OFF BECAUSE THE OTHER DRAWS HIS SWORD AND ZING!
IT'S WAY COOL
ON TOP OF THAT THERE'S A CERTAIN WAY TO DRAW AND SHEATHE YOUR SWORD WHILE GRIPPING THE BLADE SO'S TO WIPE OFF THE BLOOD.
HOONK
HOONK
HOONK
NOW IF YOU DID THAT IN JAPAN, YOU'D HAVE BEEN THROWN OUT OF THE RESTAURANT LONG AGO.
BLOWING YOUR NOSE IS THE ULTIMATE IN BAD MANNERS.
ON THE STREETS OF TOKYO, THERE ARE PEOPLE WHO GIVE OUT LITTLE PAPER HANDKERCHIEFS AND THE JAPANESE USE THEM TO WIPE THEIR RUNNY NOSES.
AND THEY'RE ALWAYS SNIFFLING.

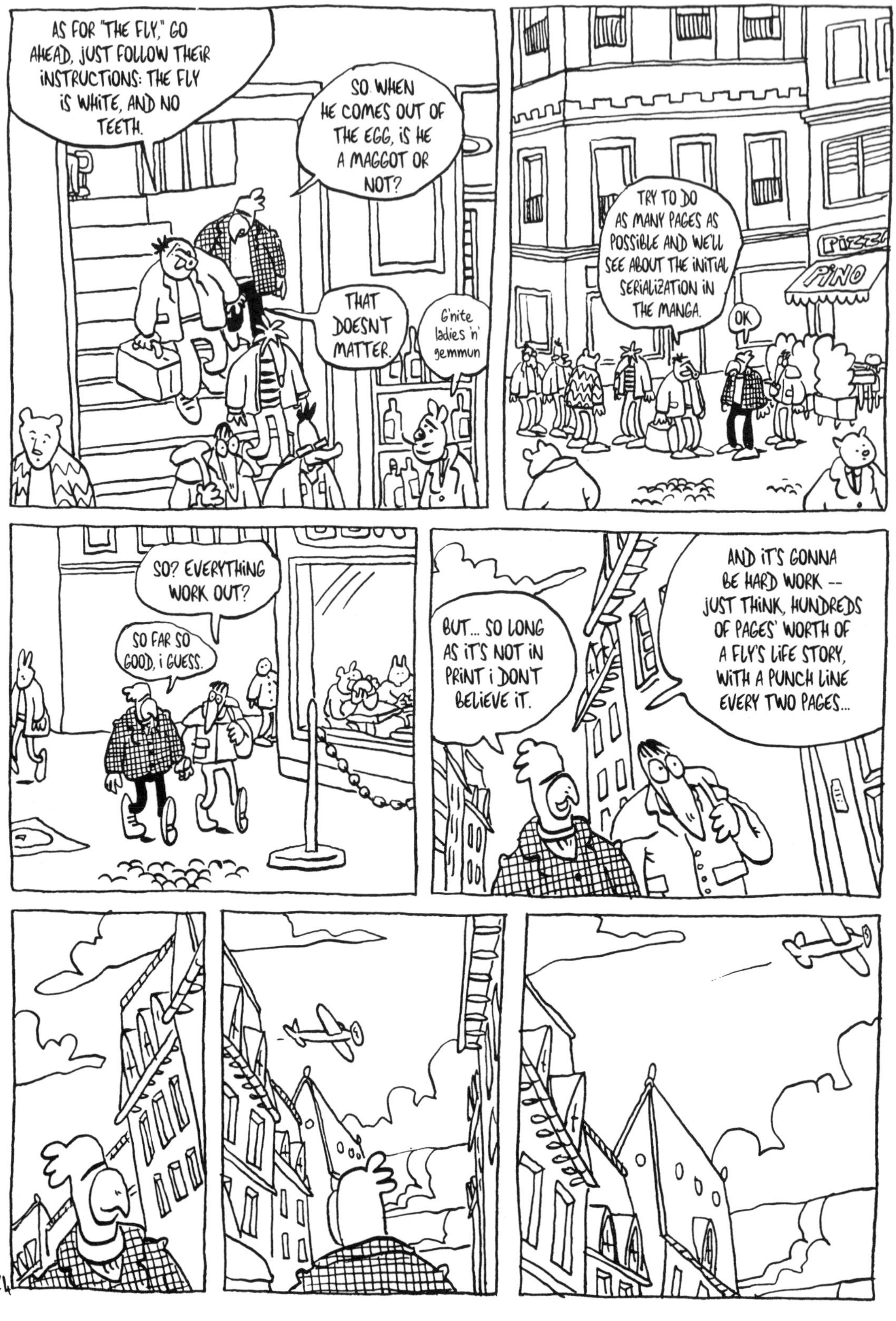
AS FOR "THE FLY," GO AHEAD, JUST FOLLOW THEIR INSTRUCTIONS: THE FLY IS WHITE, AND NO TEETH.
SO WHEN HE COMES OUT OF THE EGG, IS HE A MAGGOT OR NOT?
THAT DOESN'T MATTER.
G'nite ladies 'n' gemmun
TRY TO DO AS MANY PAGES AS POSSIBLE AND WE'LL SEE ABOUT THE INITIAL SERIALIZATION IN THE MANGA.
OK
PIZZA
PINO
SO? EVERYTHING WORK OUT?
SO FAR SO GOOD, I GUESS.
BUT... SO LONG AS IT'S NOT IN PRINT I DON'T BELIEVE IT.
AND IT'S GONNA BE HARD WORK -- JUST THINK, HUNDREDS OF PAGES' WORTH OF A FLY'S LIFE STORY, WITH A PUNCH LINE EVERY TWO PAGES...

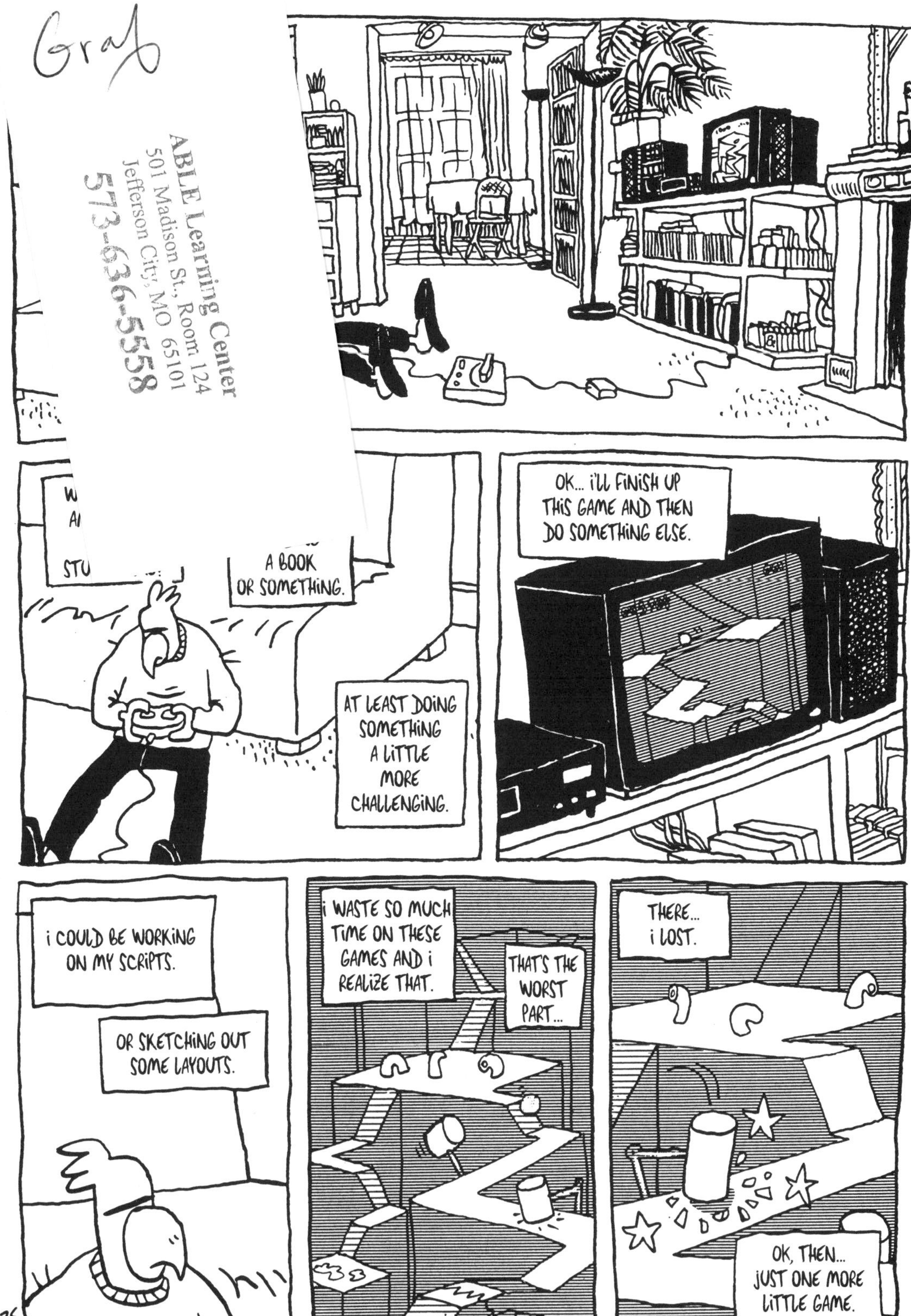
A BOOK
OR SOMETHING.
AT LEAST DOING SOMETHING A LITTLE MORE CHALLENGING.
OK... I'LL FINISH UP THIS GAME AND THEN DO SOMETHING ELSE.
I COULD BE WORKING ON MY SCRIPTS.
OR SKETCHING OUT SOME LAYOUTS.
I WASTE SO MUCH TIME ON THESE GAMES AND I REALIZE THAT.
THAT'S THE WORST PART...
THERE... I LOST.
OK, THEN... JUST ONE MORE LITTLE GAME.

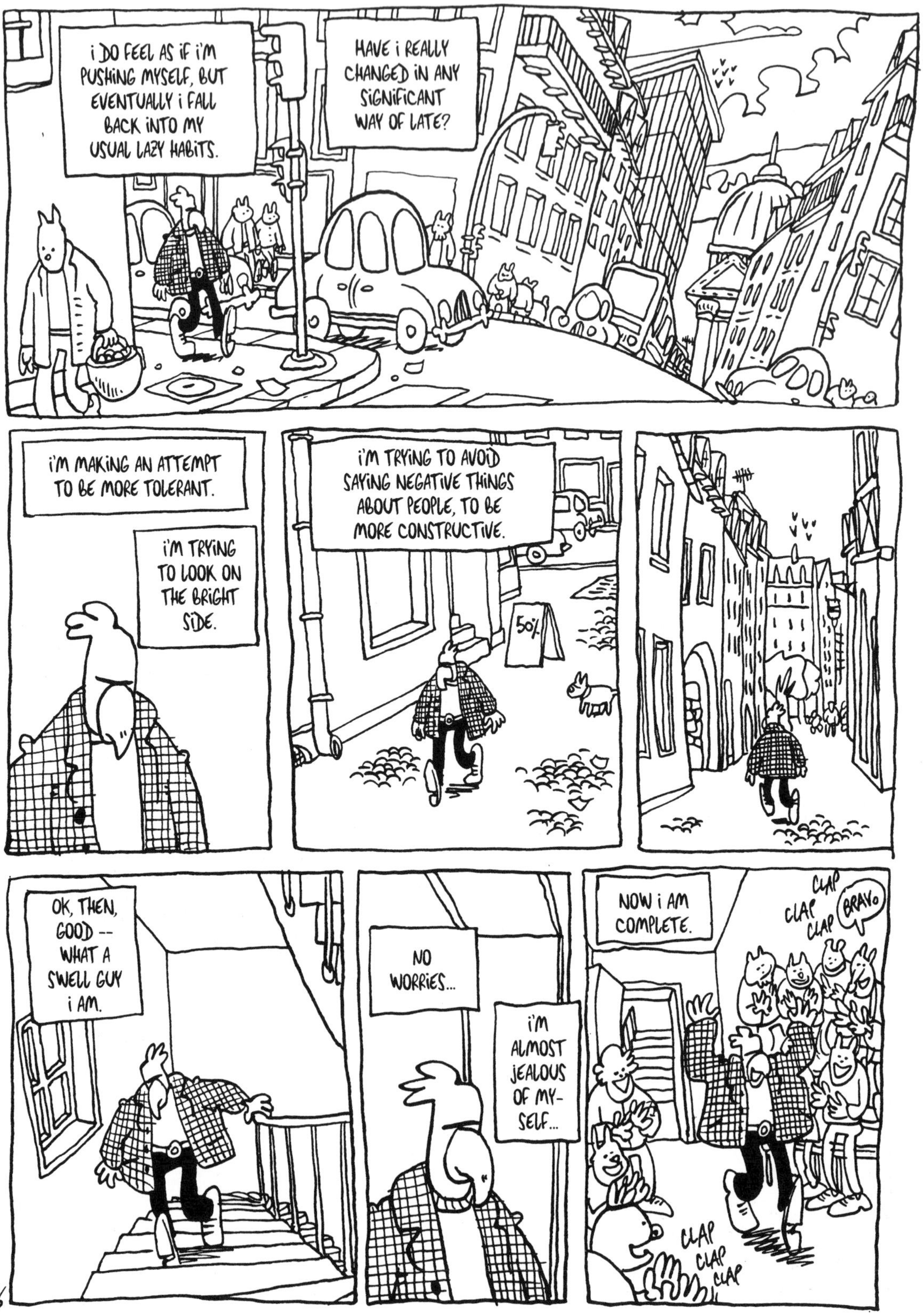
I DO FEEL AS IF I'M PUSHING MYSELF, BUT EVENTUALLY I FALL BACK INTO MY USUAL LAZY HABITS.
HAVE I REALLY CHANGED IN ANY SIGNIFICANT WAY OF LATE?
I'M MAKING AN ATTEMPT TO BE MORE TOLERANT.
I'M TRYING TO LOOK ON THE BRIGHT SIDE.
I'M TRYING TO AVOID SAYING NEGATIVE THINGS ABOUT PEOPLE, TO BE MORE CONSTRUCTIVE.
50%
OK, THEN, GOOD -- WHAT A SWELL GUY I AM.
NO WORRIES...
I'M ALMOST JEALOUS OF MY-SELF...
NOW I AM COMPLETE.
CLAP CLAP CLAP
BRAVO
CLAP CLAP CLAP

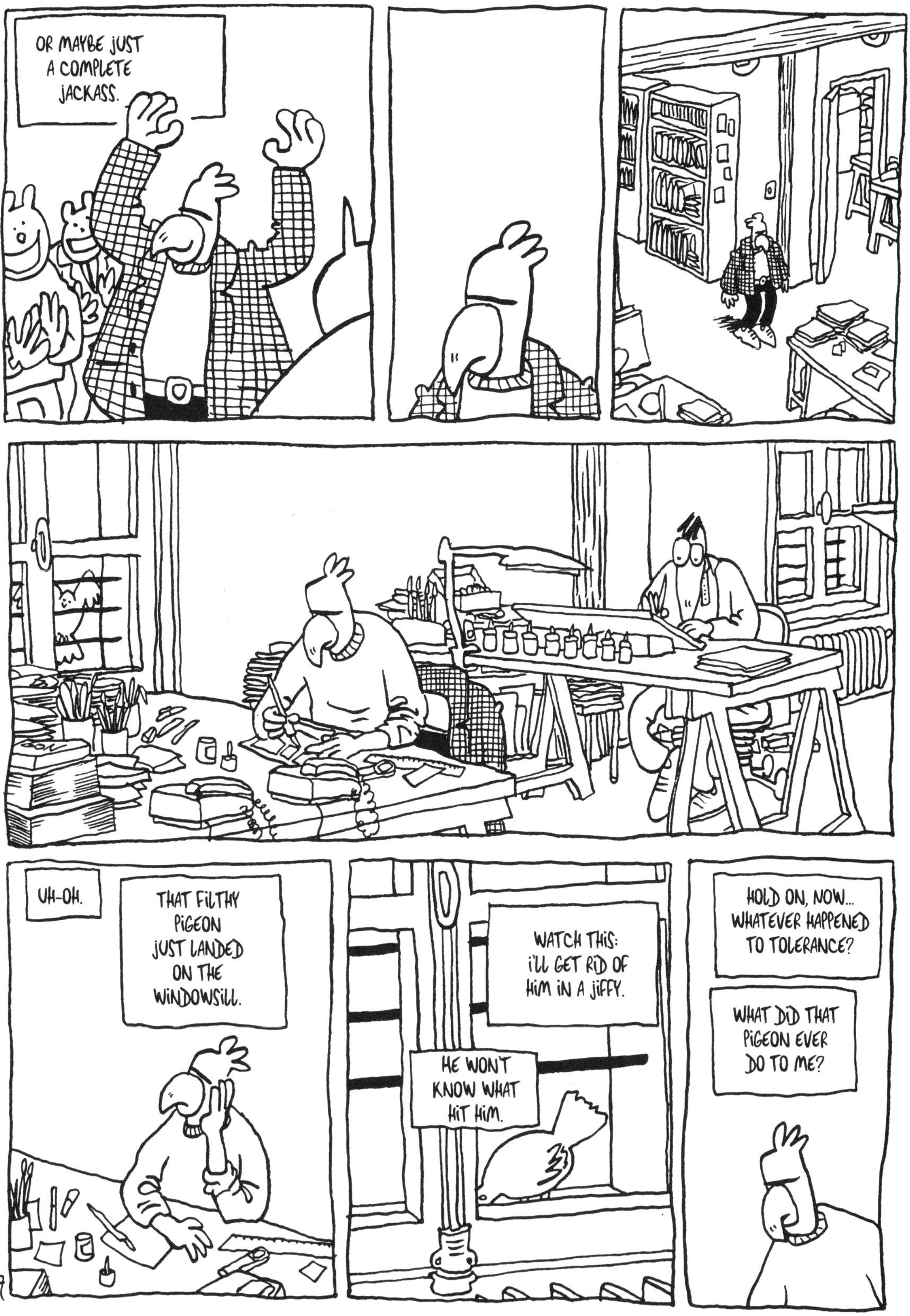
OR MAYBE JUST A COMPLETE JACKASS.
UH-OH.
THAT FILTHY PIGEON JUST LANDED ON THE WINDOWSILL.
WATCH THIS: I'LL GET RID OF HIM IN A JIFFY.
HE WON'T KNOW WHAT HIT HIM.
HOLD ON, NOW... WHATEVER HAPPENED TO TOLERANCE?
WHAT DID THAT PIGEON EVER DO TO ME?

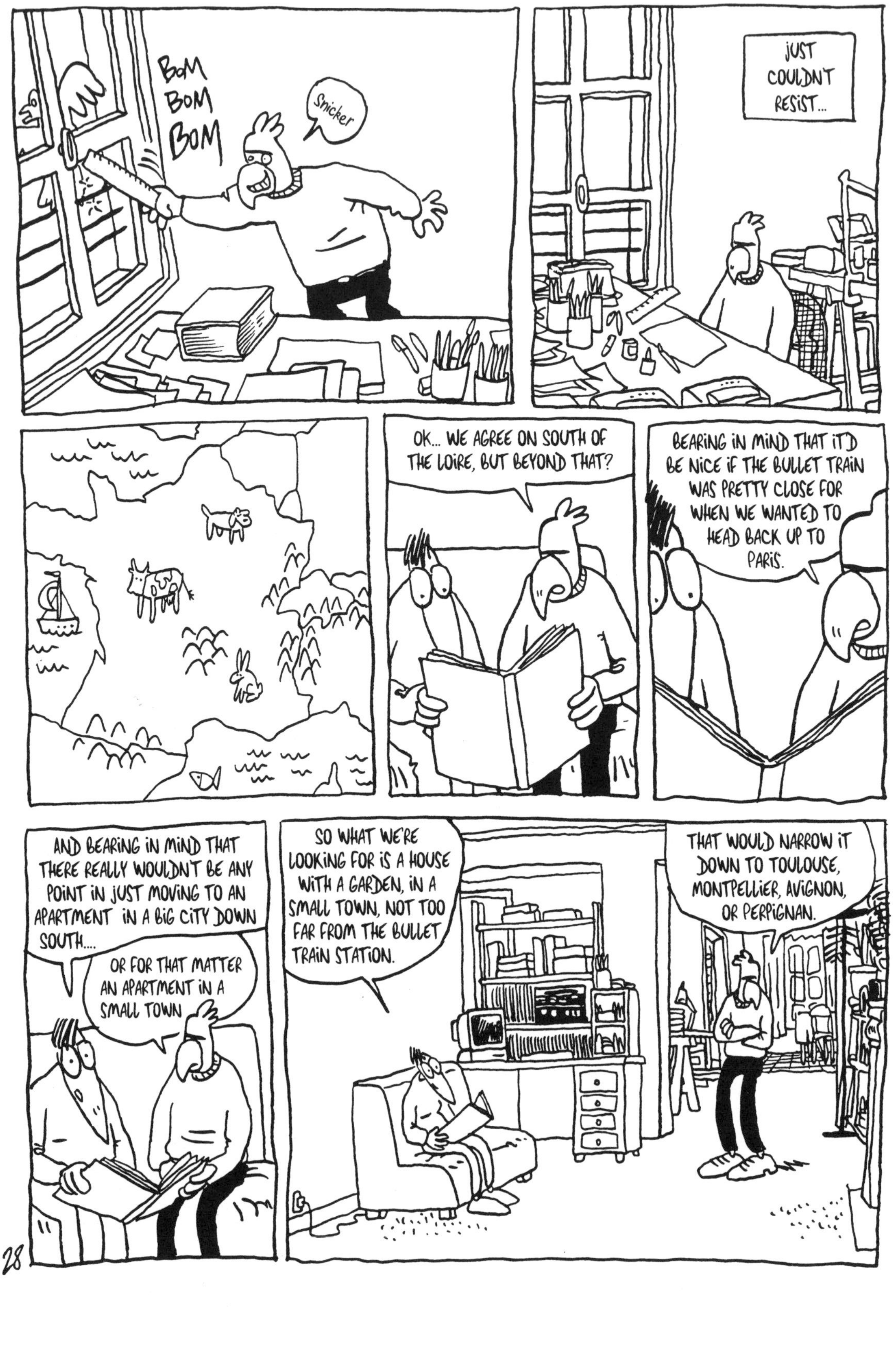
BOM
BOM
BOM
Snicker
JUST COULDN'T RESIST...
OK... WE AGREE ON SOUTH OF THE LOIRE, BUT BEYOND THAT?
BEARING IN MIND THAT IT'D BE NICE IF THE BULLET TRAIN WAS PRETTY CLOSE FOR WHEN WE WANTED TO HEAD BACK UP TO PARIS.
AND BEARING IN MIND THAT THERE REALLY WOULDN'T BE ANY POINT IN JUST MOVING TO AN APARTMENT IN A BIG CITY DOWN SOUTH....
OR FOR THAT MATTER AN APARTMENT IN A SMALL TOWN
SO WHAT WE'RE LOOKING FOR IS A HOUSE WITH A GARDEN, IN A SMALL TOWN, NOT TOO FAR FROM THE BULLET TRAIN STATION.
THAT WOULD NARROW IT DOWN TO TOULOUSE, MONTPELLIER, AVIGNON, OR PERPIGNAN.

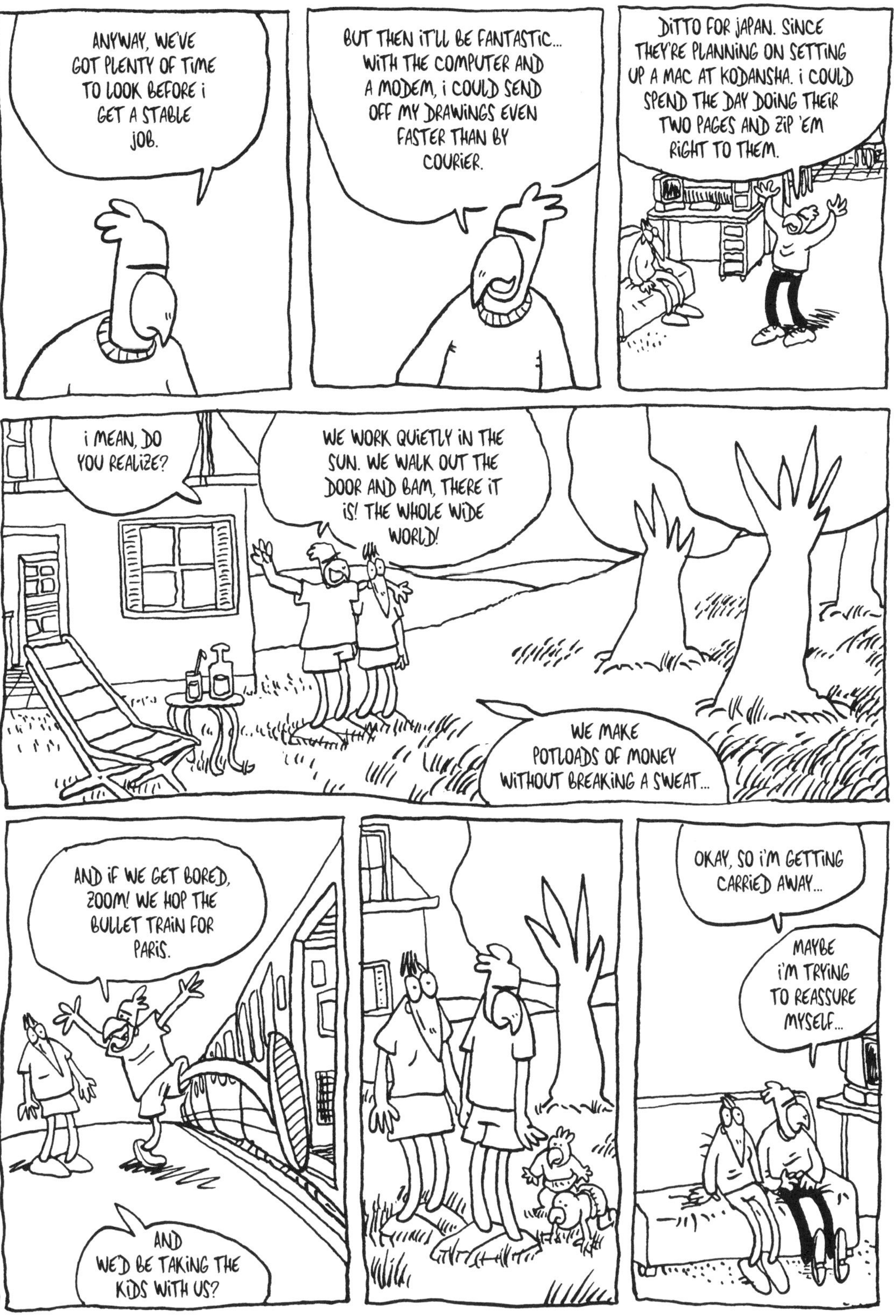
ANYWAY, WE'VE GOT PLENTY OF TIME TO LOOK BEFORE I GET A STABLE JOB.
BUT THEN IT'LL BE FANTASTIC... WITH THE COMPUTER AND A MODEM, I COULD SEND OFF MY DRAWINGS EVEN FASTER THAN BY COURIER.
DITTO FOR JAPAN. SINCE THEY'RE PLANNING ON SETTING UP A MAC AT KODANSHA. I COULD SPEND THE DAY DOING THEIR TWO PAGES AND ZIP 'EM RIGHT TO THEM.
I MEAN, DO YOU REALIZE?
WE WORK QUIETLY IN THE SUN. WE WALK OUT THE DOOR AND BAM, THERE IT IS! THE WHOLE WIDE WORLD!
WE MAKE POTLOADS OF MONEY WITHOUT BREAKING A SWEAT...
AND IF WE GET BORED, ZOOM! WE HOP THE BULLET TRAIN FOR PARIS.
AND WE'D BE TAKING THE KIDS WITH US?
OKAY, SO I'M GETTING CARRIED AWAY...
MAYBE I'M TRYING TO REASSURE MYSELF...

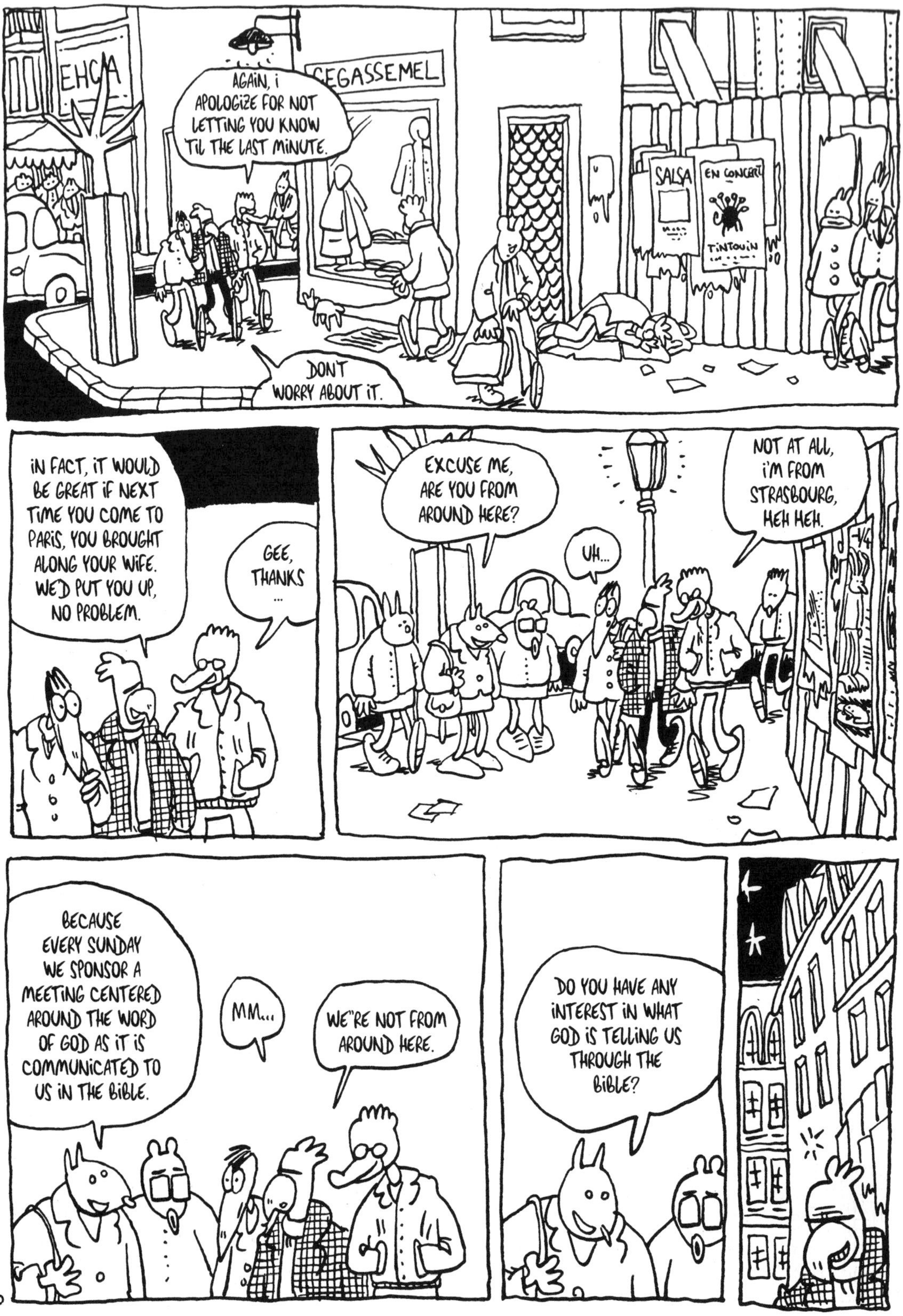
EHCA
GEGASSEMEL
AGAIN, I APOLOGIZE FOR NOT LETTING YOU KNOW TIL THE LAST MINUTE.
SALSA
EN CONCERT
TINTOUIN
DON'T WORRY ABOUT IT.
IN FACT, IT WOULD BE GREAT IF NEXT TIME YOU COME TO PARIS, YOU BROUGHT ALONG YOUR WIFE. WE'D PUT YOU UP, NO PROBLEM.
GEE, THANKS ...
EXCUSE ME, ARE YOU FROM AROUND HERE?
UH...
NOT AT ALL, I'M FROM STRASBOURG, HEH HEH.
BECAUSE EVERY SUNDAY WE SPONSOR A MEETING CENTERED AROUND THE WORD OF GOD AS IT IS COMMUNICATED TO US IN THE BIBLE.
MM...
WE'RE NOT FROM AROUND HERE.
DO YOU HAVE ANY INTEREST IN WHAT GOD IS TELLING US THROUGH THE BIBLE?

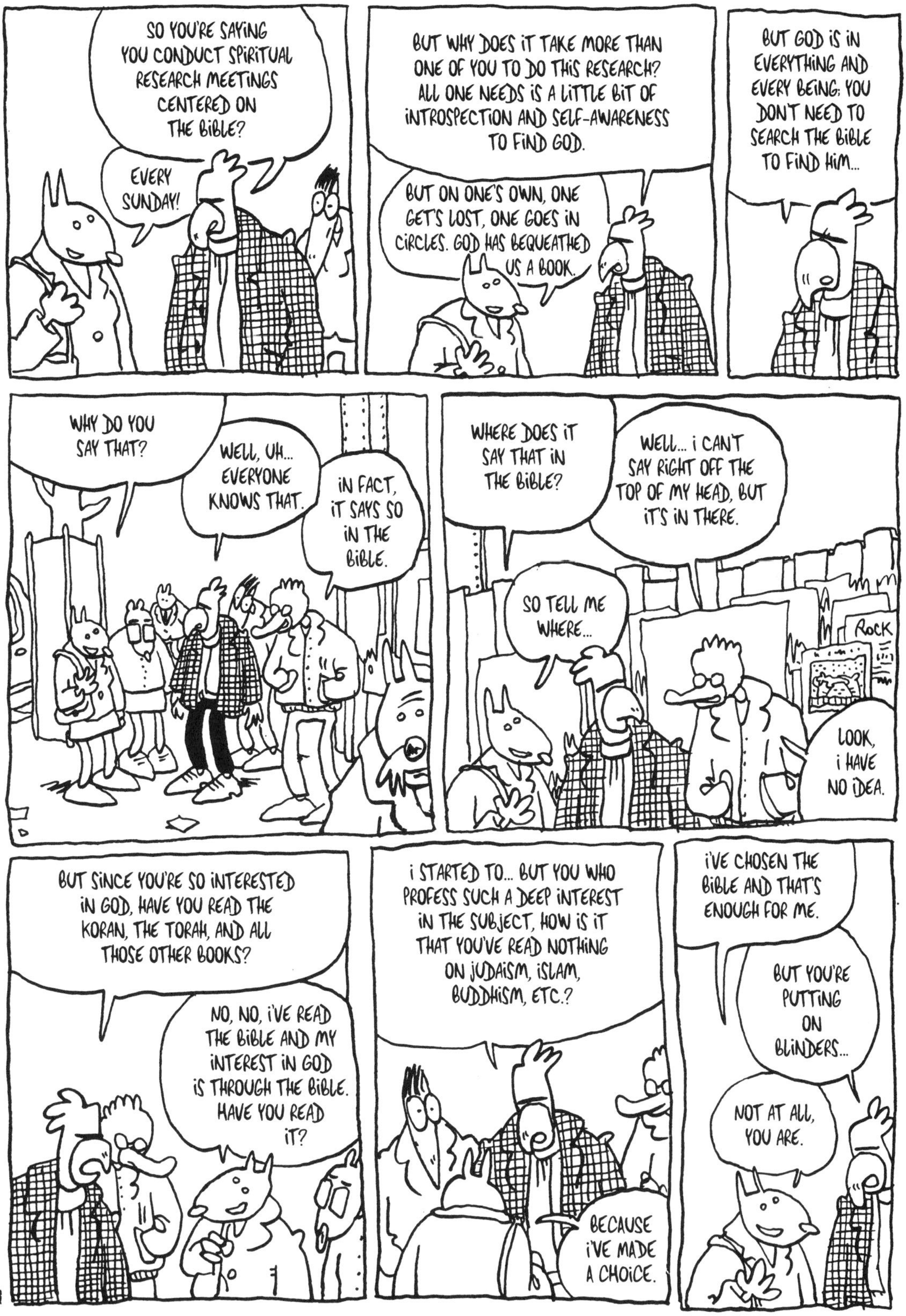

SO YOU'RE SAYING YOU CONDUCT SPIRITUAL RESEARCH MEETINGS CENTERED ON THE BIBLE?
EVERY SUNDAY!
BUT WHY DOES IT TAKE MORE THAN ONE OF YOU TO DO THIS RESEARCH? ALL ONE NEEDS IS A LITTLE BIT OF INTROSPECTION AND SELF-AWARENESS TO FIND GOD.
BUT ON ONE'S OWN, ONE GETS LOST, ONE GOES IN CIRCLES. GOD HAS BEQUEATHED US A BOOK.
BUT GOD IS IN EVERYTHING AND EVERY BEING; YOU DON'T NEED TO SEARCH THE BIBLE TO FIND HIM...
WHY DO YOU SAY THAT?
WELL, UH... EVERYONE KNOWS THAT.
IN FACT, IT SAYS SO IN THE BIBLE.
WHERE DOES IT SAY THAT IN THE BIBLE?
WELL... I CAN'T SAY RIGHT OFF THE TOP OF MY HEAD, BUT IT'S IN THERE.
SO TELL ME WHERE...
LOOK, I HAVE NO IDEA.
ROCK
BUT SINCE YOU'RE SO INTERESTED IN GOD, HAVE YOU READ THE KORAN, THE TORAH, AND ALL THOSE OTHER BOOKS?
NO, NO, I'VE READ THE BIBLE AND MY INTEREST IN GOD IS THROUGH THE BIBLE. HAVE YOU READ IT?
I STARTED TO... BUT YOU WHO PROFESS SUCH A DEEP INTEREST IN THE SUBJECT, HOW IS IT THAT YOU'VE READ NOTHING ON JUDAISM, ISLAM, BUDDHISM, ETC.?
BECAUSE I'VE MADE A CHOICE.
I'VE CHOSEN THE BIBLE AND THAT'S ENOUGH FOR ME.
BUT YOU'RE PUTTING ON BLINDERS...
NOT AT ALL, YOU ARE.

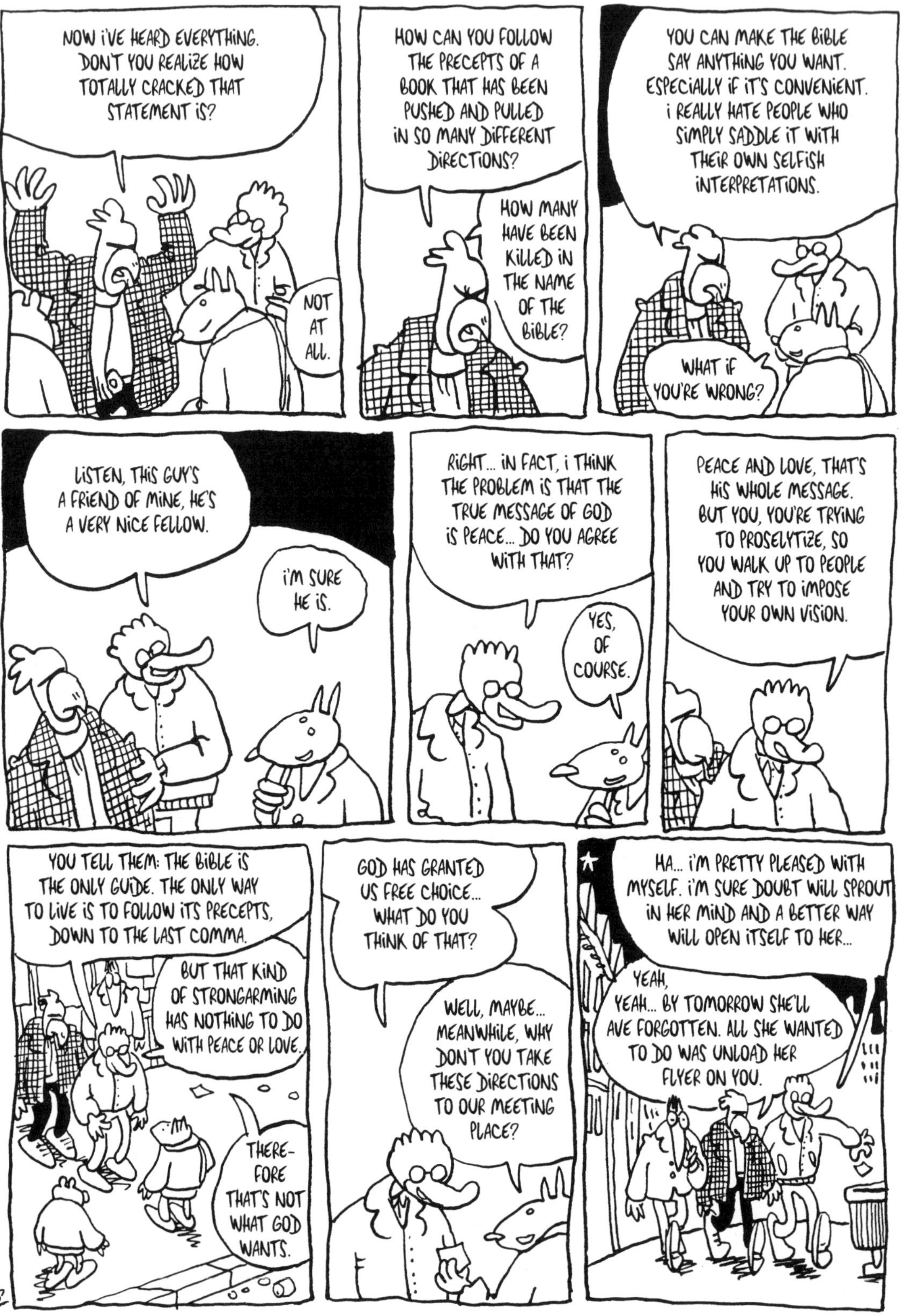
NOW I'VE HEARD EVERYTHING. DON'T YOU REALIZE HOW TOTALLY CRACKED THAT STATEMENT IS?
NOT AT ALL.
HOW CAN YOU FOLLOW THE PRECEPTS OF A BOOK THAT HAS BEEN PUSHED AND PULLED IN SO MANY DIFFERENT DIRECTIONS?
HOW MANY HAVE BEEN KILLED IN THE NAME OF THE BIBLE?
YOU CAN MAKE THE BIBLE SAY ANYTHING YOU WANT. ESPECIALLY IF IT'S CONVENIENT. I REALLY HATE PEOPLE WHO SIMPLY SADDLE IT WITH THEIR OWN SELFISH INTERPRETATIONS.
WHAT IF YOU'RE WRONG?
LISTEN, THIS GUY'S A FRIEND OF MINE, HE'S A VERY NICE FELLOW.
I'M SURE HE IS.
RIGHT... IN FACT, I THINK THE PROBLEM IS THAT THE TRUE MESSAGE OF GOD IS PEACE... DO YOU AGREE WITH THAT?
YES, OF COURSE.
PEACE AND LOVE, THAT'S HIS WHOLE MESSAGE. BUT YOU, YOU'RE TRYING TO PROSELYTIZE, SO YOU WALK UP TO PEOPLE AND TRY TO IMPOSE YOUR OWN VISION.
YOU TELL THEM: THE BIBLE IS THE ONLY GUIDE. THE ONLY WAY TO LIVE IS TO FOLLOW ITS PRECEPTS, DOWN TO THE LAST COMMA.
BUT THAT KIND OF STRONGARMING HAS NOTHING TO DO WITH PEACE OR LOVE.
THEREFORE THAT'S NOT WHAT GOD WANTS.
GOD HAS GRANTED US FREE CHOICE... WHAT DO YOU THINK OF THAT?
WELL, MAYBE... MEANWHILE, WHY DON'T YOU TAKE THESE DIRECTIONS TO OUR MEETING PLACE?
HA... I'M PRETTY PLEASED WITH MYSELF. I'M SURE DOUBT WILL SPROUT IN HER MIND AND A BETTER WAY WILL OPEN ITSELF TO HER...
YEAH, YEAH... BY TOMORROW SHE'LL AVE FORGOTTEN. ALL SHE WANTED TO DO WAS UNLOAD HER FLYER ON YOU.

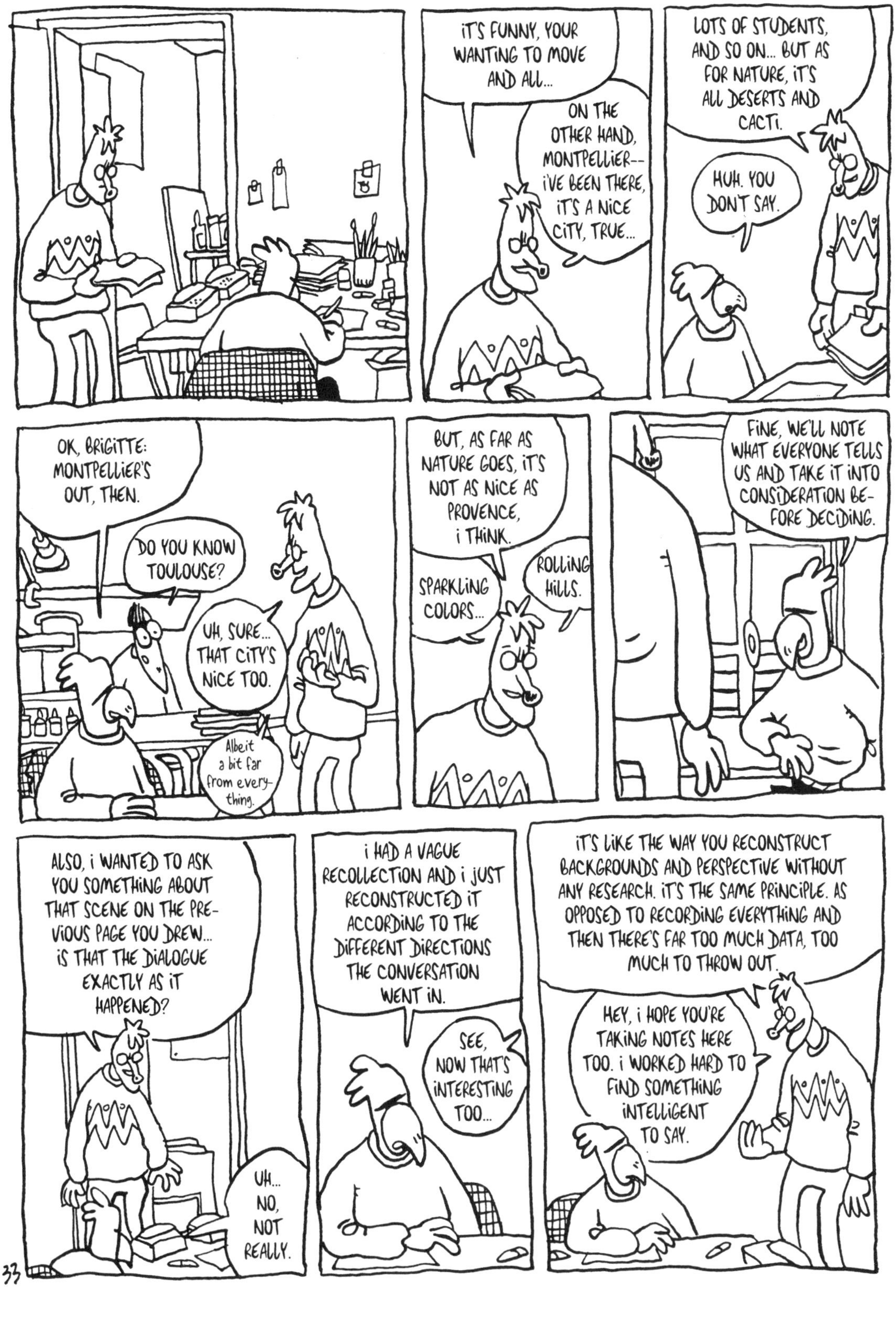

IT'S FUNNY, YOUR WANTING TO MOVE AND ALL...
ON THE OTHER HAND, MONTPELLIER-- I'VE BEEN THERE, IT'S A NICE CITY, TRUE...
LOTS OF STUDENTS, AND SO ON... BUT AS FOR NATURE, IT'S ALL DESERTS AND CACTI.
HUH. YOU DON'T SAY.
OK, BRIGITTE: MONTPELLIER'S OUT, THEN.
DO YOU KNOW TOULOUSE?
UH, SURE... THAT CITY'S NICE TOO.
Albeit a bit far from every-thing.
BUT, AS FAR AS NATURE GOES, IT'S NOT AS NICE AS PROVENCE, I THINK.
SPARKLING COLORS...
ROLLING HILLS.
FINE, WE'LL NOTE WHAT EVERYONE TELLS US AND TAKE IT INTO CONSIDERATION BE-FORE DECIDING.
ALSO, I WANTED TO ASK YOU SOMETHING ABOUT THAT SCENE ON THE PRE-VIOUS PAGE YOU DREW... IS THAT THE DIALOGUE EXACTLY AS IT HAPPENED?
UH... NO, NOT REALLY.
I HAD A VAGUE RECOLLECTION AND I JUST RECONSTRUCTED IT ACCORDING TO THE DIFFERENT DIRECTIONS THE CONVERSATION WENT IN.
SEE, NOW THAT'S INTERESTING TOO...
IT'S LIKE THE WAY YOU RECONSTRUCT BACKGROUNDS AND PERSPECTIVE WITHOUT ANY RESEARCH. IT'S THE SAME PRINCIPLE. AS OPPOSED TO RECORDING EVERYTHING AND THEN THERE'S FAR TOO MUCH DATA, TOO MUCH TO THROW OUT.
HEY, I HOPE YOU'RE TAKING NOTES HERE TOO. I WORKED HARD TO FIND SOMETHING INTELLIGENT TO SAY.

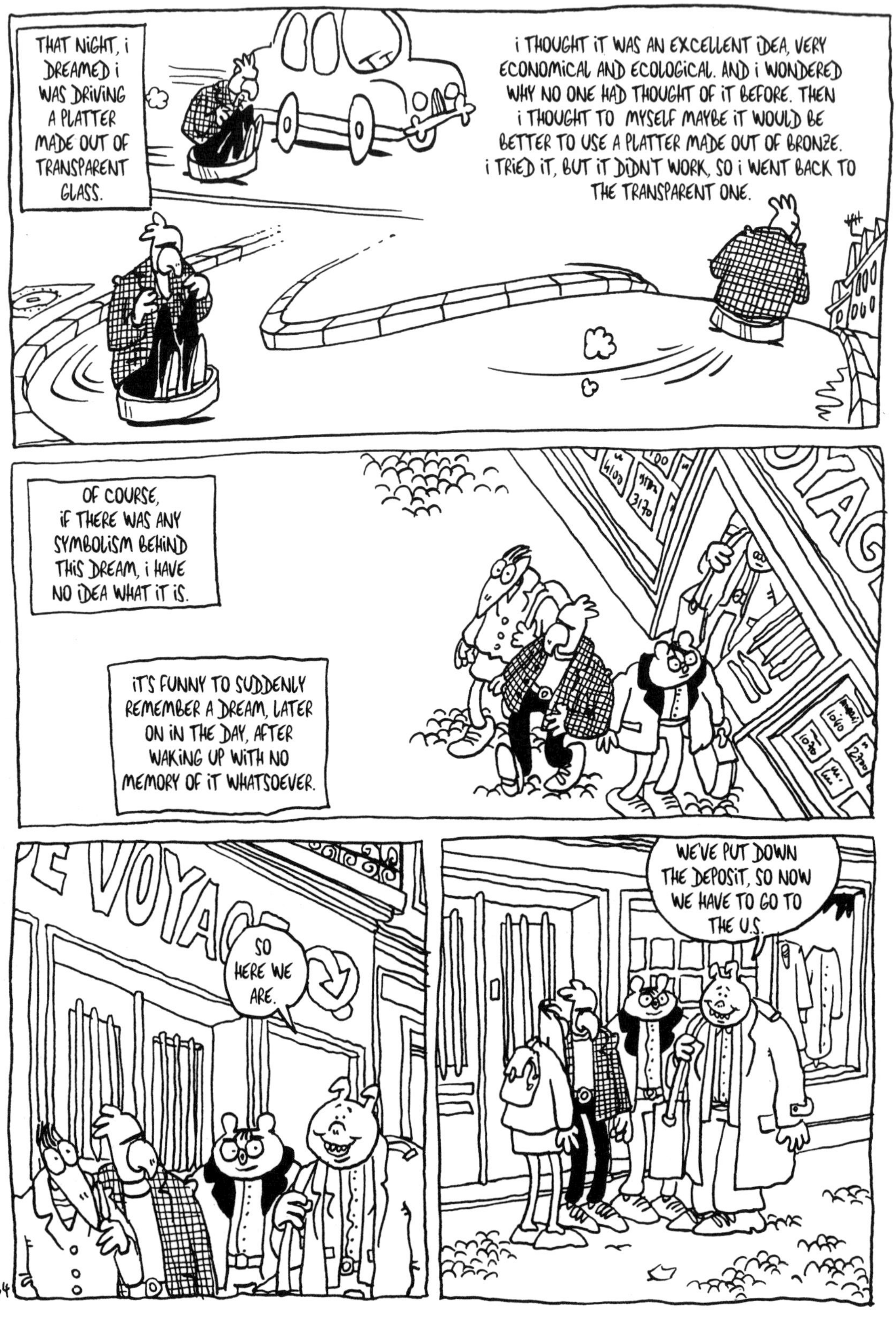
THAT NIGHT, i DREAMED i WAS DRIVING A PLATTER MADE OUT OF TRANSPARENT GLASS.
i THOUGHT iT WAS AN EXCELLENT iDEA, VERY ECONOMICAL AND ECOLOGICAL. AND i WONDERED WHY NO ONE HAD THOUGHT OF iT BEFORE. THEN i THOUGHT TO MYSELF MAYBE iT WOULD BE BETTER TO USE A PLATTER MADE OUT OF BRONZE. i TRiED iT, BUT iT DiDN'T WORK, SO i WENT BACK TO THE TRANSPARENT ONE.
OF COURSE, iF THERE WAS ANY SYMBOLiSM BEHiND THiS DREAM, i HAVE NO iDEA WHAT iT iS.
iT'S FUNNY TO SUDDENLY REMEMBER A DREAM, LATER ON iN THE DAY, AFTER WAKiNG UP WiTH NO MEMORY OF iT WHATSOEVER.
VOYAG
SO HERE WE ARE.
WE'VE PUT DOWN THE DEPOSiT, SO NOW WE HAVE TO GO TO THE U.S.

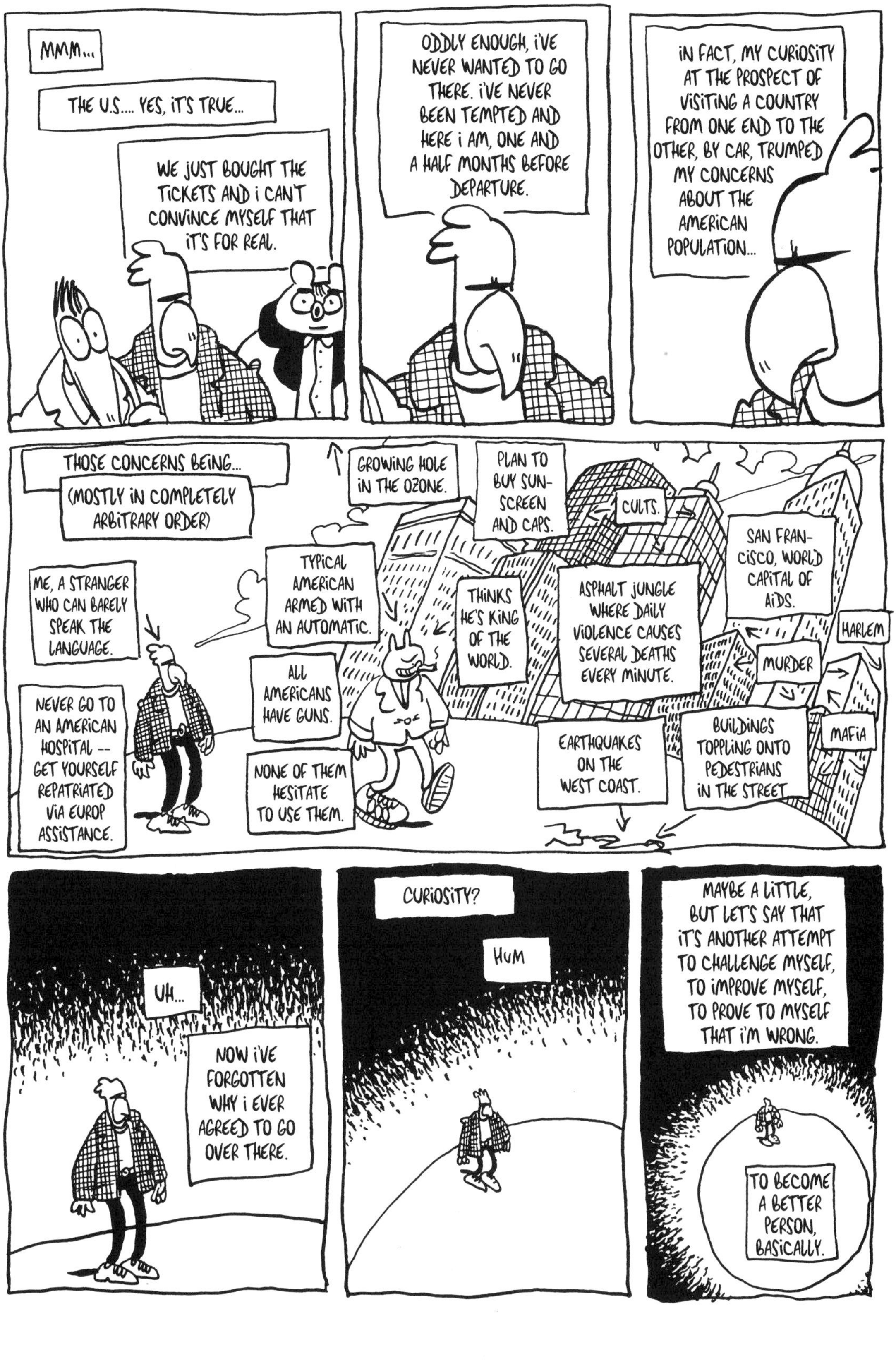

MMM...
THE U.S.... YES, IT'S TRUE...
WE JUST BOUGHT THE TICKETS AND I CAN'T CONVINCE MYSELF THAT IT'S FOR REAL.
ODDLY ENOUGH, I'VE NEVER WANTED TO GO THERE. I'VE NEVER BEEN TEMPTED AND HERE I AM, ONE AND A HALF MONTHS BEFORE DEPARTURE.
IN FACT, MY CURIOSITY AT THE PROSPECT OF VISITING A COUNTRY FROM ONE END TO THE OTHER, BY CAR, TRUMPED MY CONCERNS ABOUT THE AMERICAN POPULATION...
THOSE CONCERNS BEING...
(MOSTLY IN COMPLETELY ARBITRARY ORDER)
GROWING HOLE IN THE OZONE.
PLAN TO BUY SUN-SCREEN AND CAPS.
CULTS.
SAN FRAN-CISCO, WORLD CAPITAL OF AIDS.
ME, A STRANGER WHO CAN BARELY SPEAK THE LANGUAGE.
TYPICAL AMERICAN ARMED WITH AN AUTOMATIC.
THINKS HE'S KING OF THE WORLD.
ASPHALT JUNGLE WHERE DAILY VIOLENCE CAUSES SEVERAL DEATHS EVERY MINUTE.
HARLEM
MURDER
NEVER GO TO AN AMERICAN HOSPITAL -- GET YOURSELF REPATRIATED VIA EUROP ASSISTANCE.
ALL AMERICANS HAVE GUNS.
NONE OF THEM HESITATE TO USE THEM.
EARTHQUAKES ON THE WEST COAST.
BUILDINGS TOPPLING ONTO PEDESTRIANS IN THE STREET.
MAFIA
UH...
NOW I'VE FORGOTTEN WHY I EVER AGREED TO GO OVER THERE.
CURIOSITY?
HUM
MAYBE A LITTLE, BUT LET'S SAY THAT IT'S ANOTHER ATTEMPT TO CHALLENGE MYSELF, TO IMPROVE MYSELF, TO PROVE TO MYSELF THAT I'M WRONG.
TO BECOME A BETTER PERSON, BASICALLY.

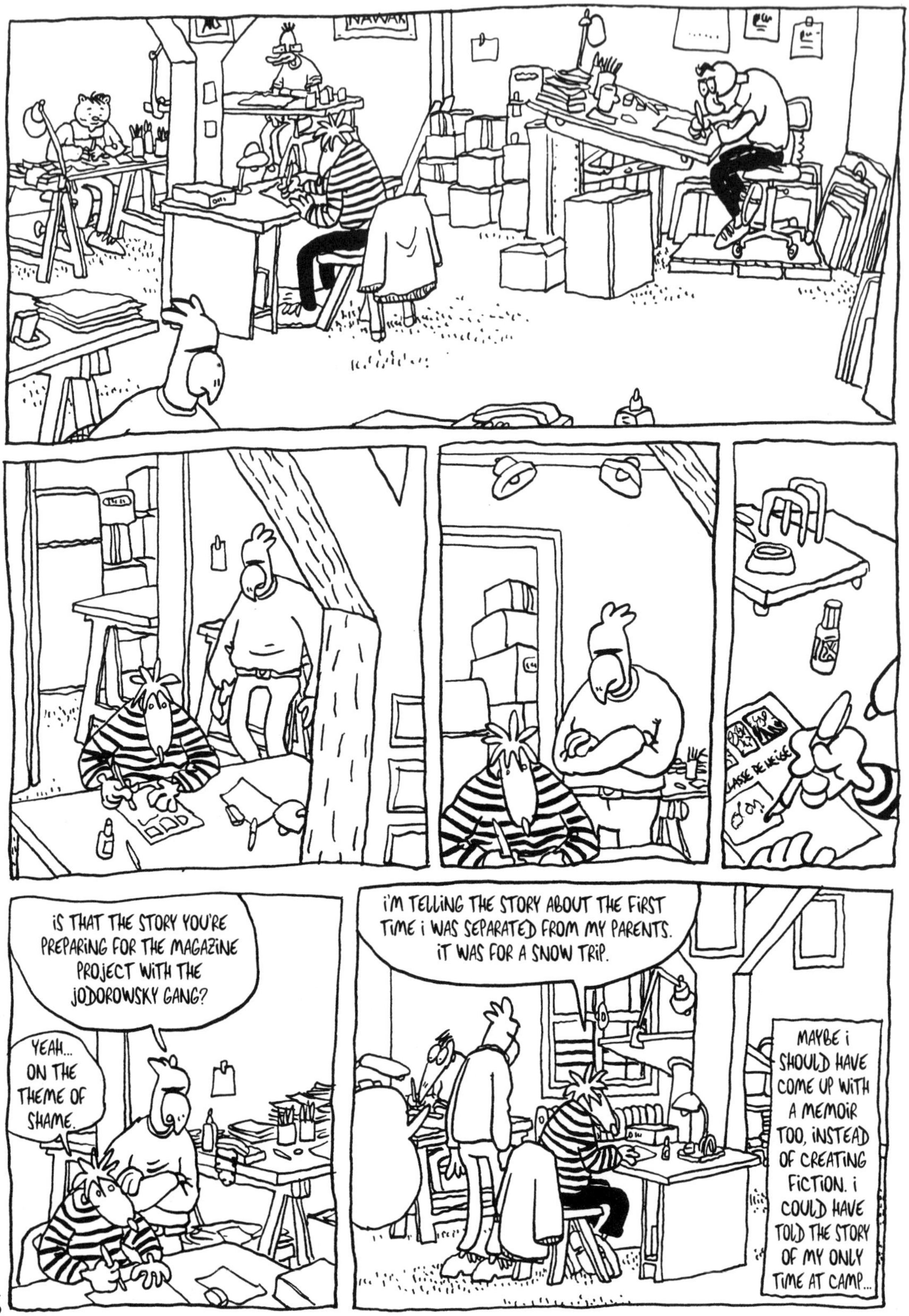
NAWAK
IS THAT THE STORY YOU'RE PREPARING FOR THE MAGAZINE PROJECT WITH THE JODOROWSKY GANG?
YEAH... ON THE THEME OF SHAME.
I'M TELLING THE STORY ABOUT THE FIRST TIME I WAS SEPARATED FROM MY PARENTS. IT WAS FOR A SNOW TRIP.
MAYBE I SHOULD HAVE COME UP WITH A MEMOIR TOO, INSTEAD OF CREATING FICTION. I COULD HAVE TOLD THE STORY OF MY ONLY TIME AT CAMP...

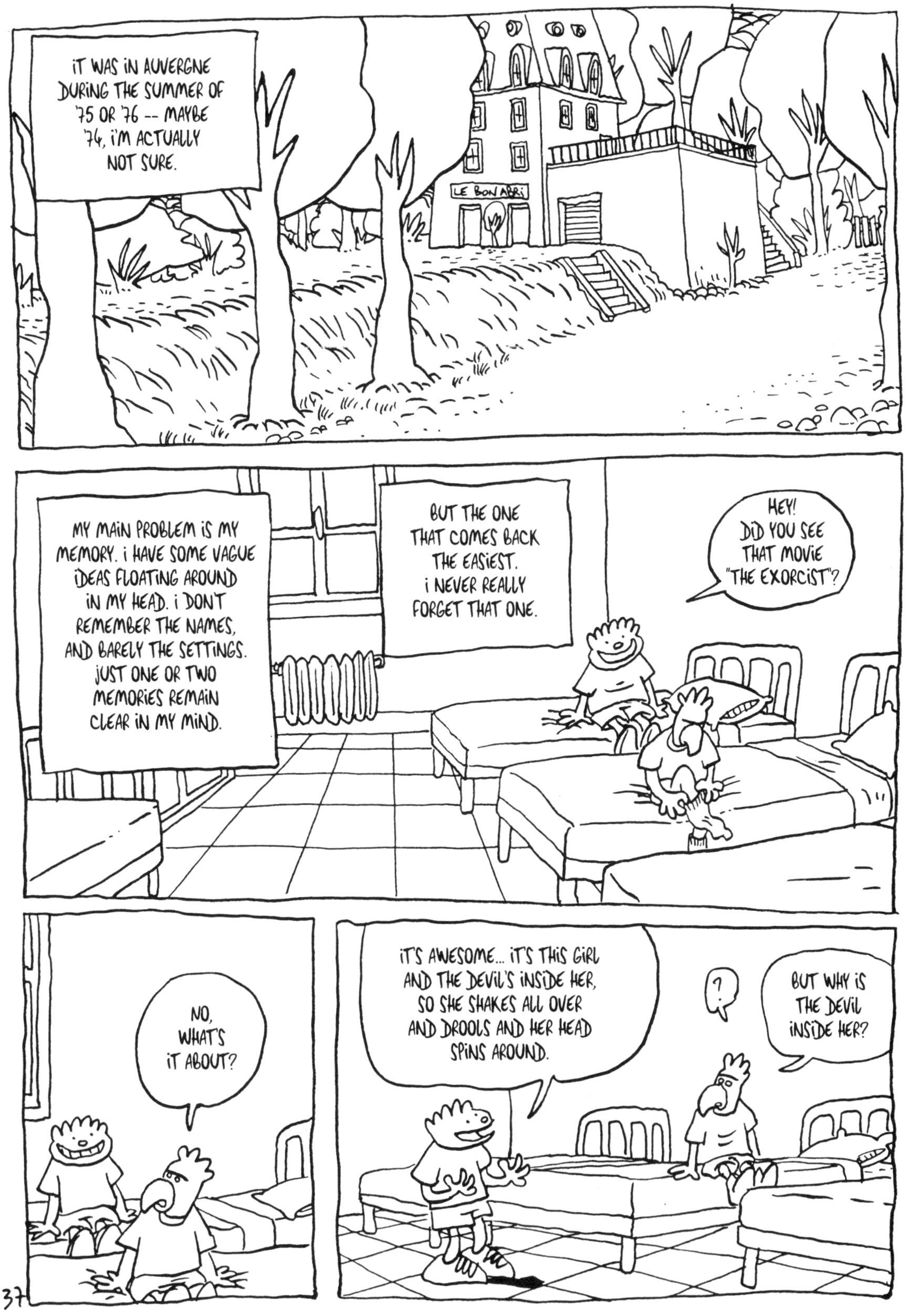
IT WAS IN AUVERGNE DURING THE SUMMER OF '75 OR '76 -- MAYBE '74, I'M ACTUALLY NOT SURE.
LE BON ABRI
MY MAIN PROBLEM IS MY MEMORY. I HAVE SOME VAGUE IDEAS FLOATING AROUND IN MY HEAD. I DON'T REMEMBER THE NAMES, AND BARELY THE SETTINGS. JUST ONE OR TWO MEMORIES REMAIN CLEAR IN MY MIND.
BUT THE ONE THAT COMES BACK THE EASIEST. I NEVER REALLY FORGET THAT ONE.
HEY! DID YOU SEE THAT MOVIE "THE EXORCIST"?
NO, WHAT'S IT ABOUT?
IT'S AWESOME... IT'S THIS GIRL AND THE DEVIL'S INSIDE HER, SO SHE SHAKES ALL OVER AND DROOLS AND HER HEAD SPINS AROUND.
?
BUT WHY IS THE DEVIL INSIDE HER?

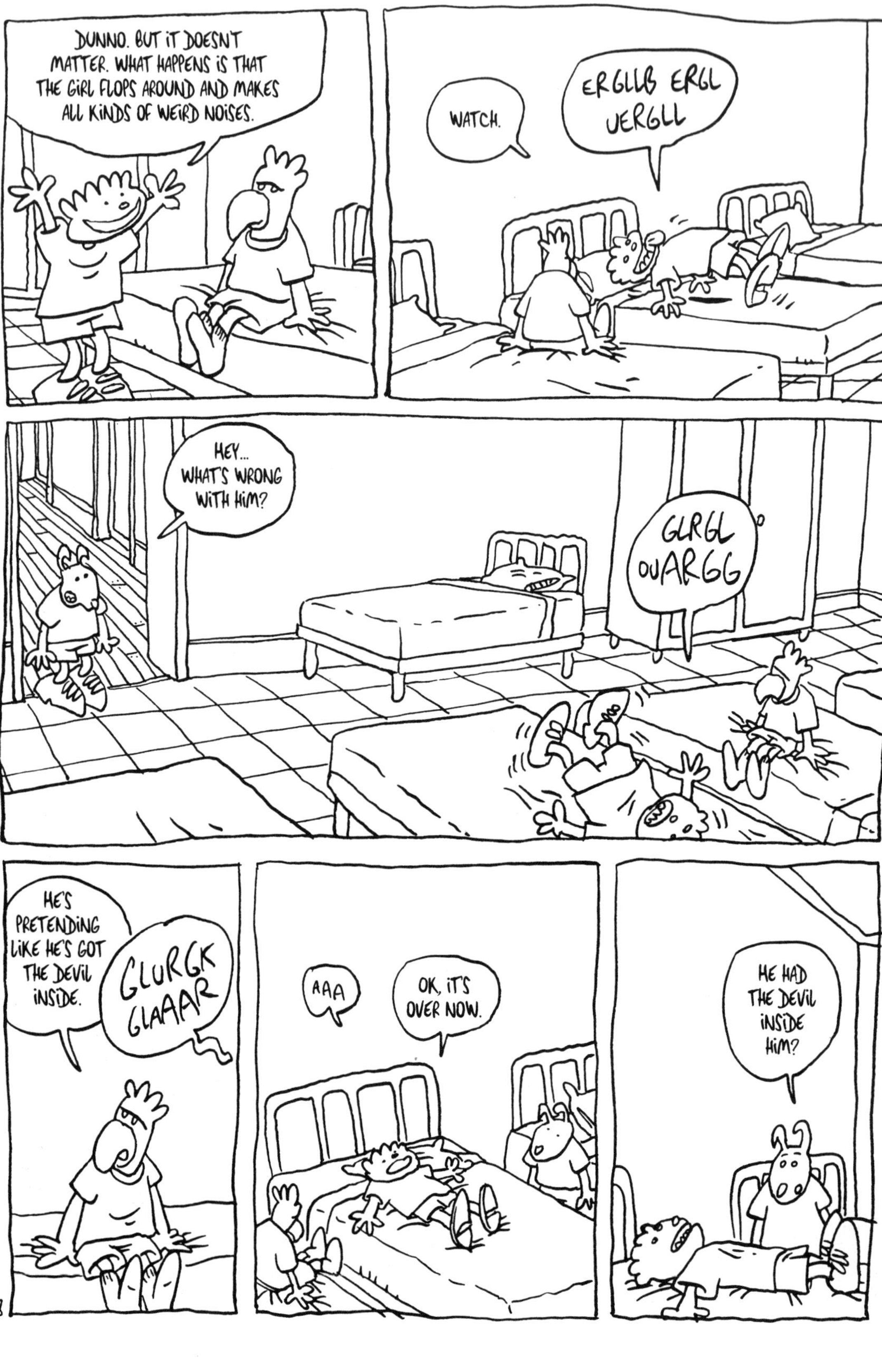
DUNNO. BUT IT DOESN'T MATTER. WHAT HAPPENS IS THAT THE GIRL FLOPS AROUND AND MAKES ALL KINDS OF WEIRD NOISES.
WATCH.
ERGLLB ERGL UERGLL
HEY... WHAT'S WRONG WITH HIM?
GLRGL OUARGG
HE'S PRETENDING LIKE HE'S GOT THE DEVIL INSIDE.
GLURGK GLAAAR
AAA
OK, IT'S OVER NOW.
HE HAD THE DEVIL INSIDE HIM?

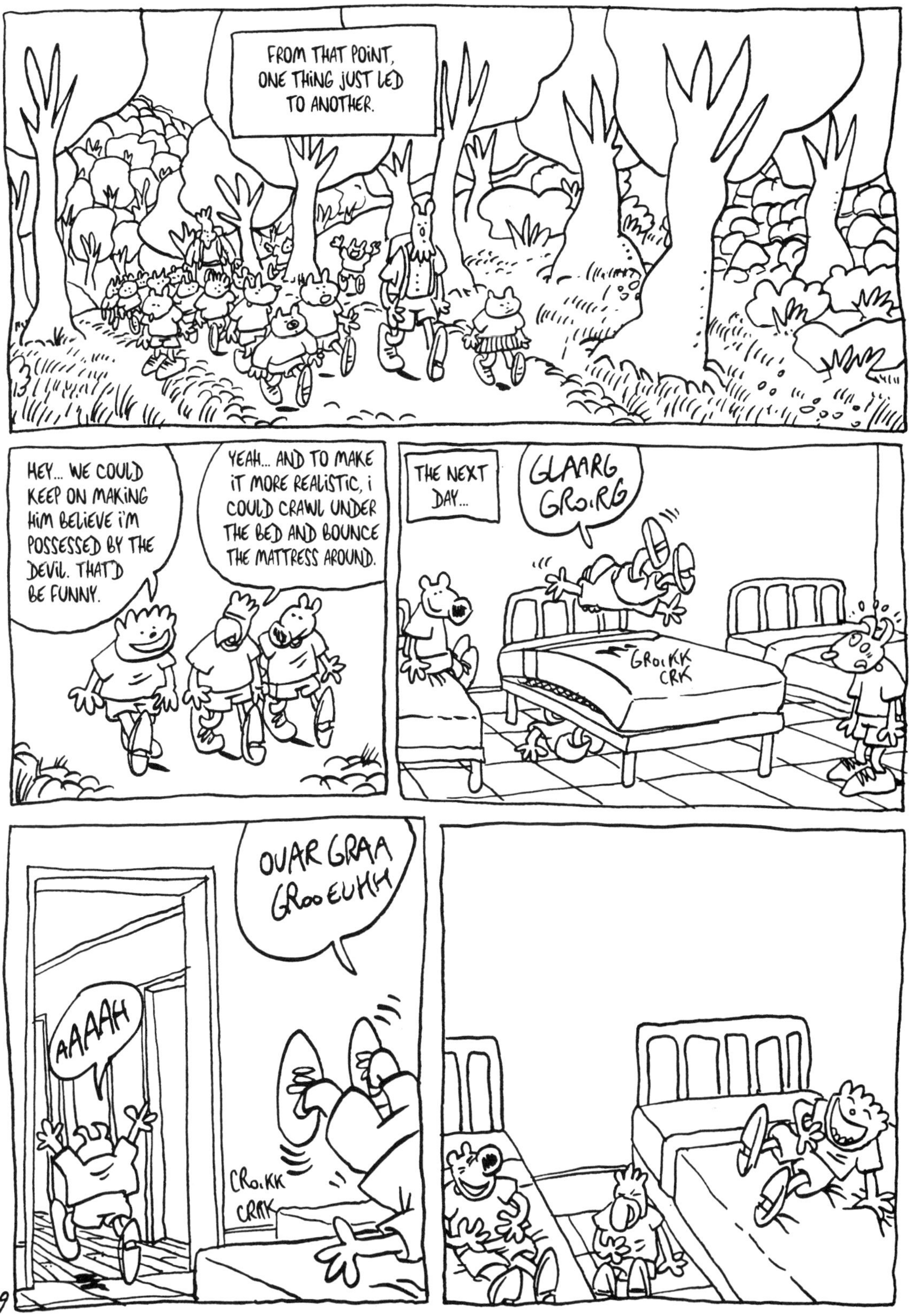
FROM THAT POINT, ONE THING JUST LED TO ANOTHER.
HEY... WE COULD KEEP ON MAKING HIM BELIEVE I'M POSSESSED BY THE DEVIL. THAT'D BE FUNNY.
YEAH... AND TO MAKE IT MORE REALISTIC, I COULD CRAWL UNDER THE BED AND BOUNCE THE MATTRESS AROUND.
THE NEXT DAY...
GLAARG GROIRG
GROIKK CRK
OUAR GRAA GROOEUHH
AAAAH
CROIKK CRRK

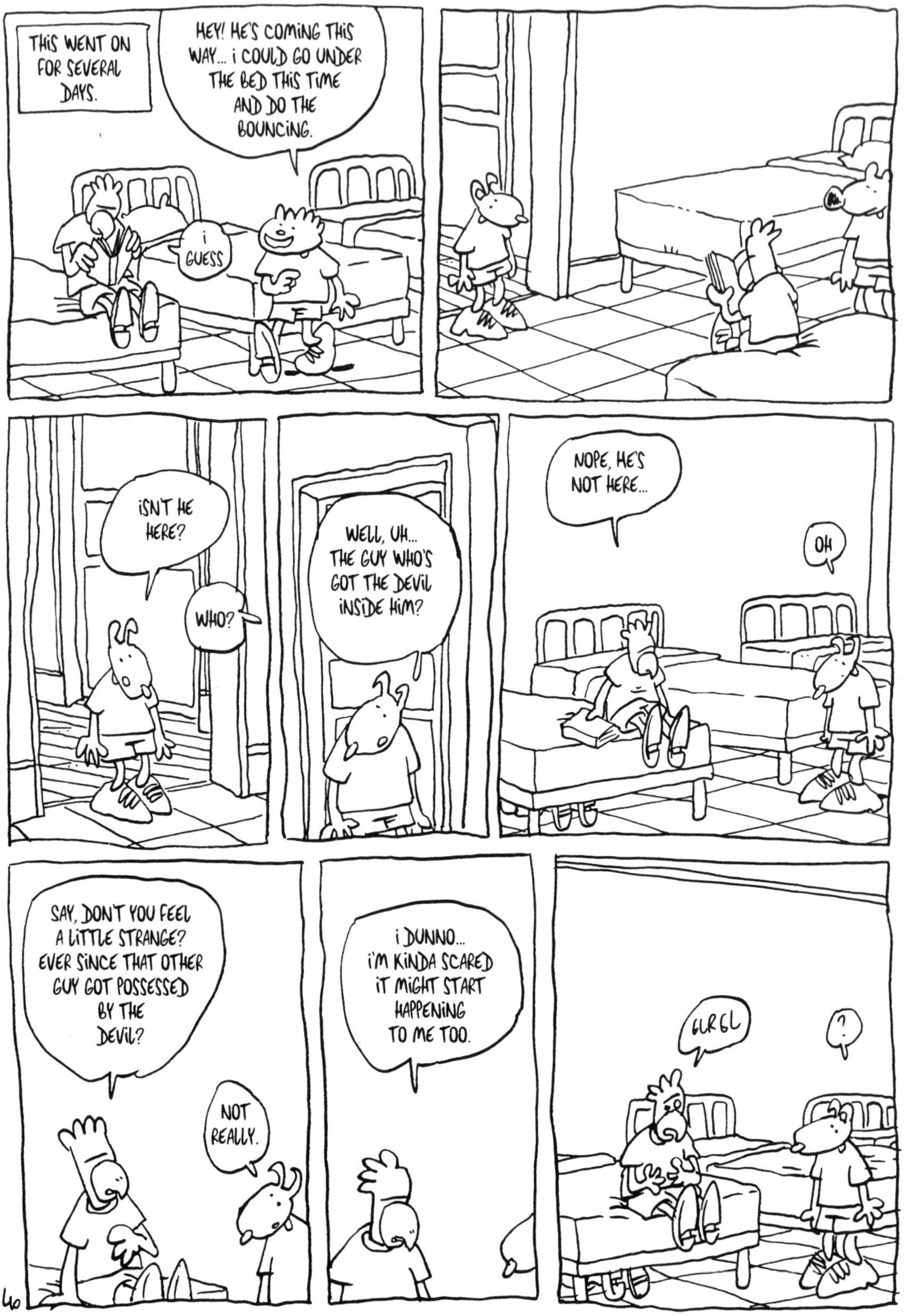
THIS WENT ON FOR SEVERAL DAYS.
HEY! HE'S COMING THIS WAY... I COULD GO UNDER THE BED THIS TIME AND DO THE BOUNCING.
I GUESS
ISN'T HE HERE?
WHO?
WELL, UH... THE GUY WHO'S GOT THE DEVIL INSIDE HIM?
NOPE, HE'S NOT HERE...
OH
SAY, DON'T YOU FEEL A LITTLE STRANGE? EVER SINCE THAT OTHER GUY GOT POSSESSED BY THE DEVIL?
NOT REALLY.
I DUNNO... I'M KINDA SCARED IT MIGHT START HAPPENING TO ME TOO.
GLRGL
?

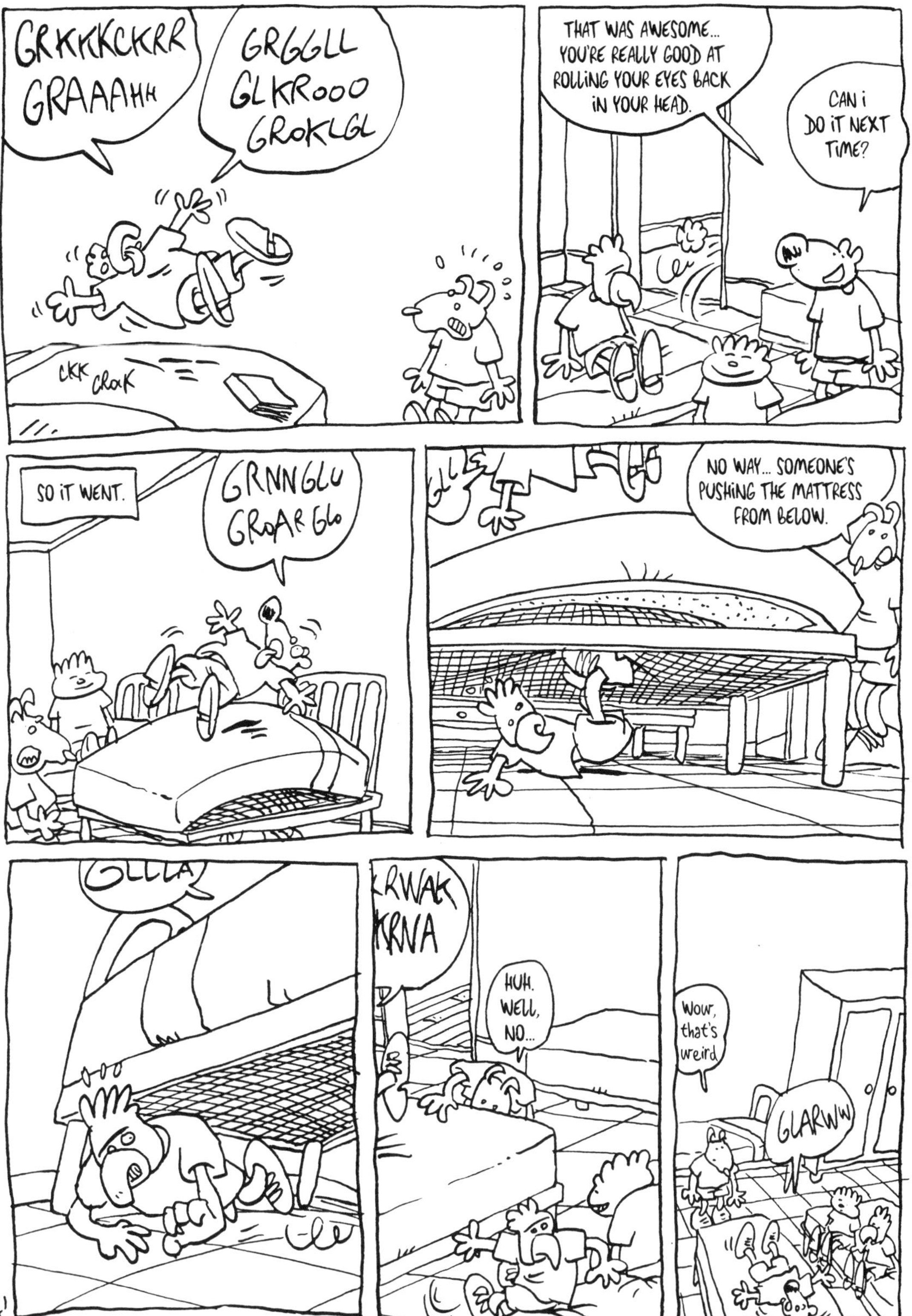
GRKKKCKRR GRAAAHH
GRGGLL GLKROOO GROKLGL
CKK CRAK
THAT WAS AWESOME... YOU'RE REALLY GOOD AT ROLLING YOUR EYES BACK IN YOUR HEAD.
CAN I DO IT NEXT TIME?
SO IT WENT.
GRNNGLU GROAR GLO
NO WAY... SOMEONE'S PUSHING THE MATTRESS FROM BELOW.
KRWAK KRNA
HUH. WELL, NO...
Wow, that's weird
GLARWW

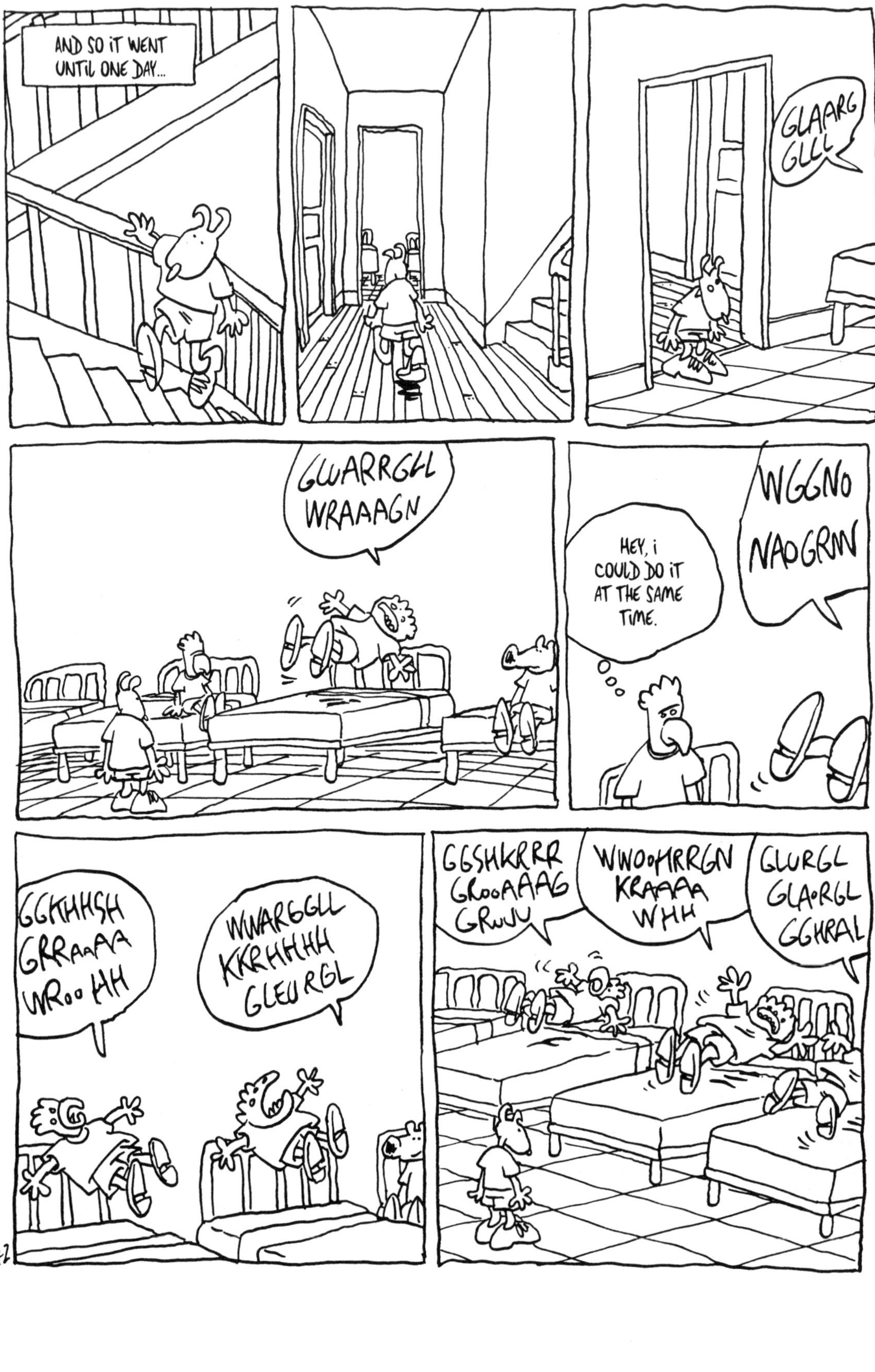
AND SO IT WENT UNTIL ONE DAY...
GLAARG GLLL
GWARRGLL WRAAAGN
HEY, I COULD DO IT AT THE SAME TIME.
WGGNO NAOGRW
GGKHHSH GRRAAAA WROO HH
WWARGGLL KKRHHHH GLEURGL
GGSHKRRR GROOAAAG GRUUU
WWOOHRRGN KRAAAA WHH
GLURGL GLAORGL GGHRAL

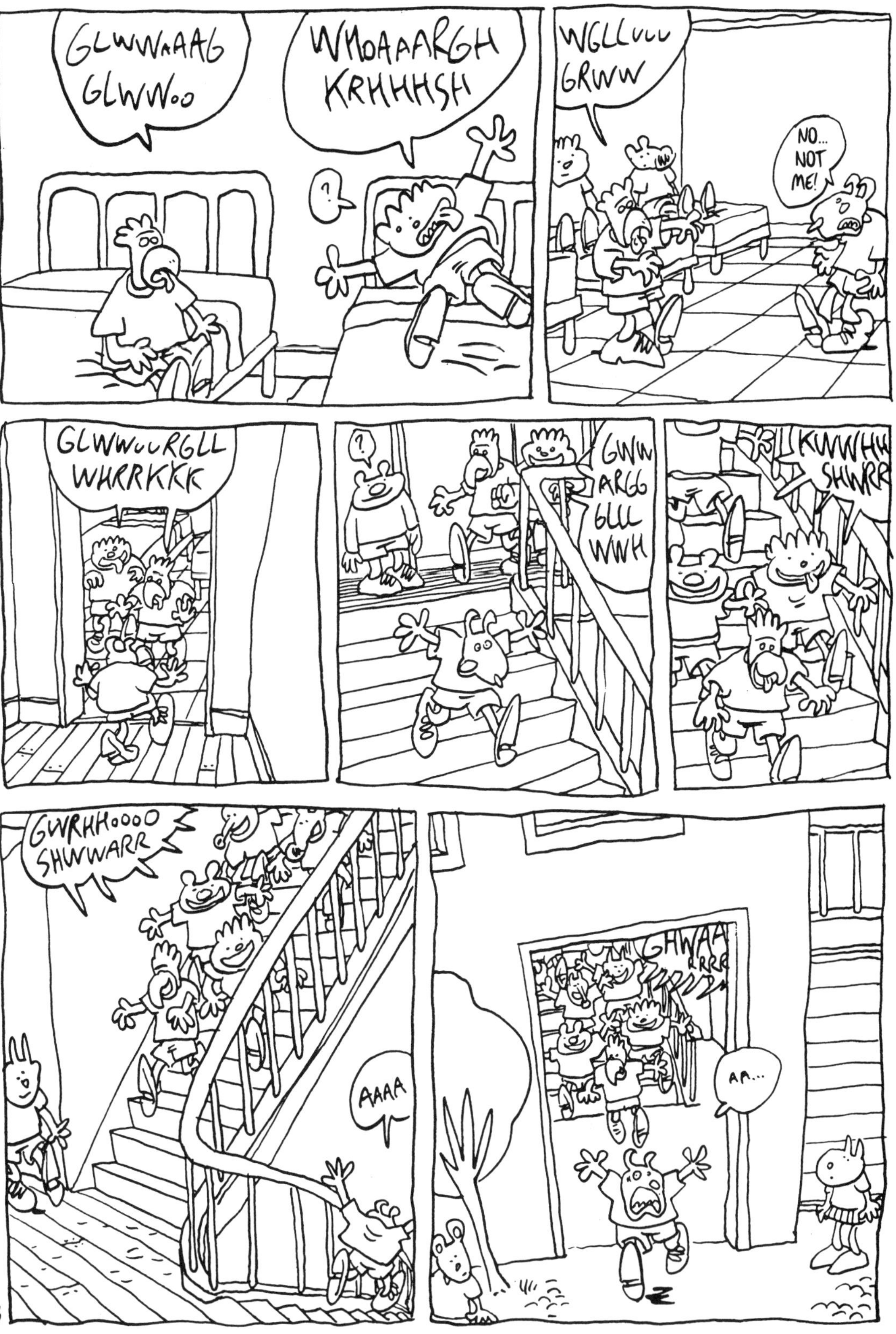
GLWWAAAG GLWWOO
WHOAAARGH KRHHHSH
?
WGLLUUU GRWW
NO... NOT ME!
GLWWUURGLL WHRRKKK
?
GWW ARGG GLLL WWH
KWWHH SHWRR
GWRHHOOOO SHWWARR
AAAA
GHWAA RRRR
AA...

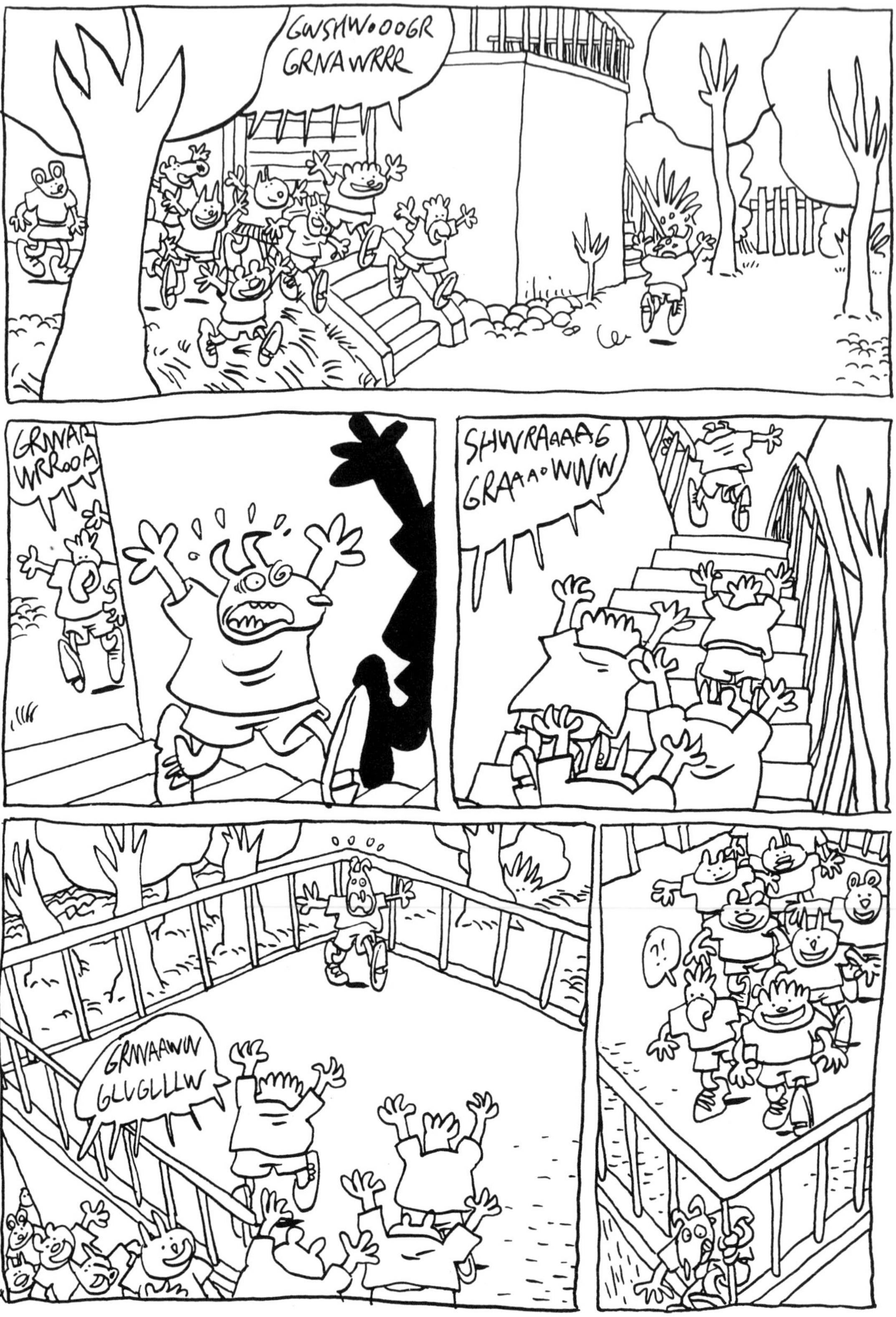
GWSHWoOOGR GRNAWRRR
GRNAR WRRoOA
SHWRAAAAG GRAAAoWWW
GRNAAWW GLUGLLLW
?!

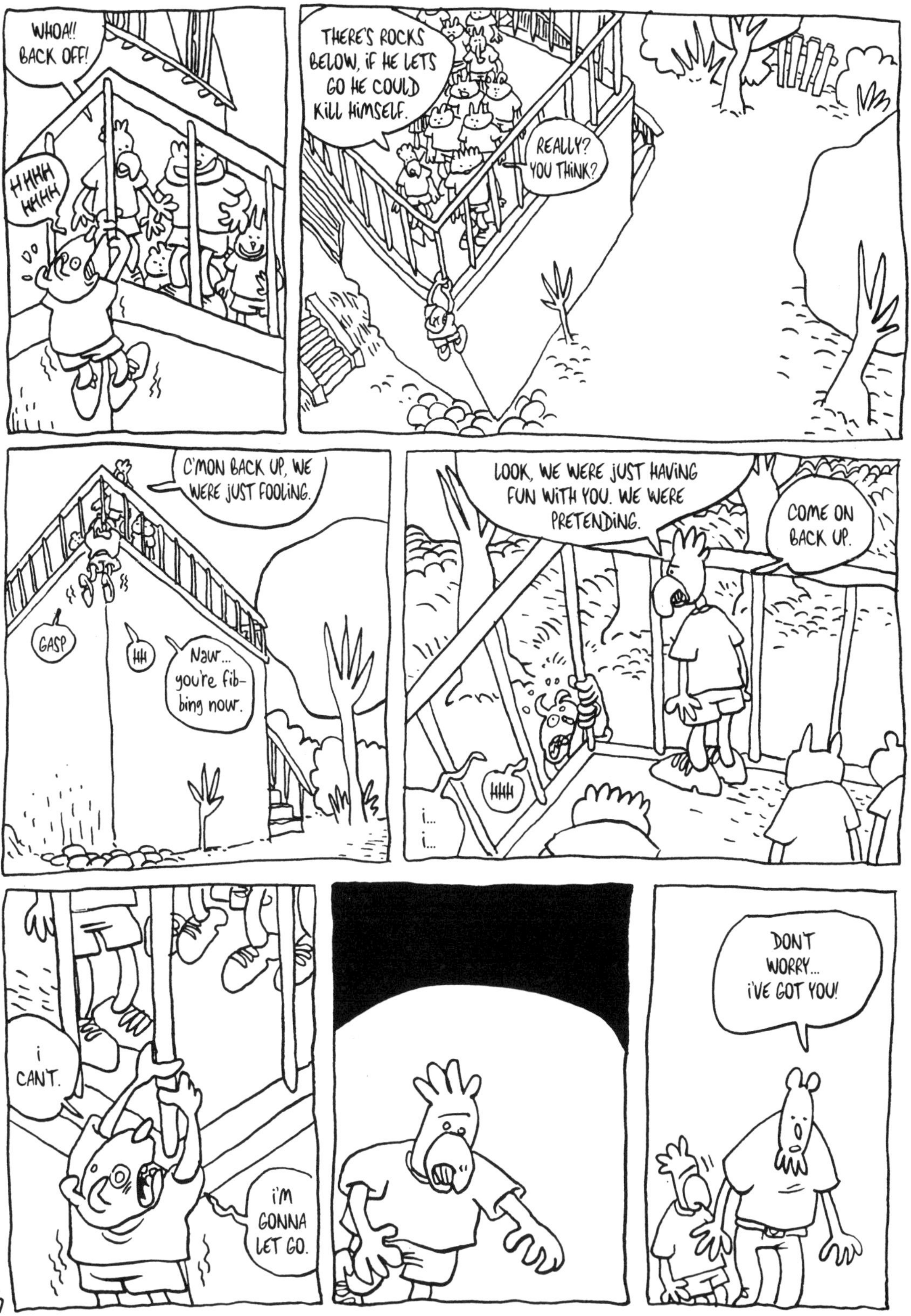
WHOA!! BACK OFF!
HHHH HHHH
THERE'S ROCKS BELOW, iF HE LETS GO HE COULD KiLL HiMSELF.
REALLY? YOU THiNK?
C'MON BACK UP, WE WERE JUST FOOLiNG.
GASP
HH
Naw... you're fib-bing now.
LOOK, WE WERE JUST HAViNG FUN WiTH YOU. WE WERE PRETENDiNG.
COME ON BACK UP.
HHH
i... i...
i CAN'T.
i'M GONNA LET GO.
DON'T WORRY... i'VE GOT YOU!

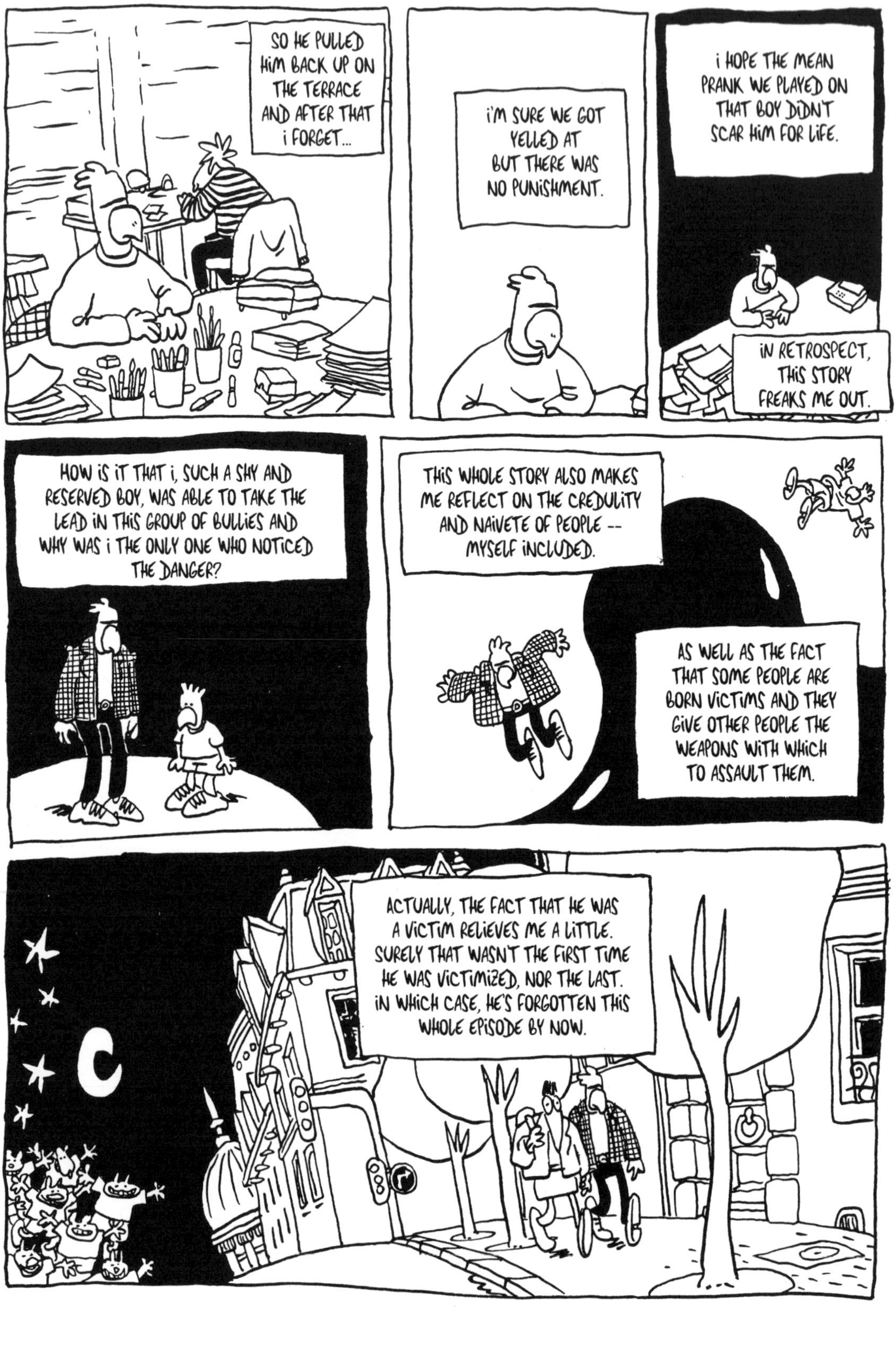
SO HE PULLED HIM BACK UP ON THE TERRACE AND AFTER THAT I FORGET...
I'M SURE WE GOT YELLED AT BUT THERE WAS NO PUNISHMENT.
I HOPE THE MEAN PRANK WE PLAYED ON THAT BOY DIDN'T SCAR HIM FOR LIFE.
IN RETROSPECT, THIS STORY FREAKS ME OUT.
HOW IS IT THAT I, SUCH A SHY AND RESERVED BOY, WAS ABLE TO TAKE THE LEAD IN THIS GROUP OF BULLIES AND WHY WAS I THE ONLY ONE WHO NOTICED THE DANGER?
THIS WHOLE STORY ALSO MAKES ME REFLECT ON THE CREDULITY AND NAIVETE OF PEOPLE -- MYSELF INCLUDED.
AS WELL AS THE FACT THAT SOME PEOPLE ARE BORN VICTIMS AND THEY GIVE OTHER PEOPLE THE WEAPONS WITH WHICH TO ASSAULT THEM.
ACTUALLY, THE FACT THAT HE WAS A VICTIM RELIEVES ME A LITTLE. SURELY THAT WASN'T THE FIRST TIME HE WAS VICTIMIZED, NOR THE LAST. IN WHICH CASE, HE'S FORGOTTEN THIS WHOLE EPISODE BY NOW.

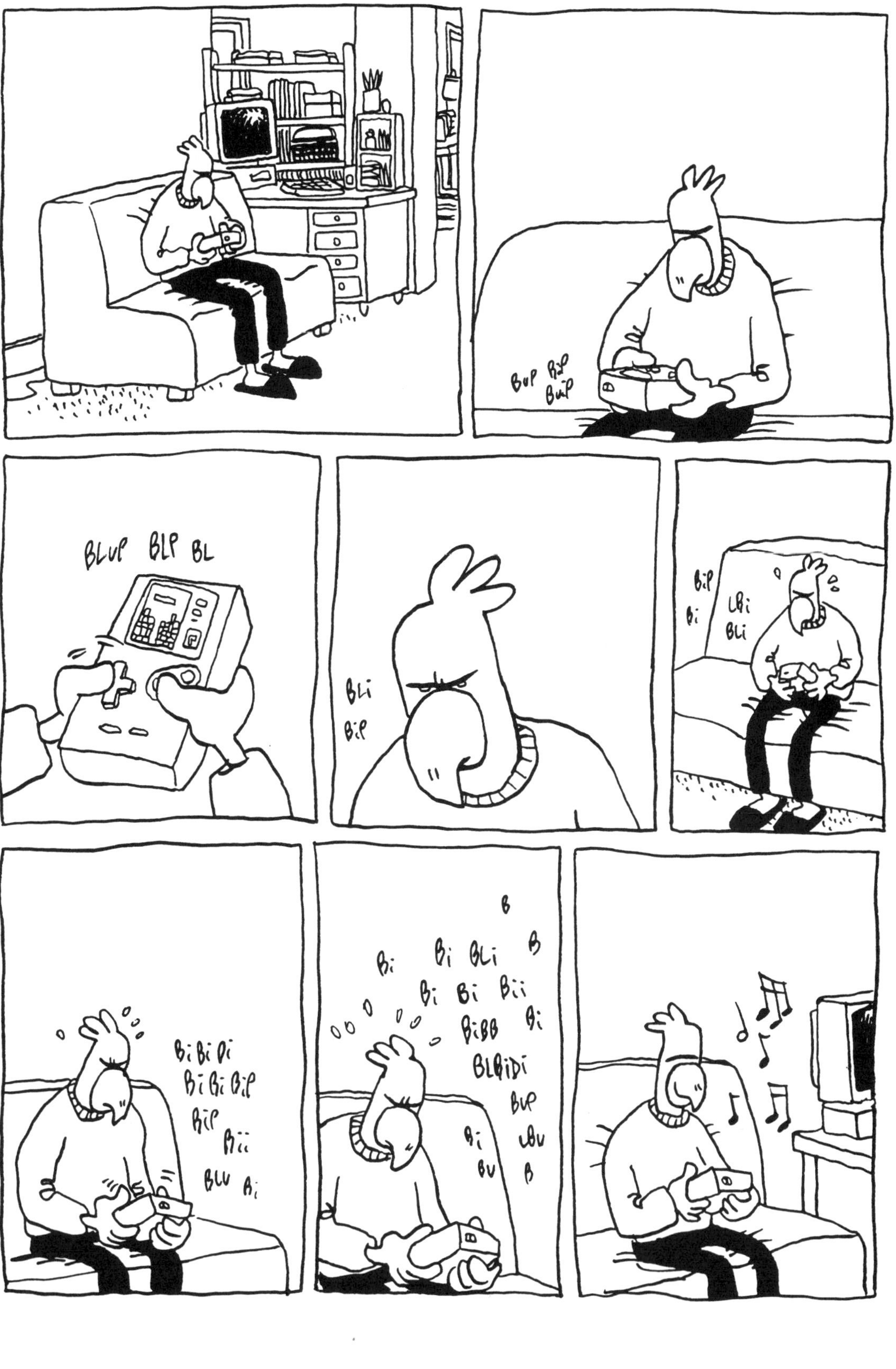
BLUP BLP BL
BLi
BiP
BiP
Bi
LBi
BLi
BiBiDi
BiBiBiP
BiP
Bii
BLU
Bi
B
Bi
Bi BLi
B
Bi Bi Bii
BiBB
Bi
BLBiDi
BUP
Bi
LBU
BU
B

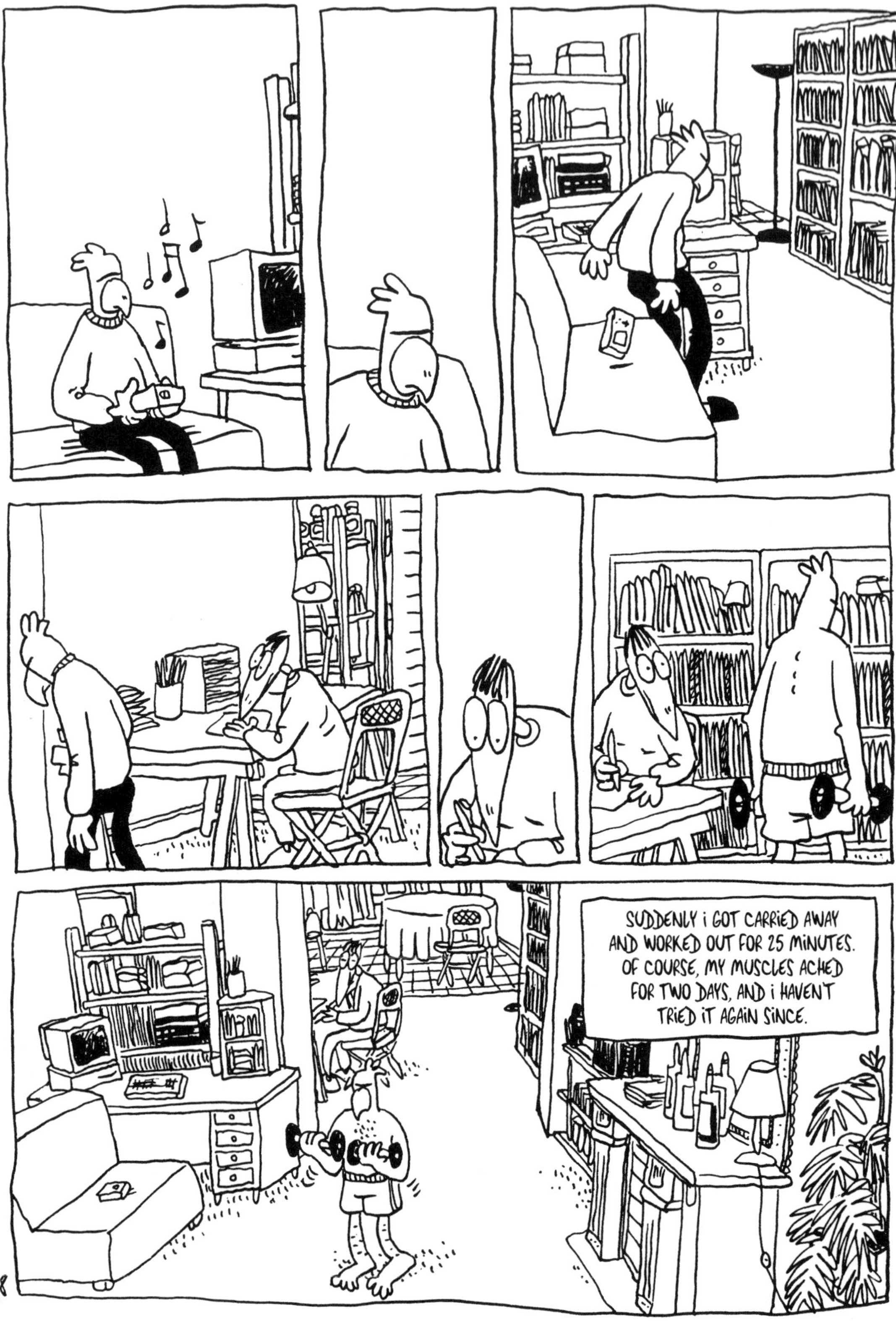
SUDDENLY i GOT CARRIED AWAY AND WORKED OUT FOR 25 MINUTES. OF COURSE, MY MUSCLES ACHED FOR TWO DAYS, AND i HAVEN'T TRIED IT AGAIN SINCE.

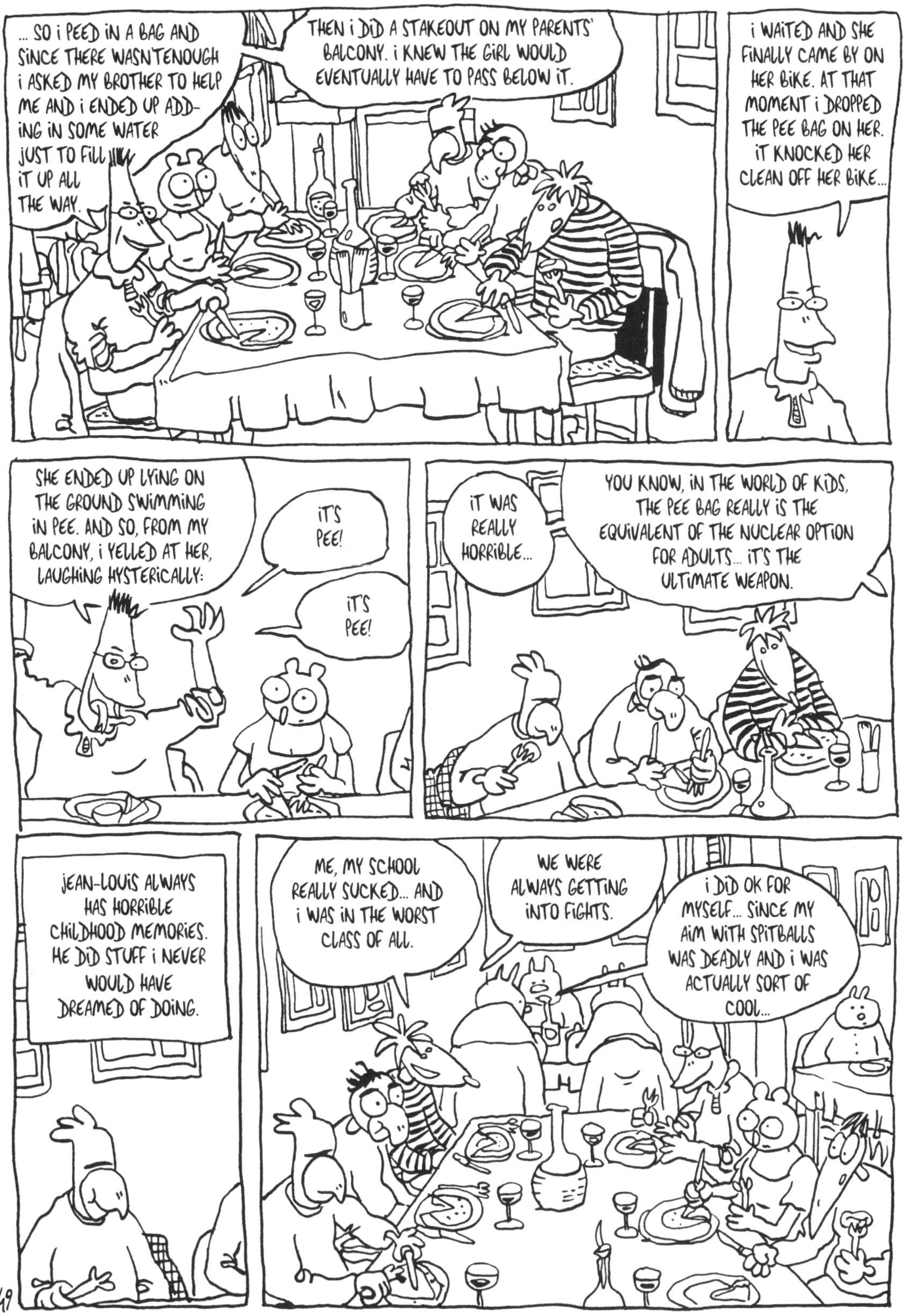
... SO i PEED iN A BAG AND SiNCE THERE WASN'T ENOUGH i ASKED MY BROTHER TO HELP ME AND i ENDED UP ADD-iNG iN SOME WATER JUST TO FiLL iT UP ALL THE WAY.
THEN i DiD A STAKEOUT ON MY PARENTS' BALCONY. i KNEW THE GiRL WOULD EVENTUALLY HAVE TO PASS BELOW iT.
i WAiTED AND SHE FiNALLY CAME BY ON HER BiKE. AT THAT MOMENT i DROPPED THE PEE BAG ON HER. iT KNOCKED HER CLEAN OFF HER BiKE...
SHE ENDED UP LYiNG ON THE GROUND SWiMMiNG iN PEE. AND SO, FROM MY BALCONY, i YELLED AT HER, LAUGHiNG HYSTERiCALLY:
iT'S PEE!
iT'S PEE!
iT WAS REALLY HORRiBLE...
YOU KNOW, iN THE WORLD OF KiDS, THE PEE BAG REALLY iS THE EQUiVALENT OF THE NUCLEAR OPTiON FOR ADULTS... iT'S THE ULTiMATE WEAPON.
JEAN-LOUiS ALWAYS HAS HORRiBLE CHiLDHOOD MEMORiES. HE DiD STUFF i NEVER WOULD HAVE DREAMED OF DOiNG.
ME, MY SCHOOL REALLY SUCKED... AND i WAS iN THE WORST CLASS OF ALL.
WE WERE ALWAYS GETTiNG iNTO FiGHTS.
i DiD OK FOR MYSELF... SiNCE MY AiM WiTH SPiTBALLS WAS DEADLY AND i WAS ACTUALLY SORT OF COOL...

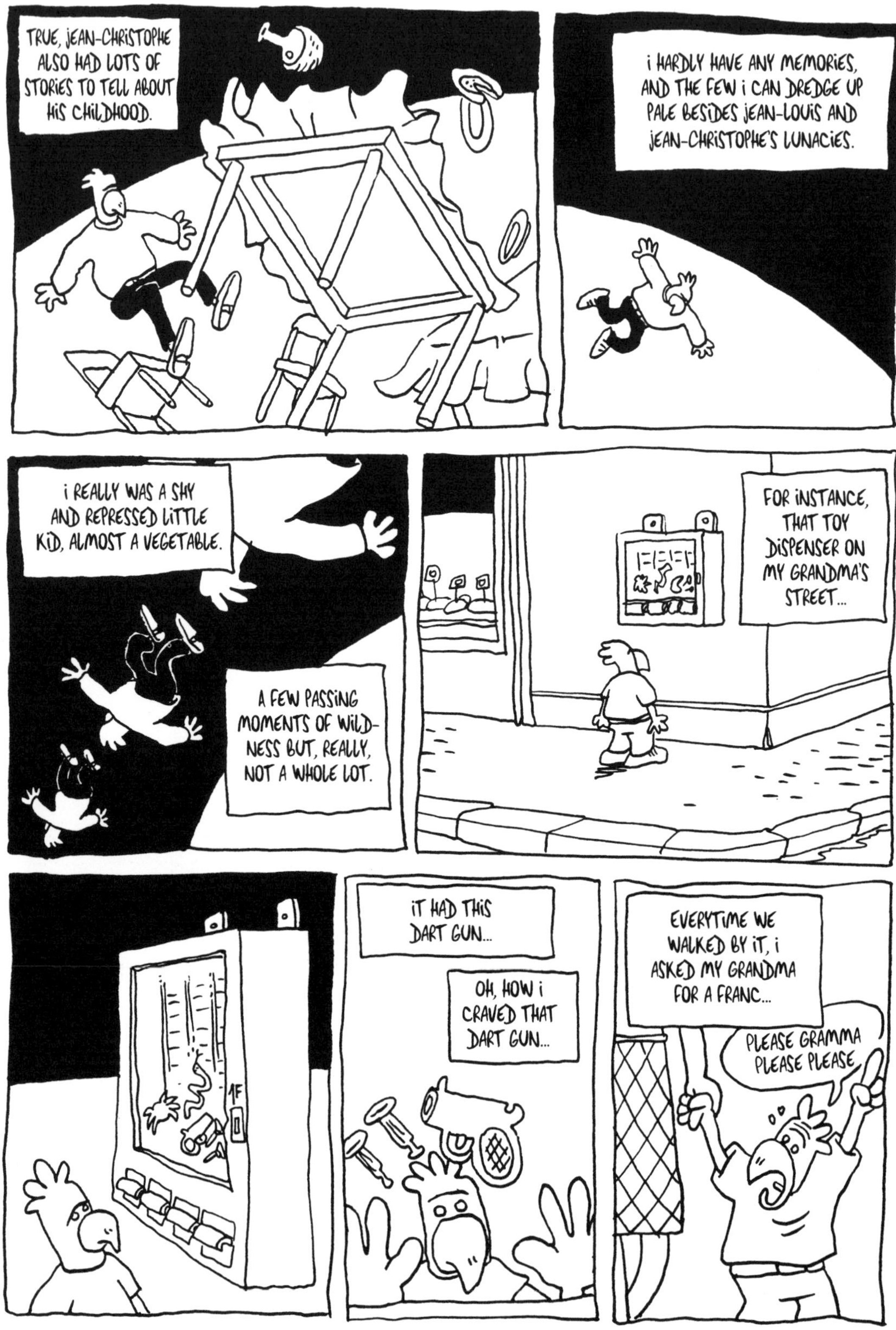
TRUE, JEAN-CHRISTOPHE ALSO HAD LOTS OF STORIES TO TELL ABOUT HIS CHILDHOOD.
I HARDLY HAVE ANY MEMORIES, AND THE FEW I CAN DREDGE UP PALE BESIDES JEAN-LOUIS AND JEAN-CHRISTOPHE'S LUNACIES.
I REALLY WAS A SHY AND REPRESSED LITTLE KID, ALMOST A VEGETABLE.
A FEW PASSING MOMENTS OF WILD-NESS BUT, REALLY, NOT A WHOLE LOT.
FOR INSTANCE, THAT TOY DISPENSER ON MY GRANDMA'S STREET...
1F
IT HAD THIS DART GUN...
OH, HOW I CRAVED THAT DART GUN...
EVERYTIME WE WALKED BY IT, I ASKED MY GRANDMA FOR A FRANC...
PLEASE GRAMMA PLEASE PLEASE

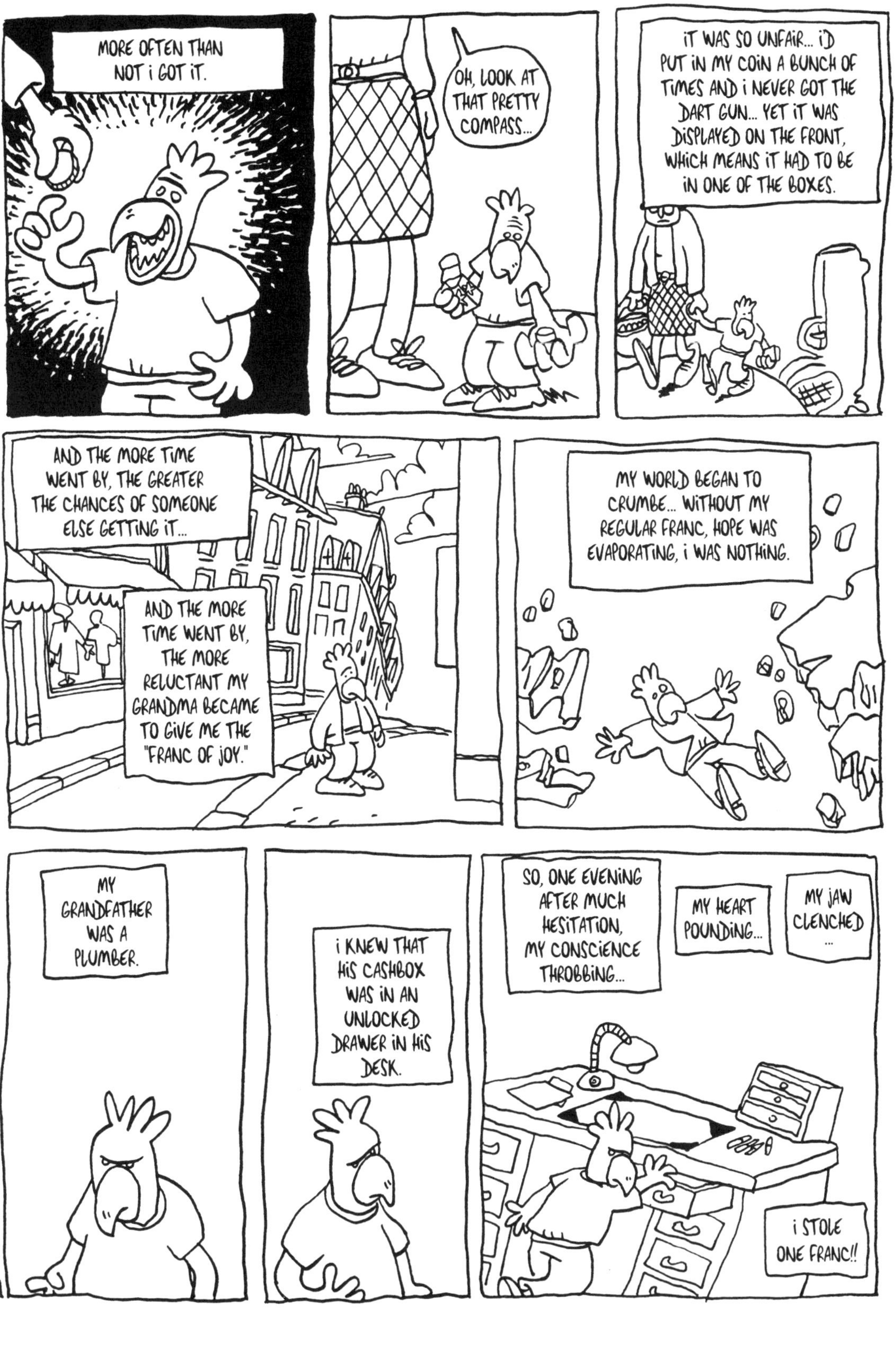
MORE OFTEN THAN NOT i GOT iT.
OH, LOOK AT THAT PRETTY COMPASS...
iT WAS SO UNFAiR... i'D PUT iN MY COiN A BUNCH OF TiMES AND i NEVER GOT THE DART GUN... YET iT WAS DiSPLAYED ON THE FRONT, WHiCH MEANS iT HAD TO BE iN ONE OF THE BOXES.
AND THE MORE TiME WENT BY, THE GREATER THE CHANCES OF SOMEONE ELSE GETTiNG iT...
AND THE MORE TiME WENT BY, THE MORE RELUCTANT MY GRANDMA BECAME TO GiVE ME THE "FRANC OF JOY."
MY WORLD BEGAN TO CRUMBE... WiTHOUT MY REGULAR FRANC, HOPE WAS EVAPORATiNG, i WAS NOTHiNG.
MY GRANDFATHER WAS A PLUMBER.
i KNEW THAT HiS CASHBOX WAS iN AN UNLOCKED DRAWER iN HiS DESK.
SO, ONE EVENiNG AFTER MUCH HESiTATiON, MY CONSCiENCE THROBBiNG...
MY HEART POUNDiNG...
MY JAW CLENCHED ...
i STOLE ONE FRANC!!

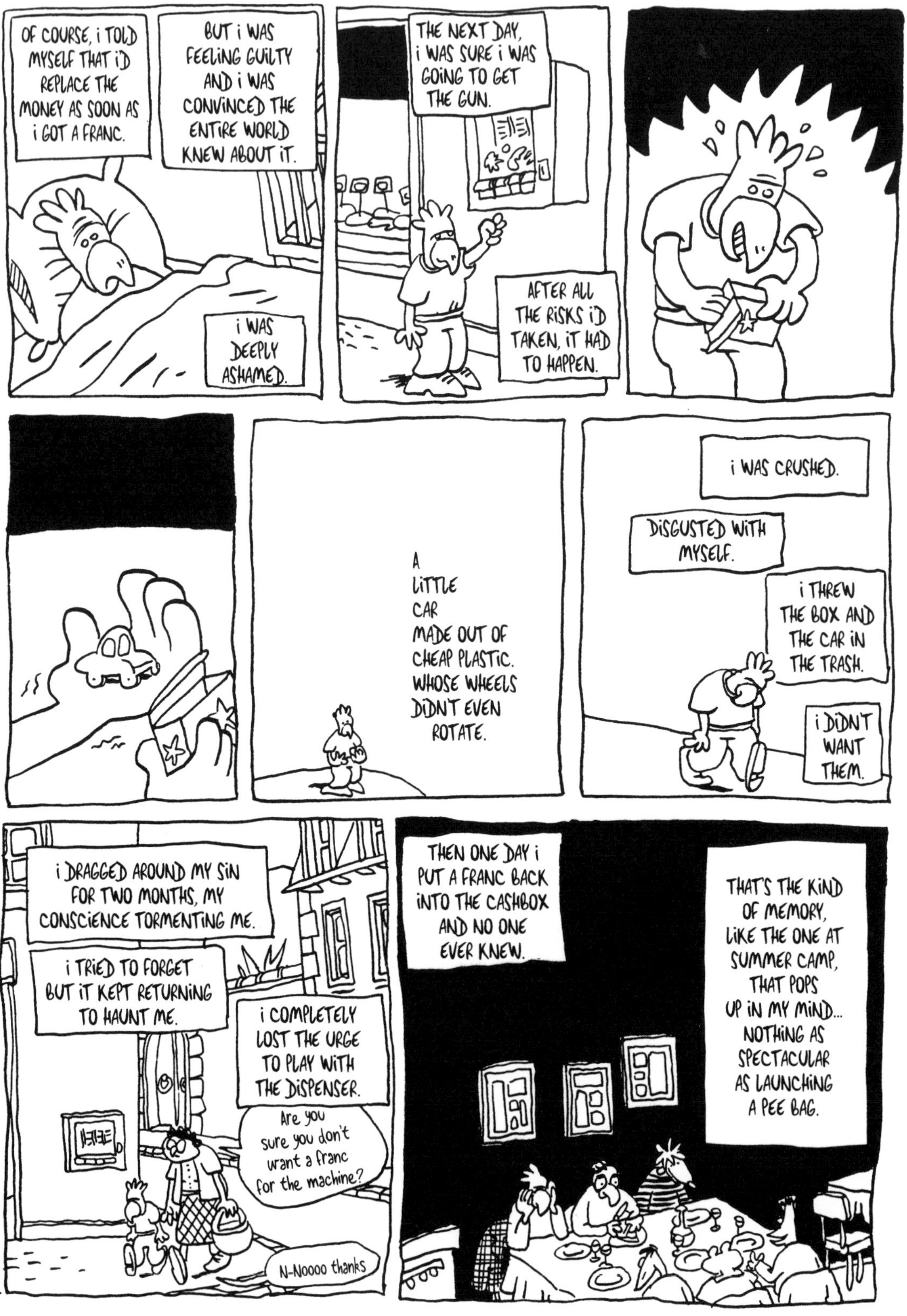
OF COURSE, i TOLD MYSELF THAT i'D REPLACE THE MONEY AS SOON AS i GOT A FRANC.
BUT i WAS FEELING GUILTY AND i WAS CONVINCED THE ENTIRE WORLD KNEW ABOUT iT.
i WAS DEEPLY ASHAMED.
THE NEXT DAY, i WAS SURE i WAS GOING TO GET THE GUN.
AFTER ALL THE RISKS i'D TAKEN, IT HAD TO HAPPEN.
A LITTLE CAR MADE OUT OF CHEAP PLASTIC. WHOSE WHEELS DIDN'T EVEN ROTATE.
i WAS CRUSHED.
DISGUSTED WITH MYSELF.
i THREW THE BOX AND THE CAR IN THE TRASH.
i DIDN'T WANT THEM.
i DRAGGED AROUND MY SiN FOR TWO MONTHS, MY CONSCIENCE TORMENTING ME.
i TRIED TO FORGET BUT iT KEPT RETURNING TO HAUNT ME.
i COMPLETELY LOST THE URGE TO PLAY WITH THE DISPENSER.
Are you sure you don't want a franc for the machine?
N-Noooo thanks
THEN ONE DAY i PUT A FRANC BACK INTO THE CASHBOX AND NO ONE EVER KNEW.
THAT'S THE KIND OF MEMORY, LIKE THE ONE AT SUMMER CAMP, THAT POPS UP IN MY MIND... NOTHING AS SPECTACULAR AS LAUNCHING A PEE BAG.

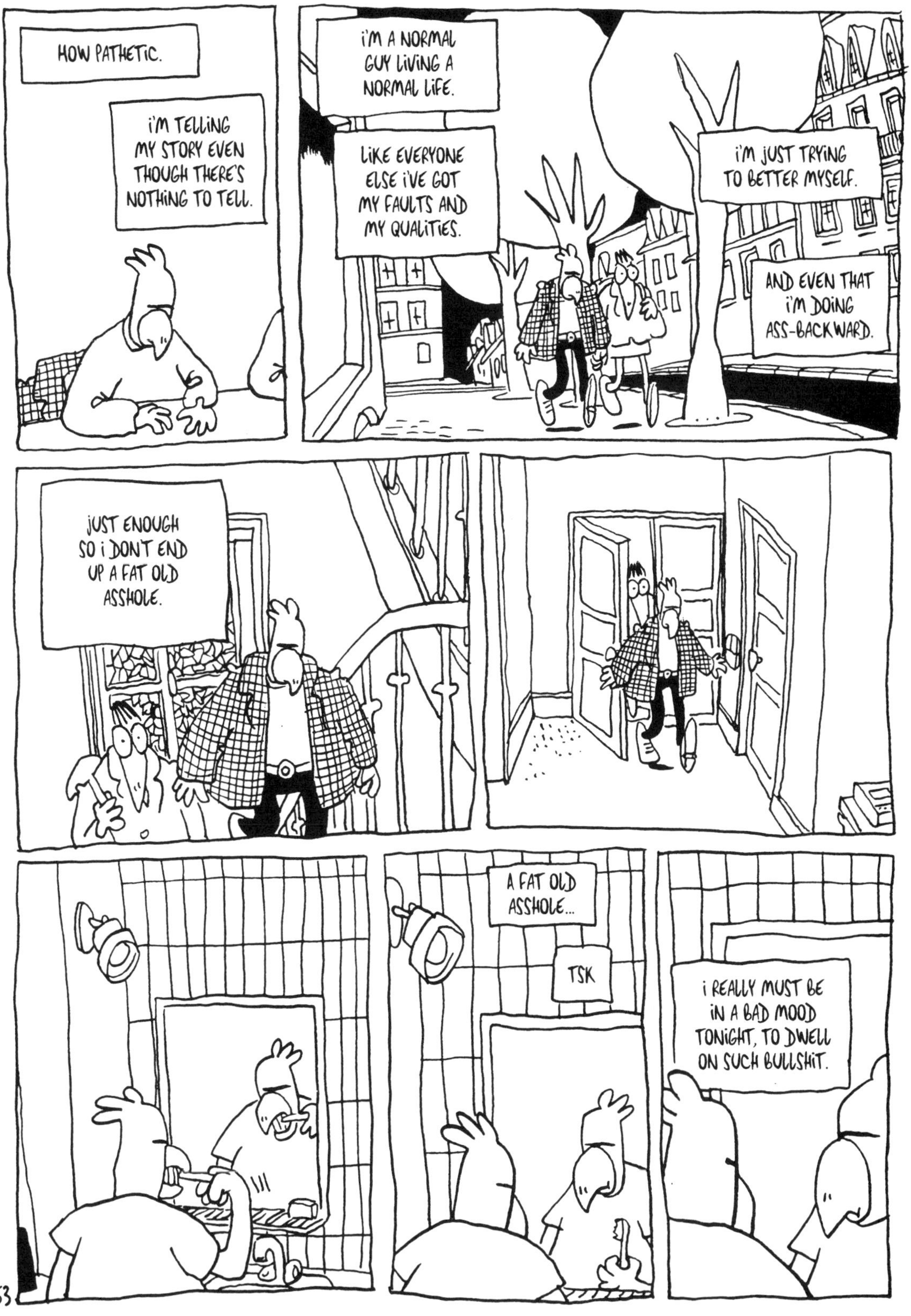
HOW PATHETIC.
i'M TELLiNG MY STORY EVEN THOUGH THERE'S NOTHiNG TO TELL.
i'M A NORMAL GUY LiViNG A NORMAL LiFE.
LiKE EVERYONE ELSE i'VE GOT MY FAULTS AND MY QUALiTiES.
i'M JUST TRYiNG TO BETTER MYSELF.
AND EVEN THAT i'M DOiNG ASS-BACKWARD.
JUST ENOUGH SO i DON'T END UP A FAT OLD ASSHOLE.
A FAT OLD ASSHOLE...
TSK
i REALLY MUST BE iN A BAD MOOD TONiGHT, TO DWELL ON SUCH BULLSHiT.

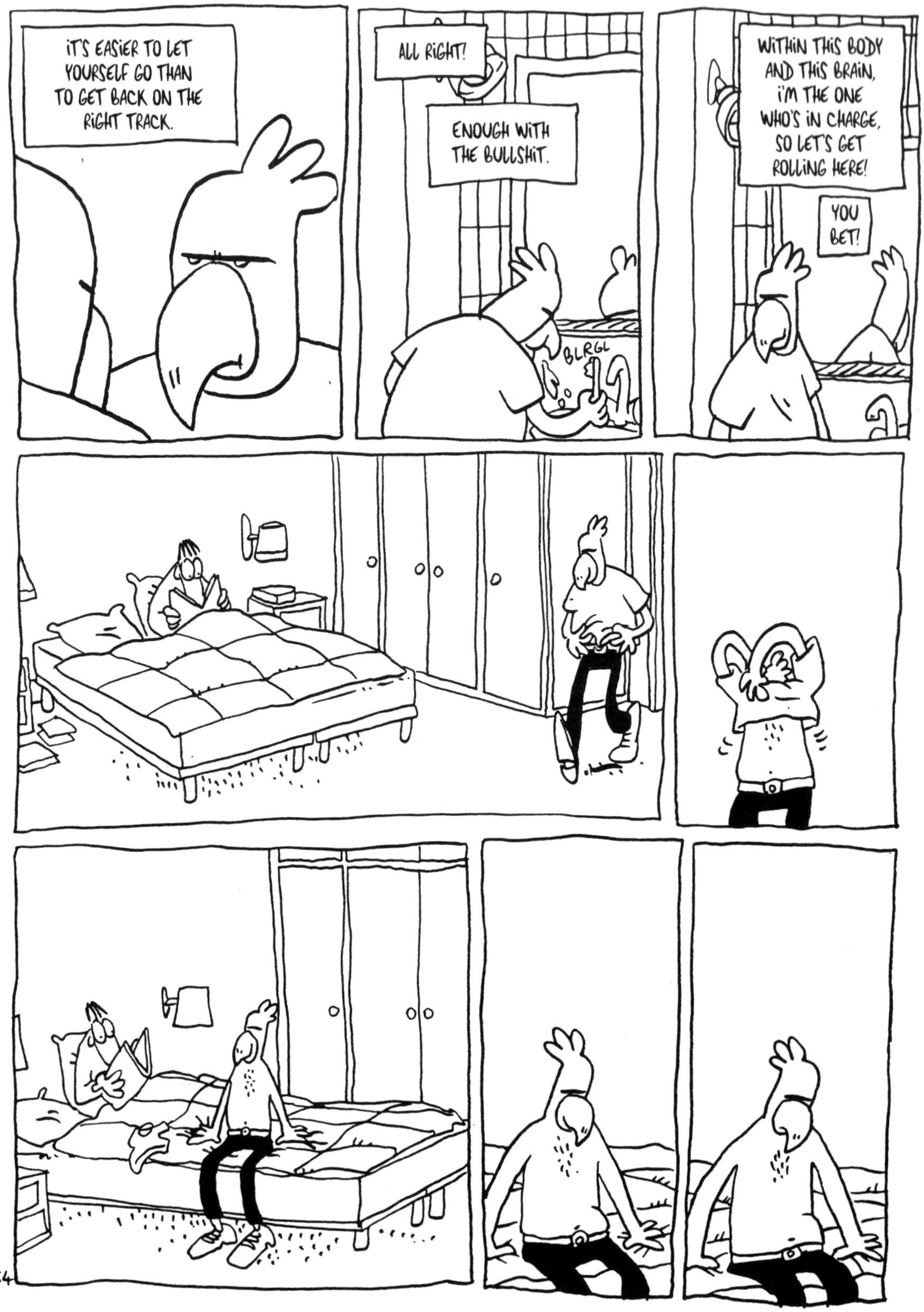
IT'S EASIER TO LET YOURSELF GO THAN TO GET BACK ON THE RIGHT TRACK.
ALL RIGHT!
ENOUGH WITH THE BULLSHIT.
BLRGL
WITHIN THIS BODY AND THIS BRAIN, I'M THE ONE WHO'S IN CHARGE, SO LET'S GET ROLLING HERE!
YOU BET!

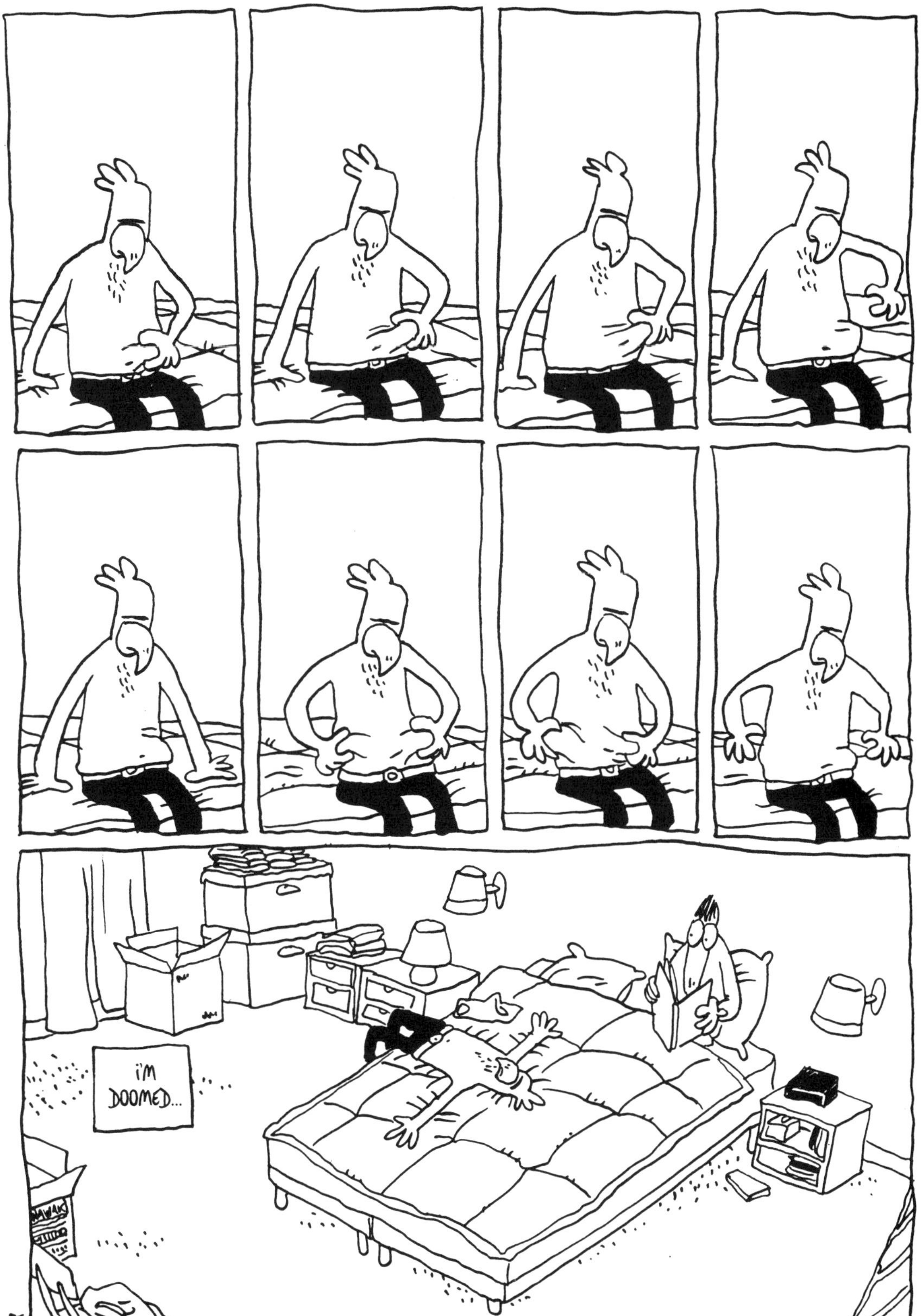
I'M
DOOMED...

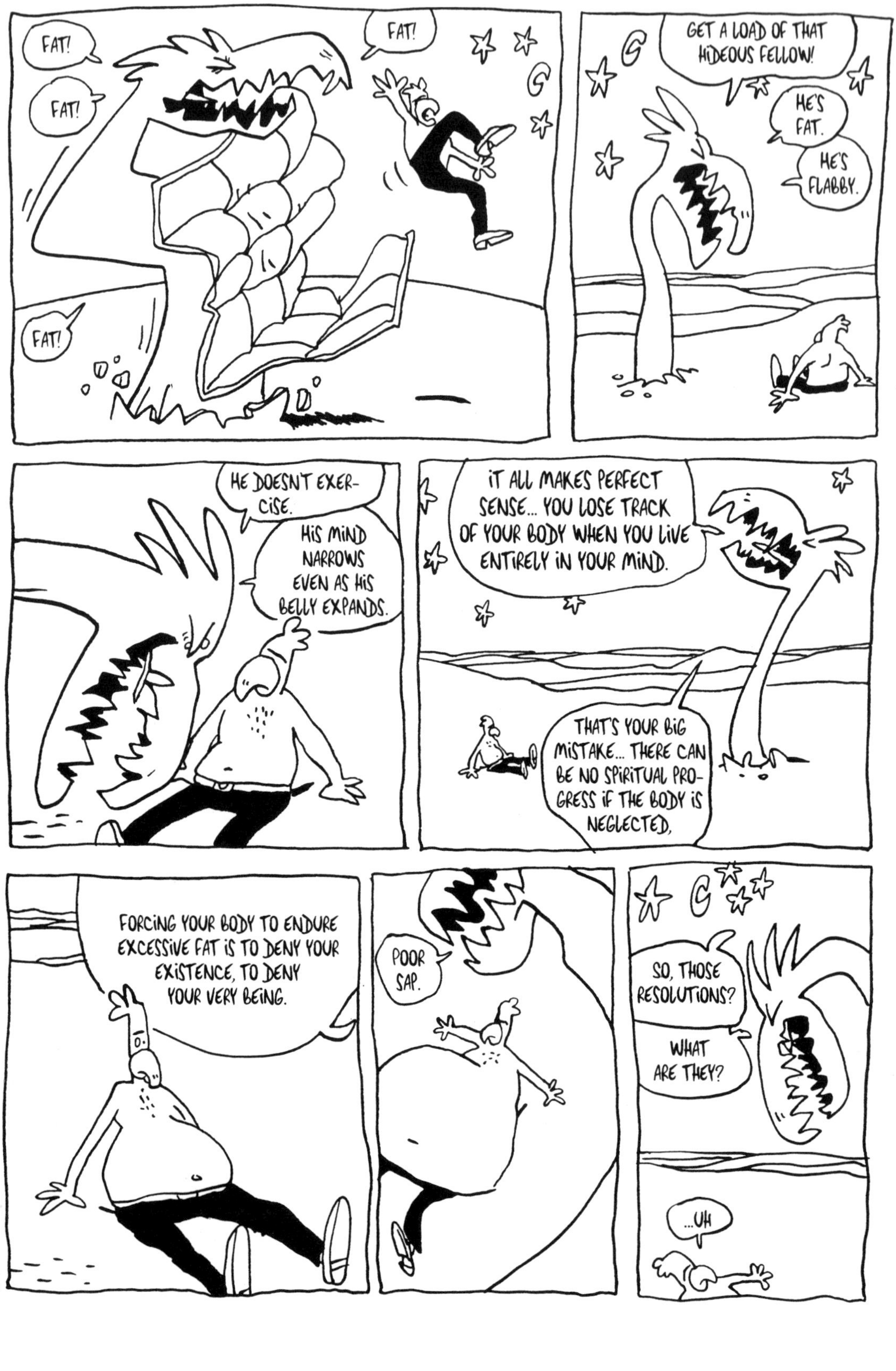
FAT!
FAT!
FAT!
FAT!
GET A LOAD OF THAT HIDEOUS FELLOW!
HE'S FAT.
HE'S FLABBY.
HE DOESN'T EXER-CISE.
HIS MIND NARROWS EVEN AS HIS BELLY EXPANDS.
IT ALL MAKES PERFECT SENSE... YOU LOSE TRACK OF YOUR BODY WHEN YOU LIVE ENTIRELY IN YOUR MIND.
THAT'S YOUR BIG MISTAKE... THERE CAN BE NO SPIRITUAL PRO-GRESS IF THE BODY IS NEGLECTED,
FORCING YOUR BODY TO ENDURE EXCESSIVE FAT IS TO DENY YOUR EXISTENCE, TO DENY YOUR VERY BEING.
POOR SAP.
SO, THOSE RESOLUTIONS?
WHAT ARE THEY?
...UH

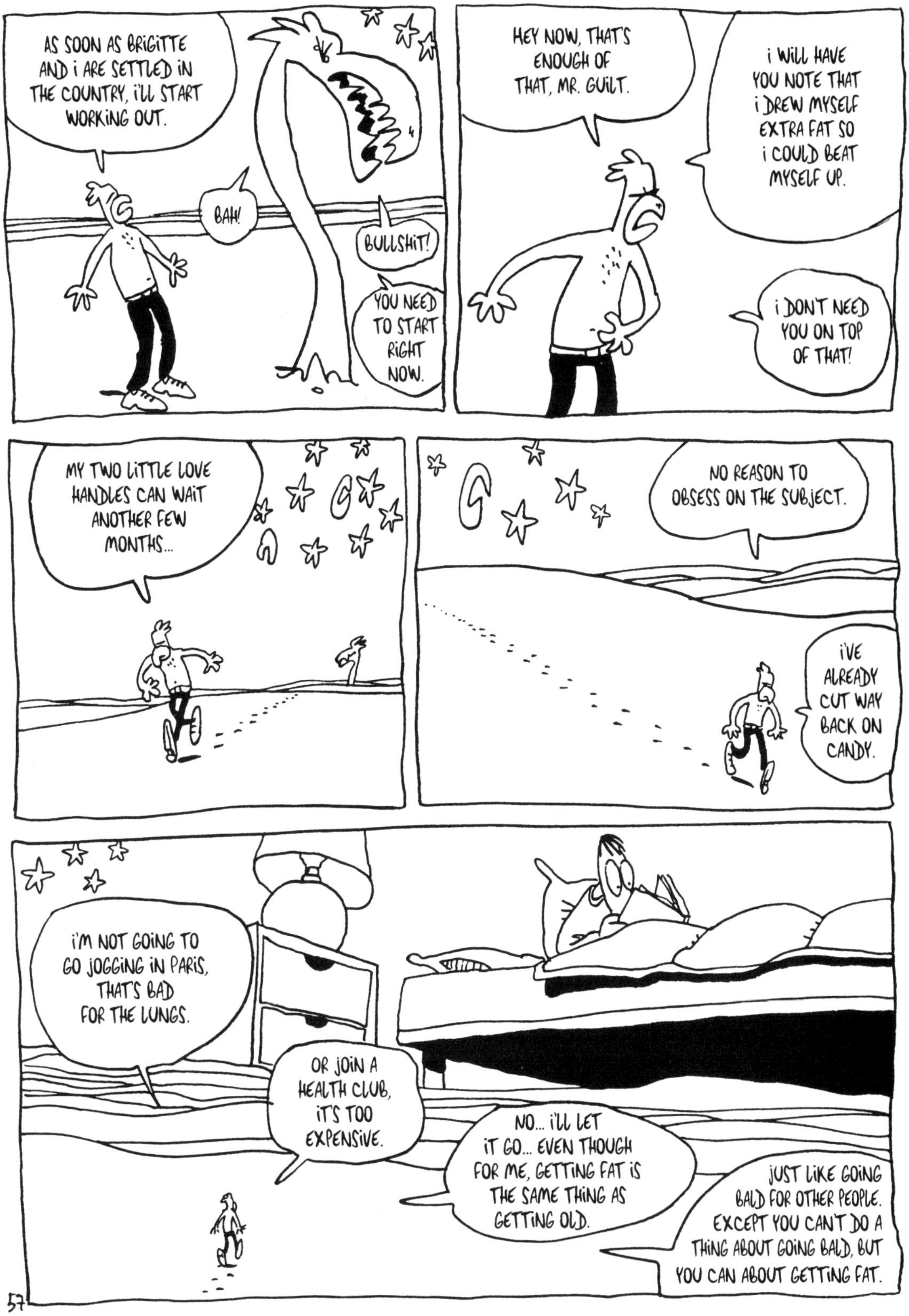
AS SOON AS BRIGITTE AND I ARE SETTLED IN THE COUNTRY, I'LL START WORKING OUT.
BAH!
BULLSHIT!
YOU NEED TO START RIGHT NOW.
HEY NOW, THAT'S ENOUGH OF THAT, MR. GUILT.
I WILL HAVE YOU NOTE THAT I DREW MYSELF EXTRA FAT SO I COULD BEAT MYSELF UP.
I DON'T NEED YOU ON TOP OF THAT!
MY TWO LITTLE LOVE HANDLES CAN WAIT ANOTHER FEW MONTHS...
NO REASON TO OBSESS ON THE SUBJECT.
I'VE ALREADY CUT WAY BACK ON CANDY.
I'M NOT GOING TO GO JOGGING IN PARIS, THAT'S BAD FOR THE LUNGS.
OR JOIN A HEALTH CLUB, IT'S TOO EXPENSIVE.
NO... I'LL LET IT GO... EVEN THOUGH FOR ME, GETTING FAT IS THE SAME THING AS GETTING OLD.
JUST LIKE GOING BALD FOR OTHER PEOPLE. EXCEPT YOU CAN'T DO A THING ABOUT GOING BALD, BUT YOU CAN ABOUT GETTING FAT.

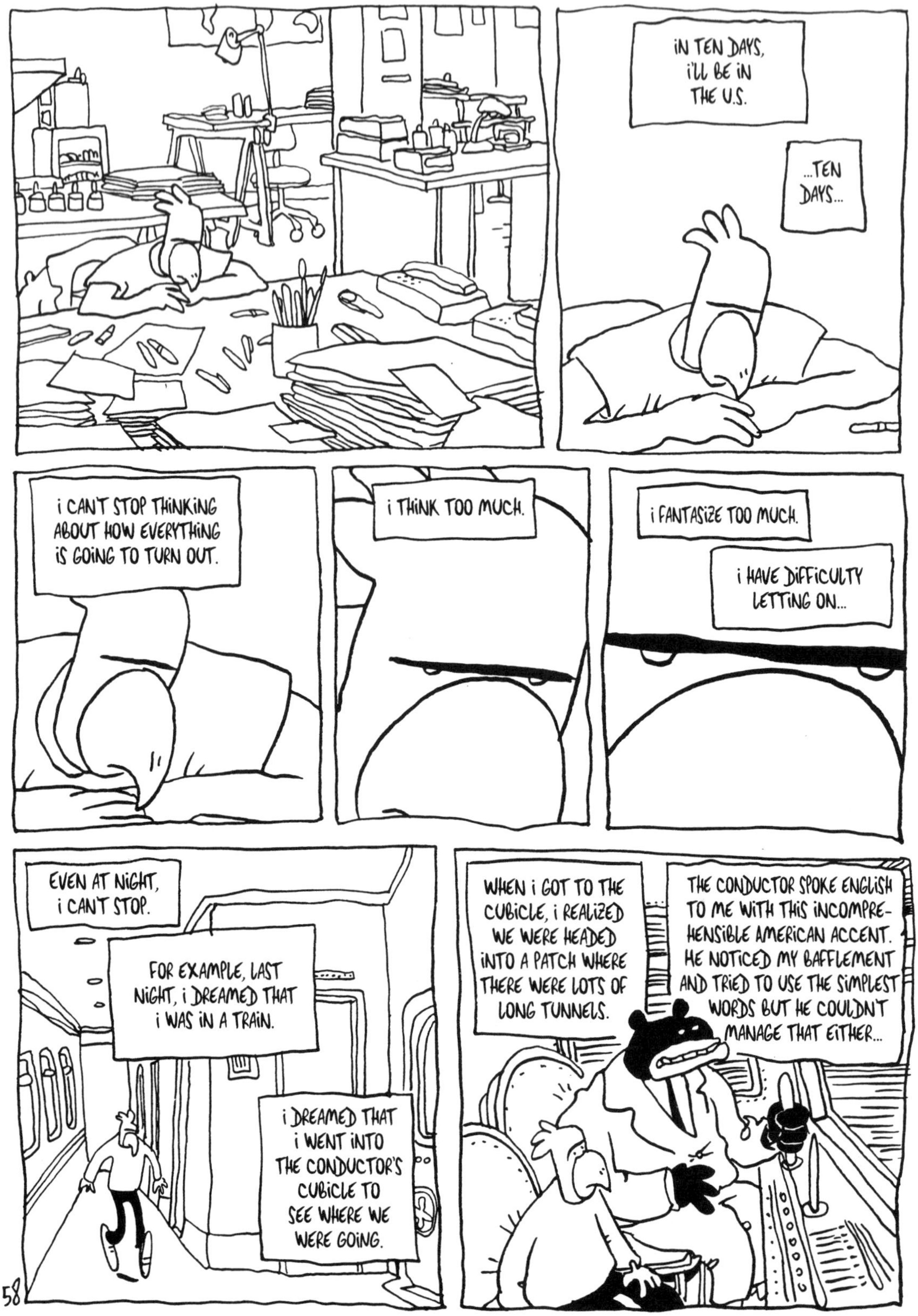
IN TEN DAYS,
I'LL BE IN
THE U.S.
...TEN
DAYS...
I CAN'T STOP THINKING ABOUT HOW EVERYTHING IS GOING TO TURN OUT.
I THINK TOO MUCH.
I FANTASIZE TOO MUCH.
I HAVE DIFFICULTY LETTING ON...
EVEN AT NIGHT, I CAN'T STOP.
FOR EXAMPLE, LAST NIGHT, I DREAMED THAT I WAS IN A TRAIN.
I DREAMED THAT I WENT INTO THE CONDUCTOR'S CUBICLE TO SEE WHERE WE WERE GOING.
WHEN I GOT TO THE CUBICLE, I REALIZED WE WERE HEADED INTO A PATCH WHERE THERE WERE LOTS OF LONG TUNNELS.
THE CONDUCTOR SPOKE ENGLISH TO ME WITH THIS INCOMPRE-HENSIBLE AMERICAN ACCENT. HE NOTICED MY BAFFLEMENT AND TRIED TO USE THE SIMPLEST WORDS BUT HE COULDN'T MANAGE THAT EITHER...

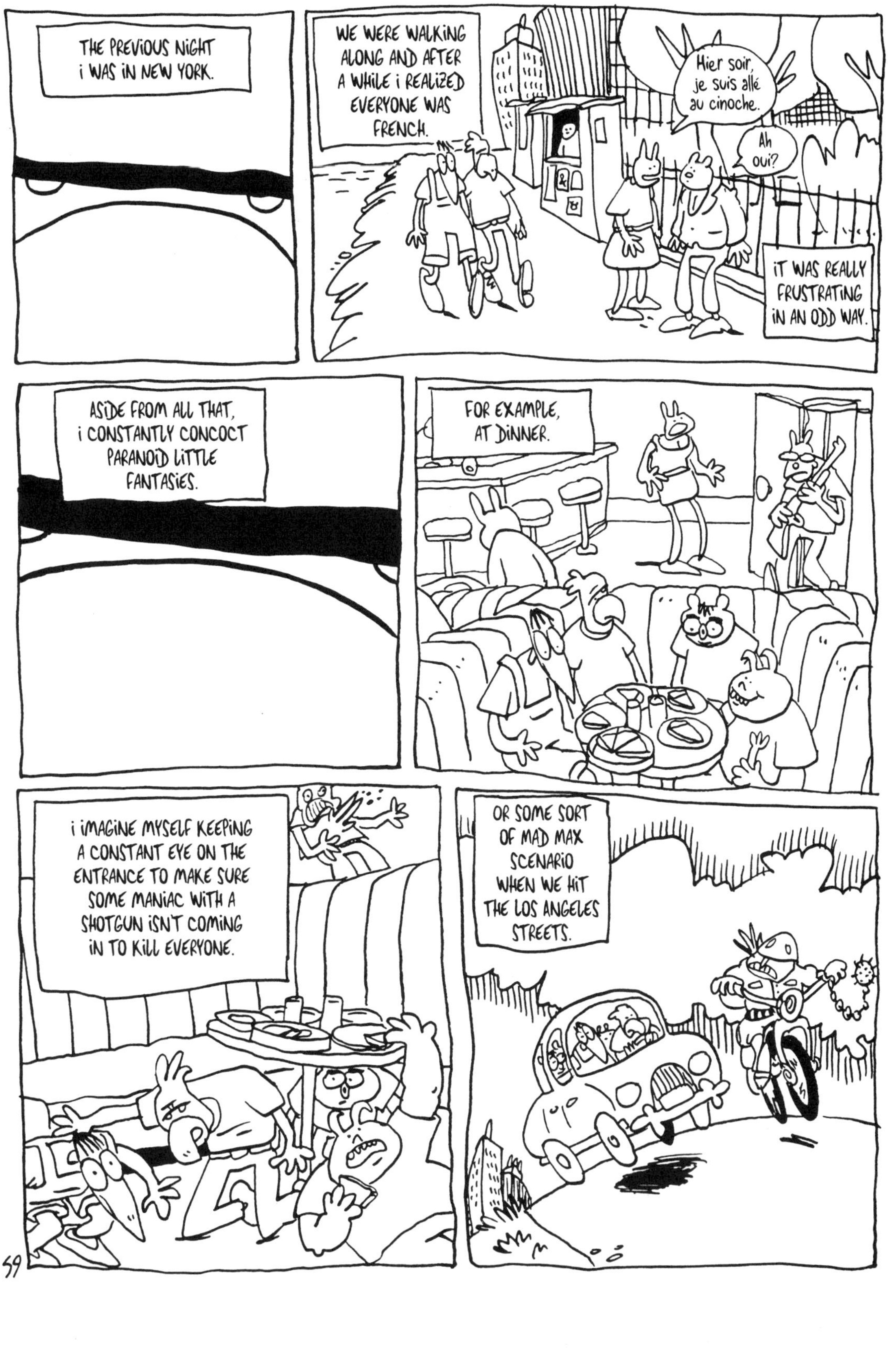
THE PREVIOUS NIGHT i WAS IN NEW YORK.
WE WERE WALKING ALONG AND AFTER A WHILE i REALIZED EVERYONE WAS FRENCH.
Hier soir, je suis allé au cinoche.
Ah oui?
iT WAS REALLY FRUSTRATING IN AN ODD WAY.
ASiDE FROM ALL THAT, i CONSTANTLY CONCOCT PARANOID LiTTLE FANTASiES.
FOR EXAMPLE, AT DiNNER.
i iMAGINE MYSELF KEEPING A CONSTANT EYE ON THE ENTRANCE TO MAKE SURE SOME MANiAC WITH A SHOTGUN iSN'T COMiNG iN TO KiLL EVERYONE.
OR SOME SORT OF MAD MAX SCENARIO WHEN WE HIT THE LOS ANGELES STREETS.

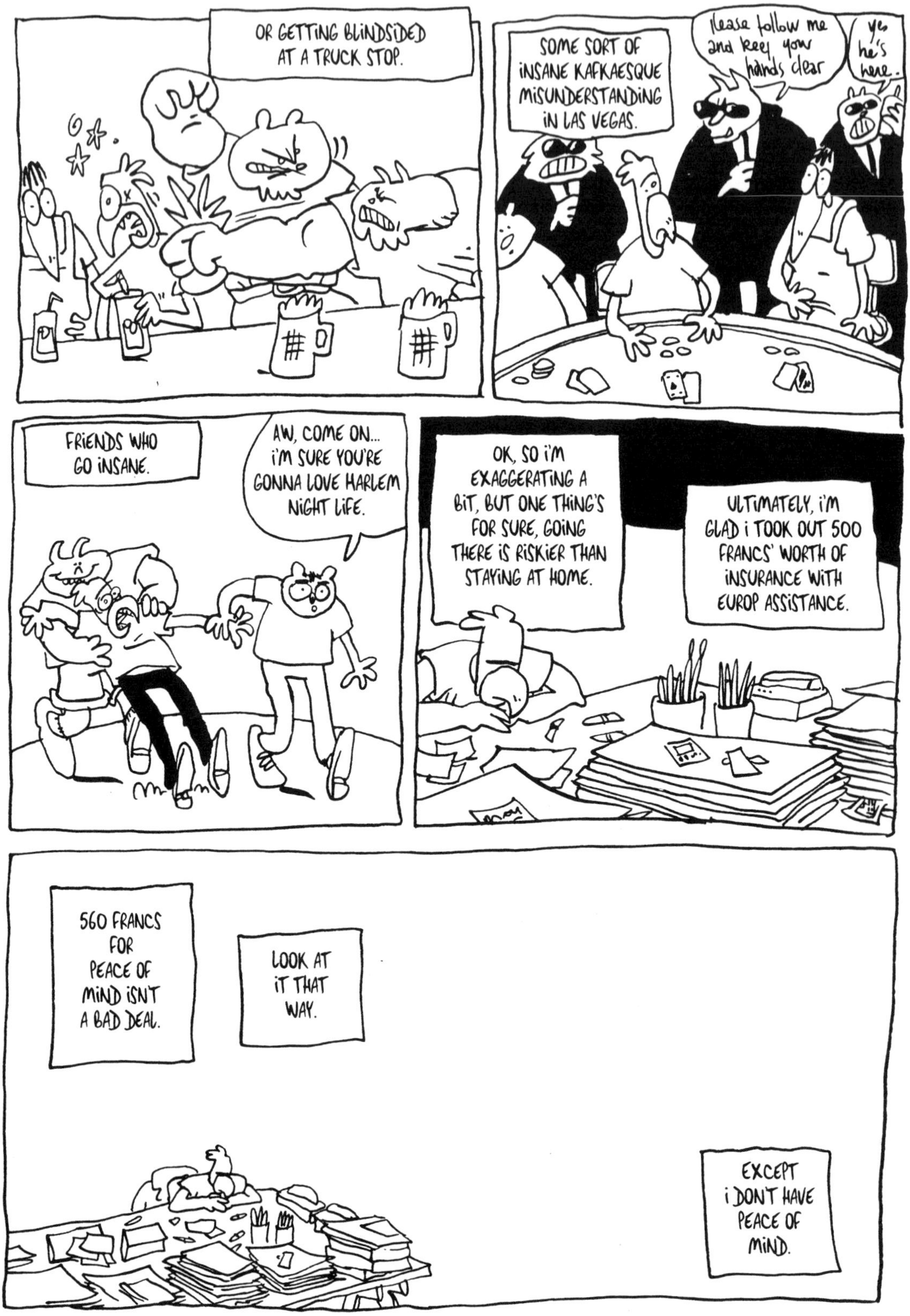
OR GETTING BLINDSIDED AT A TRUCK STOP.
SOME SORT OF INSANE KAFKAESQUE MISUNDERSTANDING IN LAS VEGAS.
Please follow me and keep your hands clear
yes he's here.
FRIENDS WHO GO INSANE.
AW, COME ON... I'M SURE YOU'RE GONNA LOVE HARLEM NIGHT LIFE.
OK, SO I'M EXAGGERATING A BIT, BUT ONE THING'S FOR SURE, GOING THERE IS RISKIER THAN STAYING AT HOME.
ULTIMATELY, I'M GLAD I TOOK OUT 500 FRANCS' WORTH OF INSURANCE WITH EUROP ASSISTANCE.
560 FRANCS FOR PEACE OF MIND ISN'T A BAD DEAL.
LOOK AT IT THAT WAY.
EXCEPT I DON'T HAVE PEACE OF MIND.

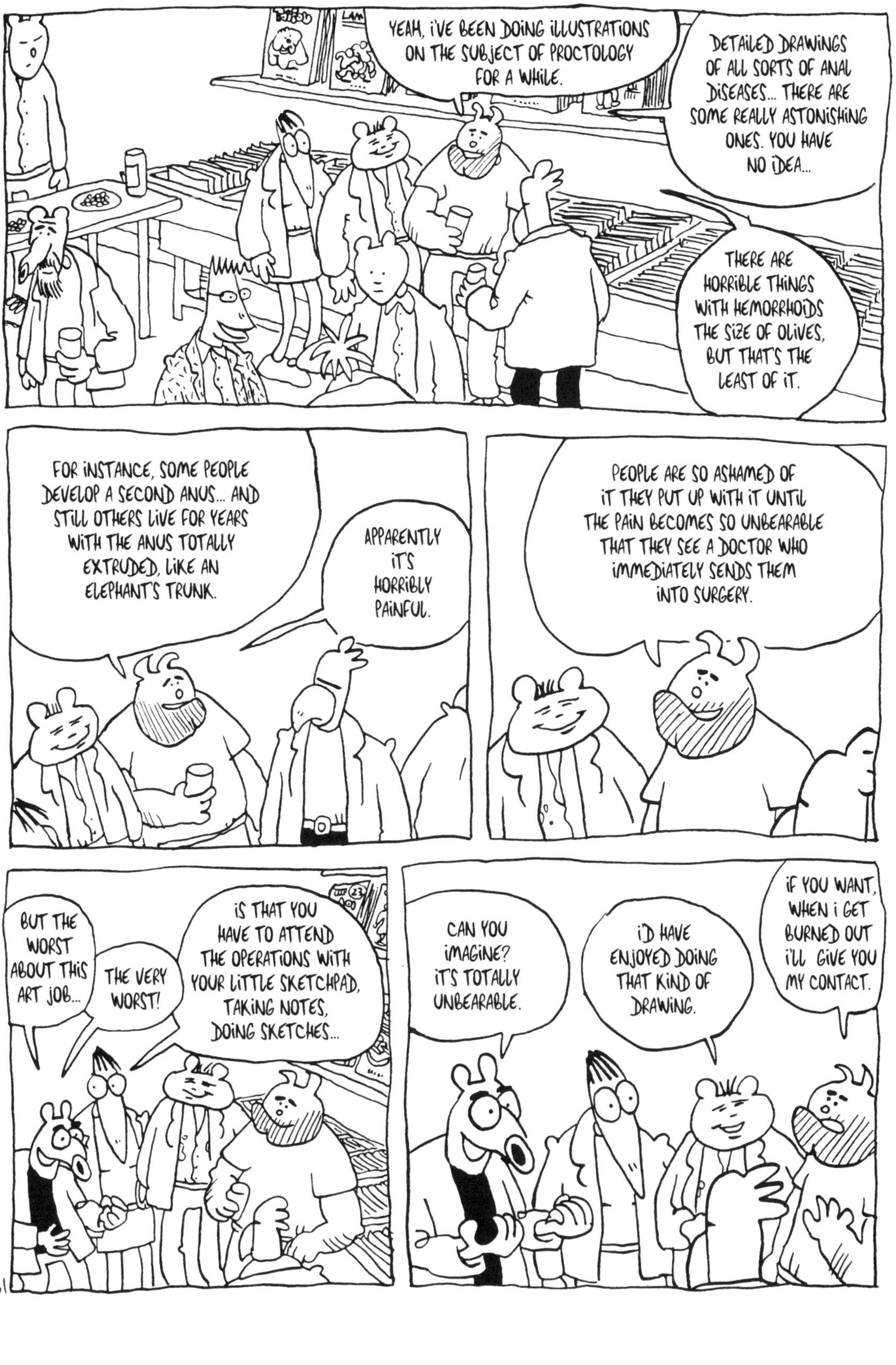
YEAH, I'VE BEEN DOING ILLUSTRATIONS ON THE SUBJECT OF PROCTOLOGY FOR A WHILE.
DETAILED DRAWINGS OF ALL SORTS OF ANAL DISEASES... THERE ARE SOME REALLY ASTONISHING ONES. YOU HAVE NO IDEA...
THERE ARE HORRIBLE THINGS WITH HEMORRHOIDS THE SIZE OF OLIVES, BUT THAT'S THE LEAST OF IT.
FOR INSTANCE, SOME PEOPLE DEVELOP A SECOND ANUS... AND STILL OTHERS LIVE FOR YEARS WITH THE ANUS TOTALLY EXTRUDED, LIKE AN ELEPHANT'S TRUNK.
APPARENTLY IT'S HORRIBLY PAINFUL.
PEOPLE ARE SO ASHAMED OF IT THEY PUT UP WITH IT UNTIL THE PAIN BECOMES SO UNBEARABLE THAT THEY SEE A DOCTOR WHO IMMEDIATELY SENDS THEM INTO SURGERY.
BUT THE WORST ABOUT THIS ART JOB...
THE VERY WORST!
IS THAT YOU HAVE TO ATTEND THE OPERATIONS WITH YOUR LITTLE SKETCHPAD, TAKING NOTES, DOING SKETCHES...
CAN YOU IMAGINE? IT'S TOTALLY UNBEARABLE.
I'D HAVE ENJOYED DOING THAT KIND OF DRAWING.
IF YOU WANT, WHEN I GET BURNED OUT I'LL GIVE YOU MY CONTACT.

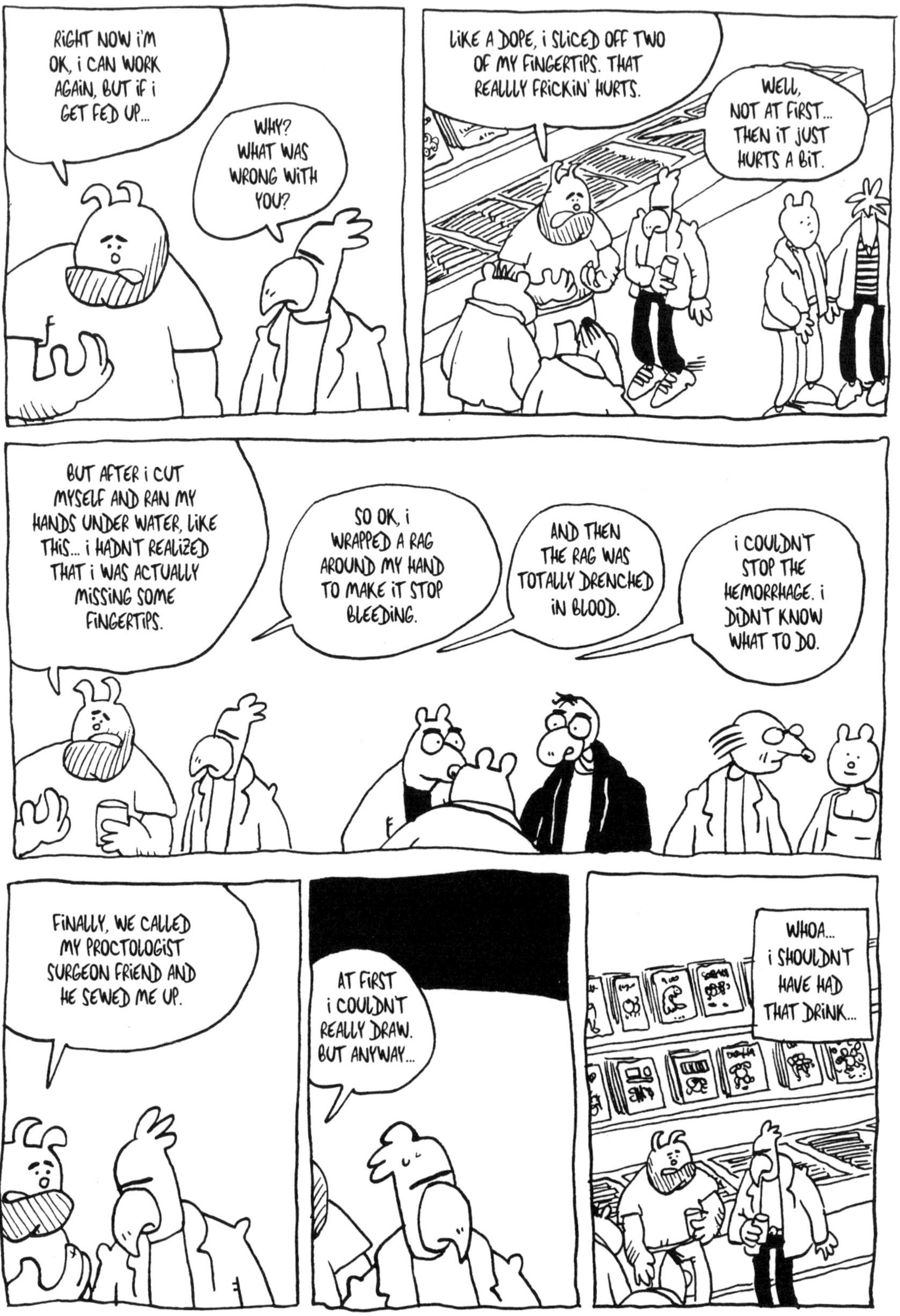
RIGHT NOW I'M OK, I CAN WORK AGAIN, BUT IF I GET FED UP...
WHY? WHAT WAS WRONG WITH YOU?
LIKE A DOPE, I SLICED OFF TWO OF MY FINGERTIPS. THAT REALLY FRICKIN' HURTS.
WELL, NOT AT FIRST... THEN IT JUST HURTS A BIT.
BUT AFTER I CUT MYSELF AND RAN MY HANDS UNDER WATER, LIKE THIS... I HADN'T REALIZED THAT I WAS ACTUALLY MISSING SOME FINGERTIPS.
SO OK, I WRAPPED A RAG AROUND MY HAND TO MAKE IT STOP BLEEDING.
AND THEN THE RAG WAS TOTALLY DRENCHED IN BLOOD.
I COULDN'T STOP THE HEMORRHAGE. I DIDN'T KNOW WHAT TO DO.
FINALLY, WE CALLED MY PROCTOLOGIST SURGEON FRIEND AND HE SEWED ME UP.
AT FIRST I COULDN'T REALLY DRAW. BUT ANYWAY...
WHOA... I SHOULDN'T HAVE HAD THAT DRINK...

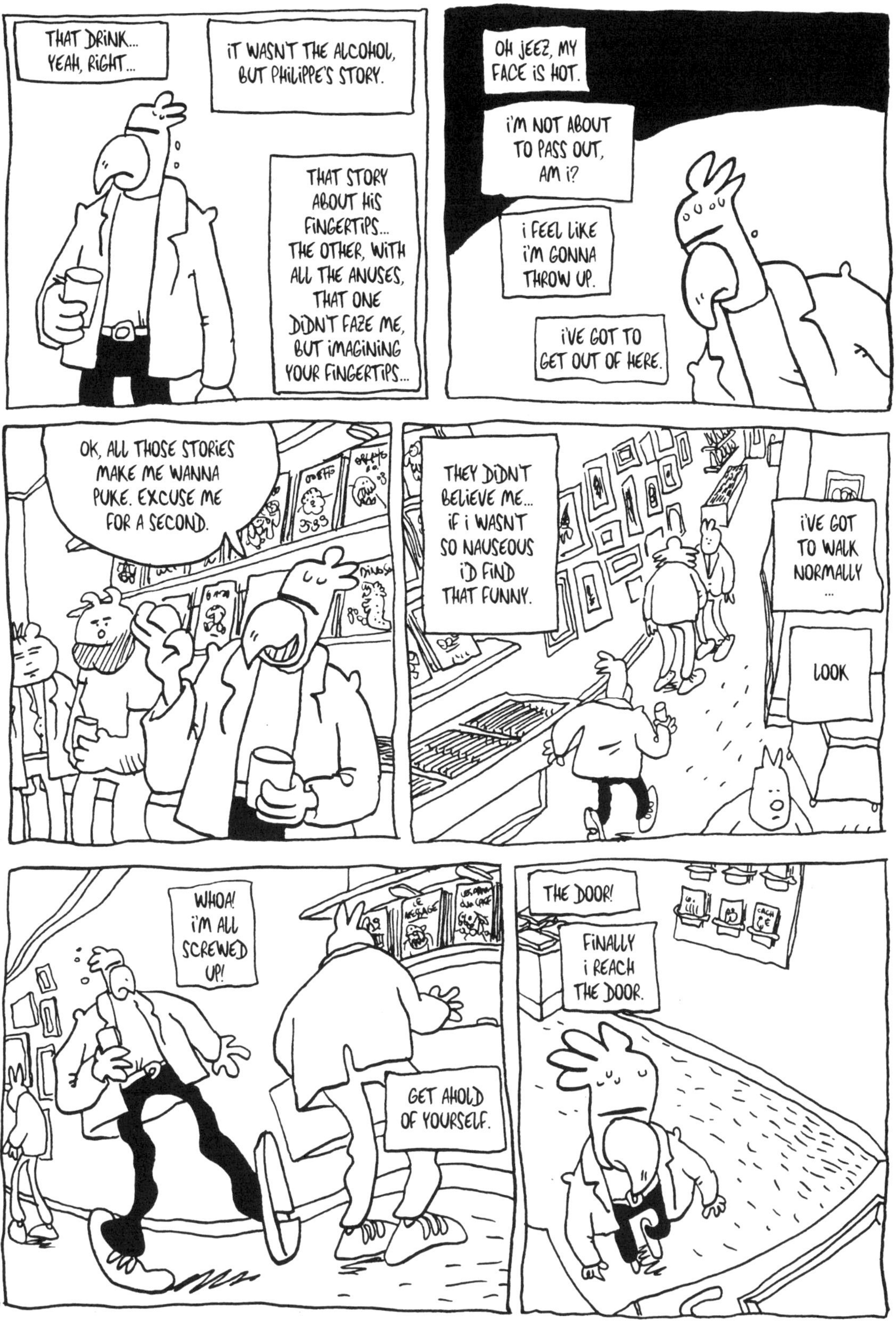
THAT DRINK... YEAH, RIGHT...
IT WASN'T THE ALCOHOL, BUT PHILIPPE'S STORY.
THAT STORY ABOUT HIS FINGERTIPS... THE OTHER, WITH ALL THE ANUSES, THAT ONE DIDN'T FAZE ME, BUT IMAGINING YOUR FINGERTIPS...
OH JEEZ, MY FACE IS HOT.
I'M NOT ABOUT TO PASS OUT, AM I?
I FEEL LIKE I'M GONNA THROW UP.
I'VE GOT TO GET OUT OF HERE.
OK, ALL THOSE STORIES MAKE ME WANNA PUKE. EXCUSE ME FOR A SECOND.
THEY DIDN'T BELIEVE ME... IF I WASN'T SO NAUSEOUS I'D FIND THAT FUNNY.
I'VE GOT TO WALK NORMALLY ...
LOOK
WHOA! I'M ALL SCREWED UP!
GET AHOLD OF YOURSELF.
THE DOOR!
FINALLY I REACH THE DOOR.

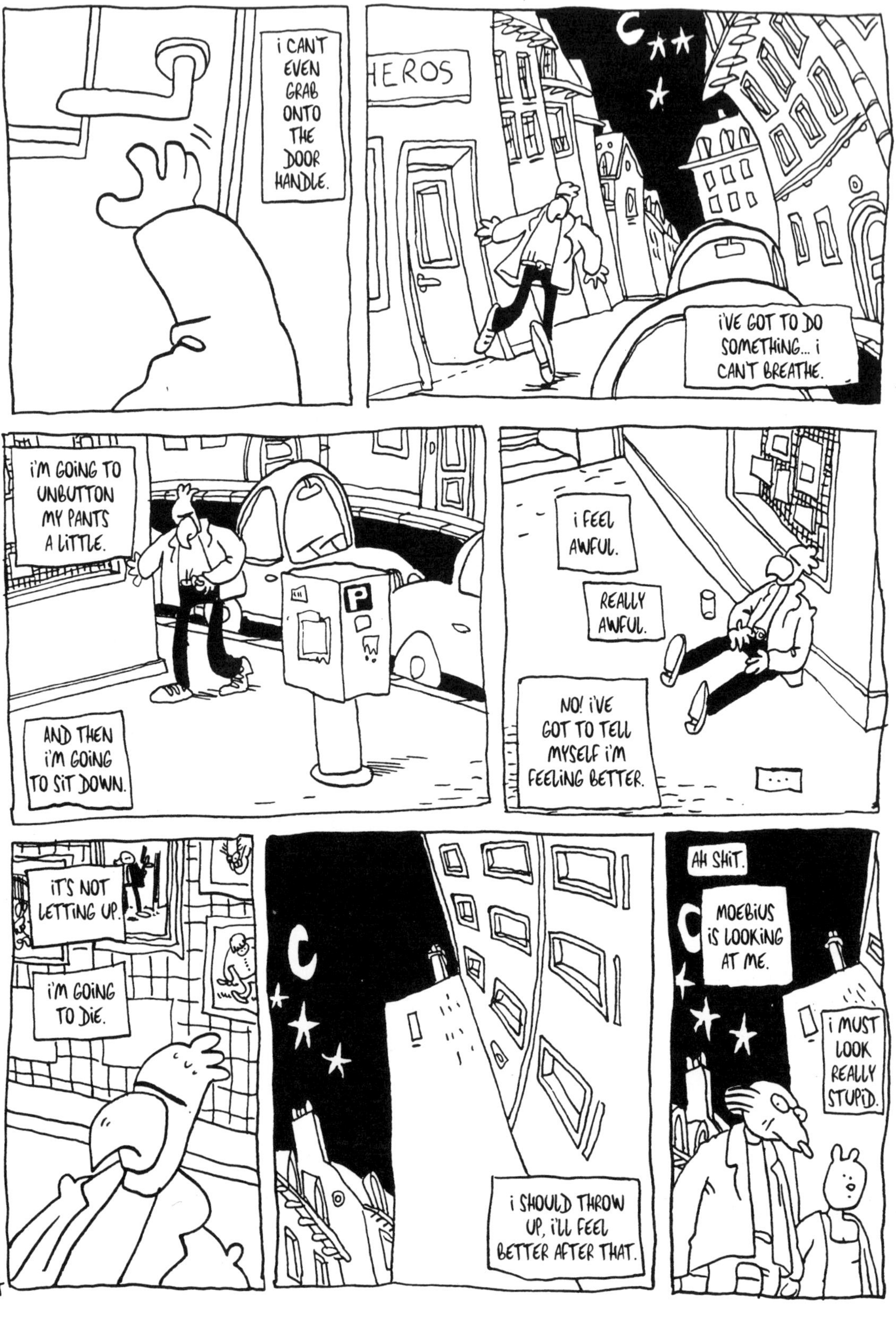

i CAN'T EVEN GRAB ONTO THE DOOR HANDLE.
HEROS
i'VE GOT TO DO SOMETHiNG... i CAN'T BREATHE.
i'M GOiNG TO UNBUTTON MY PANTS A LiTTLE.
AND THEN i'M GOiNG TO SiT DOWN.
P
i FEEL AWFUL.
REALLY AWFUL.
NO! i'VE GOT TO TELL MYSELF i'M FEELiNG BETTER.
...
iT'S NOT LETTiNG UP.
i'M GOiNG TO DiE.
i SHOULD THROW UP, i'LL FEEL BETTER AFTER THAT.
AH SHiT.
MOEBiUS iS LOOKiNG AT ME.
i MUST LOOK REALLY STUPiD.

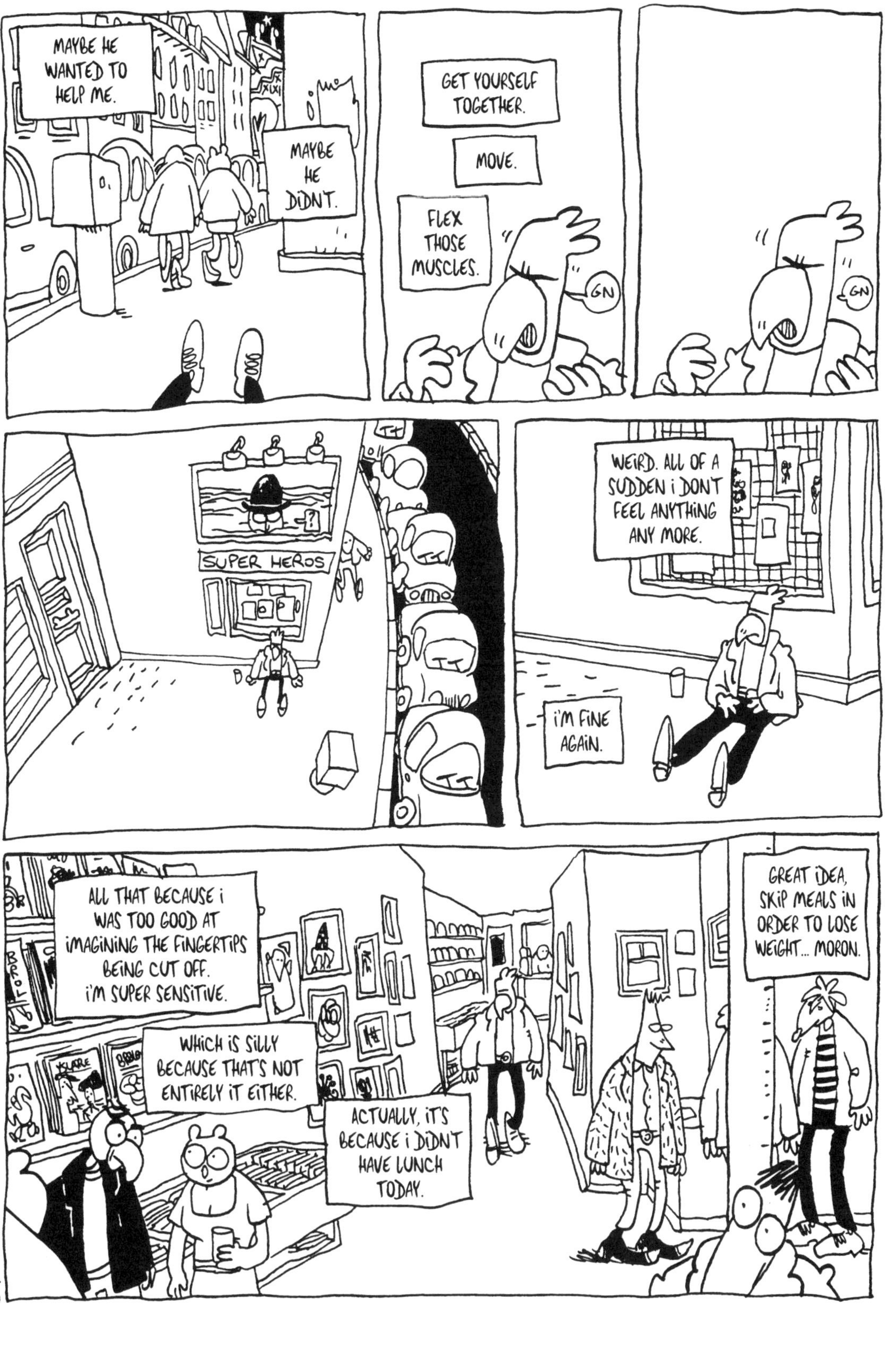

MAYBE HE WANTED TO HELP ME.
MAYBE HE DIDN'T.
GET YOURSELF TOGETHER.
MOVE.
FLEX THOSE MUSCLES.
GN
GN
SUPER HEROS
WEIRD. ALL OF A SUDDEN I DON'T FEEL ANYTHING ANY MORE.
I'M FINE AGAIN.
ALL THAT BECAUSE I WAS TOO GOOD AT IMAGINING THE FINGERTIPS BEING CUT OFF. I'M SUPER SENSITIVE.
WHICH IS SILLY BECAUSE THAT'S NOT ENTIRELY IT EITHER.
ACTUALLY, IT'S BECAUSE I DIDN'T HAVE LUNCH TODAY.
GREAT IDEA, SKIP MEALS IN ORDER TO LOSE WEIGHT... MORON.

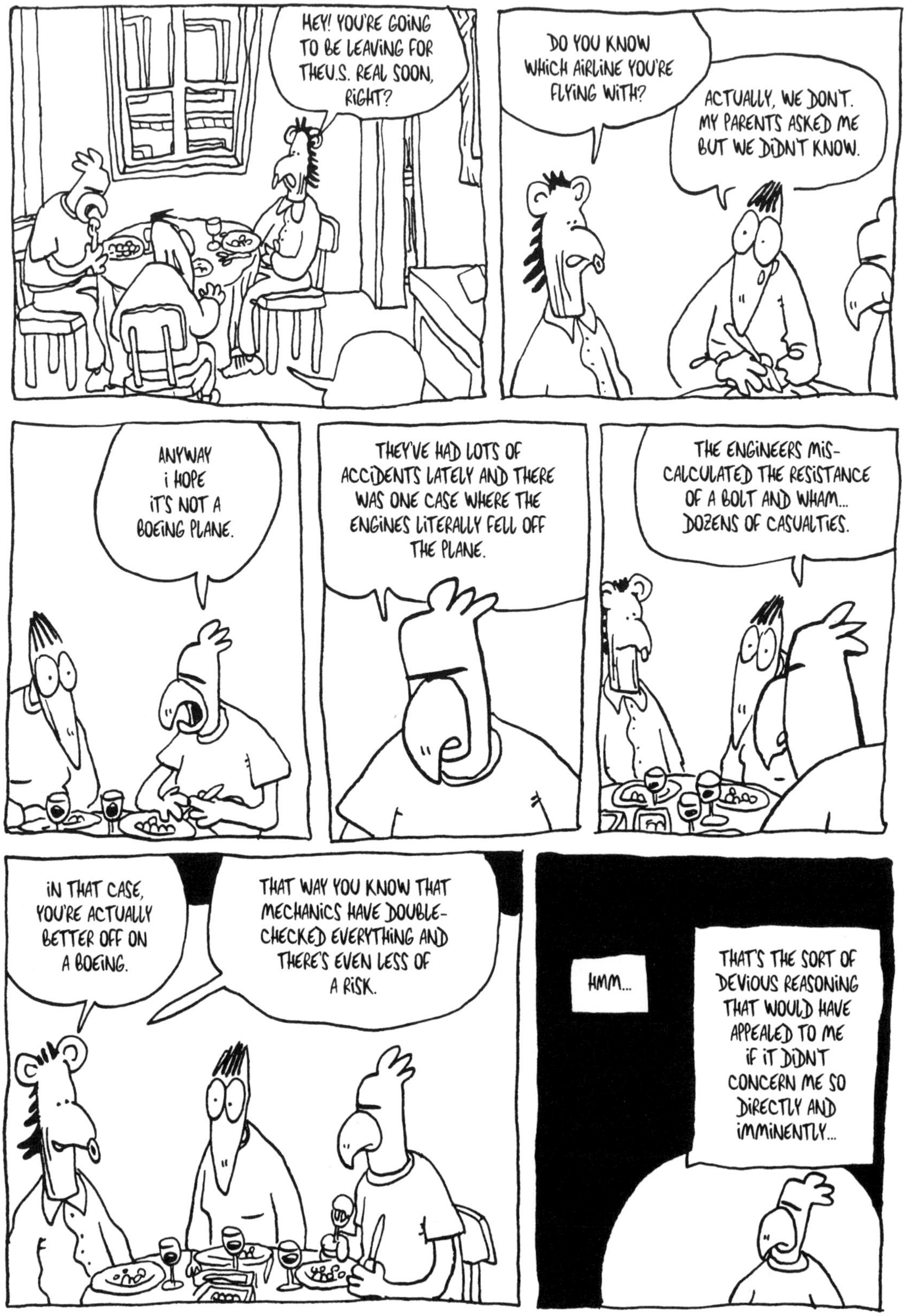
HEY! YOU'RE GOING TO BE LEAVING FOR THE U.S. REAL SOON, RIGHT?
DO YOU KNOW WHICH AIRLINE YOU'RE FLYING WITH?
ACTUALLY, WE DON'T. MY PARENTS ASKED ME BUT WE DIDN'T KNOW.
ANYWAY I HOPE IT'S NOT A BOEING PLANE.
THEY'VE HAD LOTS OF ACCIDENTS LATELY AND THERE WAS ONE CASE WHERE THE ENGINES LITERALLY FELL OFF THE PLANE.
THE ENGINEERS MIS-CALCULATED THE RESISTANCE OF A BOLT AND WHAM... DOZENS OF CASUALTIES.
IN THAT CASE, YOU'RE ACTUALLY BETTER OFF ON A BOEING.
THAT WAY YOU KNOW THAT MECHANICS HAVE DOUBLE-CHECKED EVERYTHING AND THERE'S EVEN LESS OF A RISK.
HMM...
THAT'S THE SORT OF DEVIOUS REASONING THAT WOULD HAVE APPEALED TO ME IF IT DIDN'T CONCERN ME SO DIRECTLY AND IMMINENTLY...

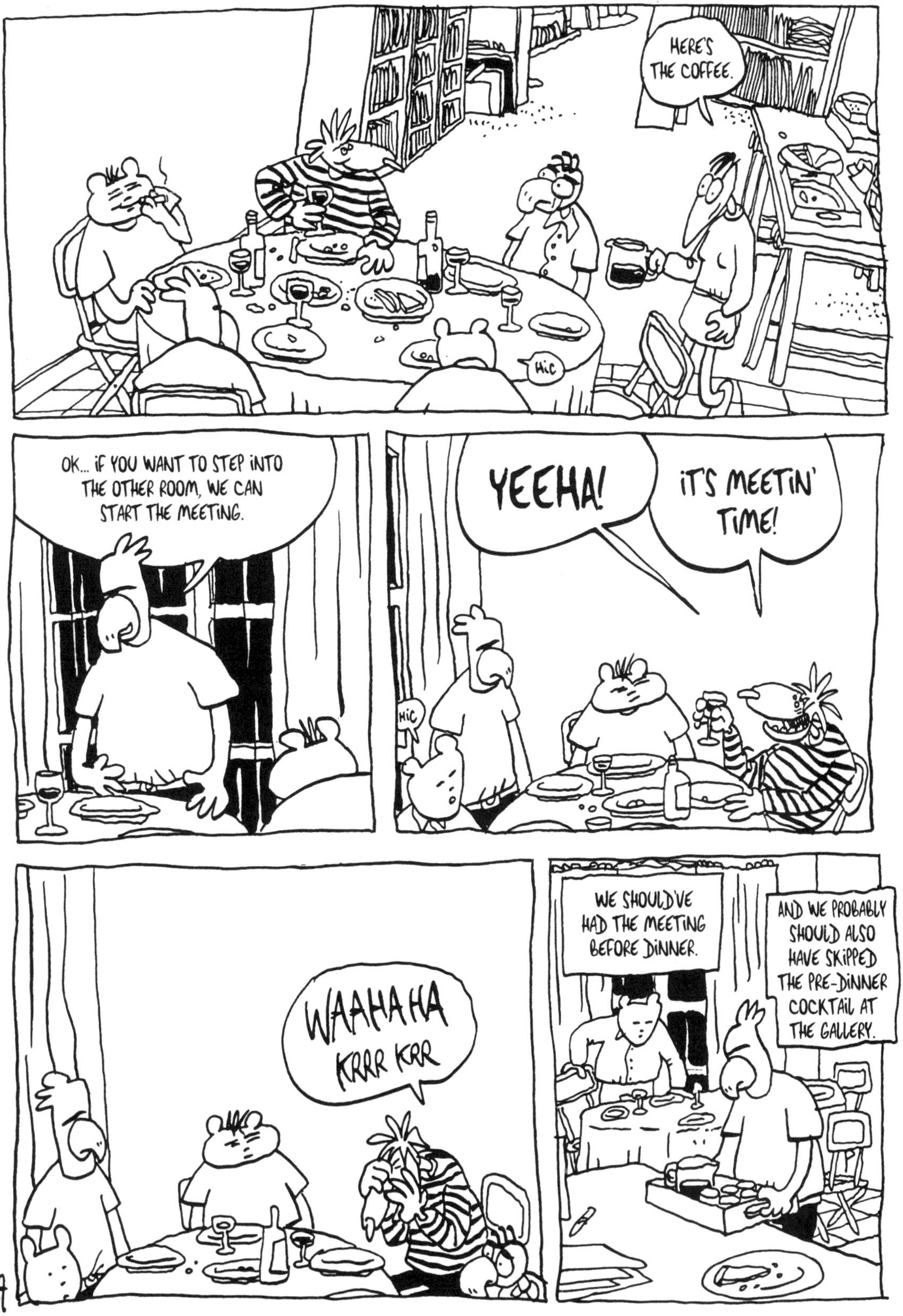
HERE'S THE COFFEE.
HIC
OK... IF YOU WANT TO STEP INTO THE OTHER ROOM, WE CAN START THE MEETING.
YEEHA!
IT'S MEETIN' TIME!
HIC
WAAHAHA KRRR KRR
WE SHOULD'VE HAD THE MEETING BEFORE DINNER.
AND WE PROBABLY SHOULD ALSO HAVE SKIPPED THE PRE-DINNER COCKTAIL AT THE GALLERY.

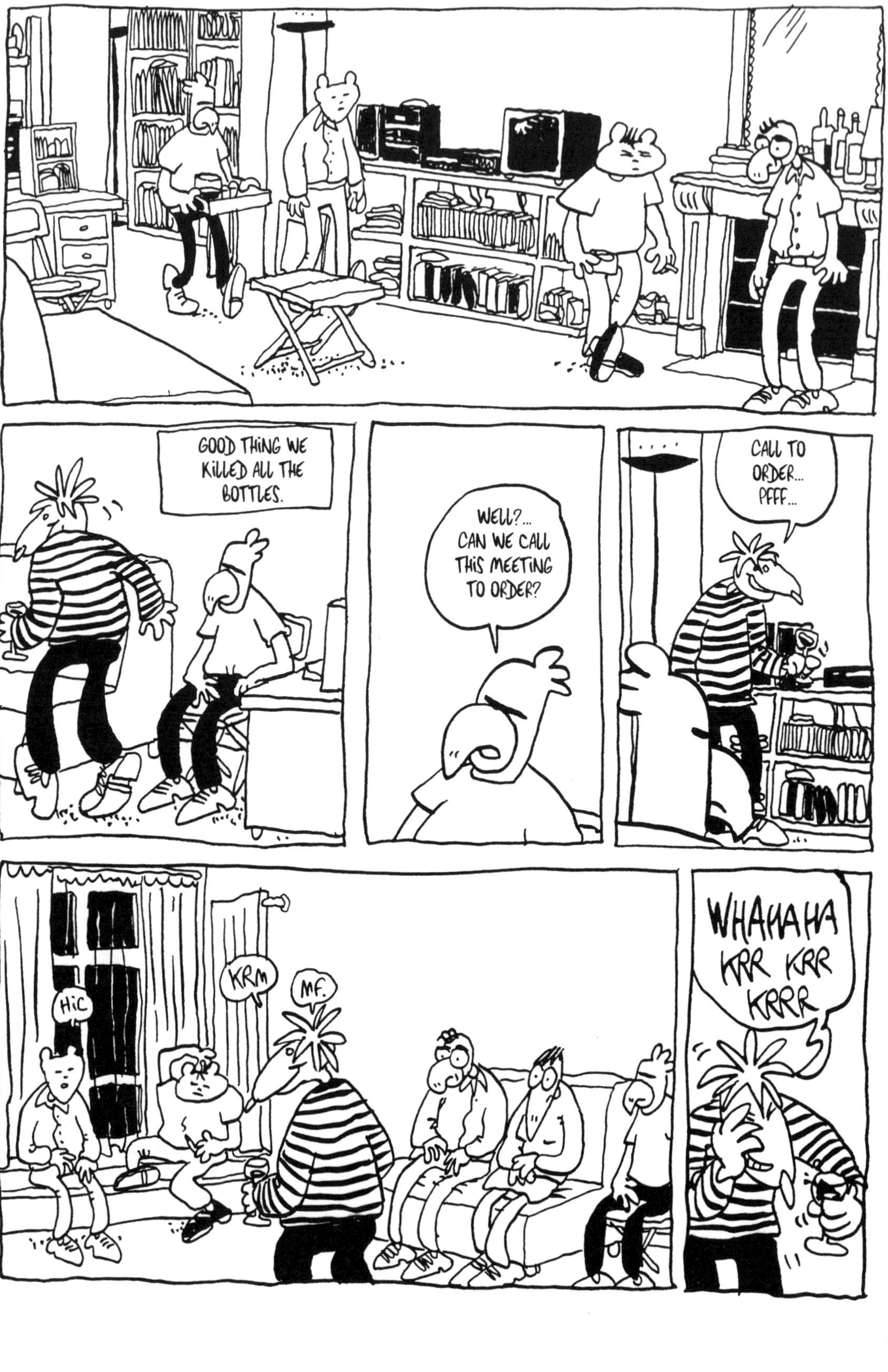
GOOD THING WE KILLED ALL THE BOTTLES.
WELL?... CAN WE CALL THIS MEETING TO ORDER?
CALL TO ORDER... PFFF...
HiC
KRM
MF.
WHAHAHA KRR KRR KRRR

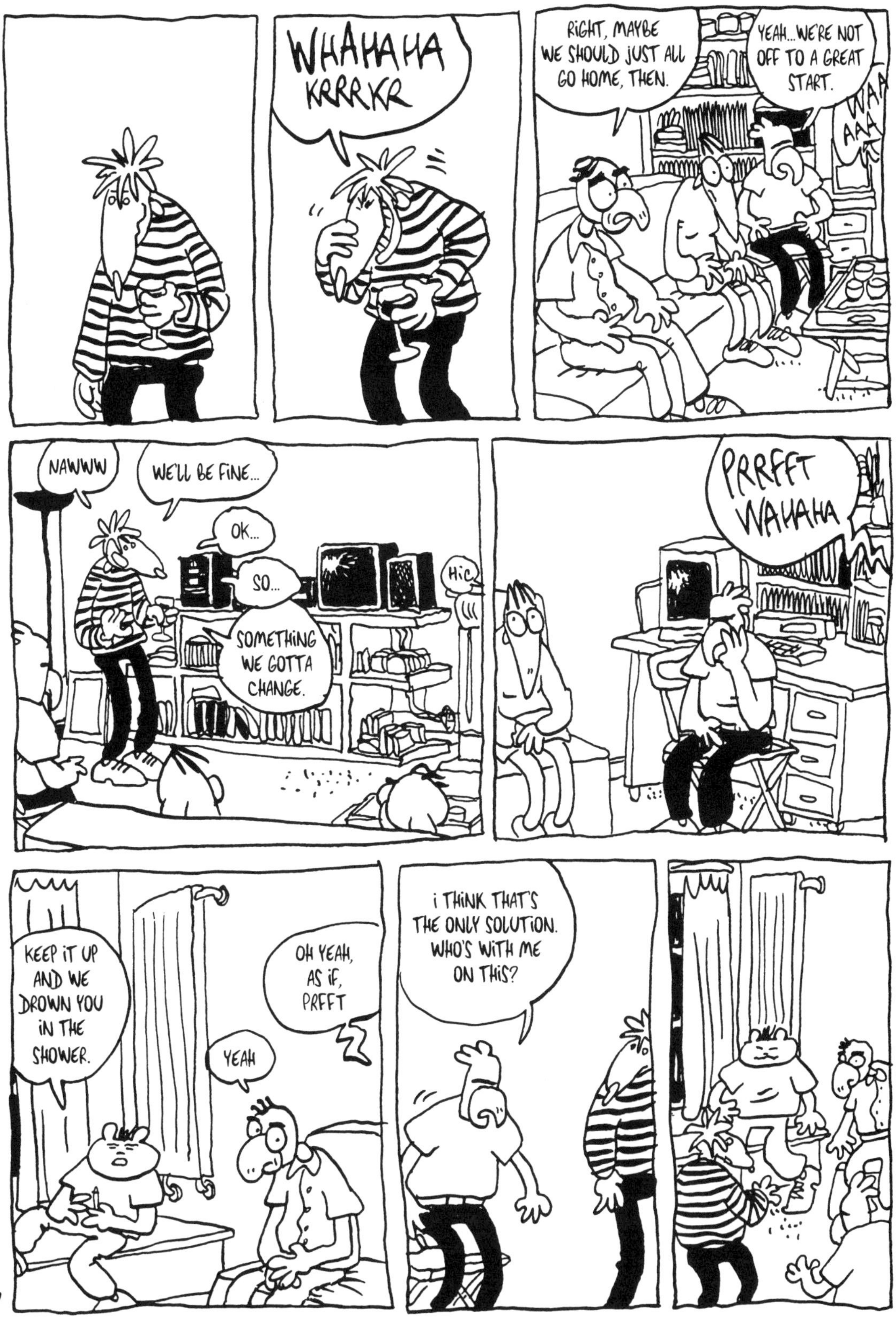
WHAHAHA KRRRKR
RIGHT, MAYBE WE SHOULD JUST ALL GO HOME, THEN.
YEAH... WE'RE NOT OFF TO A GREAT START.
WAA AAA
NAWWW
WE'LL BE FINE...
OK...
SO...
SOMETHING WE GOTTA CHANGE.
HIC
PRRFFT WAHAHA
KEEP IT UP AND WE DROWN YOU IN THE SHOWER.
YEAH
OH YEAH, AS IF, PRFFT
I THINK THAT'S THE ONLY SOLUTION. WHO'S WITH ME ON THIS?

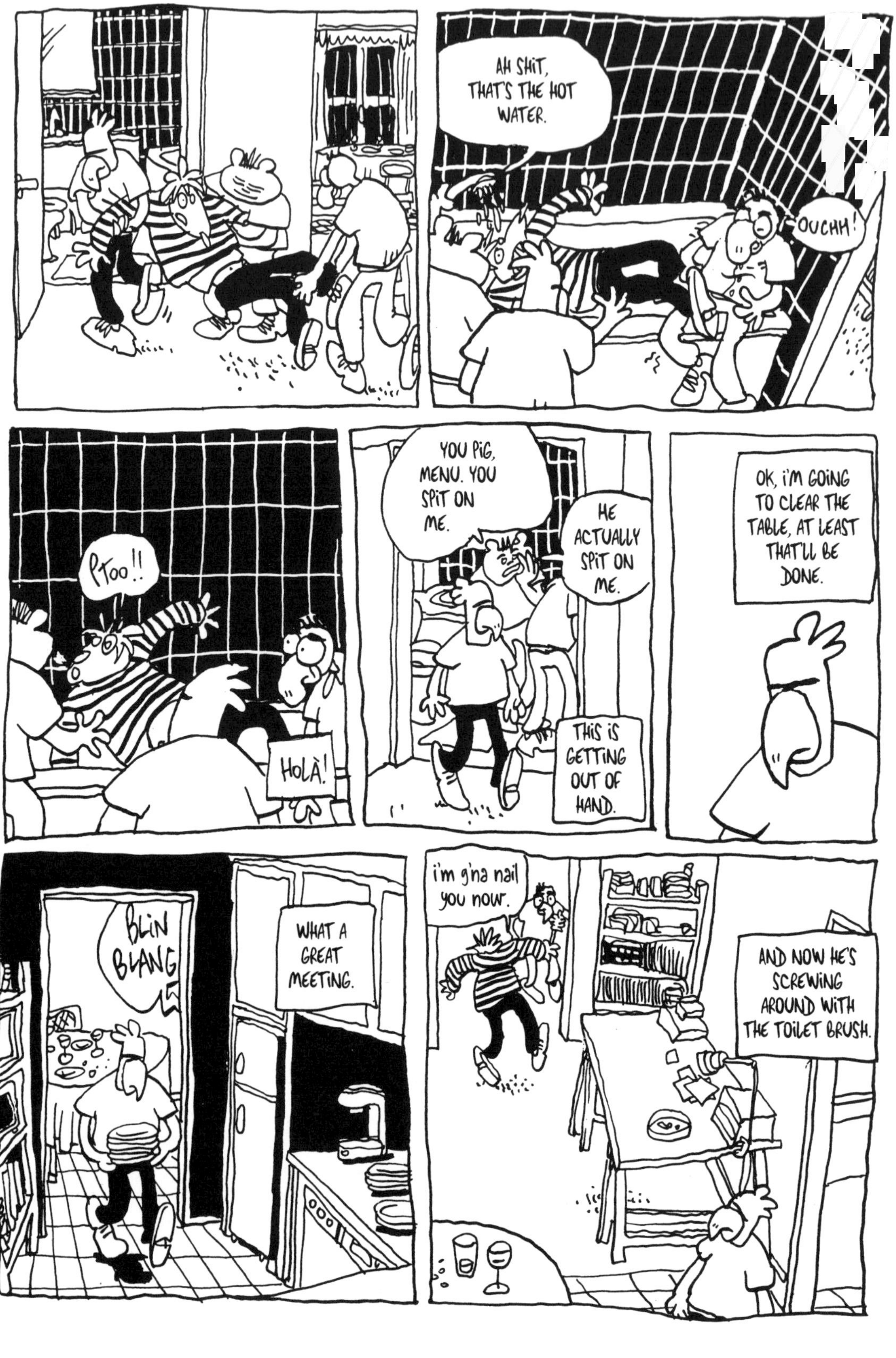
AH SHIT, THAT'S THE HOT WATER.
OUCHH!
PTOO!!
HOLÀ!
YOU PIG, MENU. YOU SPIT ON ME.
HE ACTUALLY SPIT ON ME.
THIS IS GETTING OUT OF HAND.
OK, I'M GOING TO CLEAR THE TABLE, AT LEAST THAT'LL BE DONE.
BLIN BLANG
WHAT A GREAT MEETING.
i'm g'na nail you now.
AND NOW HE'S SCREWING AROUND WITH THE TOILET BRUSH.

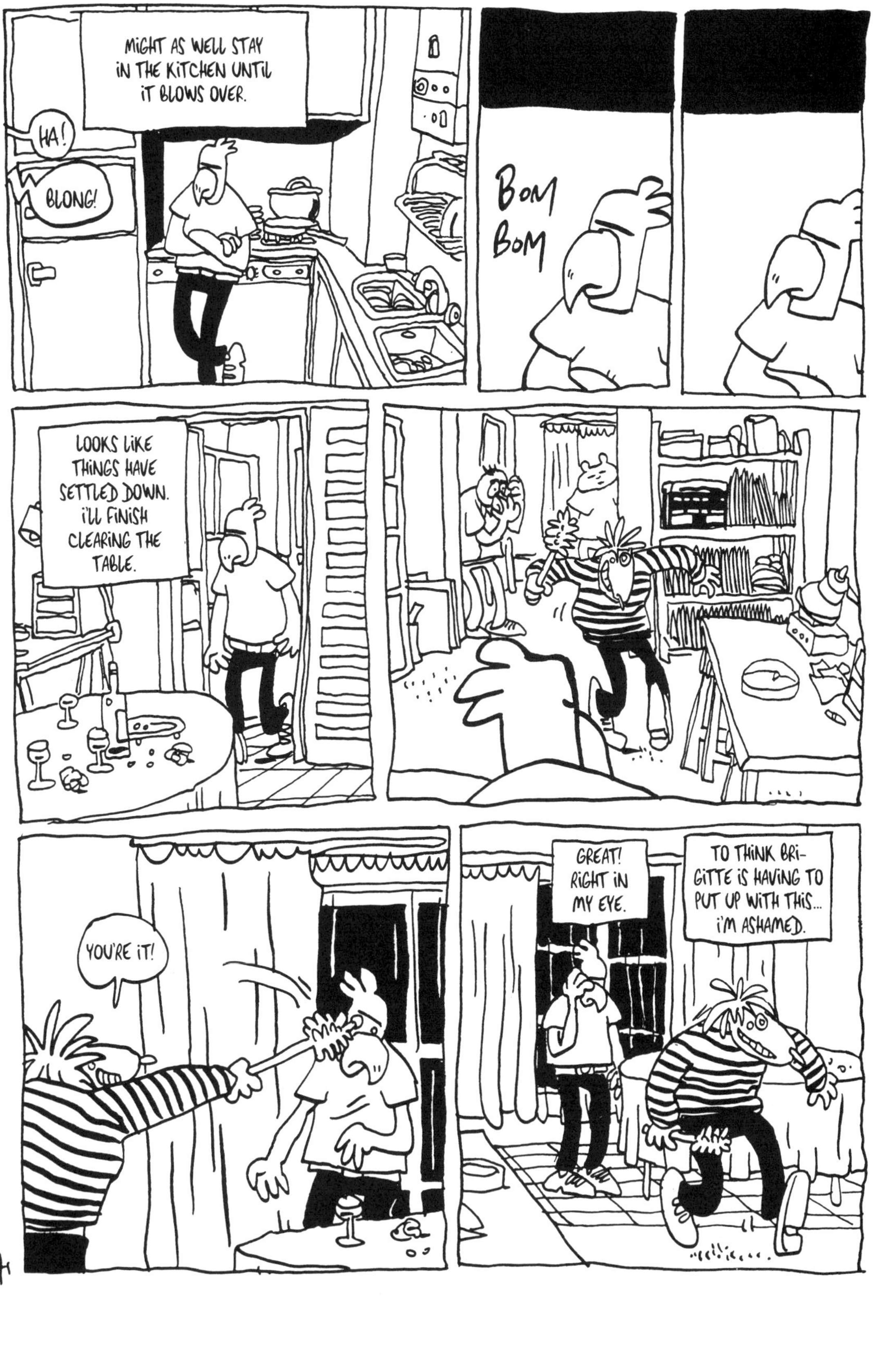
MIGHT AS WELL STAY IN THE KITCHEN UNTIL IT BLOWS OVER.
HA!
BLONG!
BOM BOM
LOOKS LIKE THINGS HAVE SETTLED DOWN. I'LL FINISH CLEARING THE TABLE.
YOU'RE IT!
GREAT! RIGHT IN MY EYE.
TO THINK BRI-GITTE IS HAVING TO PUT UP WITH THIS... I'M ASHAMED.

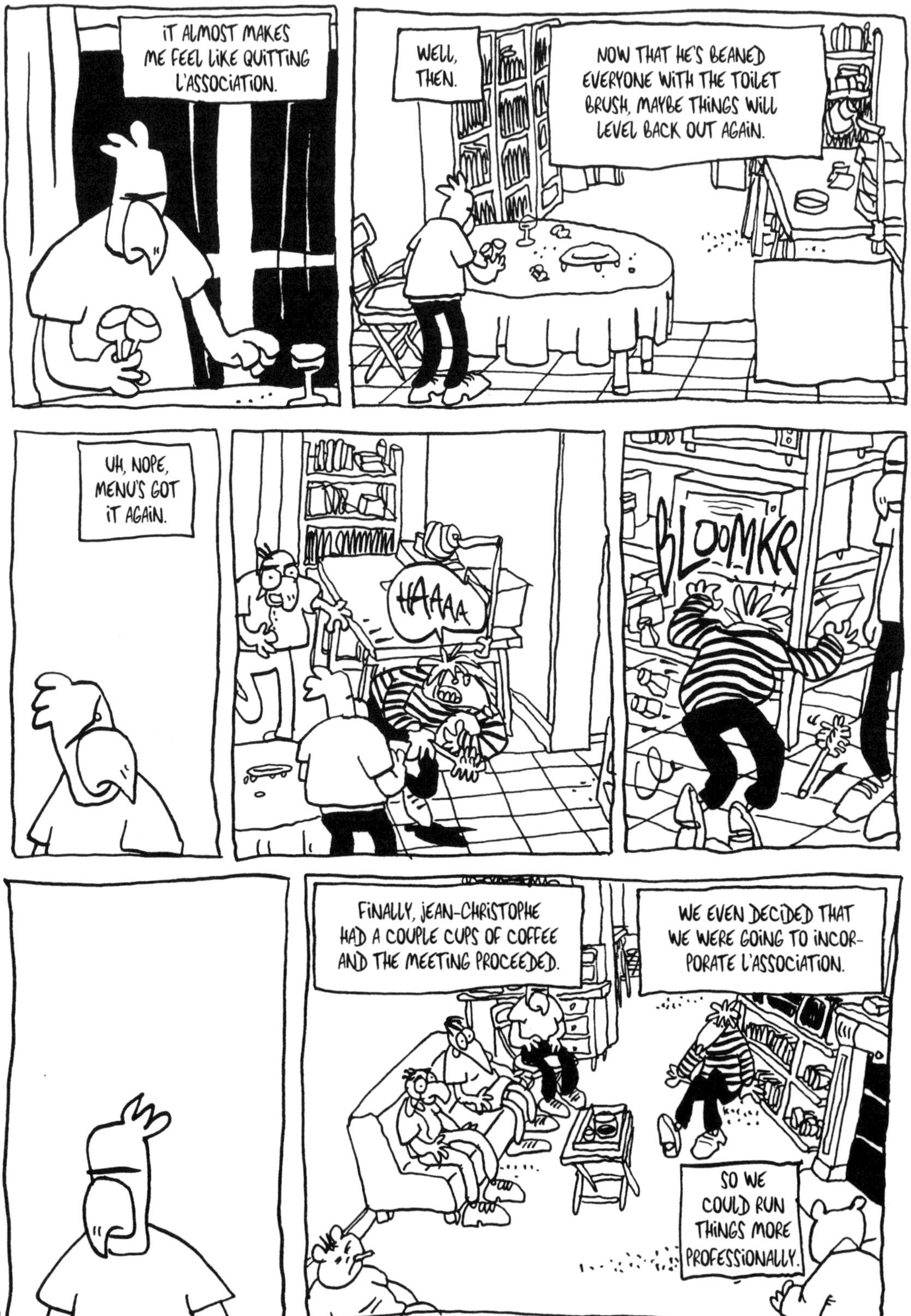

IT ALMOST MAKES ME FEEL LIKE QUITTING L'ASSOCIATION.
WELL, THEN.
NOW THAT HE'S BEANED EVERYONE WITH THE TOILET BRUSH, MAYBE THINGS WILL LEVEL BACK OUT AGAIN.
UH, NOPE, MENU'S GOT IT AGAIN.
HAAAA
BLOOMKR
FINALLY, JEAN-CHRISTOPHE HAD A COUPLE CUPS OF COFFEE AND THE MEETING PROCEEDED.
WE EVEN DECIDED THAT WE WERE GOING TO INCORPORATE L'ASSOCIATION.
SO WE COULD RUN THINGS MORE PROFESSIONALLY.

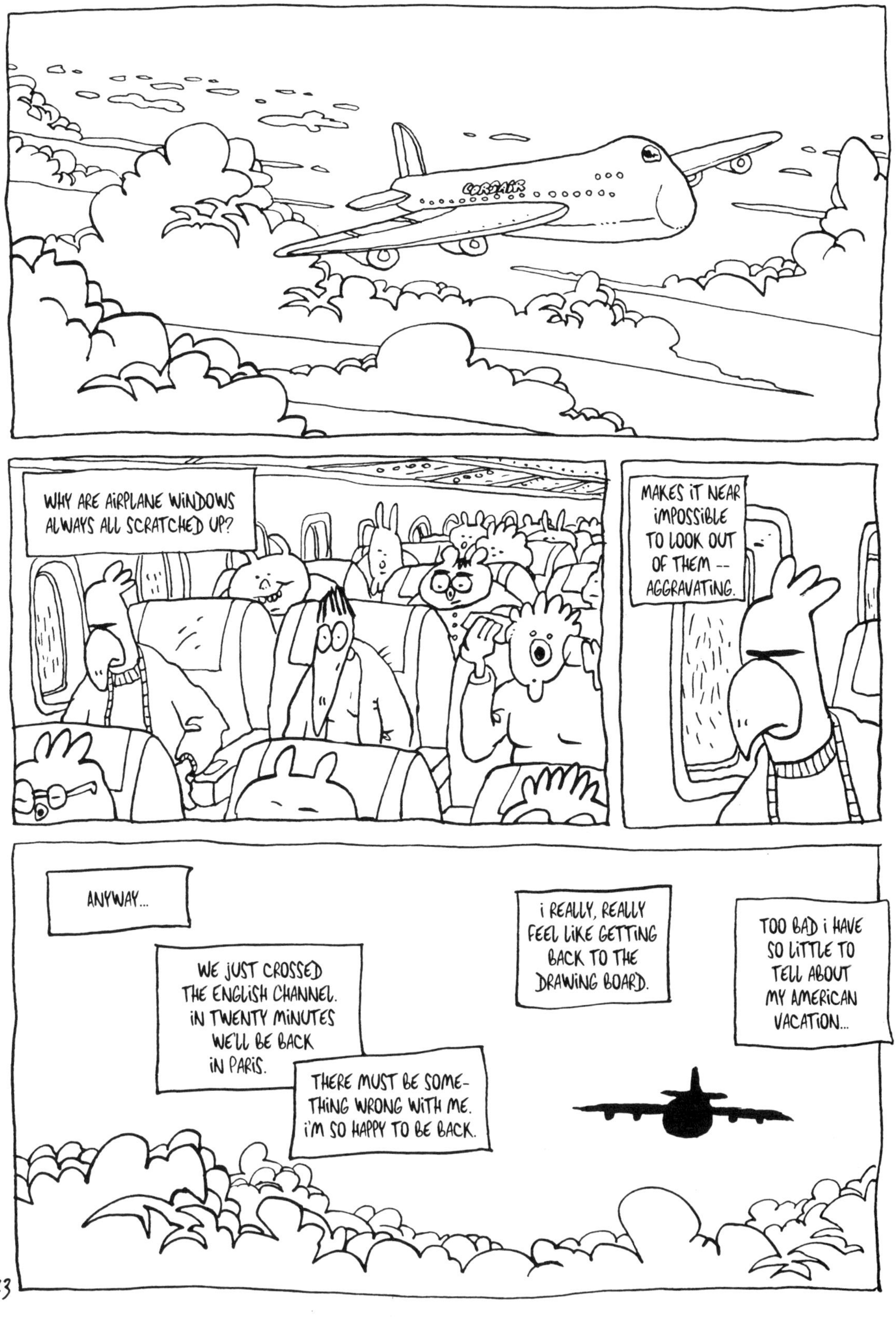

WHY ARE AIRPLANE WINDOWS ALWAYS ALL SCRATCHED UP?
MAKES IT NEAR IMPOSSIBLE TO LOOK OUT OF THEM -- AGGRAVATING.
ANYWAY...
WE JUST CROSSED THE ENGLISH CHANNEL. IN TWENTY MINUTES WE'LL BE BACK IN PARIS.
THERE MUST BE SOME-THING WRONG WITH ME. I'M SO HAPPY TO BE BACK.
I REALLY, REALLY FEEL LIKE GETTING BACK TO THE DRAWING BOARD.
TOO BAD I HAVE SO LITTLE TO TELL ABOUT MY AMERICAN VACATION...

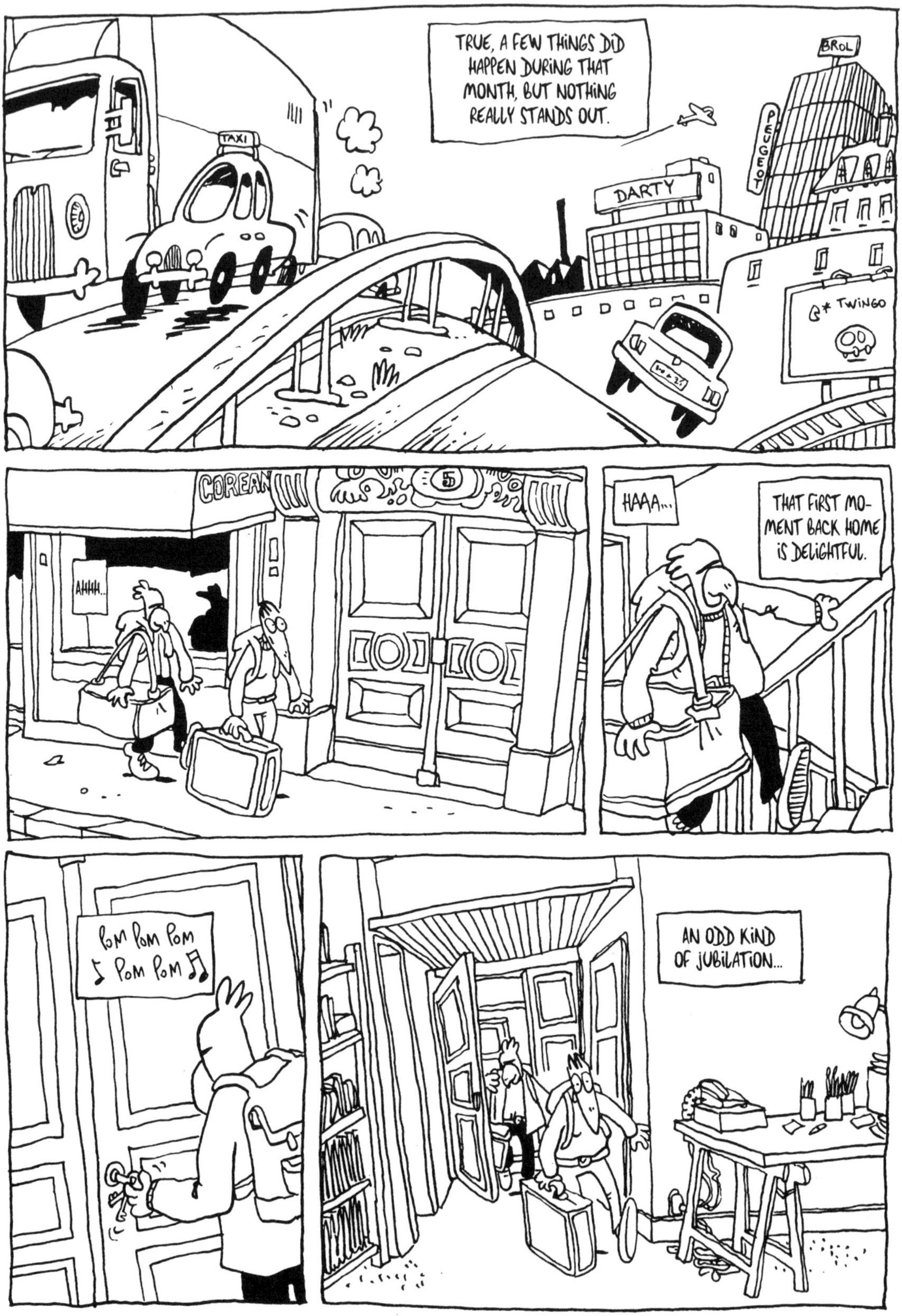
TRUE, A FEW THINGS DID HAPPEN DURING THAT MONTH, BUT NOTHING REALLY STANDS OUT.
TAXI
BROL
PEUGEOT
DARTY
TWINGO
COREAN
5
AHHH...
HAAA...
THAT FIRST MOMENT BACK HOME IS DELIGHTFUL.
POM POM POM
POM POM
AN ODD KIND OF JUBILATION...

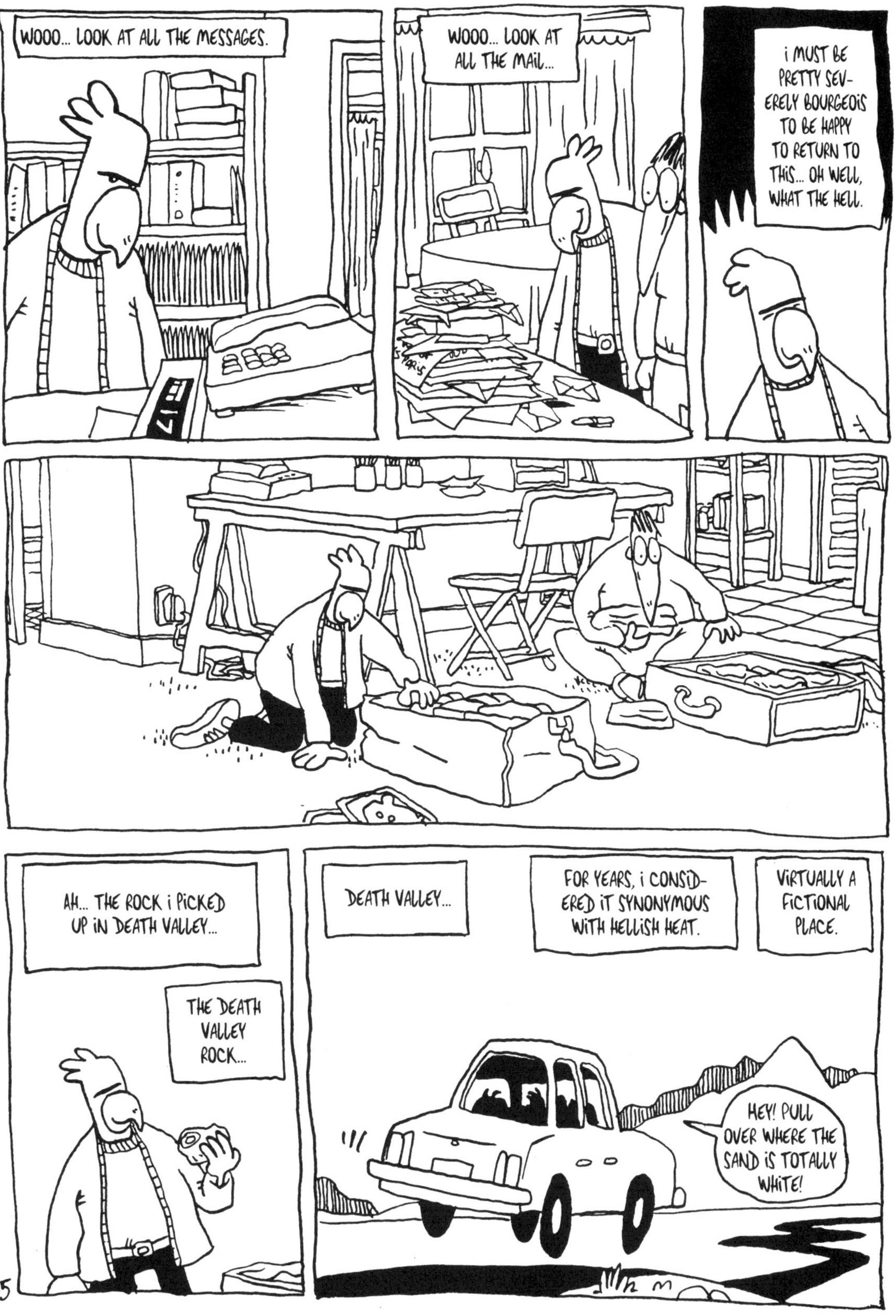
WOOO... LOOK AT ALL THE MESSAGES.
WOOO... LOOK AT ALL THE MAIL...
i MUST BE PRETTY SEV-ERELY BOURGEOiS TO BE HAPPY TO RETURN TO THiS... OH WELL, WHAT THE HELL.
AH... THE ROCK i PiCKED UP iN DEATH VALLEY...
THE DEATH VALLEY ROCK...
DEATH VALLEY...
FOR YEARS, i CONSiD-ERED iT SYNONYMOUS WiTH HELLiSH HEAT.
ViRTUALLY A FiCTiONAL PLACE.
HEY! PULL OVER WHERE THE SAND iS TOTALLY WHiTE!

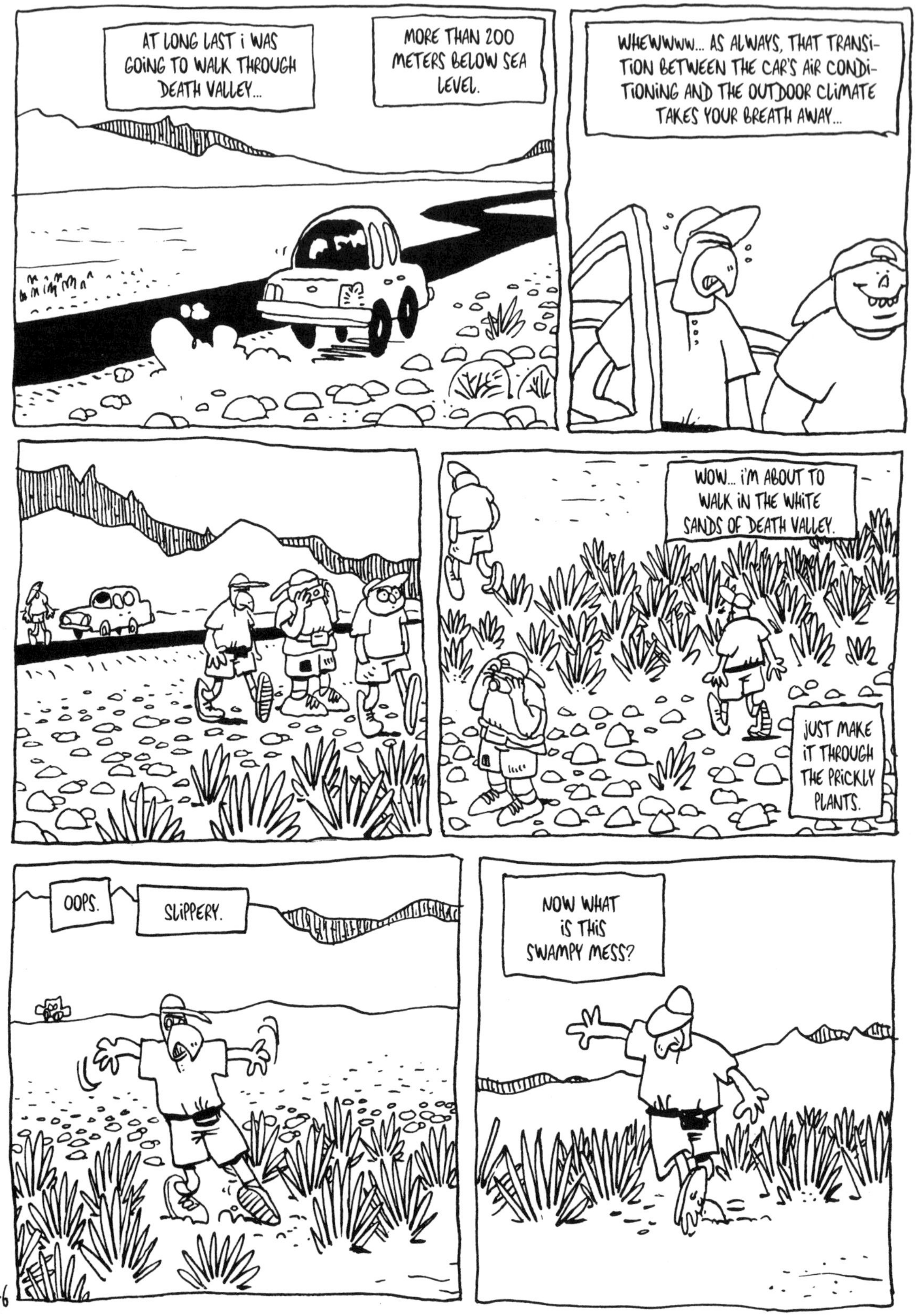
AT LONG LAST i WAS GOING TO WALK THROUGH DEATH VALLEY...
MORE THAN 200 METERS BELOW SEA LEVEL.
WHEWWWW... AS ALWAYS, THAT TRANSITION BETWEEN THE CAR'S AIR CONDITIONING AND THE OUTDOOR CLIMATE TAKES YOUR BREATH AWAY...
WOW... i'M ABOUT TO WALK IN THE WHITE SANDS OF DEATH VALLEY.
JUST MAKE IT THROUGH THE PRICKLY PLANTS.
OOPS.
SLIPPERY.
NOW WHAT IS THIS SWAMPY MESS?

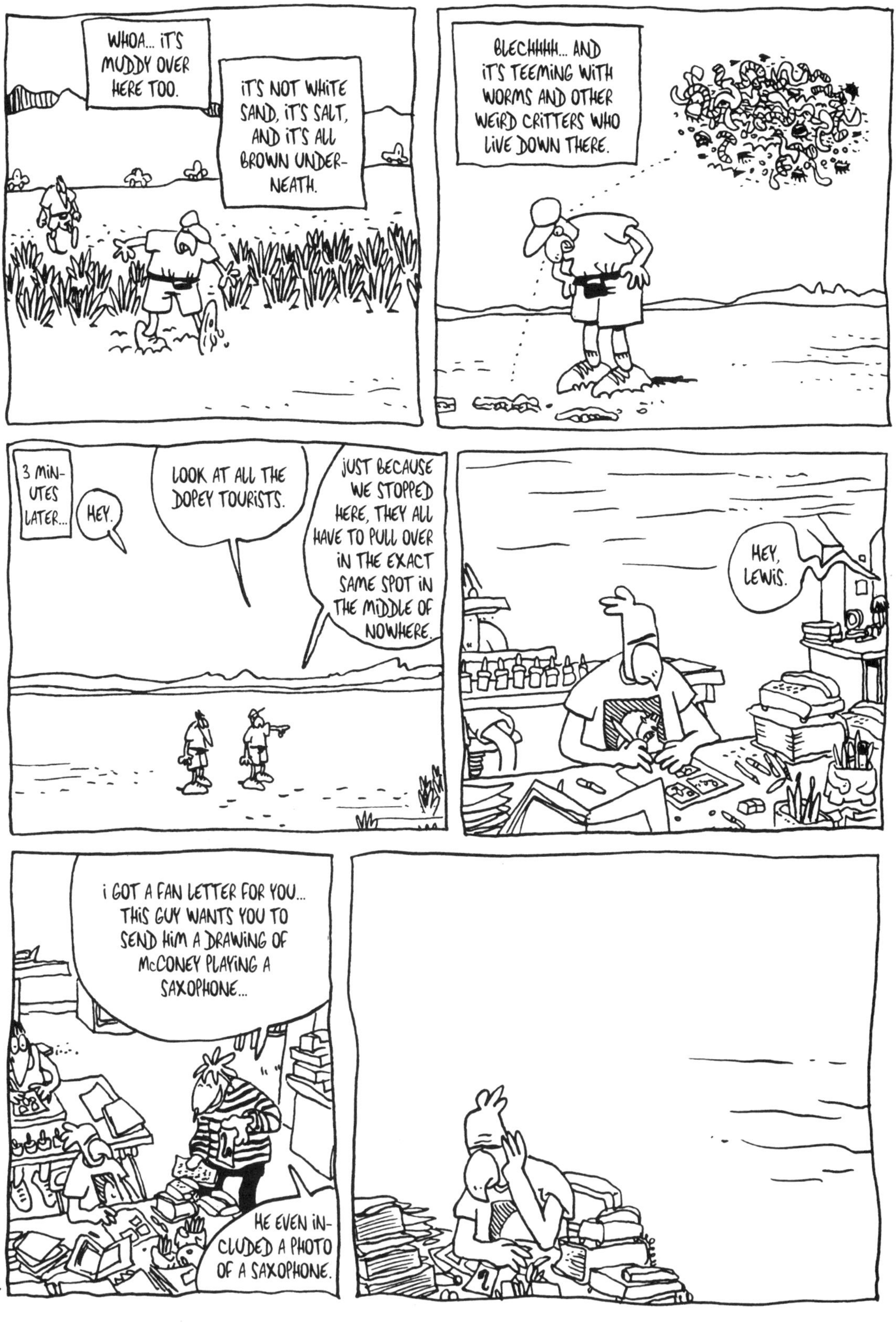
WHOA... IT'S MUDDY OVER HERE TOO.
IT'S NOT WHITE SAND, IT'S SALT, AND IT'S ALL BROWN UNDER-NEATH.
BLECHHHH... AND IT'S TEEMING WITH WORMS AND OTHER WEIRD CRITTERS WHO LIVE DOWN THERE.
3 MIN-UTES LATER...
HEY.
LOOK AT ALL THE DOPEY TOURISTS.
JUST BECAUSE WE STOPPED HERE, THEY ALL HAVE TO PULL OVER IN THE EXACT SAME SPOT IN THE MIDDLE OF NOWHERE.
HEY, LEWIS.
I GOT A FAN LETTER FOR YOU... THIS GUY WANTS YOU TO SEND HIM A DRAWING OF McCONEY PLAYING A SAXOPHONE...
HE EVEN IN-CLUDED A PHOTO OF A SAXOPHONE.

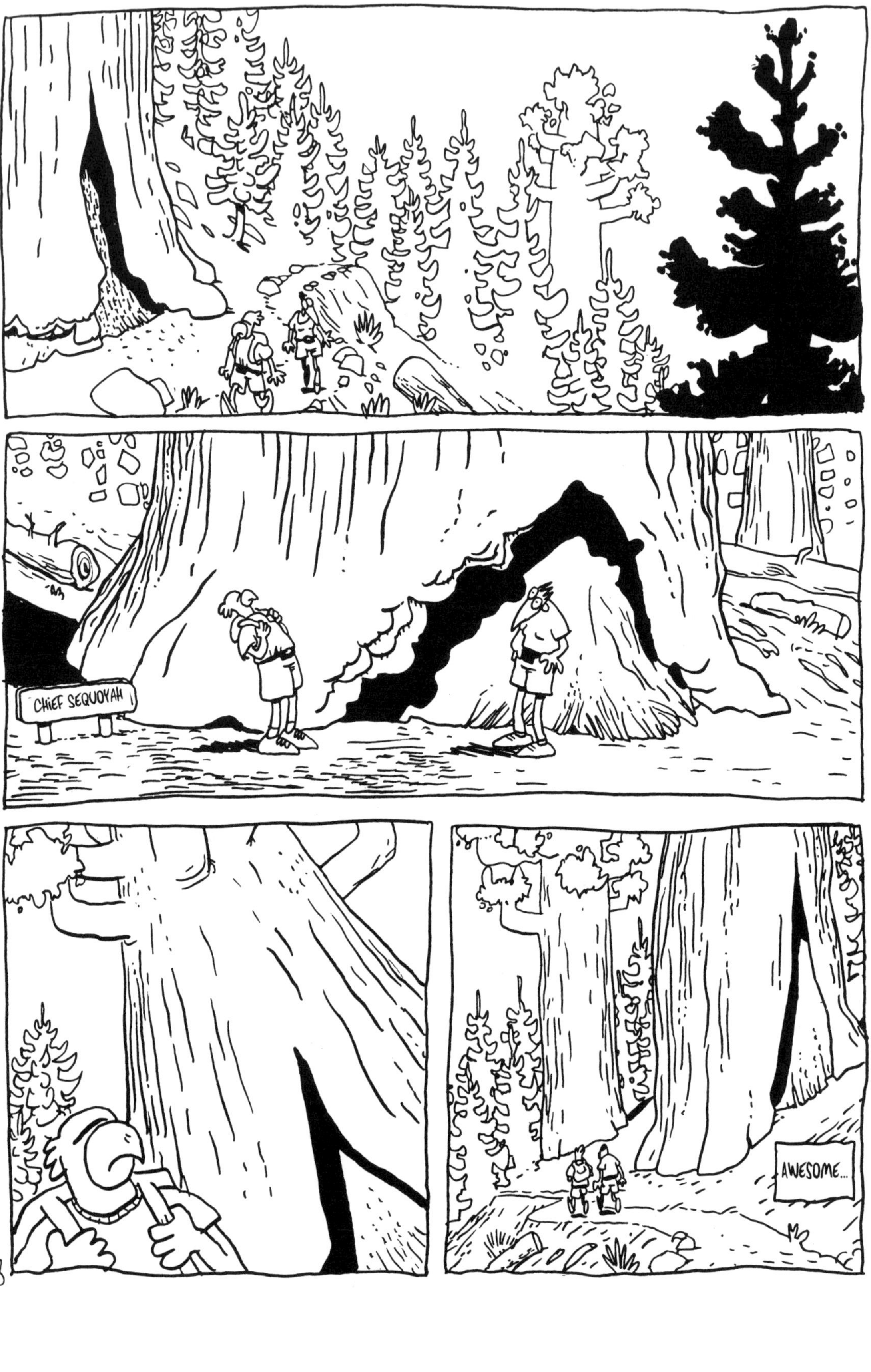
CHIEF SEQUOYAH
AWESOME...

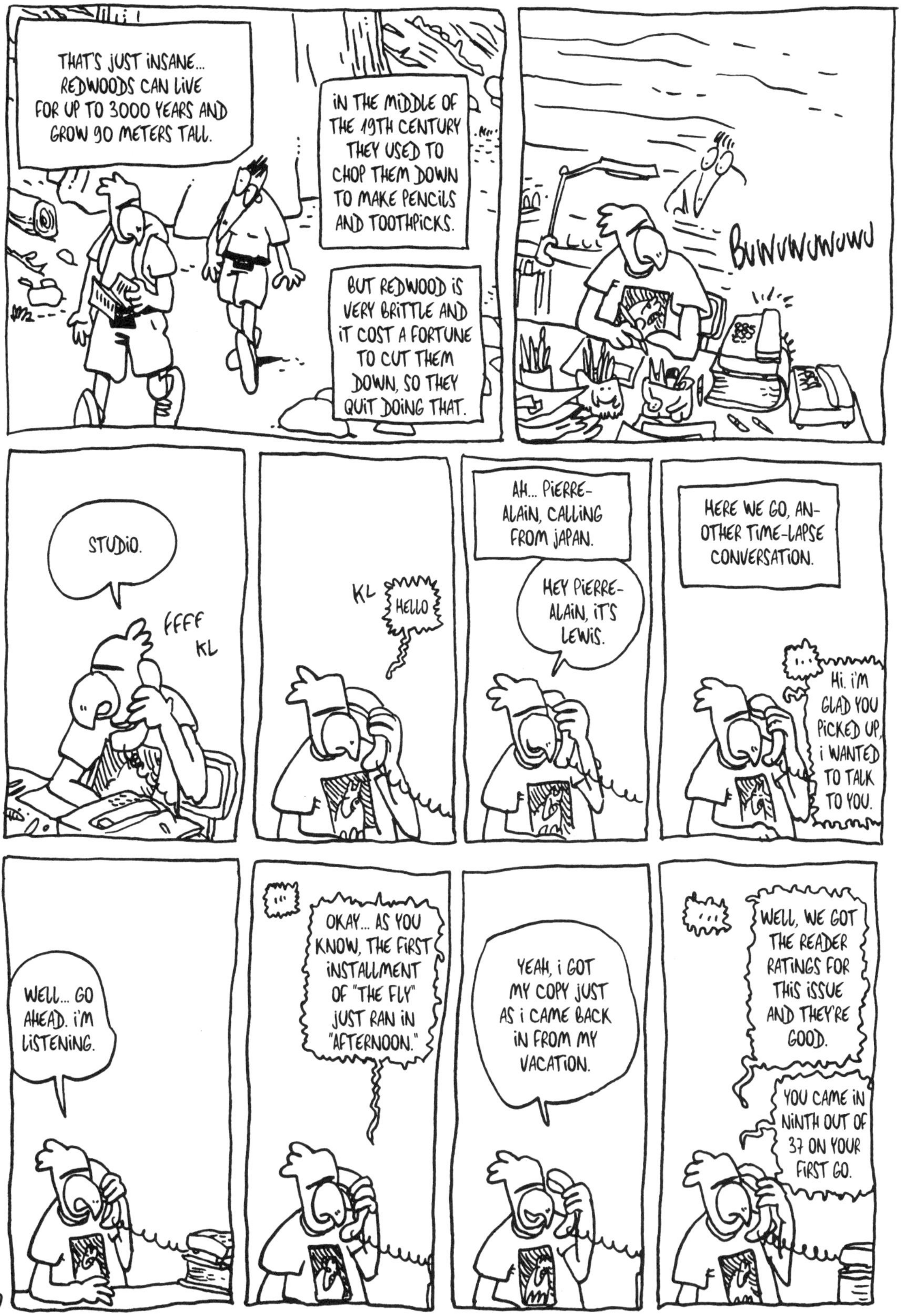
THAT'S JUST INSANE... REDWOODS CAN LIVE FOR UP TO 3000 YEARS AND GROW 90 METERS TALL.
IN THE MIDDLE OF THE 19TH CENTURY THEY USED TO CHOP THEM DOWN TO MAKE PENCILS AND TOOTHPICKS.
BUT REDWOOD IS VERY BRITTLE AND IT COST A FORTUNE TO CUT THEM DOWN, SO THEY QUIT DOING THAT.
BUWUWUWUWU
STUDIO.
FFFF
KL
KL
HELLO
AH... PIERRE-ALAIN, CALLING FROM JAPAN.
HEY PIERRE-ALAIN, IT'S LEWIS.
HERE WE GO, ANOTHER TIME-LAPSE CONVERSATION.
...
HI. I'M GLAD YOU PICKED UP, I WANTED TO TALK TO YOU.
WELL... GO AHEAD. I'M LISTENING.
...
OKAY... AS YOU KNOW, THE FIRST INSTALLMENT OF "THE FLY" JUST RAN IN "AFTERNOON."
YEAH, I GOT MY COPY JUST AS I CAME BACK IN FROM MY VACATION.
....
WELL, WE GOT THE READER RATINGS FOR THIS ISSUE AND THEY'RE GOOD.
YOU CAME IN NINTH OUT OF 37 ON YOUR FIRST GO.

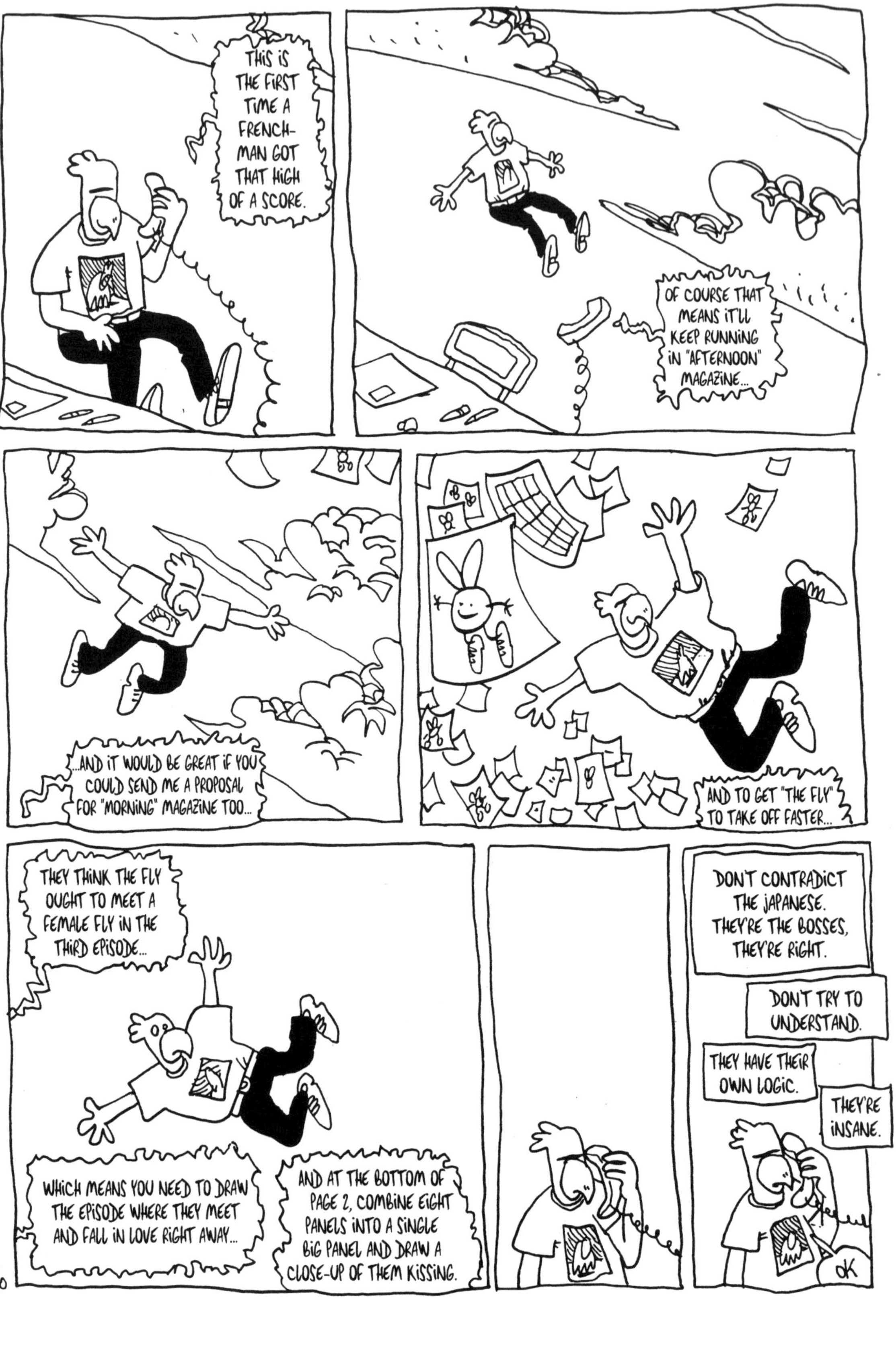
THIS IS THE FIRST TIME A FRENCH-MAN GOT THAT HIGH OF A SCORE.
OF COURSE THAT MEANS IT'LL KEEP RUNNING IN "AFTERNOON" MAGAZINE...
...AND IT WOULD BE GREAT IF YOU COULD SEND ME A PROPOSAL FOR "MORNING" MAGAZINE TOO...
AND TO GET "THE FLY" TO TAKE OFF FASTER...
THEY THINK THE FLY OUGHT TO MEET A FEMALE FLY IN THE THIRD EPISODE...
WHICH MEANS YOU NEED TO DRAW THE EPISODE WHERE THEY MEET AND FALL IN LOVE RIGHT AWAY...
AND AT THE BOTTOM OF PAGE 2, COMBINE EIGHT PANELS INTO A SINGLE BIG PANEL AND DRAW A CLOSE-UP OF THEM KISSING.
DON'T CONTRADICT THE JAPANESE. THEY'RE THE BOSSES, THEY'RE RIGHT.
DON'T TRY TO UNDERSTAND.
THEY HAVE THEIR OWN LOGIC.
THEY'RE INSANE.
OK

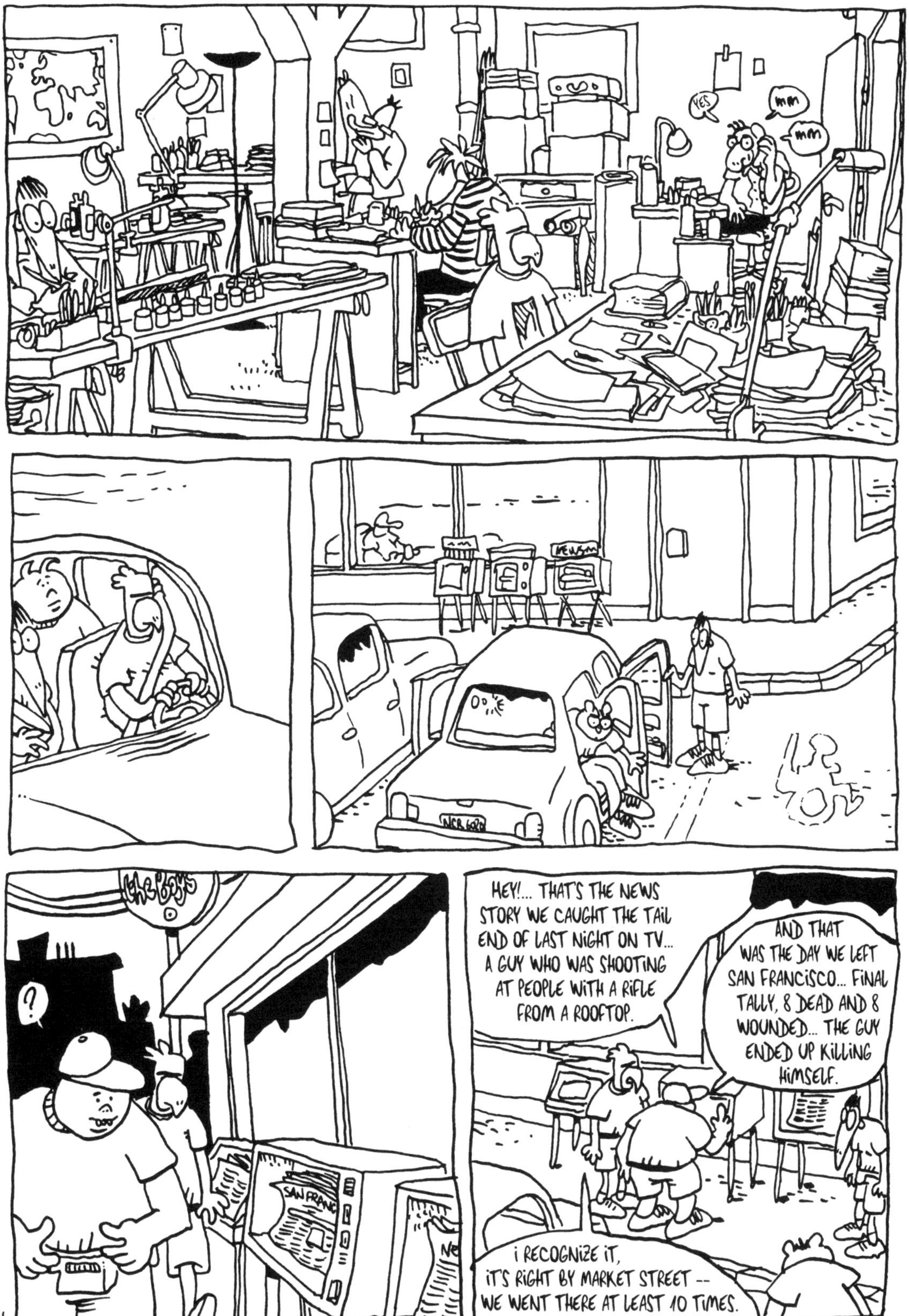
YES
mm
mm
HEY!... THAT'S THE NEWS STORY WE CAUGHT THE TAIL END OF LAST NIGHT ON TV... A GUY WHO WAS SHOOTING AT PEOPLE WITH A RIFLE FROM A ROOFTOP.
AND THAT WAS THE DAY WE LEFT SAN FRANCISCO... FINAL TALLY, 8 DEAD AND 8 WOUNDED... THE GUY ENDED UP KILLING HIMSELF.
I RECOGNIZE IT, IT'S RIGHT BY MARKET STREET -- WE WENT THERE AT LEAST 10 TIMES.

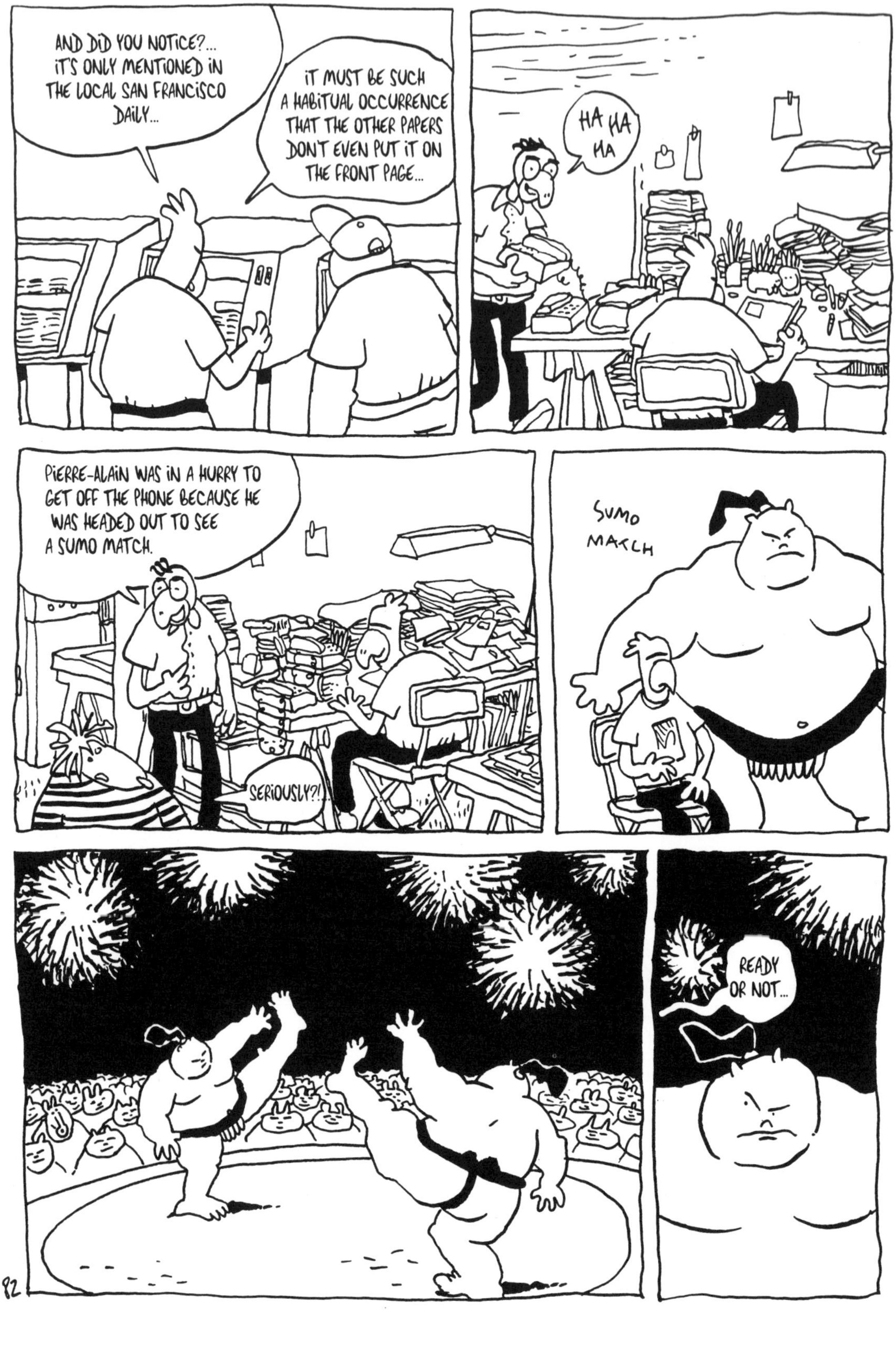
AND DID YOU NOTICE?... IT'S ONLY MENTIONED IN THE LOCAL SAN FRANCISCO DAILY...
IT MUST BE SUCH A HABITUAL OCCURRENCE THAT THE OTHER PAPERS DON'T EVEN PUT IT ON THE FRONT PAGE...
HA HA HA
PIERRE-ALAIN WAS IN A HURRY TO GET OFF THE PHONE BECAUSE HE WAS HEADED OUT TO SEE A SUMO MATCH.
SERIOUSLY?!...
SUMO MATCH
READY OR NOT...

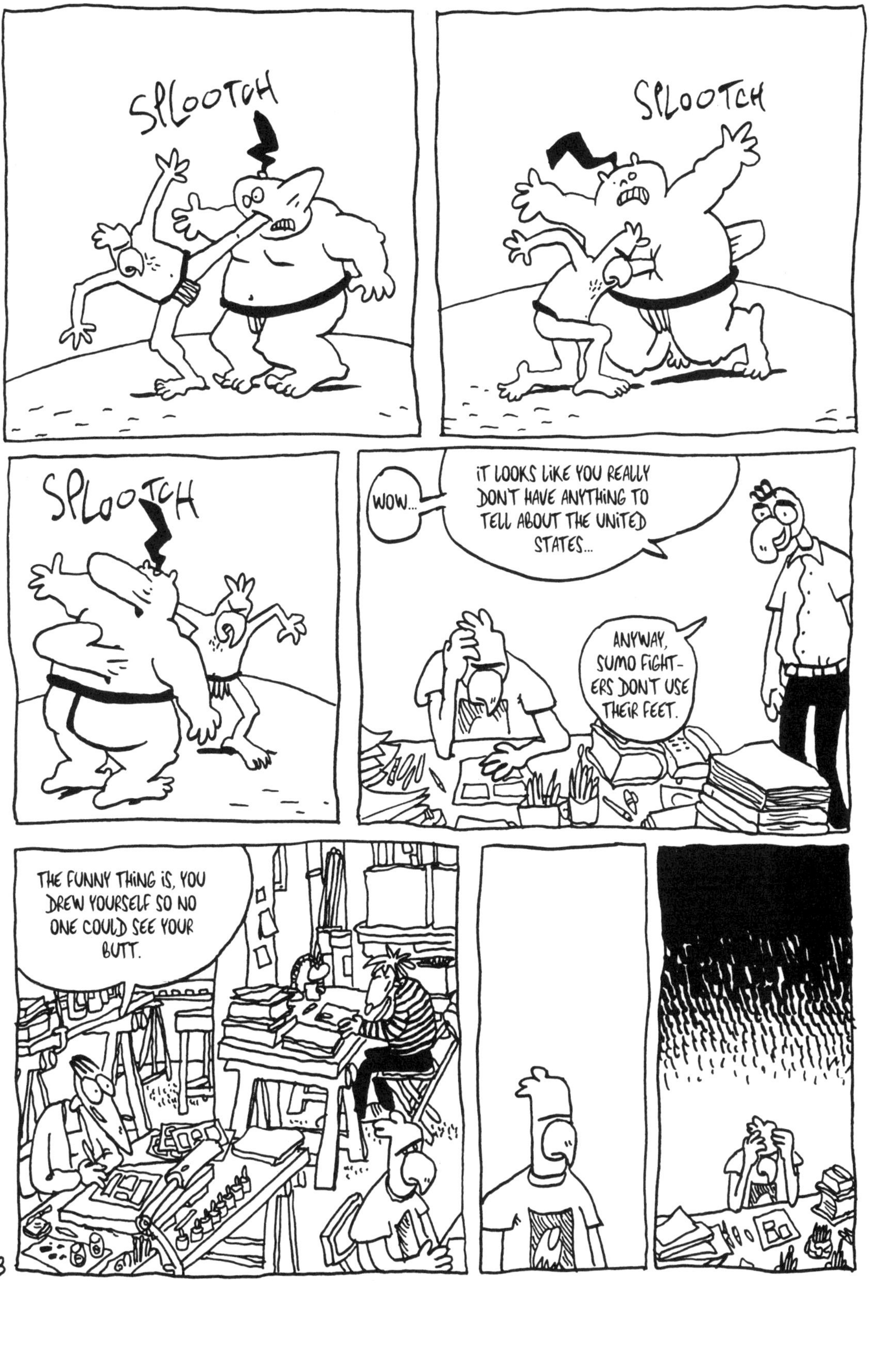
SPLOOTCH
SPLOOTCH
SPLOOTCH
WOW...
IT LOOKS LIKE YOU REALLY DON'T HAVE ANYTHING TO TELL ABOUT THE UNITED STATES...
ANYWAY, SUMO FIGHT-ERS DON'T USE THEIR FEET.
THE FUNNY THING IS, YOU DREW YOURSELF SO NO ONE COULD SEE YOUR BUTT.

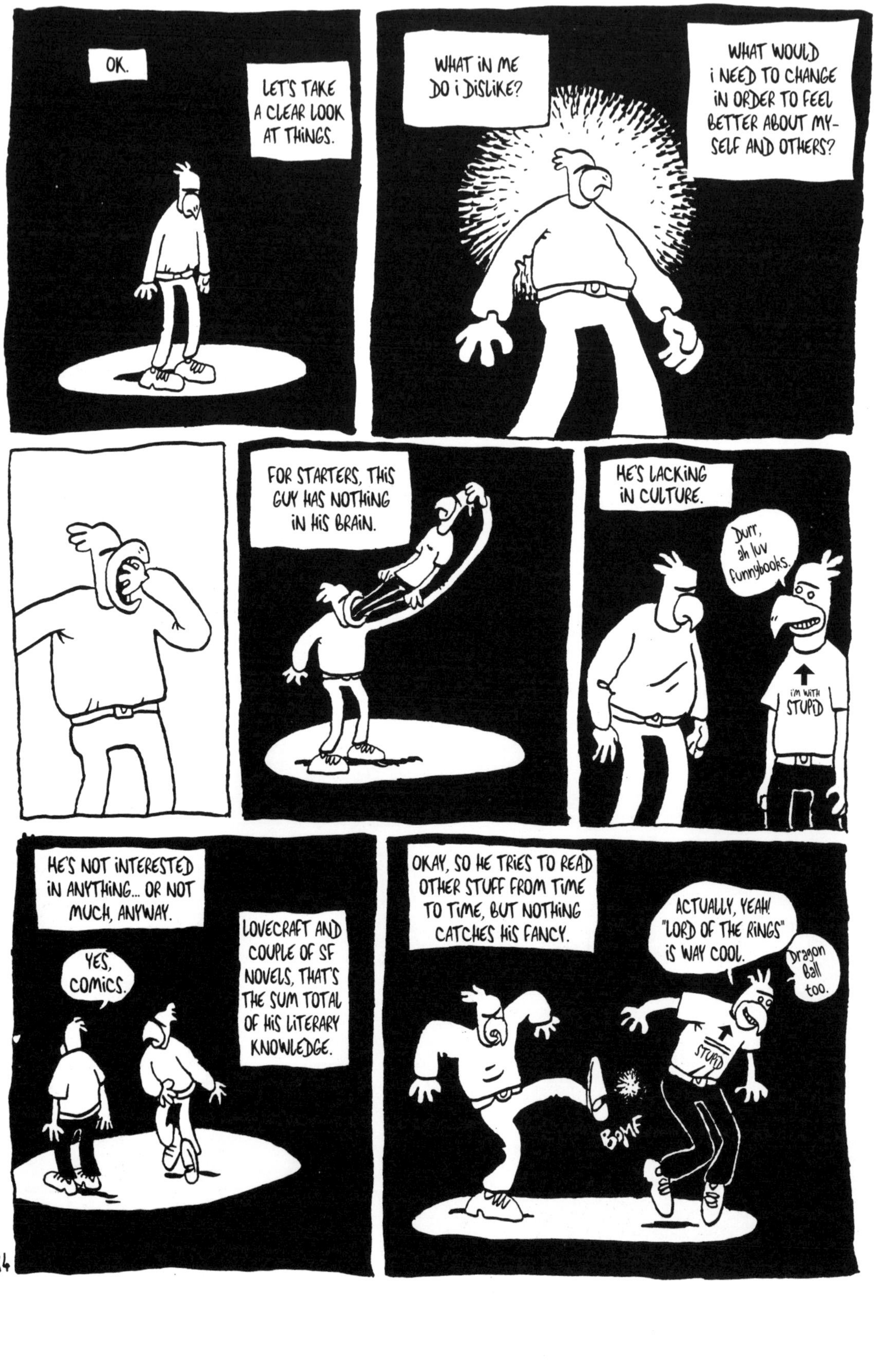
OK.
LET'S TAKE A CLEAR LOOK AT THINGS.
WHAT IN ME DO I DISLIKE?
WHAT WOULD I NEED TO CHANGE IN ORDER TO FEEL BETTER ABOUT MY-SELF AND OTHERS?
FOR STARTERS, THIS GUY HAS NOTHING IN HIS BRAIN.
HE'S LACKING IN CULTURE.
Durr, ah luv funnybooks.
I'M WITH STUPID
HE'S NOT INTERESTED IN ANYTHING... OR NOT MUCH, ANYWAY.
YES, COMICS.
LOVECRAFT AND COUPLE OF SF NOVELS, THAT'S THE SUM TOTAL OF HIS LITERARY KNOWLEDGE.
OKAY, SO HE TRIES TO READ OTHER STUFF FROM TIME TO TIME, BUT NOTHING CATCHES HIS FANCY.
ACTUALLY, YEAH! "LORD OF THE RINGS" IS WAY COOL.
Dragon Ball too.
STUPID
BOMF

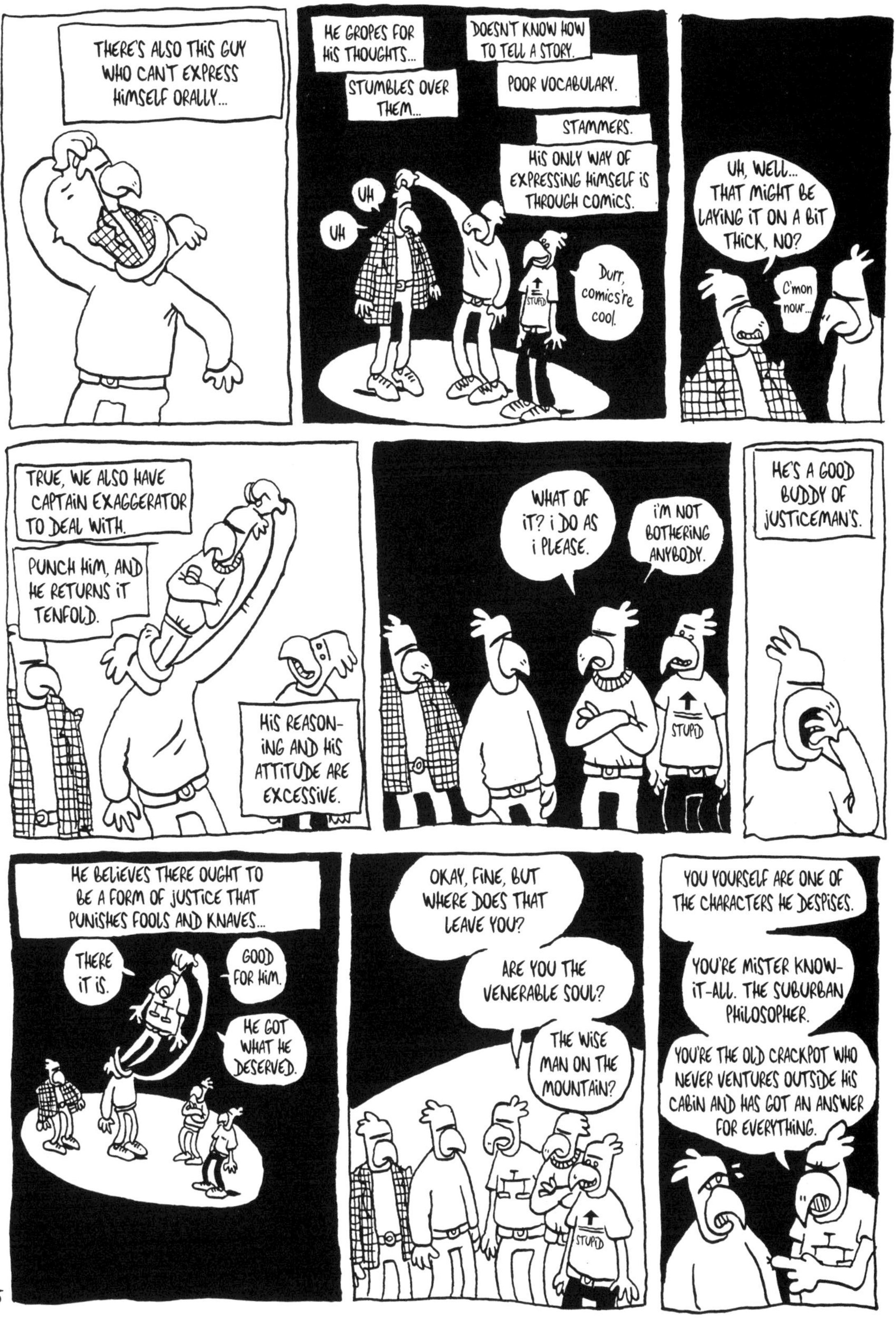
THERE'S ALSO THIS GUY WHO CAN'T EXPRESS HIMSELF ORALLY...
HE GROPES FOR HIS THOUGHTS...
STUMBLES OVER THEM...
DOESN'T KNOW HOW TO TELL A STORY.
POOR VOCABULARY.
STAMMERS.
HIS ONLY WAY OF EXPRESSING HIMSELF IS THROUGH COMICS.
UH
UH
STUPID
Durr, comics're cool.
UH, WELL... THAT MIGHT BE LAYING IT ON A BIT THICK, NO?
C'mon now...
TRUE, WE ALSO HAVE CAPTAIN EXAGGERATOR TO DEAL WITH.
PUNCH HIM, AND HE RETURNS IT TENFOLD.
HIS REASONING AND HIS ATTITUDE ARE EXCESSIVE.
WHAT OF IT? I DO AS I PLEASE.
I'M NOT BOTHERING ANYBODY.
STUPID
HE'S A GOOD BUDDY OF JUSTICEMAN'S.
HE BELIEVES THERE OUGHT TO BE A FORM OF JUSTICE THAT PUNISHES FOOLS AND KNAVES...
THERE IT IS.
GOOD FOR HIM.
HE GOT WHAT HE DESERVED.
OKAY, FINE, BUT WHERE DOES THAT LEAVE YOU?
ARE YOU THE VENERABLE SOUL?
THE WISE MAN ON THE MOUNTAIN?
STUPID
YOU YOURSELF ARE ONE OF THE CHARACTERS HE DESPISES.
YOU'RE MISTER KNOW-IT-ALL. THE SUBURBAN PHILOSOPHER.
YOU'RE THE OLD CRACKPOT WHO NEVER VENTURES OUTSIDE HIS CABIN AND HAS GOT AN ANSWER FOR EVERYTHING.

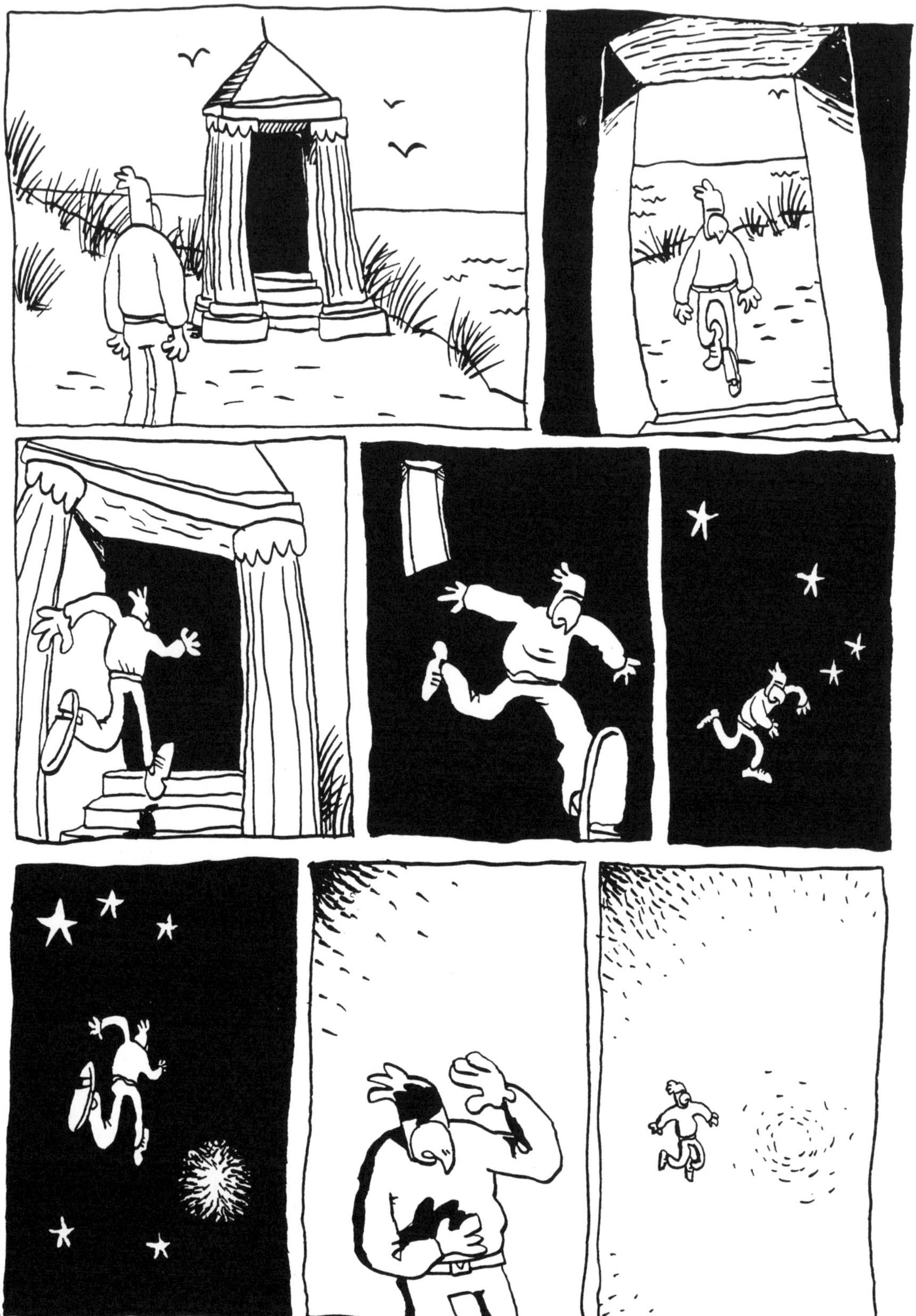

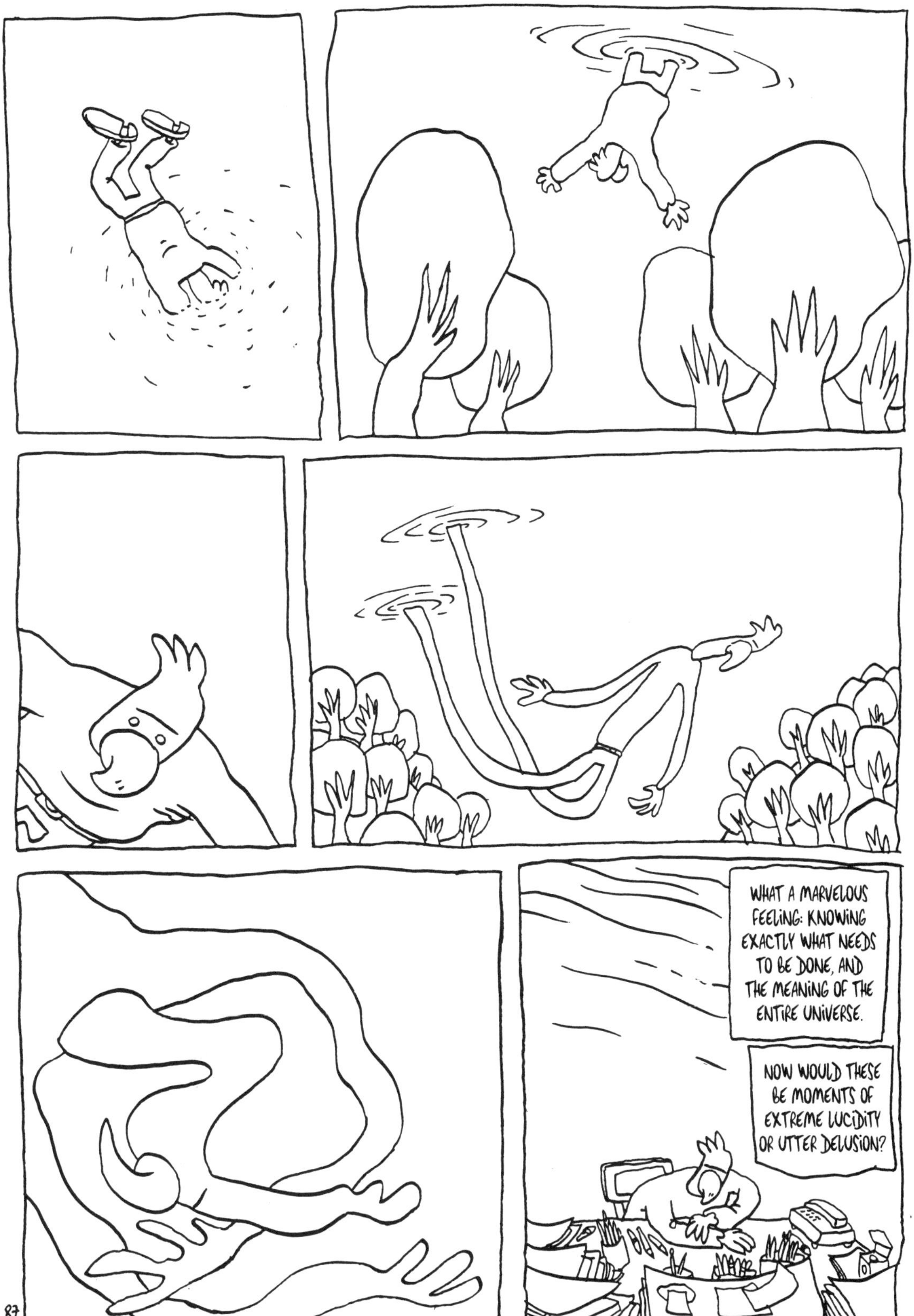
WHAT A MARVELOUS FEELING: KNOWING EXACTLY WHAT NEEDS TO BE DONE, AND THE MEANING OF THE ENTIRE UNIVERSE.
NOW WOULD THESE BE MOMENTS OF EXTREME LUCIDITY OR UTTER DELUSION?

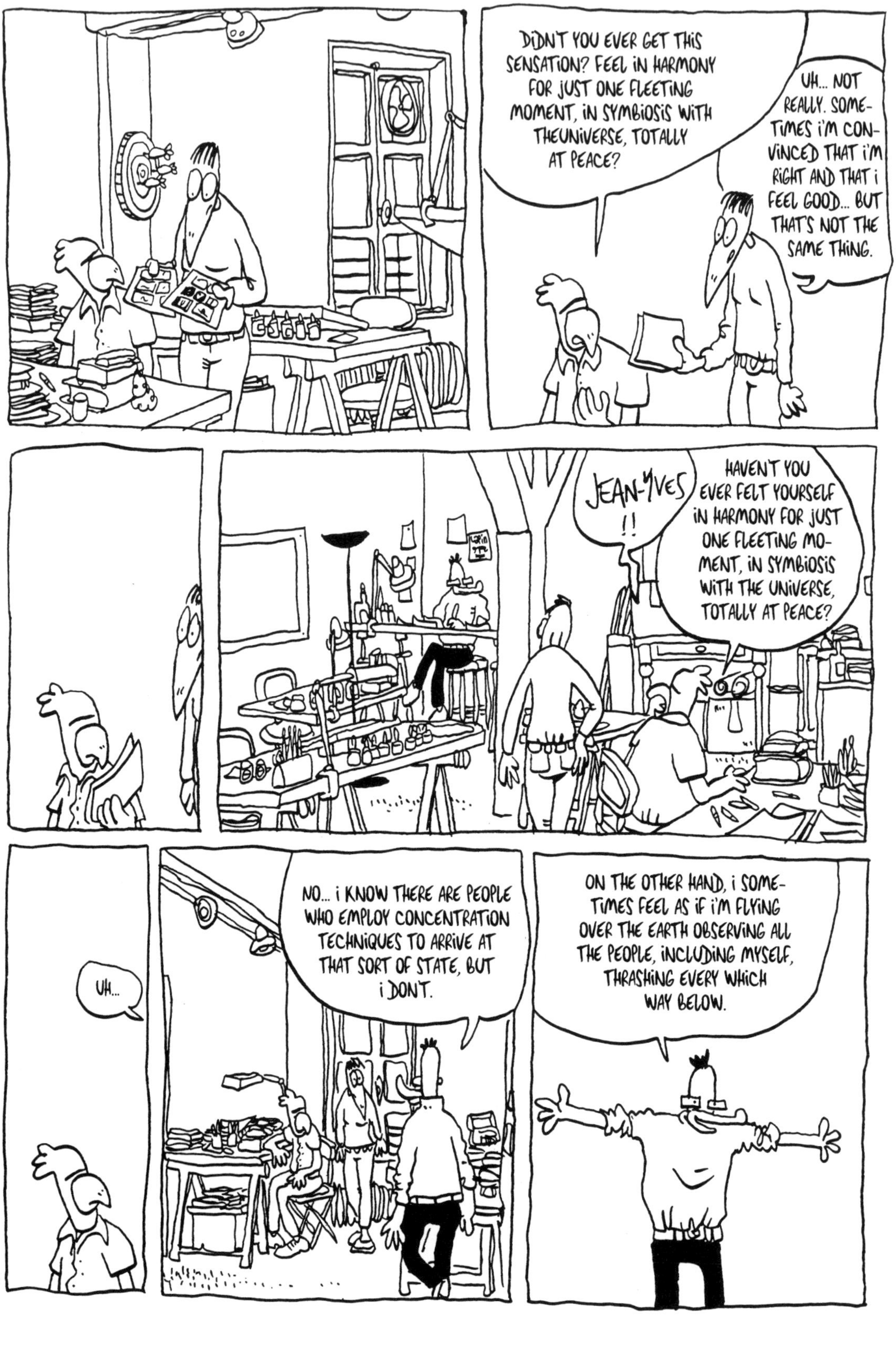
DIDN'T YOU EVER GET THIS SENSATION? FEEL IN HARMONY FOR JUST ONE FLEETING MOMENT, IN SYMBIOSIS WITH THEUNIVERSE, TOTALLY AT PEACE?
UH... NOT REALLY. SOMETIMES I'M CONVINCED THAT I'M RIGHT AND THAT I FEEL GOOD... BUT THAT'S NOT THE SAME THING.
JEAN-YVES !!
HAVEN'T YOU EVER FELT YOURSELF IN HARMONY FOR JUST ONE FLEETING MOMENT, IN SYMBIOSIS WITH THE UNIVERSE, TOTALLY AT PEACE?
UH...
NO... I KNOW THERE ARE PEOPLE WHO EMPLOY CONCENTRATION TECHNIQUES TO ARRIVE AT THAT SORT OF STATE, BUT I DON'T.
ON THE OTHER HAND, I SOMETIMES FEEL AS IF I'M FLYING OVER THE EARTH OBSERVING ALL THE PEOPLE, INCLUDING MYSELF, THRASHING EVERY WHICH WAY BELOW.

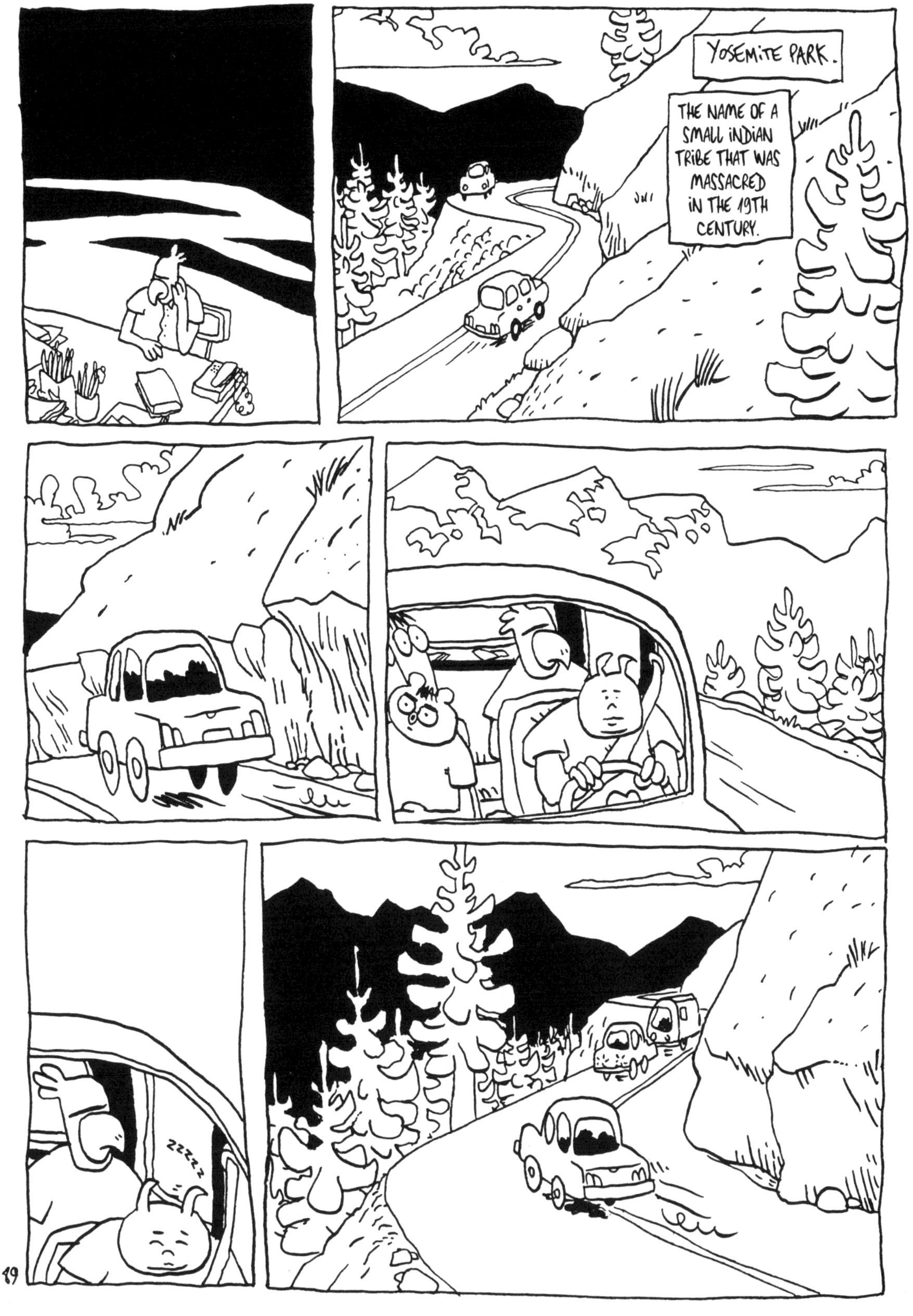
YOSEMITE PARK.
THE NAME OF A SMALL INDIAN TRIBE THAT WAS MASSACRED IN THE 19TH CENTURY.
ZZZZZ

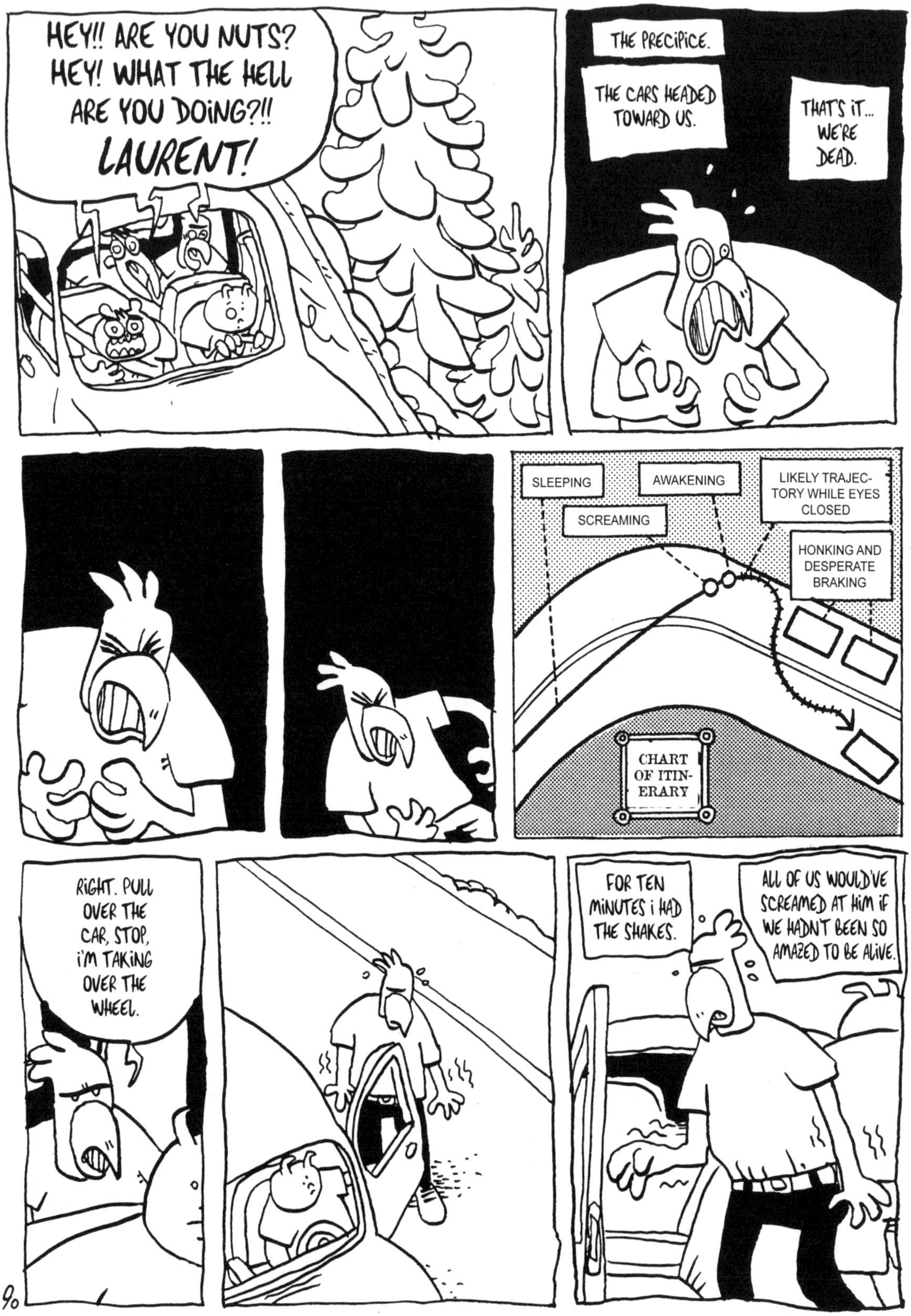
HEY!! ARE YOU NUTS? HEY! WHAT THE HELL ARE YOU DOING?!! LAURENT!
THE PRECIPICE.
THE CARS HEADED TOWARD US.
THAT'S IT... WE'RE DEAD.
SLEEPING
AWAKENING
LIKELY TRAJECTORY WHILE EYES CLOSED
SCREAMING
HONKING AND DESPERATE BRAKING
CHART OF ITINERARY
RIGHT. PULL OVER THE CAR, STOP, I'M TAKING OVER THE WHEEL.
FOR TEN MINUTES I HAD THE SHAKES.
ALL OF US WOULD'VE SCREAMED AT HIM IF WE HADN'T BEEN SO AMAZED TO BE ALIVE.

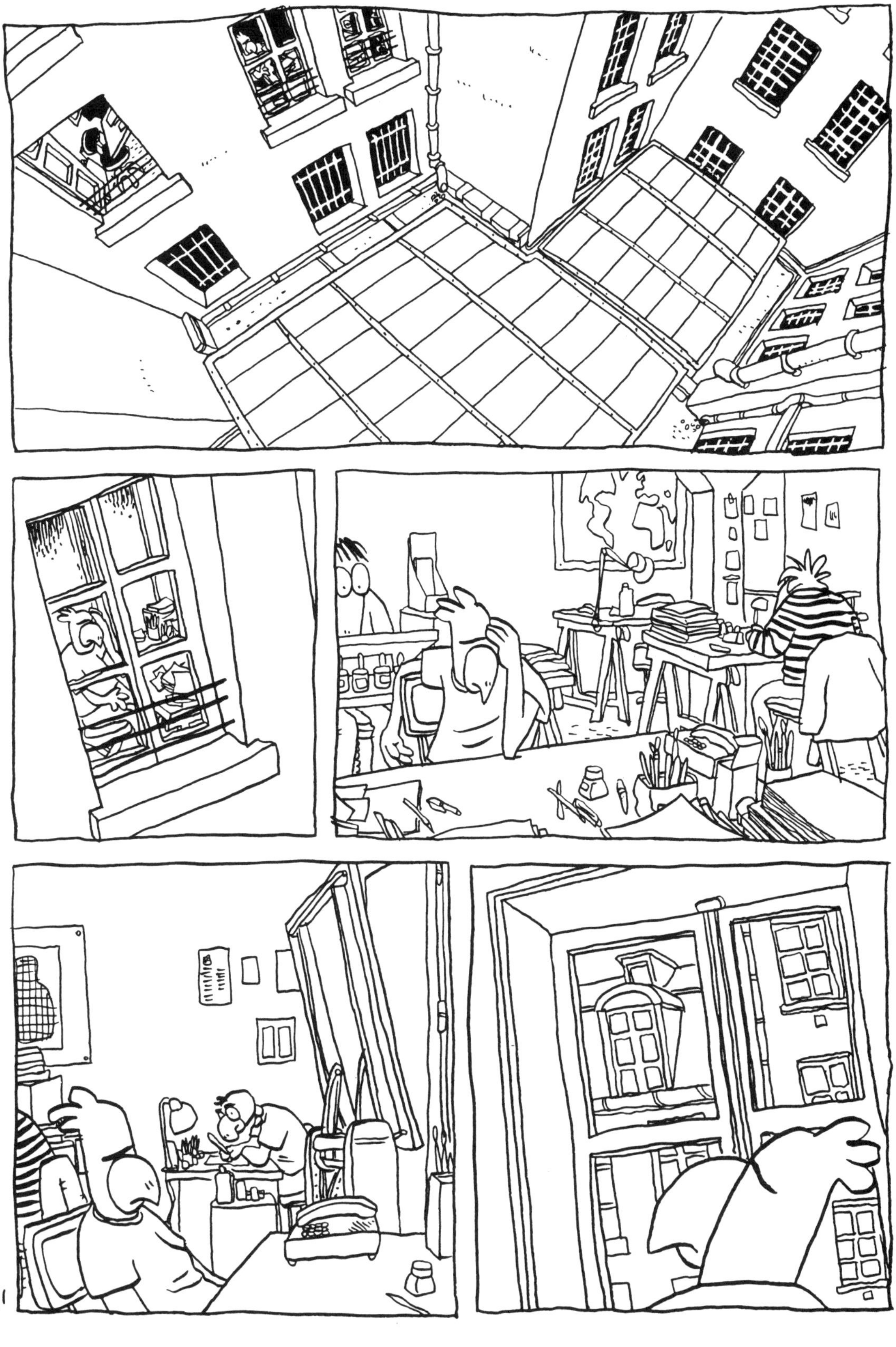

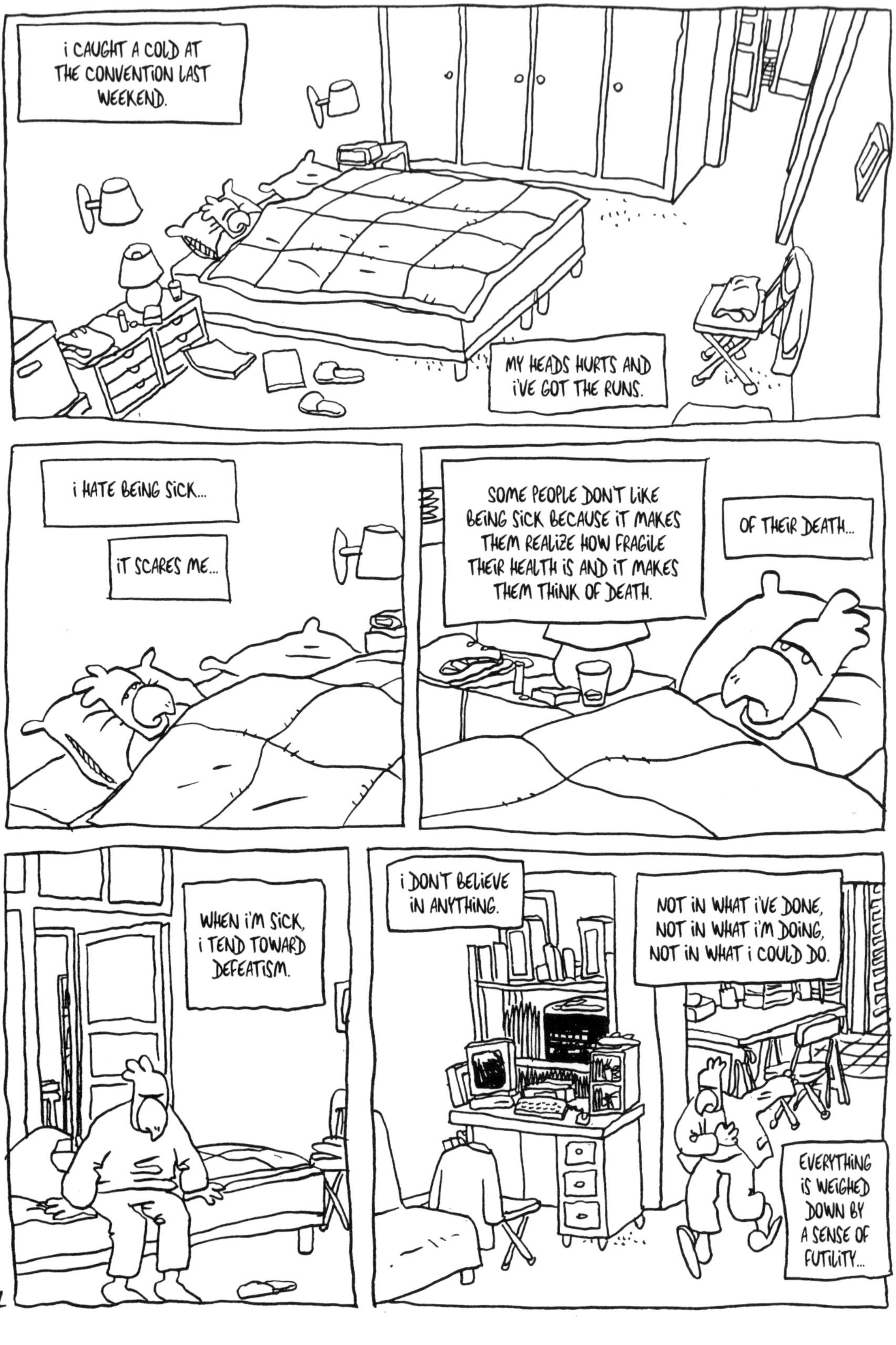
i CAUGHT A COLD AT THE CONVENTION LAST WEEKEND.
MY HEADS HURTS AND i'VE GOT THE RUNS.
i HATE BEING SICK...
iT SCARES ME...
SOME PEOPLE DON'T LIKE BEING SICK BECAUSE IT MAKES THEM REALIZE HOW FRAGILE THEIR HEALTH IS AND IT MAKES THEM THINK OF DEATH.
OF THEIR DEATH...
WHEN i'M SICK, i TEND TOWARD DEFEATISM.
i DON'T BELIEVE IN ANYTHING.
NOT IN WHAT i'VE DONE, NOT IN WHAT i'M DOING, NOT IN WHAT i COULD DO.
EVERYTHING IS WEIGHED DOWN BY A SENSE OF FUTILITY...

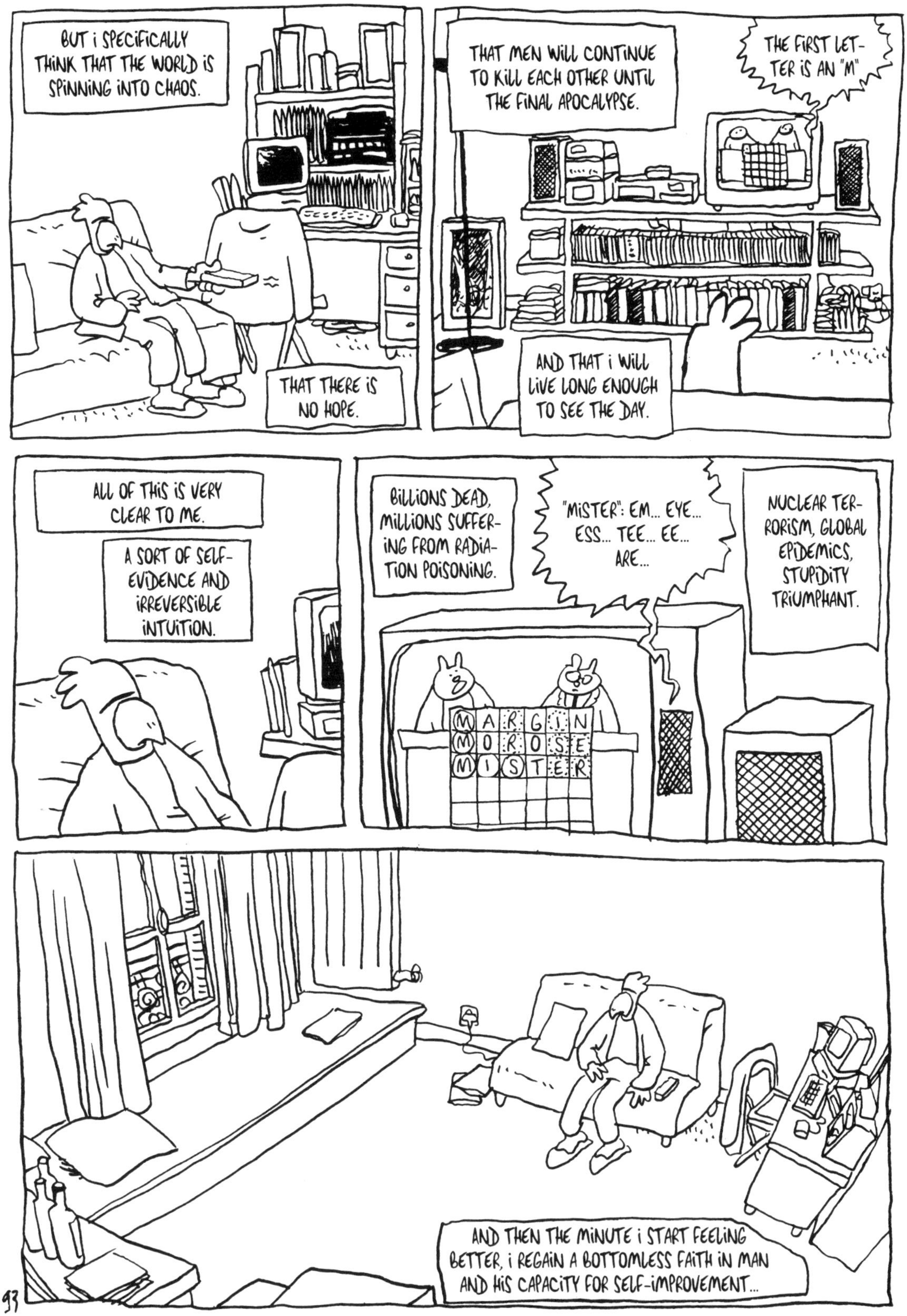
BUT I SPECIFICALLY THINK THAT THE WORLD IS SPINNING INTO CHAOS.
THAT THERE IS NO HOPE.
THAT MEN WILL CONTINUE TO KILL EACH OTHER UNTIL THE FINAL APOCALYPSE.
THE FIRST LETTER IS AN "M"
AND THAT I WILL LIVE LONG ENOUGH TO SEE THE DAY.
ALL OF THIS IS VERY CLEAR TO ME.
A SORT OF SELF-EVIDENCE AND IRREVERSIBLE INTUITION.
BILLIONS DEAD, MILLIONS SUFFERING FROM RADIATION POISONING.
"MISTER": EM... EYE... ESS... TEE... EE... ARE...
NUCLEAR TERRORISM, GLOBAL EPIDEMICS, STUPIDITY TRIUMPHANT.
MARGIN
MOROSE
MISTER
AND THEN THE MINUTE I START FEELING BETTER, I REGAIN A BOTTOMLESS FAITH IN MAN AND HIS CAPACITY FOR SELF-IMPROVEMENT...

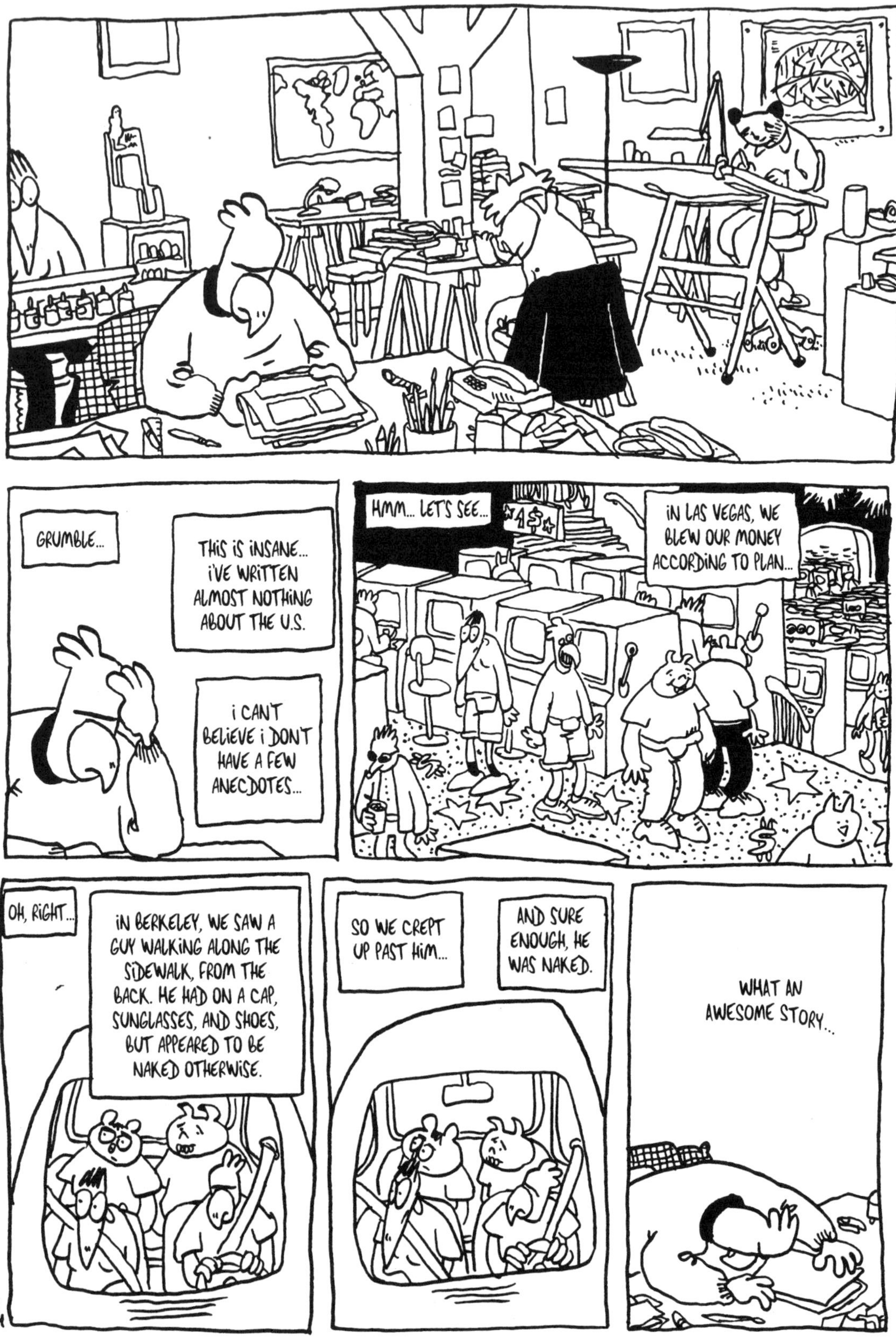
GRUMBLE...
THIS IS INSANE... I'VE WRITTEN ALMOST NOTHING ABOUT THE U.S.
I CAN'T BELIEVE I DON'T HAVE A FEW ANECDOTES...
HMM... LET'S SEE...
IN LAS VEGAS, WE BLEW OUR MONEY ACCORDING TO PLAN...
OH, RIGHT...
IN BERKELEY, WE SAW A GUY WALKING ALONG THE SIDEWALK, FROM THE BACK. HE HAD ON A CAP, SUNGLASSES, AND SHOES, BUT APPEARED TO BE NAKED OTHERWISE.
SO WE CREPT UP PAST HIM...
AND SURE ENOUGH, HE WAS NAKED.
WHAT AN AWESOME STORY...

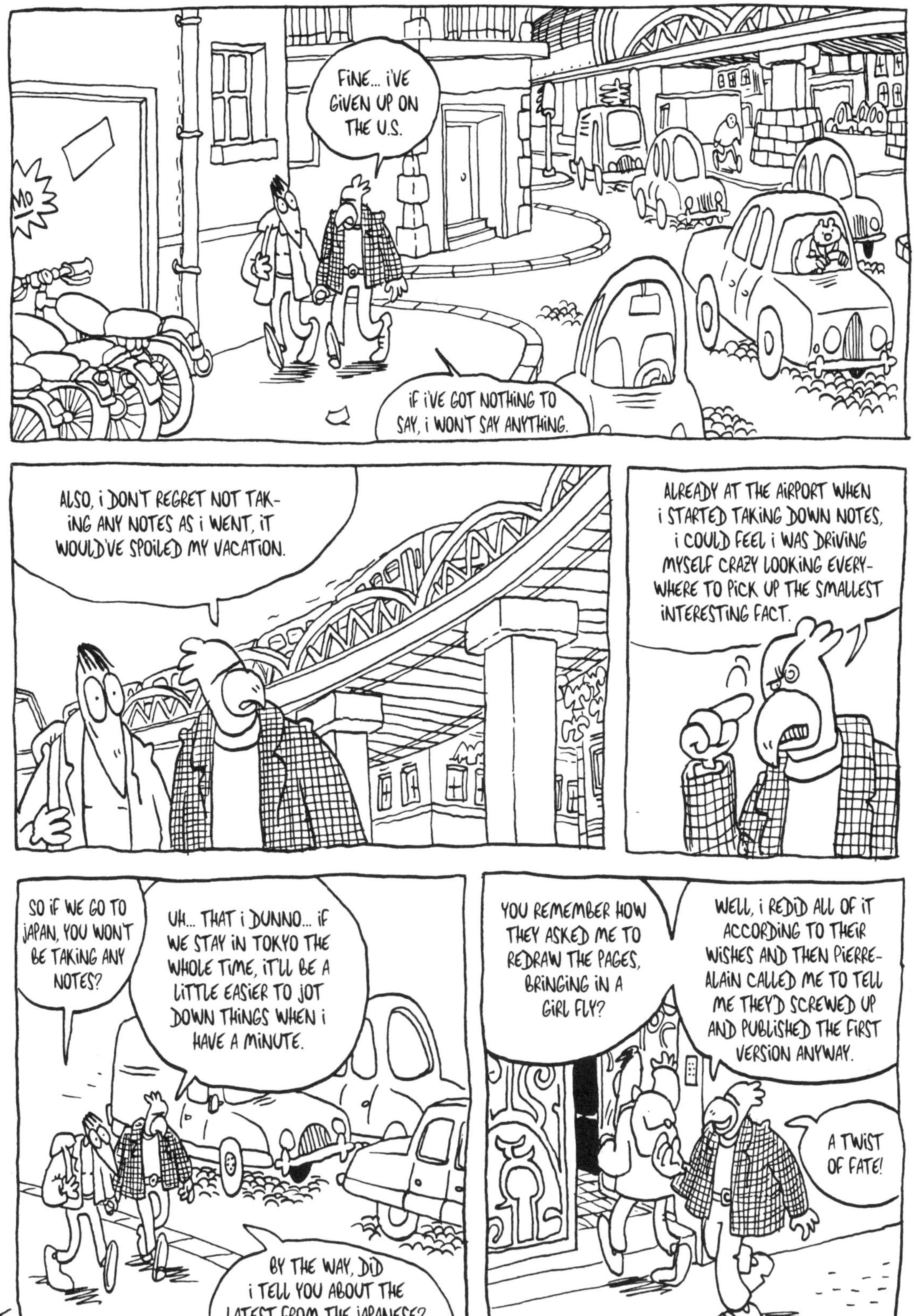

FINE... i'VE GIVEN UP ON THE U.S.
iF i'VE GOT NOTHING TO SAY, i WON'T SAY ANYTHING.
ALSO, i DON'T REGRET NOT TAKING ANY NOTES AS i WENT, iT WOULD'VE SPOiLED MY VACATiON.
ALREADY AT THE AiRPORT WHEN i STARTED TAKiNG DOWN NOTES, i COULD FEEL i WAS DRiViNG MYSELF CRAZY LOOKiNG EVERYWHERE TO PiCK UP THE SMALLEST iNTERESTiNG FACT.
SO iF WE GO TO JAPAN, YOU WON'T BE TAKiNG ANY NOTES?
UH... THAT i DUNNO... iF WE STAY iN TOKYO THE WHOLE TiME, iT'LL BE A LiTTLE EASiER TO JOT DOWN THiNGS WHEN i HAVE A MiNUTE.
BY THE WAY, DiD i TELL YOU ABOUT THE LATEST FROM THE JAPANESE?
YOU REMEMBER HOW THEY ASKED ME TO REDRAW THE PAGES, BRiNGiNG iN A GiRL FLY?
WELL, i REDiD ALL OF iT ACCORDiNG TO THEiR WiSHES AND THEN PiERRE-ALAiN CALLED ME TO TELL ME THEY'D SCREWED UP AND PUBLiSHED THE FiRST VERSiON ANYWAY.
A TWiST OF FATE!

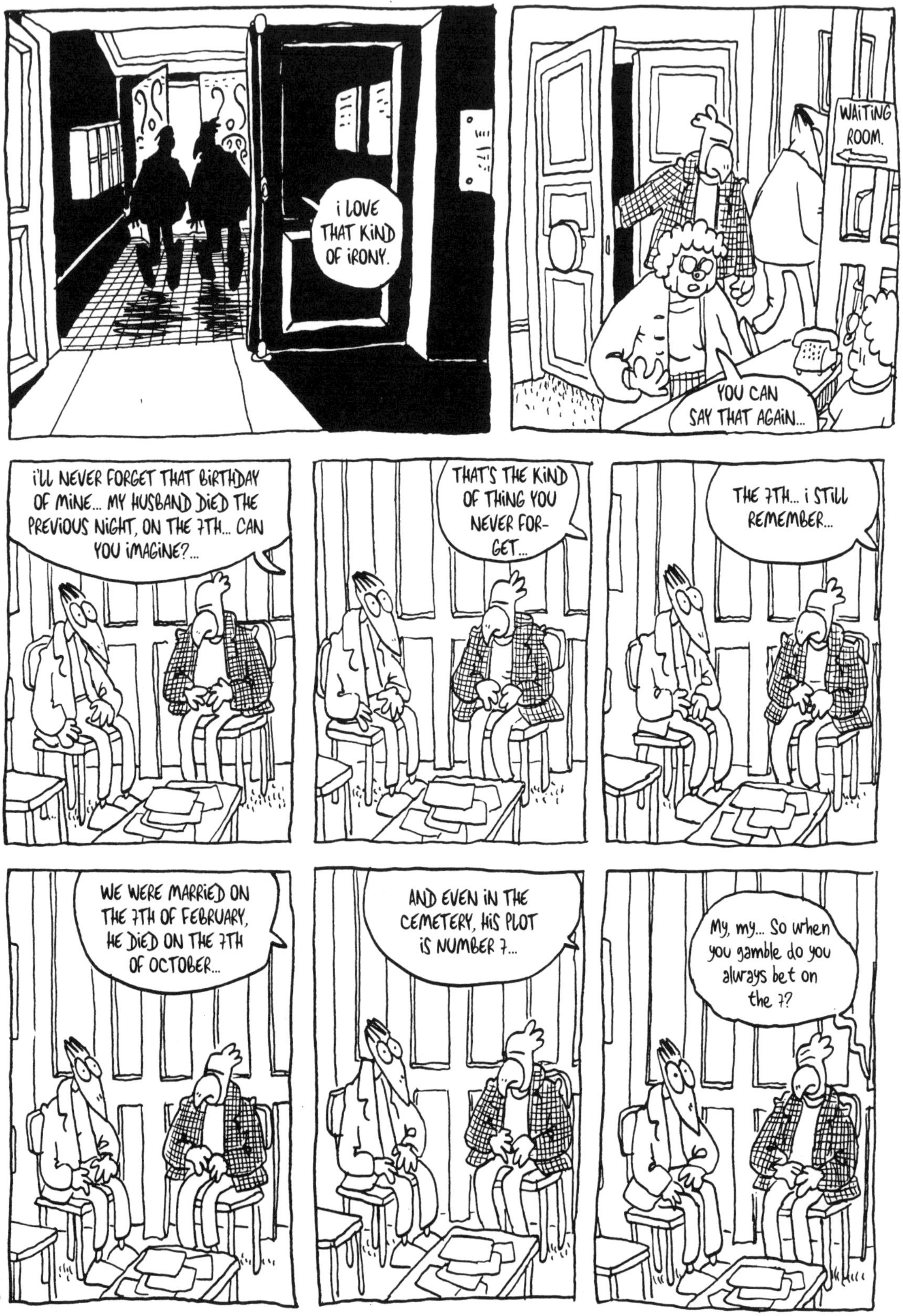
I LOVE THAT KIND OF IRONY.
WAITING ROOM.
YOU CAN SAY THAT AGAIN...
I'LL NEVER FORGET THAT BIRTHDAY OF MINE... MY HUSBAND DIED THE PREVIOUS NIGHT, ON THE 7TH... CAN YOU IMAGINE?...
THAT'S THE KIND OF THING YOU NEVER FOR-GET...
THE 7TH... I STILL REMEMBER...
WE WERE MARRIED ON THE 7TH OF FEBRUARY, HE DIED ON THE 7TH OF OCTOBER...
AND EVEN IN THE CEMETERY, HIS PLOT IS NUMBER 7...
My, my... So when you gamble do you always bet on the 7?

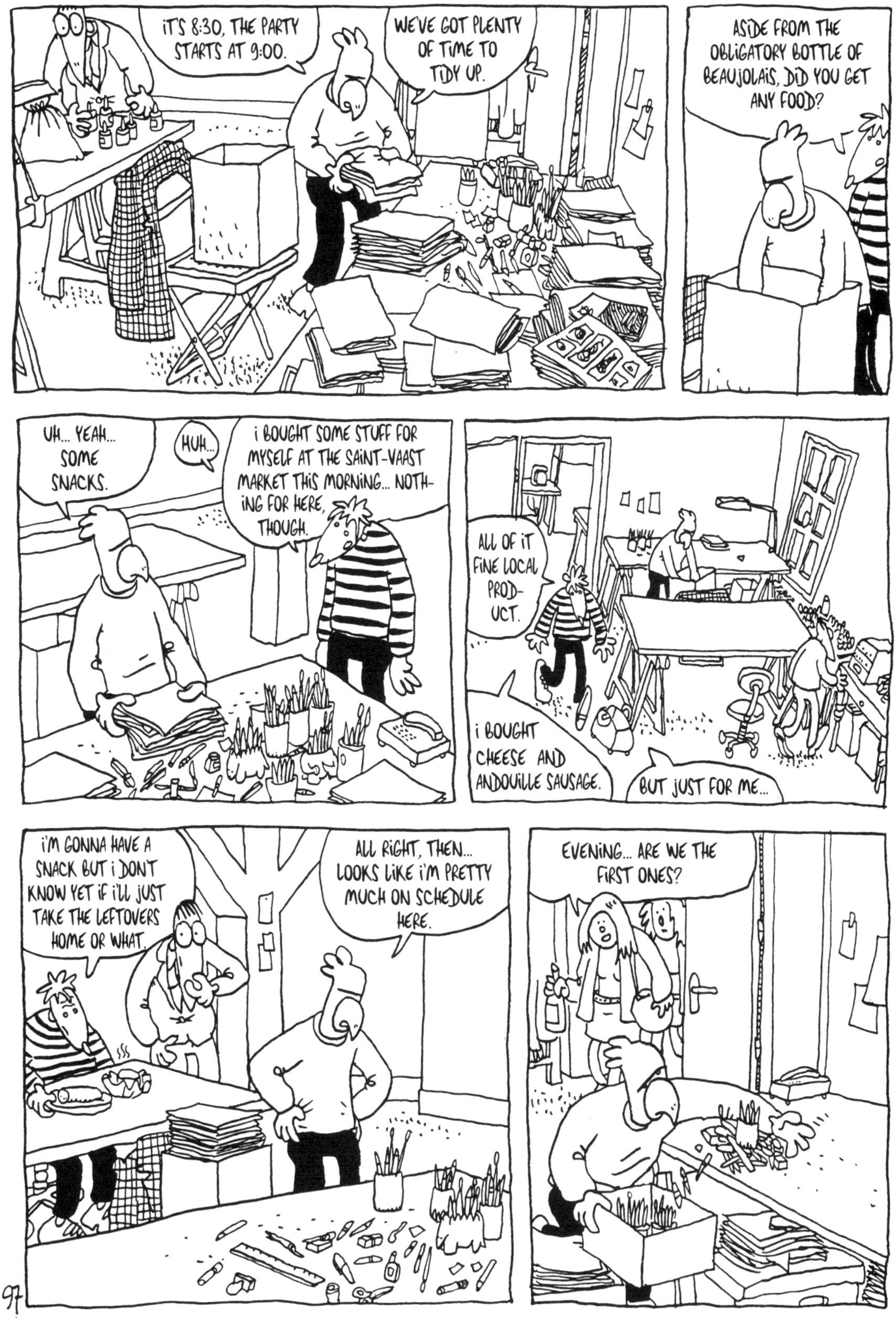
IT'S 8:30, THE PARTY STARTS AT 9:00.
WE'VE GOT PLENTY OF TIME TO TIDY UP.
ASIDE FROM THE OBLIGATORY BOTTLE OF BEAUJOLAIS, DID YOU GET ANY FOOD?
UH... YEAH... SOME SNACKS.
HUH...
I BOUGHT SOME STUFF FOR MYSELF AT THE SAINT-VAAST MARKET THIS MORNING... NOTHING FOR HERE, THOUGH.
ALL OF IT FINE LOCAL PRODUCT.
I BOUGHT CHEESE AND ANDOUILLE SAUSAGE.
BUT JUST FOR ME...
I'M GONNA HAVE A SNACK BUT I DON'T KNOW YET IF I'LL JUST TAKE THE LEFTOVERS HOME OR WHAT.
ALL RIGHT, THEN... LOOKS LIKE I'M PRETTY MUCH ON SCHEDULE HERE.
EVENING... ARE WE THE FIRST ONES?

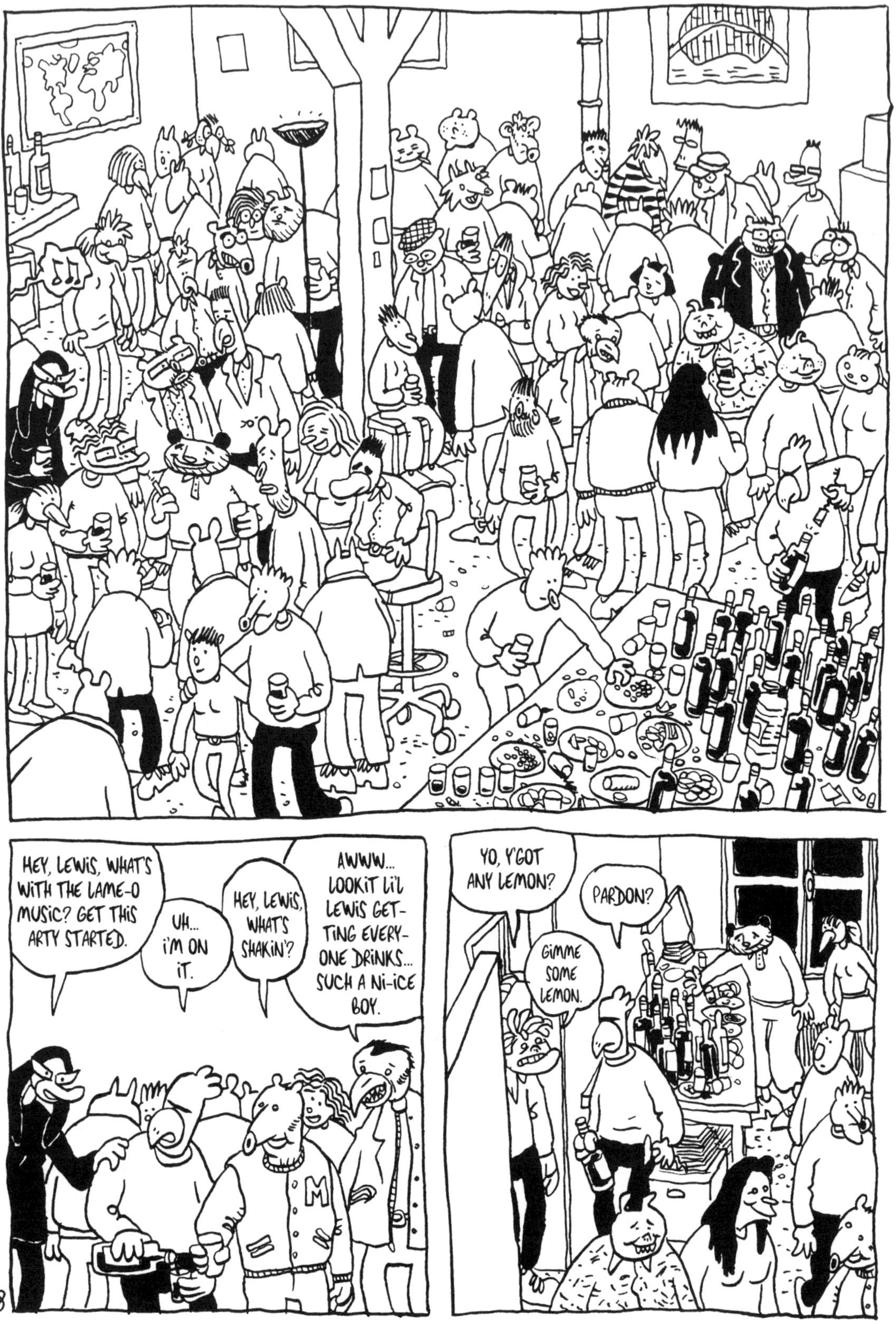
HEY, LEWIS, WHAT'S WITH THE LAME-O MUSIC? GET THIS ARTY STARTED.
UH... i'M ON iT.
HEY, LEWiS, WHAT'S SHAKiN'?
AWWW... LOOKiT Li'L LEWiS GETTiNG EVERYONE DRiNKS... SUCH A Ni-ICE BOY.
YO, Y'GOT ANY LEMON?
PARDON?
GiMME SOME LEMON.

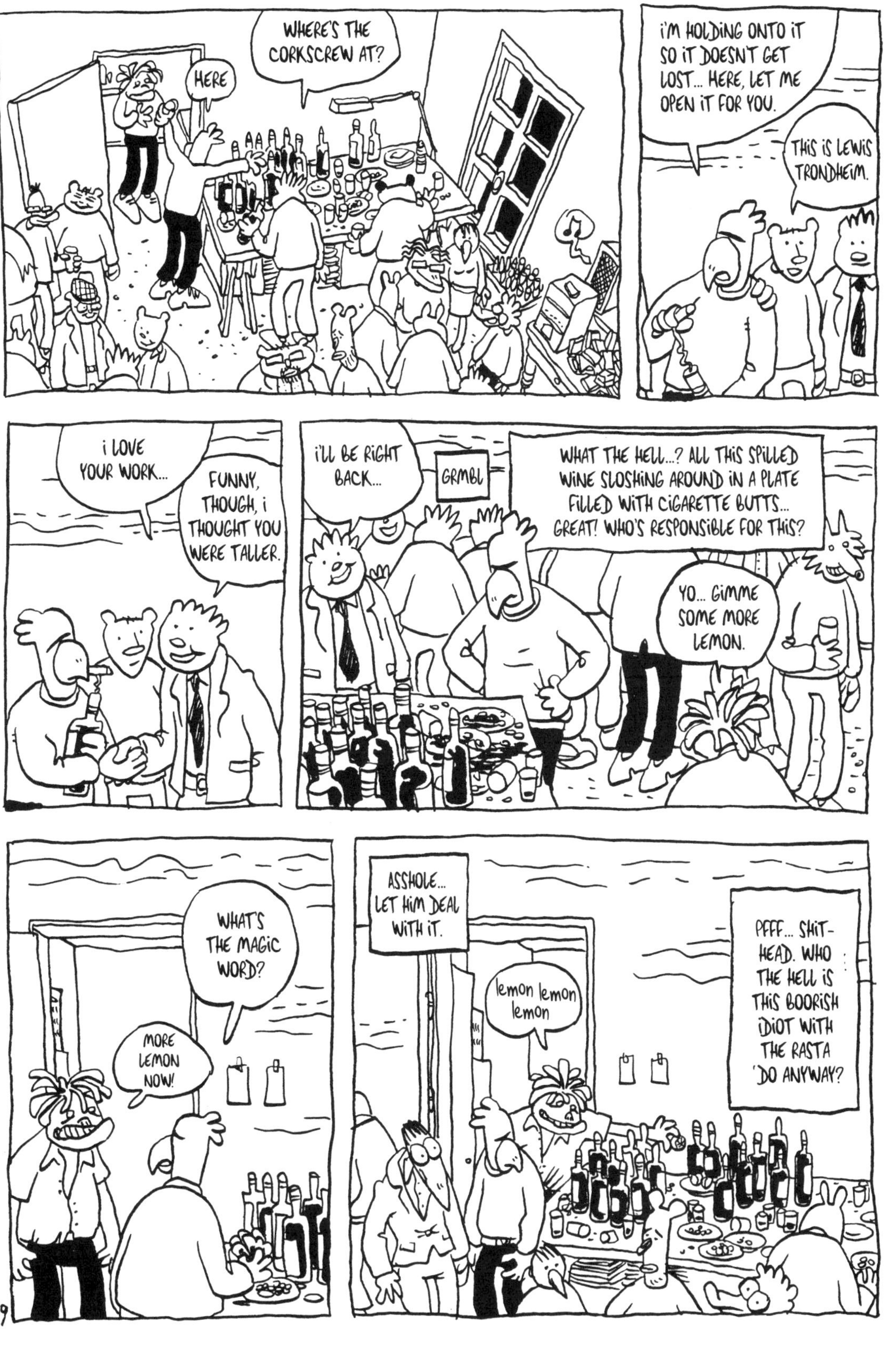
WHERE'S THE CORKSCREW AT?
HERE
i'M HOLDING ONTO iT SO iT DOESN'T GET LOST... HERE, LET ME OPEN iT FOR YOU.
THiS iS LEWiS TRONDHEiM.
i LOVE YOUR WORK...
FUNNY, THOUGH, i THOUGHT YOU WERE TALLER.
i'LL BE RiGHT BACK...
GRMBL
WHAT THE HELL...? ALL THiS SPiLLED WiNE SLOSHiNG AROUND iN A PLATE FiLLED WiTH CiGARETTE BUTTS... GREAT! WHO'S RESPONSiBLE FOR THiS?
YO... GiMME SOME MORE LEMON.
WHAT'S THE MAGiC WORD?
MORE LEMON NOW!
ASSHOLE... LET HiM DEAL WiTH iT.
lemon lemon lemon
PFFF... SHiT-HEAD. WHO THE HELL iS THiS BOORiSH iDiOT WiTH THE RASTA 'DO ANYWAY?

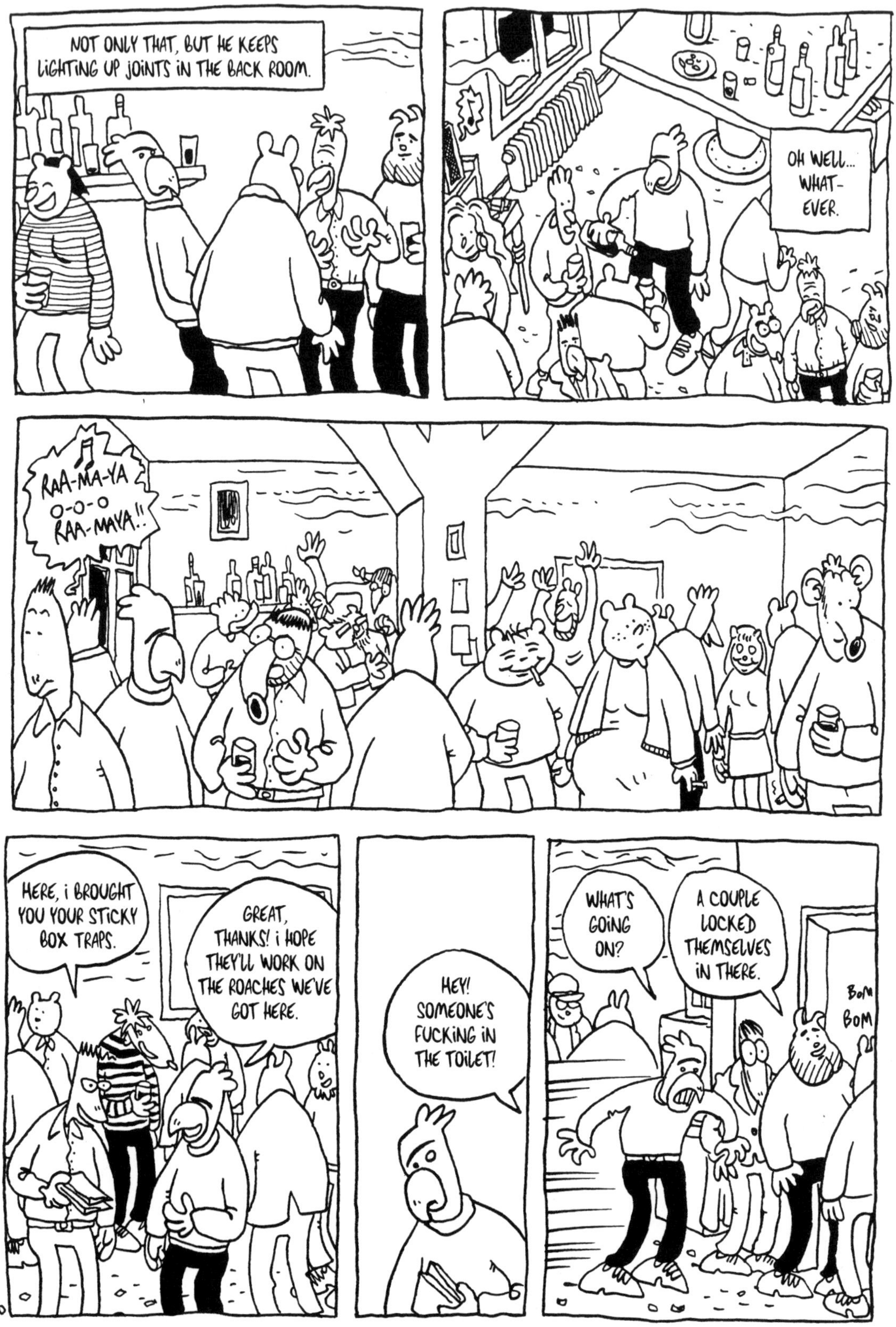
NOT ONLY THAT, BUT HE KEEPS LIGHTING UP JOINTS IN THE BACK ROOM.
OH WELL... WHAT-EVER.
RAA-MA-YA O-O-O RAA-MAYA!!
HERE, I BROUGHT YOU YOUR STICKY BOX TRAPS.
GREAT, THANKS! I HOPE THEY'LL WORK ON THE ROACHES WE'VE GOT HERE.
HEY! SOMEONE'S FUCKING IN THE TOILET!
WHAT'S GOING ON?
A COUPLE LOCKED THEMSELVES IN THERE.
BOM BOM

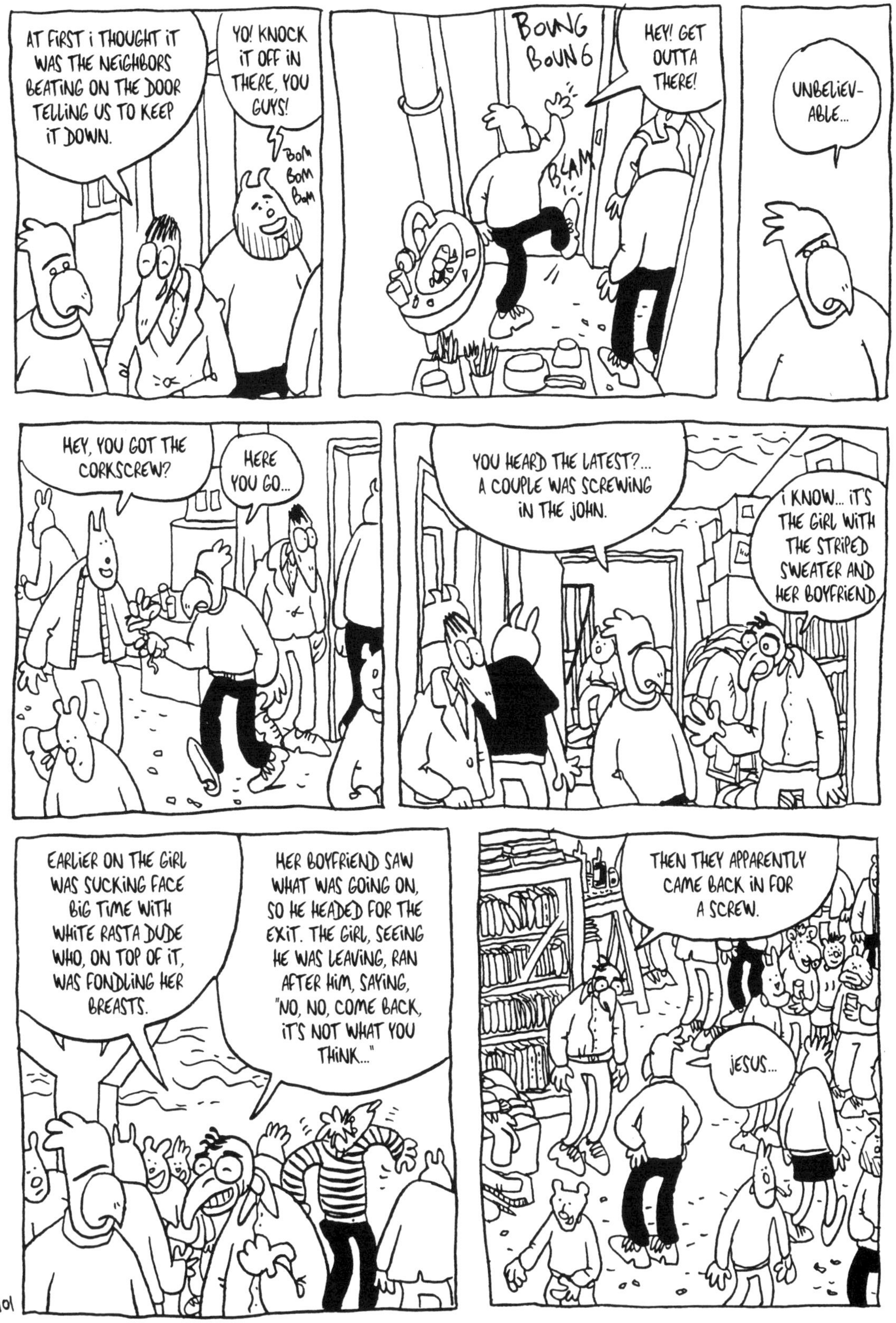

AT FIRST i THOUGHT iT WAS THE NEiGHBORS BEATiNG ON THE DOOR TELLiNG US TO KEEP iT DOWN.
YO! KNOCK iT OFF iN THERE, YOU GUYS!
BOM BOM BOM
BOUNG BOUNG
BLAM
HEY! GET OUTTA THERE!
UNBELiEV-ABLE...
HEY, YOU GOT THE CORKSCREW?
HERE YOU GO...
YOU HEARD THE LATEST?... A COUPLE WAS SCREWiNG iN THE JOHN.
i KNOW... iT'S THE GiRL WiTH THE STRiPED SWEATER AND HER BOYFRiEND.
EARLiER ON THE GiRL WAS SUCKiNG FACE BiG TiME WiTH WHiTE RASTA DUDE WHO, ON TOP OF iT, WAS FONDLiNG HER BREASTS.
HER BOYFRiEND SAW WHAT WAS GOiNG ON, SO HE HEADED FOR THE EXiT. THE GiRL, SEEiNG HE WAS LEAViNG, RAN AFTER HiM, SAYiNG, "NO, NO, COME BACK, iT'S NOT WHAT YOU THiNK..."
THEN THEY APPARENTLY CAME BACK iN FOR A SCREW.
JESUS...

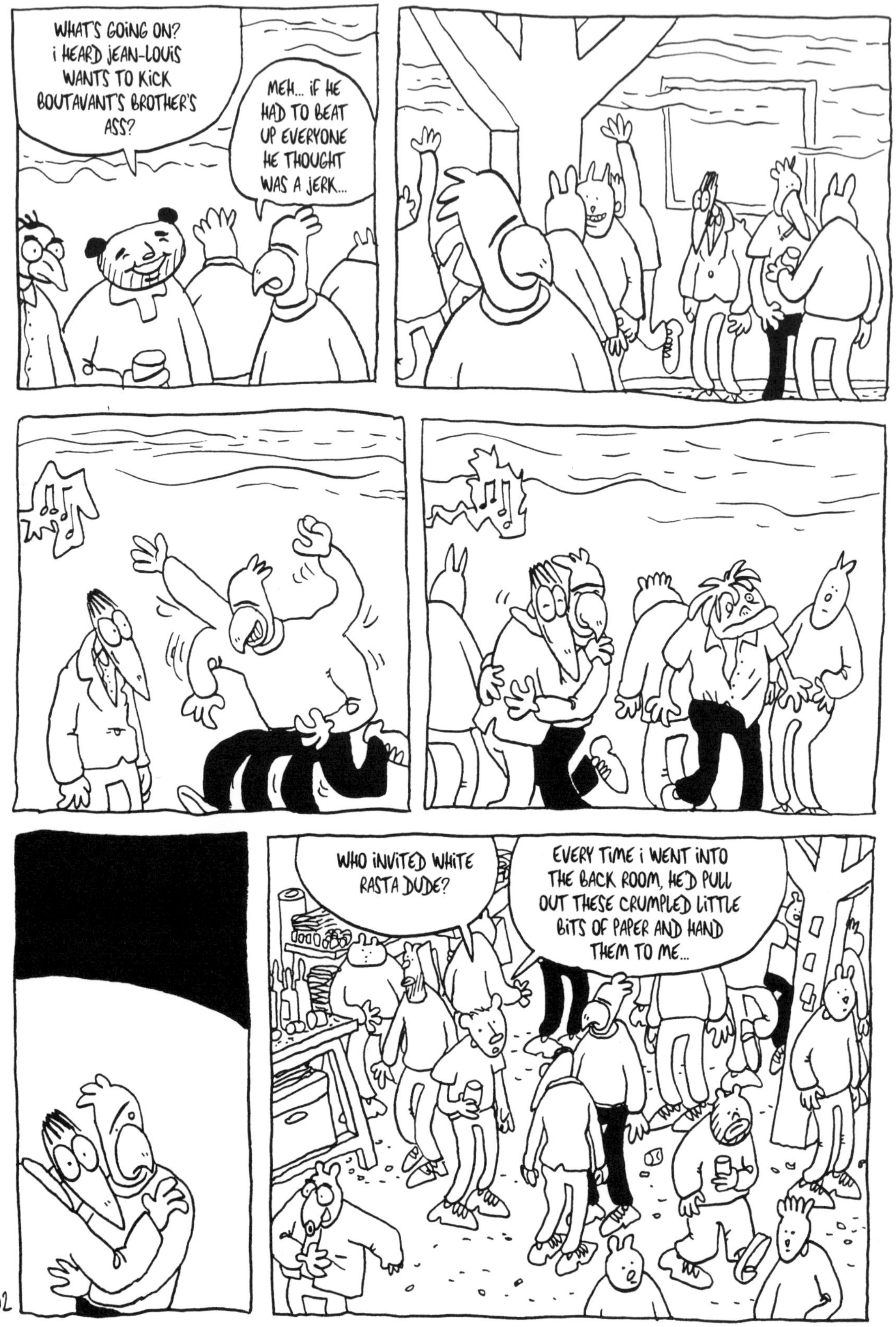
WHAT'S GOING ON? i HEARD JEAN-LOUiS WANTS TO KiCK BOUTAVANT'S BROTHER'S ASS?
MEH... iF HE HAD TO BEAT UP EVERYONE HE THOUGHT WAS A JERK...
WHO iNViTED WHiTE RASTA DUDE?
EVERY TiME i WENT iNTO THE BACK ROOM, HE'D PULL OUT THESE CRUMPLED LiTTLE BiTS OF PAPER AND HAND THEM TO ME...

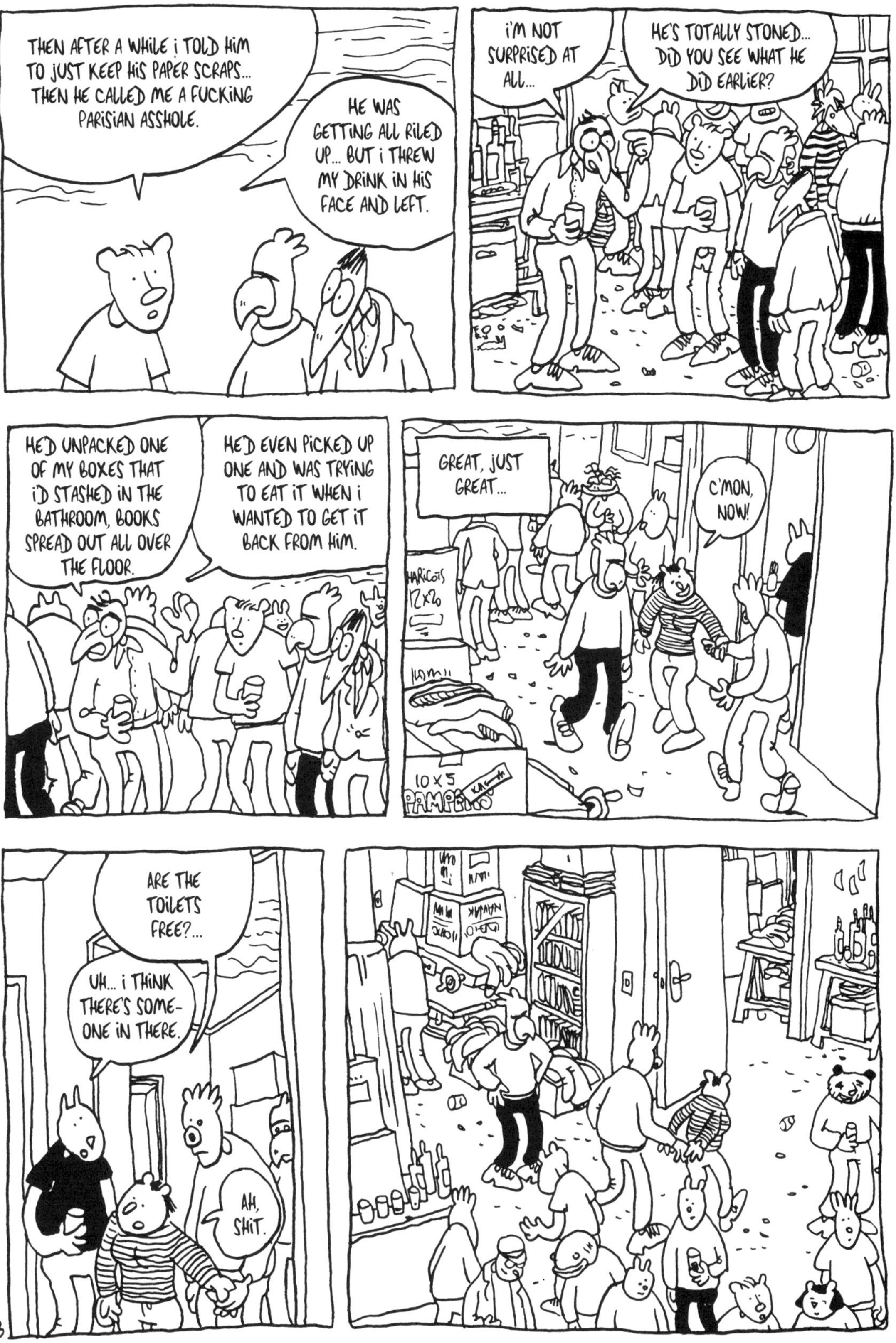
THEN AFTER A WHILE I TOLD HIM TO JUST KEEP HIS PAPER SCRAPS... THEN HE CALLED ME A FUCKING PARISIAN ASSHOLE.
HE WAS GETTING ALL RILED UP... BUT I THREW MY DRINK IN HIS FACE AND LEFT.
I'M NOT SURPRISED AT ALL...
HE'S TOTALLY STONED... DID YOU SEE WHAT HE DID EARLIER?
HE'D UNPACKED ONE OF MY BOXES THAT I'D STASHED IN THE BATHROOM, BOOKS SPREAD OUT ALL OVER THE FLOOR.
HE'D EVEN PICKED UP ONE AND WAS TRYING TO EAT IT WHEN I WANTED TO GET IT BACK FROM HIM.
GREAT, JUST GREAT...
C'MON, NOW!
HARICOTS 12x20
10 x 5
ARE THE TOILETS FREE?...
UH... I THINK THERE'S SOME-ONE IN THERE.
AH, SHIT.

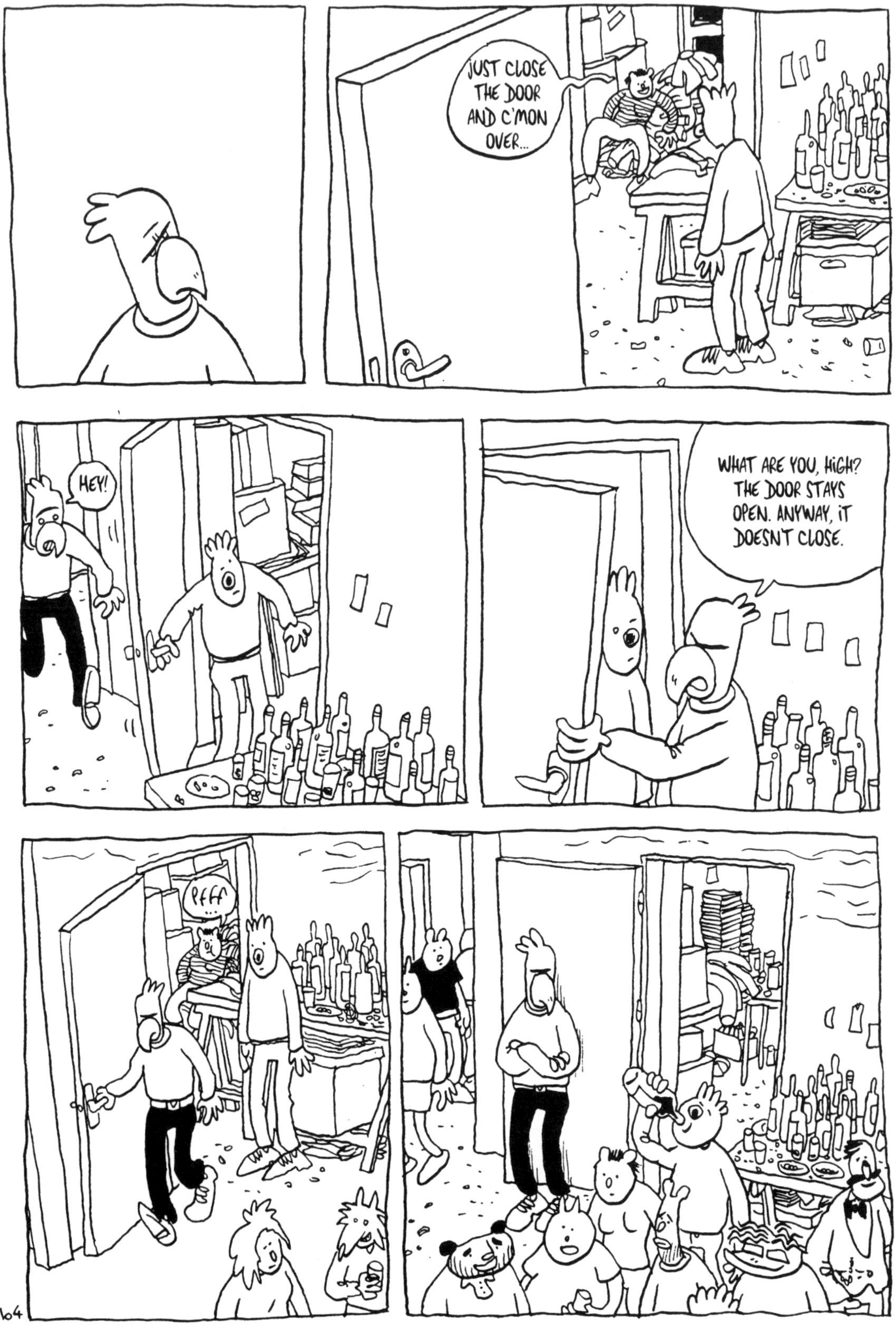
JUST CLOSE THE DOOR AND C'MON OVER...
HEY!
WHAT ARE YOU, HIGH? THE DOOR STAYS OPEN. ANYWAY, IT DOESN'T CLOSE.
PFFF...

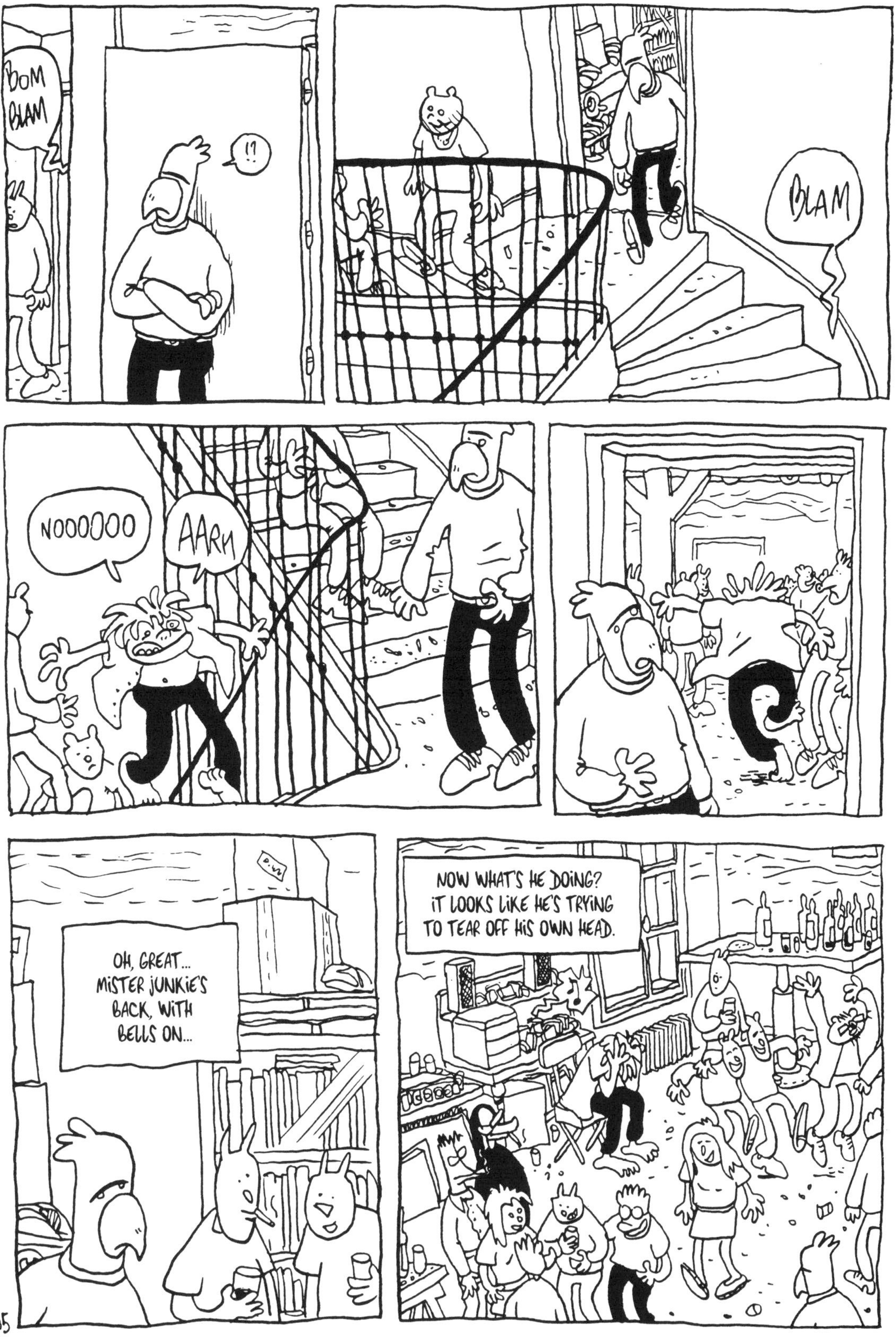
BOM BLAM
!?
BLAM
NOOOOOO
AARH
OH, GREAT... MISTER JUNKIE'S BACK, WITH BELLS ON...
NOW WHAT'S HE DOING? IT LOOKS LIKE HE'S TRYING TO TEAR OFF HIS OWN HEAD.

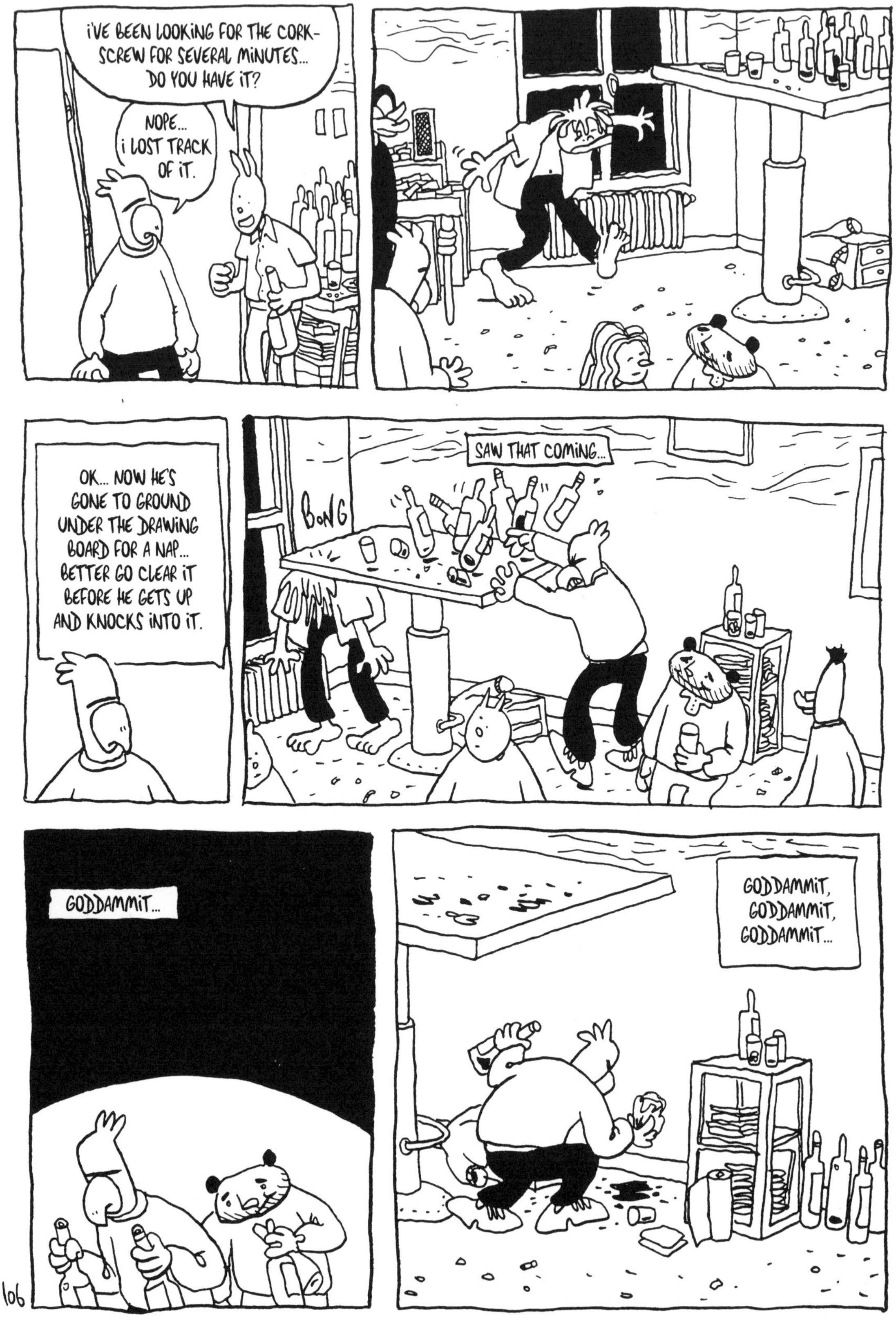
i'VE BEEN LOOKiNG FOR THE CORK-SCREW FOR SEVERAL MiNUTES... DO YOU HAVE iT?
NOPE... i LOST TRACK OF iT.
OK... NOW HE'S GONE TO GROUND UNDER THE DRAWING BOARD FOR A NAP... BETTER GO CLEAR iT BEFORE HE GETS UP AND KNOCKS iNTO iT.
BONG
SAW THAT COMiNG...
GODDAMMiT...
GODDAMMiT, GODDAMMiT, GODDAMMiT...

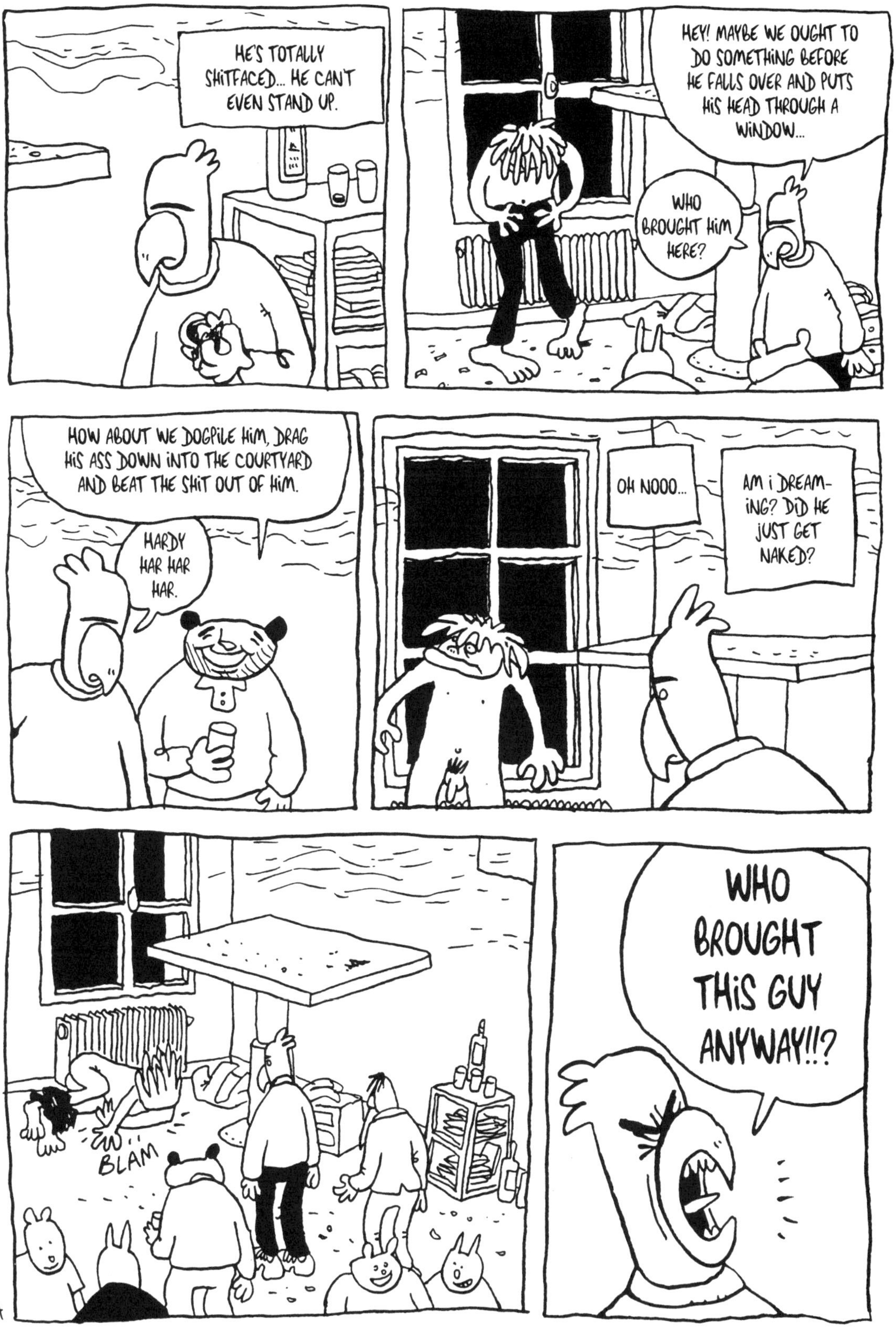
HE'S TOTALLY SHITFACED... HE CAN'T EVEN STAND UP.
HEY! MAYBE WE OUGHT TO DO SOMETHING BEFORE HE FALLS OVER AND PUTS HIS HEAD THROUGH A WINDOW...
WHO BROUGHT HIM HERE?
HOW ABOUT WE DOGPILE HIM, DRAG HIS ASS DOWN INTO THE COURTYARD AND BEAT THE SHIT OUT OF HIM.
HARDY HAR HAR HAR.
OH NOOO...
AM I DREAMING? DID HE JUST GET NAKED?
BLAM
WHO BROUGHT THIS GUY ANYWAY!!?

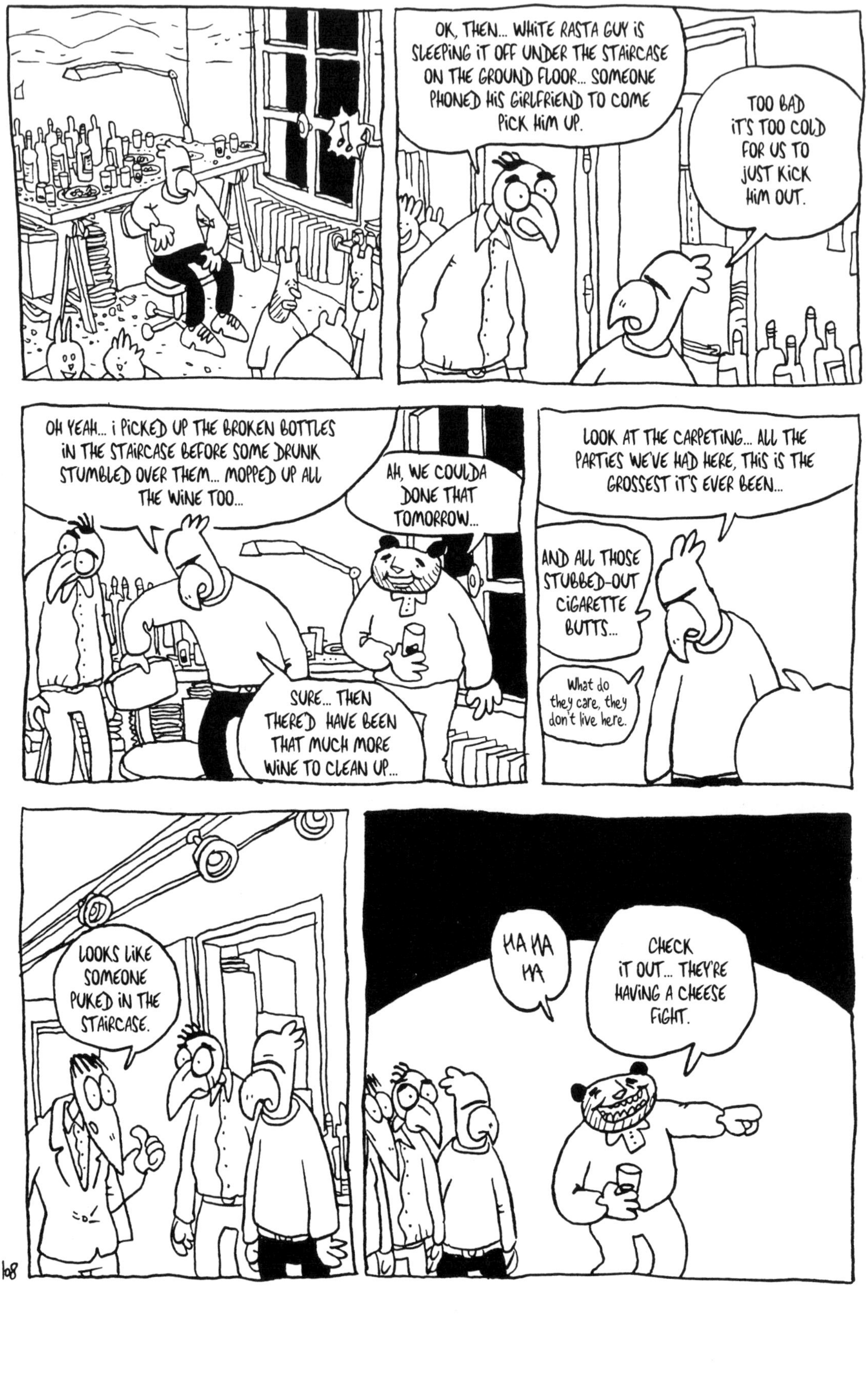
OK, THEN... WHITE RASTA GUY IS SLEEPING IT OFF UNDER THE STAIRCASE ON THE GROUND FLOOR... SOMEONE PHONED HIS GIRLFRIEND TO COME PICK HIM UP.
TOO BAD IT'S TOO COLD FOR US TO JUST KICK HIM OUT.
OH YEAH... I PICKED UP THE BROKEN BOTTLES IN THE STAIRCASE BEFORE SOME DRUNK STUMBLED OVER THEM... MOPPED UP ALL THE WINE TOO...
AH, WE COULDA DONE THAT TOMORROW...
SURE... THEN THERE'D HAVE BEEN THAT MUCH MORE WINE TO CLEAN UP...
LOOK AT THE CARPETING... ALL THE PARTIES WE'VE HAD HERE, THIS IS THE GROSSEST IT'S EVER BEEN...
AND ALL THOSE STUBBED-OUT CIGARETTE BUTTS...
What do they care, they don't live here.
LOOKS LIKE SOMEONE PUKED IN THE STAIRCASE.
HA HA HA
CHECK IT OUT... THEY'RE HAVING A CHEESE FIGHT.

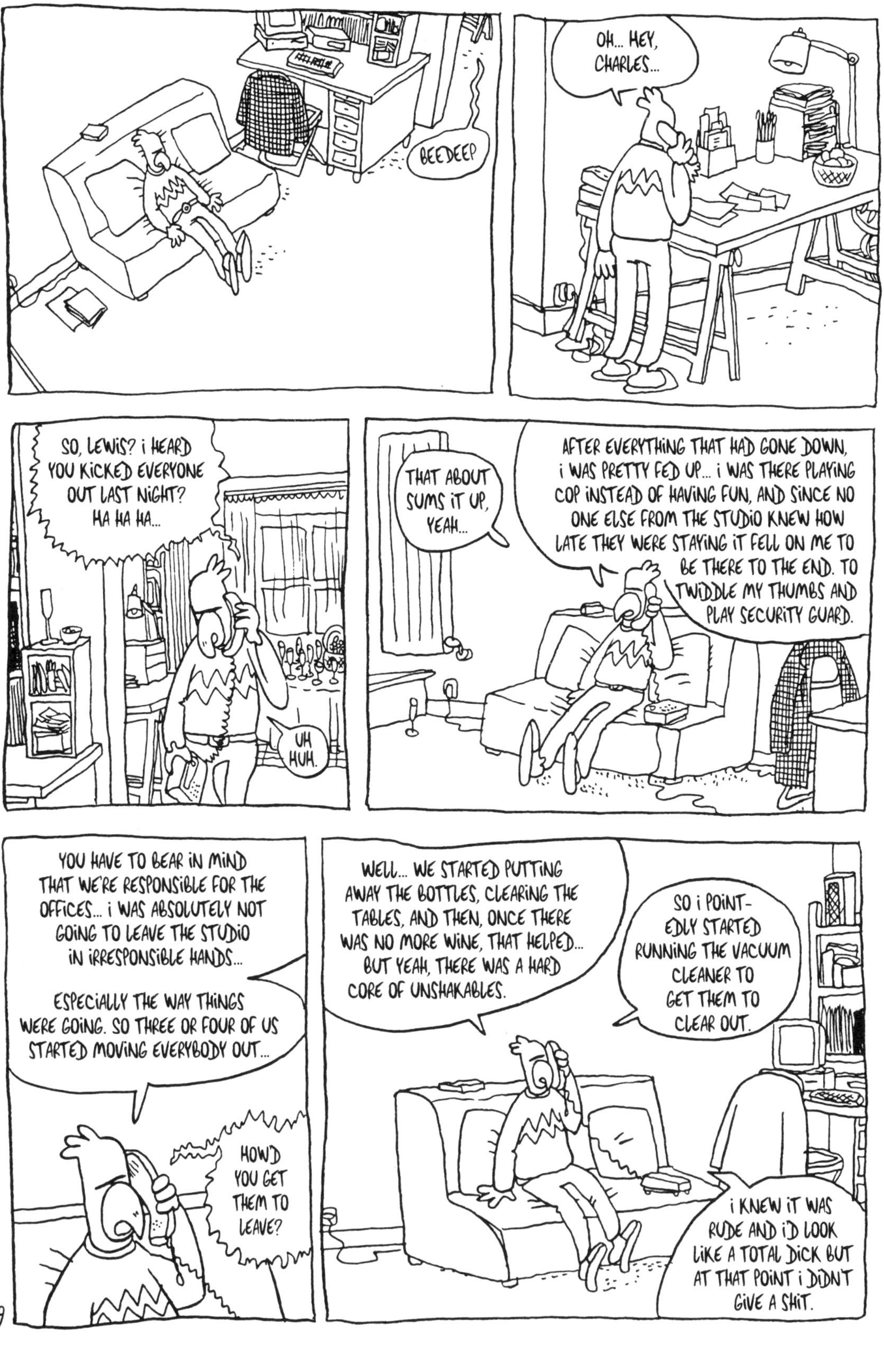
BEEDEEP
OH... HEY, CHARLES...
SO, LEWIS? i HEARD YOU KiCKED EVERYONE OUT LAST NiGHT? HA HA HA...
UH HUH.
THAT ABOUT SUMS iT UP, YEAH...
AFTER EVERYTHING THAT HAD GONE DOWN, i WAS PRETTY FED UP... i WAS THERE PLAYiNG COP iNSTEAD OF HAViNG FUN, AND SiNCE NO ONE ELSE FROM THE STUDiO KNEW HOW LATE THEY WERE STAYiNG iT FELL ON ME TO BE THERE TO THE END. TO TWiDDLE MY THUMBS AND PLAY SECURiTY GUARD.
YOU HAVE TO BEAR iN MiND THAT WE'RE RESPONSiBLE FOR THE OFFiCES... i WAS ABSOLUTELY NOT GOiNG TO LEAVE THE STUDiO iN iRRESPONSiBLE HANDS...
ESPECiALLY THE WAY THiNGS WERE GOiNG. SO THREE OR FOUR OF US STARTED MOViNG EVERYBODY OUT...
HOW'D YOU GET THEM TO LEAVE?
WELL... WE STARTED PUTTiNG AWAY THE BOTTLES, CLEARiNG THE TABLES, AND THEN, ONCE THERE WAS NO MORE WiNE, THAT HELPED... BUT YEAH, THERE WAS A HARD CORE OF UNSHAKABLES.
SO i POiNT-EDLY STARTED RUNNiNG THE VACUUM CLEANER TO GET THEM TO CLEAR OUT.
i KNEW iT WAS RUDE AND i'D LOOK LIKE A TOTAL DiCK BUT AT THAT POiNT i DiDN'T GiVE A SHiT.

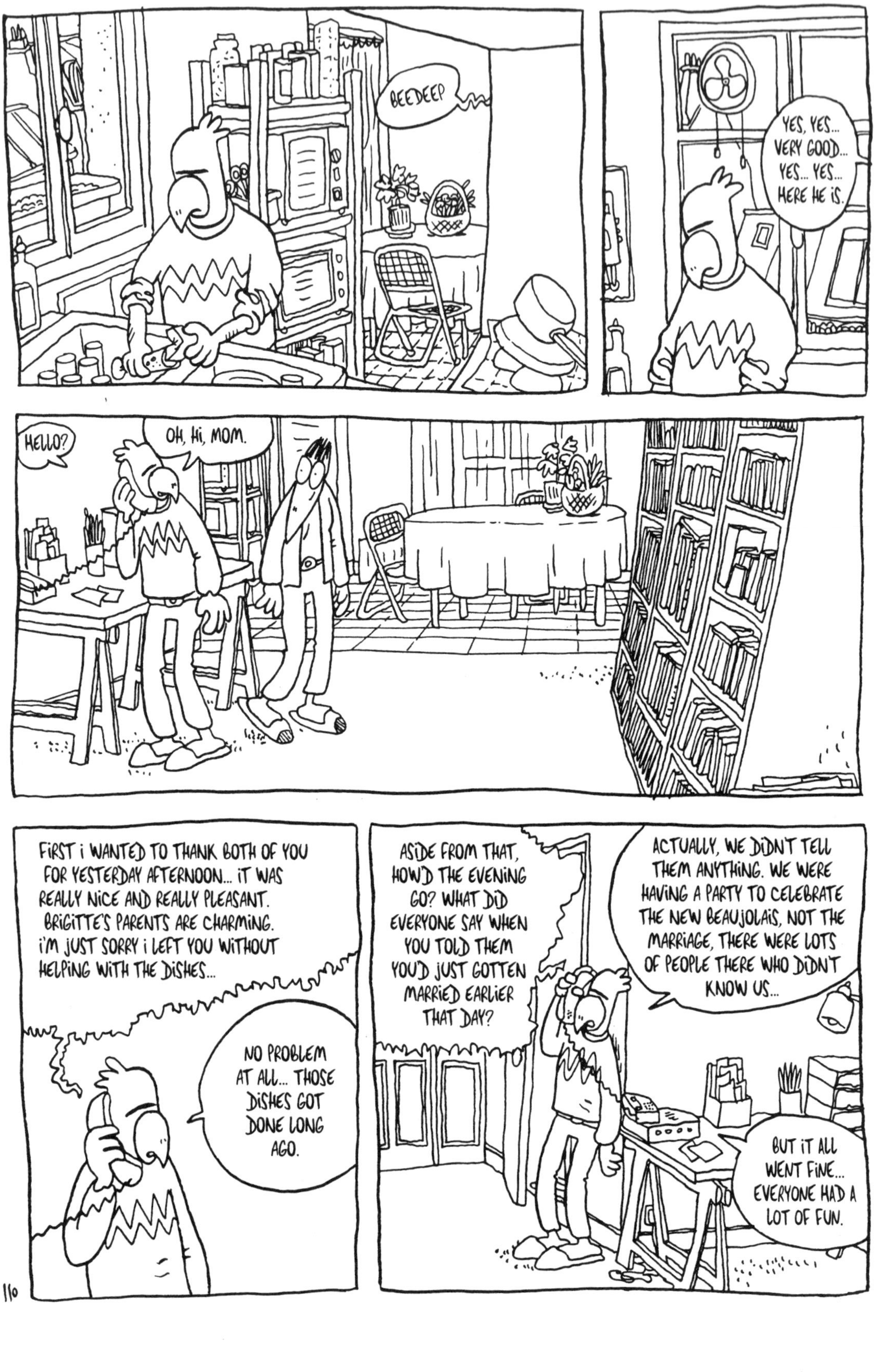
BEEDEEP
YES, YES... VERY GOOD... YES... YES... HERE HE IS.
HELLO?
OH, HI, MOM.
FIRST I WANTED TO THANK BOTH OF YOU FOR YESTERDAY AFTERNOON... IT WAS REALLY NICE AND REALLY PLEASANT. BRIGITTE'S PARENTS ARE CHARMING. I'M JUST SORRY I LEFT YOU WITHOUT HELPING WITH THE DISHES...
NO PROBLEM AT ALL... THOSE DISHES GOT DONE LONG AGO.
ASIDE FROM THAT, HOW'D THE EVENING GO? WHAT DID EVERYONE SAY WHEN YOU TOLD THEM YOU'D JUST GOTTEN MARRIED EARLIER THAT DAY?
ACTUALLY, WE DIDN'T TELL THEM ANYTHING. WE WERE HAVING A PARTY TO CELEBRATE THE NEW BEAUJOLAIS, NOT THE MARRIAGE, THERE WERE LOTS OF PEOPLE THERE WHO DIDN'T KNOW US...
BUT IT ALL WENT FINE... EVERYONE HAD A LOT OF FUN.

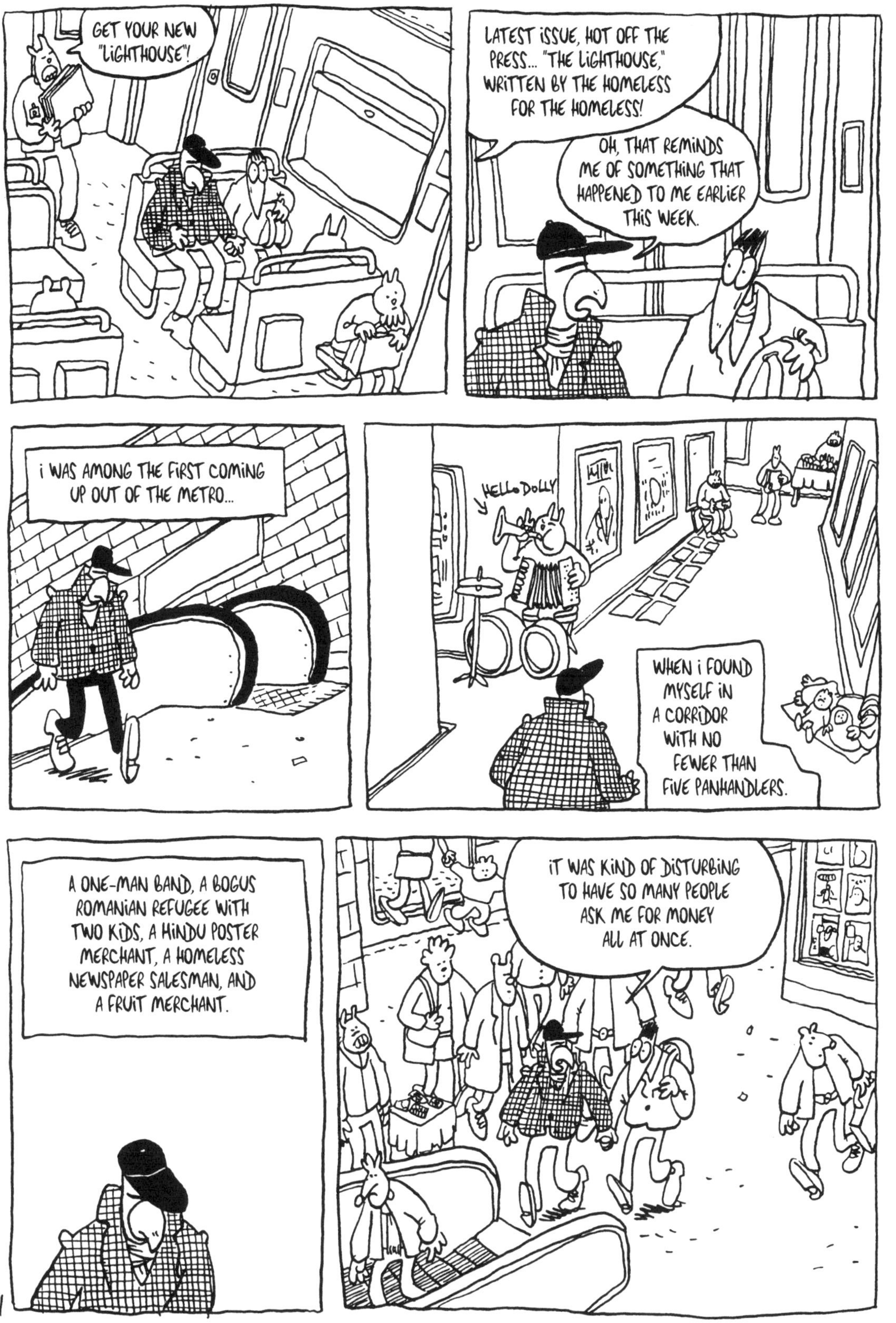
GET YOUR NEW "LIGHTHOUSE"!
LATEST ISSUE, HOT OFF THE PRESS... "THE LIGHTHOUSE," WRITTEN BY THE HOMELESS FOR THE HOMELESS!
OH, THAT REMINDS ME OF SOMETHING THAT HAPPENED TO ME EARLIER THIS WEEK.
I WAS AMONG THE FIRST COMING UP OUT OF THE METRO...
HELLO DOLLY
WHEN I FOUND MYSELF IN A CORRIDOR WITH NO FEWER THAN FIVE PANHANDLERS.
A ONE-MAN BAND, A BOGUS ROMANIAN REFUGEE WITH TWO KIDS, A HINDU POSTER MERCHANT, A HOMELESS NEWSPAPER SALESMAN, AND A FRUIT MERCHANT.
IT WAS KIND OF DISTURBING TO HAVE SO MANY PEOPLE ASK ME FOR MONEY ALL AT ONCE.

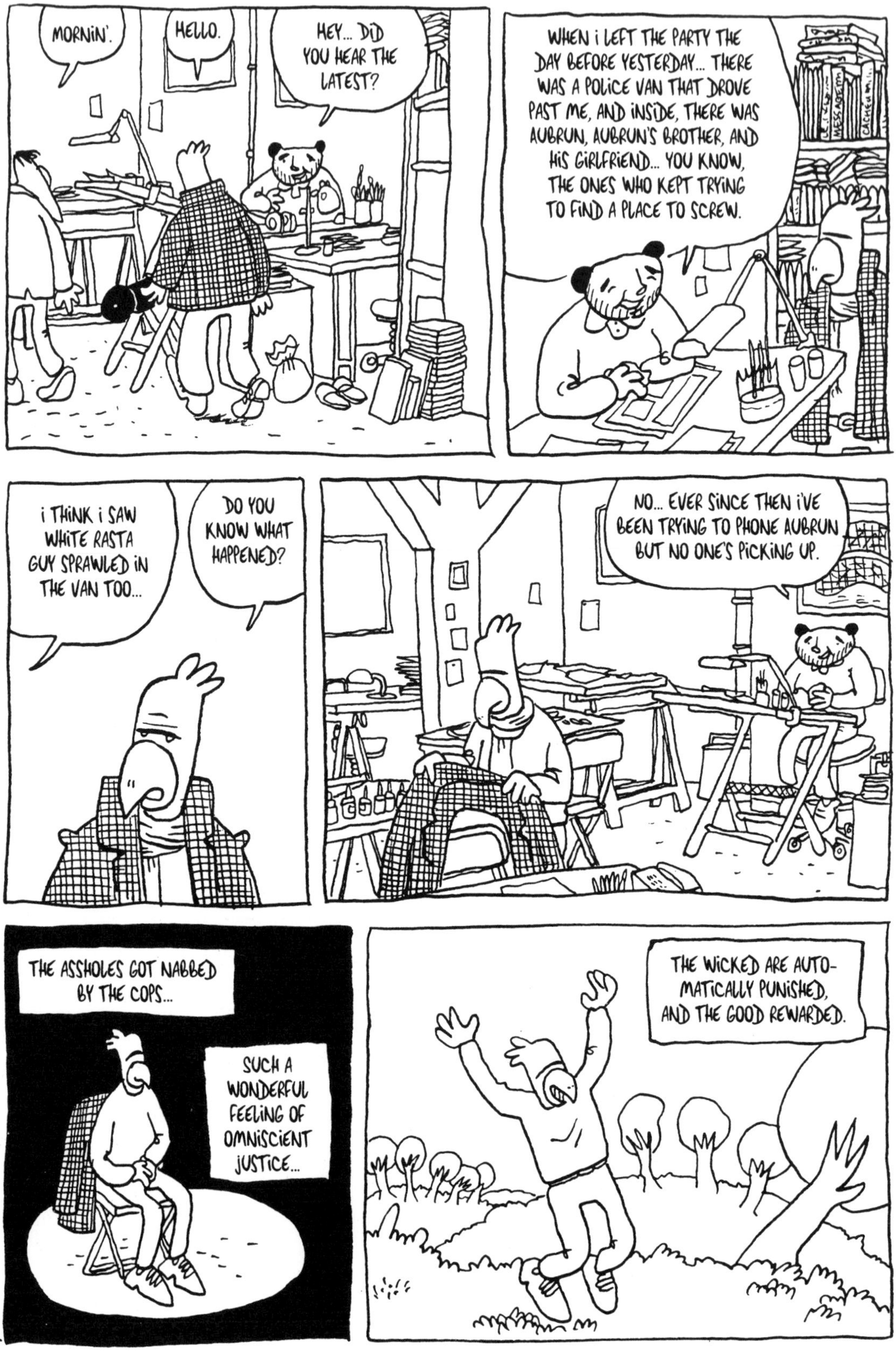
MORNIN'.
HELLO.
HEY... DID YOU HEAR THE LATEST?
WHEN i LEFT THE PARTY THE DAY BEFORE YESTERDAY... THERE WAS A POLICE VAN THAT DROVE PAST ME, AND iNSiDE, THERE WAS AUBRUN, AUBRUN'S BROTHER, AND HIS GIRLFRIEND... YOU KNOW, THE ONES WHO KEPT TRYING TO FIND A PLACE TO SCREW.
i THINK i SAW WHITE RASTA GUY SPRAWLED iN THE VAN TOO...
DO YOU KNOW WHAT HAPPENED?
NO... EVER SiNCE THEN i'VE BEEN TRYING TO PHONE AUBRUN BUT NO ONE'S PiCKiNG UP.
THE ASSHOLES GOT NABBED BY THE COPS...
SUCH A WONDERFUL FEELING OF OMNiSCiENT JUSTiCE...
THE WiCKED ARE AUTO-MATICALLY PUNiSHED, AND THE GOOD REWARDED.

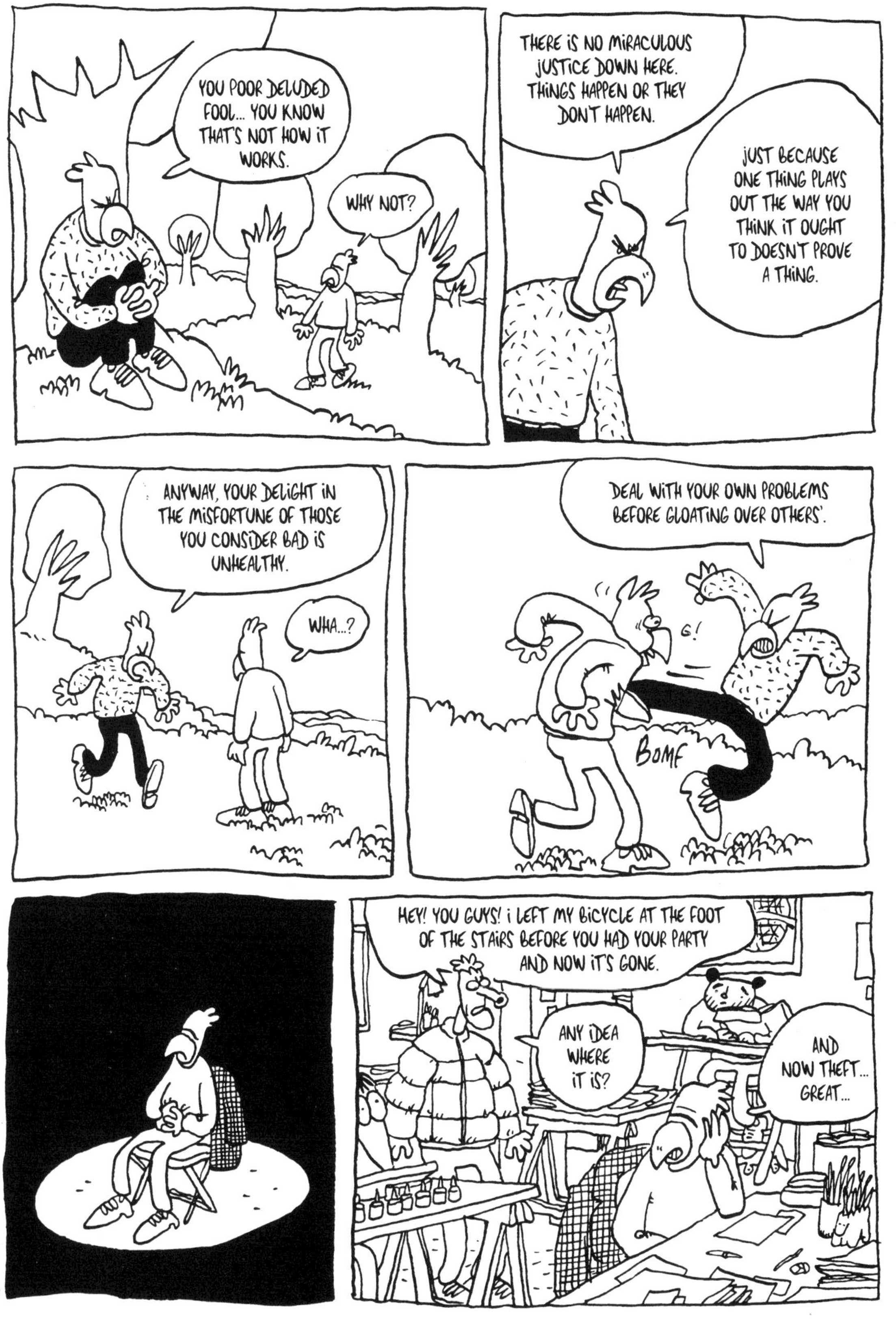
YOU POOR DELUDED FOOL... YOU KNOW THAT'S NOT HOW IT WORKS.
WHY NOT?
THERE IS NO MIRACULOUS JUSTICE DOWN HERE. THINGS HAPPEN OR THEY DON'T HAPPEN.
JUST BECAUSE ONE THING PLAYS OUT THE WAY YOU THINK IT OUGHT TO DOESN'T PROVE A THING.
ANYWAY, YOUR DELIGHT IN THE MISFORTUNE OF THOSE YOU CONSIDER BAD IS UNHEALTHY.
WHA...?
DEAL WITH YOUR OWN PROBLEMS BEFORE GLOATING OVER OTHERS'.
G!
BOMF
HEY! YOU GUYS! I LEFT MY BICYCLE AT THE FOOT OF THE STAIRS BEFORE YOU HAD YOUR PARTY AND NOW IT'S GONE.
ANY IDEA WHERE IT IS?
AND NOW THEFT... GREAT...

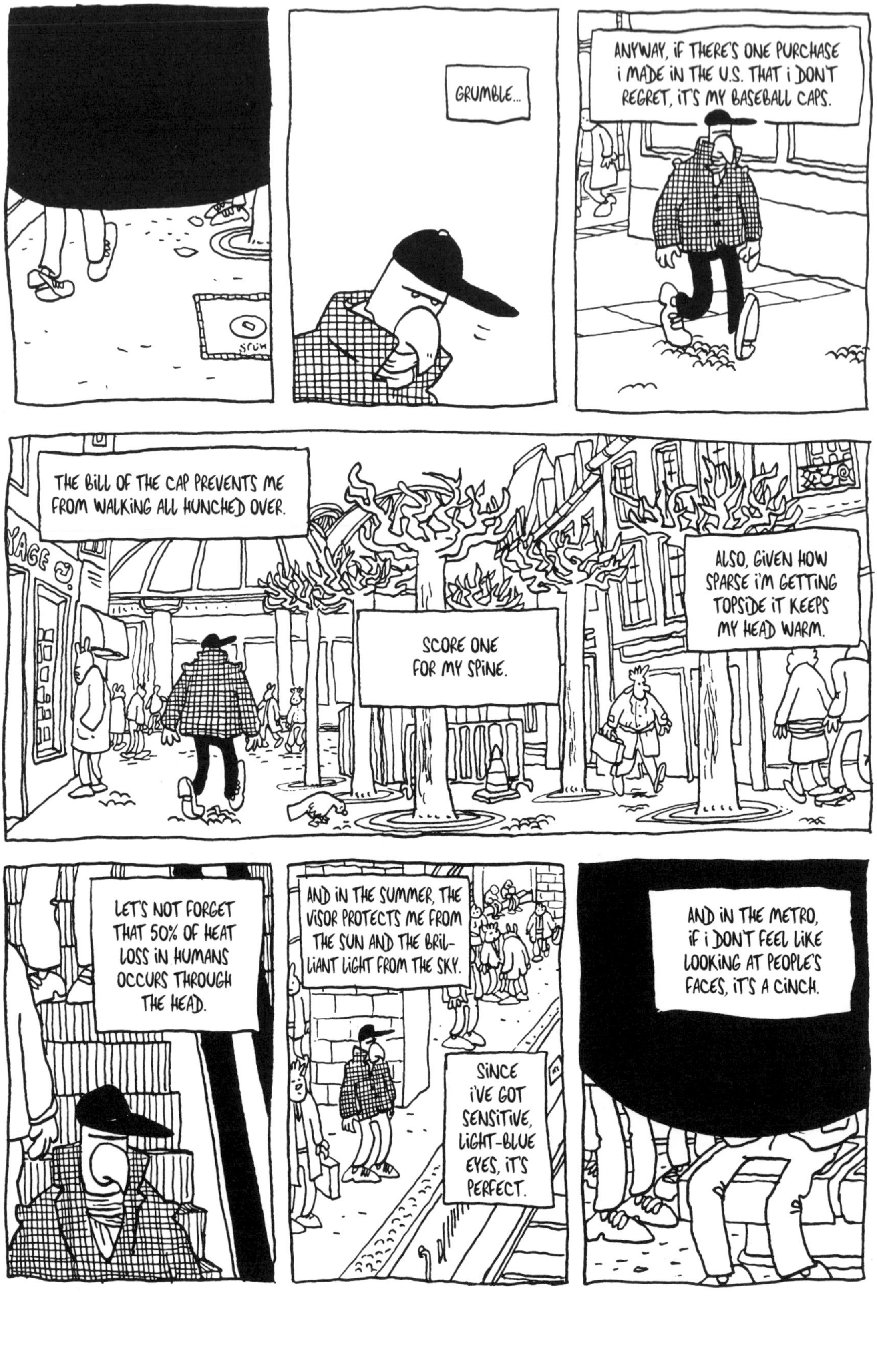

GRUMBLE...
ANYWAY, IF THERE'S ONE PURCHASE I MADE IN THE U.S. THAT I DON'T REGRET, IT'S MY BASEBALL CAPS.
THE BILL OF THE CAP PREVENTS ME FROM WALKING ALL HUNCHED OVER.
SCORE ONE FOR MY SPINE.
ALSO, GIVEN HOW SPARSE I'M GETTING TOPSIDE IT KEEPS MY HEAD WARM.
LET'S NOT FORGET THAT 50% OF HEAT LOSS IN HUMANS OCCURS THROUGH THE HEAD.
AND IN THE SUMMER, THE VISOR PROTECTS ME FROM THE SUN AND THE BRILLIANT LIGHT FROM THE SKY.
SINCE I'VE GOT SENSITIVE, LIGHT-BLUE EYES, IT'S PERFECT.
AND IN THE METRO, IF I DON'T FEEL LIKE LOOKING AT PEOPLE'S FACES, IT'S A CINCH.

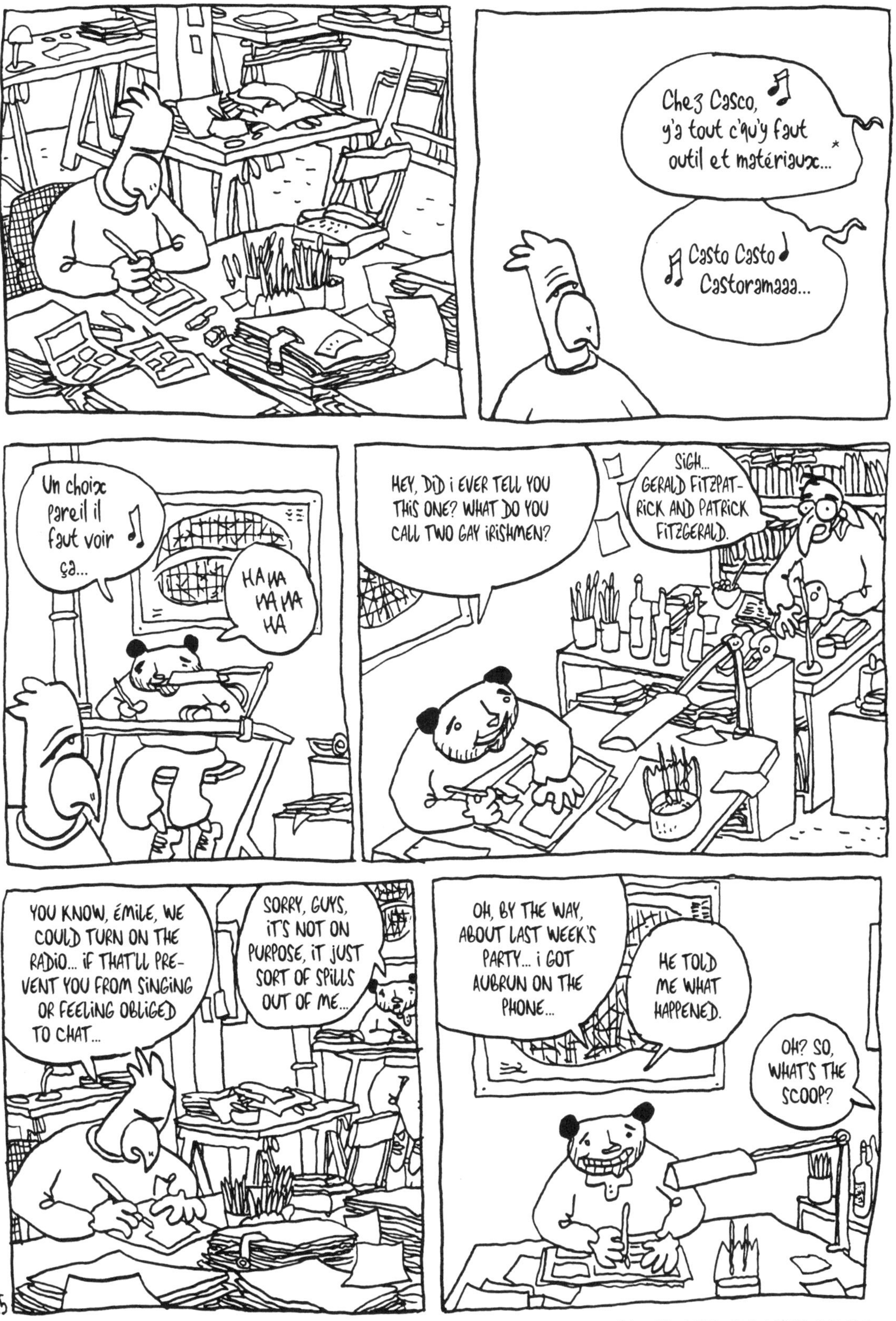
Chez Casco, y'a tout c'qu'y faut outil et matériaux...*
Casto Casto Castoramaaa...
Un choix pareil il faut voir ça...
HA HA HA HA HA
HEY, DID I EVER TELL YOU THIS ONE? WHAT DO YOU CALL TWO GAY IRISHMEN?
SIGH... GERALD FITZPATRICK AND PATRICK FITZGERALD.
YOU KNOW, ÉMILE, WE COULD TURN ON THE RADIO... IF THAT'LL PREVENT YOU FROM SINGING OR FEELING OBLIGED TO CHAT...
SORRY, GUYS, IT'S NOT ON PURPOSE, IT JUST SORT OF SPILLS OUT OF ME...
OH, BY THE WAY, ABOUT LAST WEEK'S PARTY... I GOT AUBRUN ON THE PHONE...
HE TOLD ME WHAT HAPPENED.
OH? SO, WHAT'S THE SCOOP?

* ANNOYING FRENCH ADVERTISING JINGLE

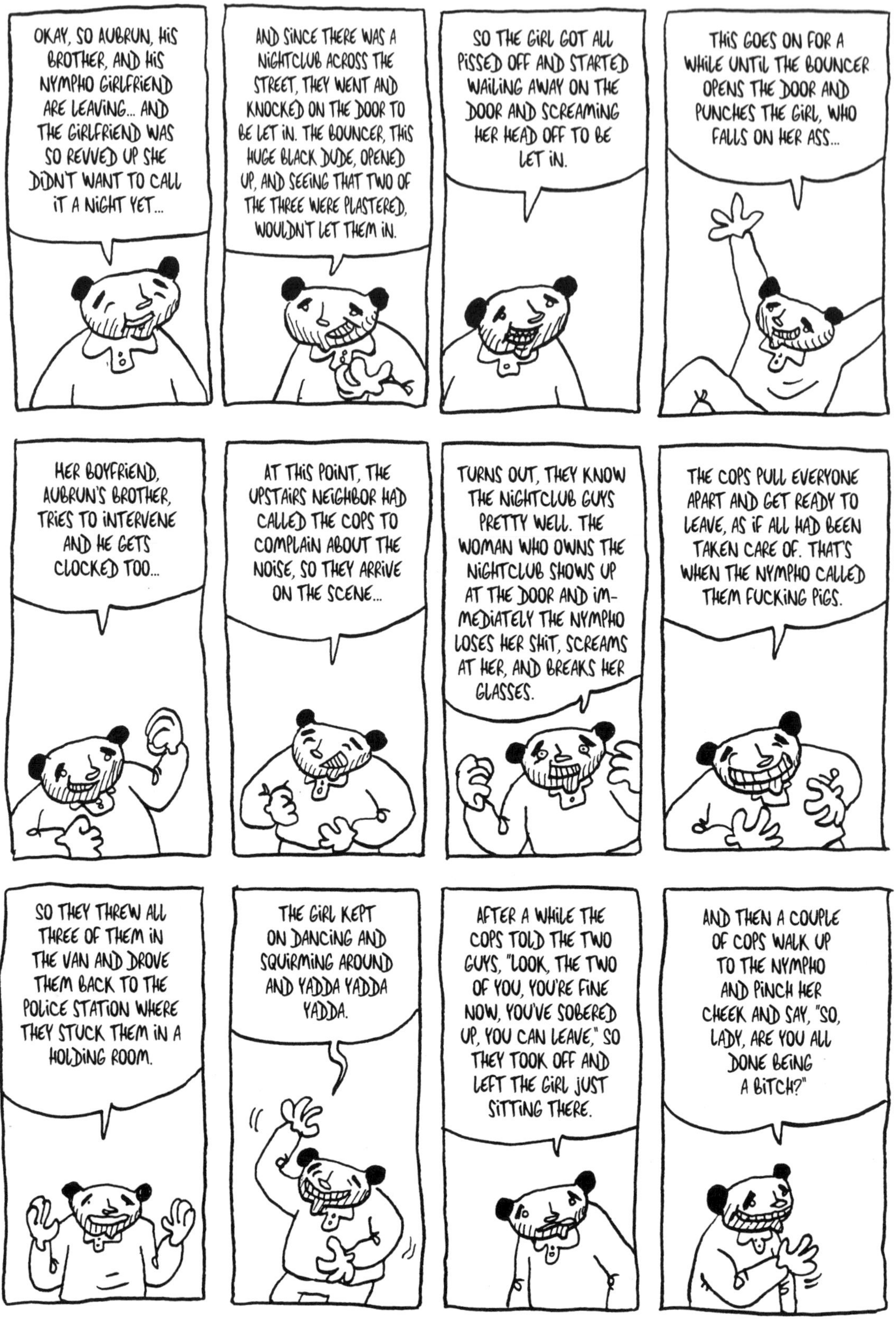
OKAY, SO AUBRUN, HIS BROTHER, AND HIS NYMPHO GIRLFRIEND ARE LEAVING... AND THE GIRLFRIEND WAS SO REVVED UP SHE DIDN'T WANT TO CALL IT A NIGHT YET...
AND SINCE THERE WAS A NIGHTCLUB ACROSS THE STREET, THEY WENT AND KNOCKED ON THE DOOR TO BE LET IN. THE BOUNCER, THIS HUGE BLACK DUDE, OPENED UP, AND SEEING THAT TWO OF THE THREE WERE PLASTERED, WOULDN'T LET THEM IN.
SO THE GIRL GOT ALL PISSED OFF AND STARTED WAILING AWAY ON THE DOOR AND SCREAMING HER HEAD OFF TO BE LET IN.
THIS GOES ON FOR A WHILE UNTIL THE BOUNCER OPENS THE DOOR AND PUNCHES THE GIRL, WHO FALLS ON HER ASS...
HER BOYFRIEND, AUBRUN'S BROTHER, TRIES TO INTERVENE AND HE GETS CLOCKED TOO...
AT THIS POINT, THE UPSTAIRS NEIGHBOR HAD CALLED THE COPS TO COMPLAIN ABOUT THE NOISE, SO THEY ARRIVE ON THE SCENE...
TURNS OUT, THEY KNOW THE NIGHTCLUB GUYS PRETTY WELL. THE WOMAN WHO OWNS THE NIGHTCLUB SHOWS UP AT THE DOOR AND IM-MEDIATELY THE NYMPHO LOSES HER SHIT, SCREAMS AT HER, AND BREAKS HER GLASSES.
THE COPS PULL EVERYONE APART AND GET READY TO LEAVE, AS IF ALL HAD BEEN TAKEN CARE OF. THAT'S WHEN THE NYMPHO CALLED THEM FUCKING PIGS.
SO THEY THREW ALL THREE OF THEM IN THE VAN AND DROVE THEM BACK TO THE POLICE STATION WHERE THEY STUCK THEM IN A HOLDING ROOM.
THE GIRL KEPT ON DANCING AND SQUIRMING AROUND AND YADDA YADDA YADDA.
AFTER A WHILE THE COPS TOLD THE TWO GUYS, "LOOK, THE TWO OF YOU, YOU'RE FINE NOW, YOU'VE SOBERED UP, YOU CAN LEAVE," SO THEY TOOK OFF AND LEFT THE GIRL JUST SITTING THERE.
AND THEN A COUPLE OF COPS WALK UP TO THE NYMPHO AND PINCH HER CHEEK AND SAY, "SO, LADY, ARE YOU ALL DONE BEING A BITCH?"

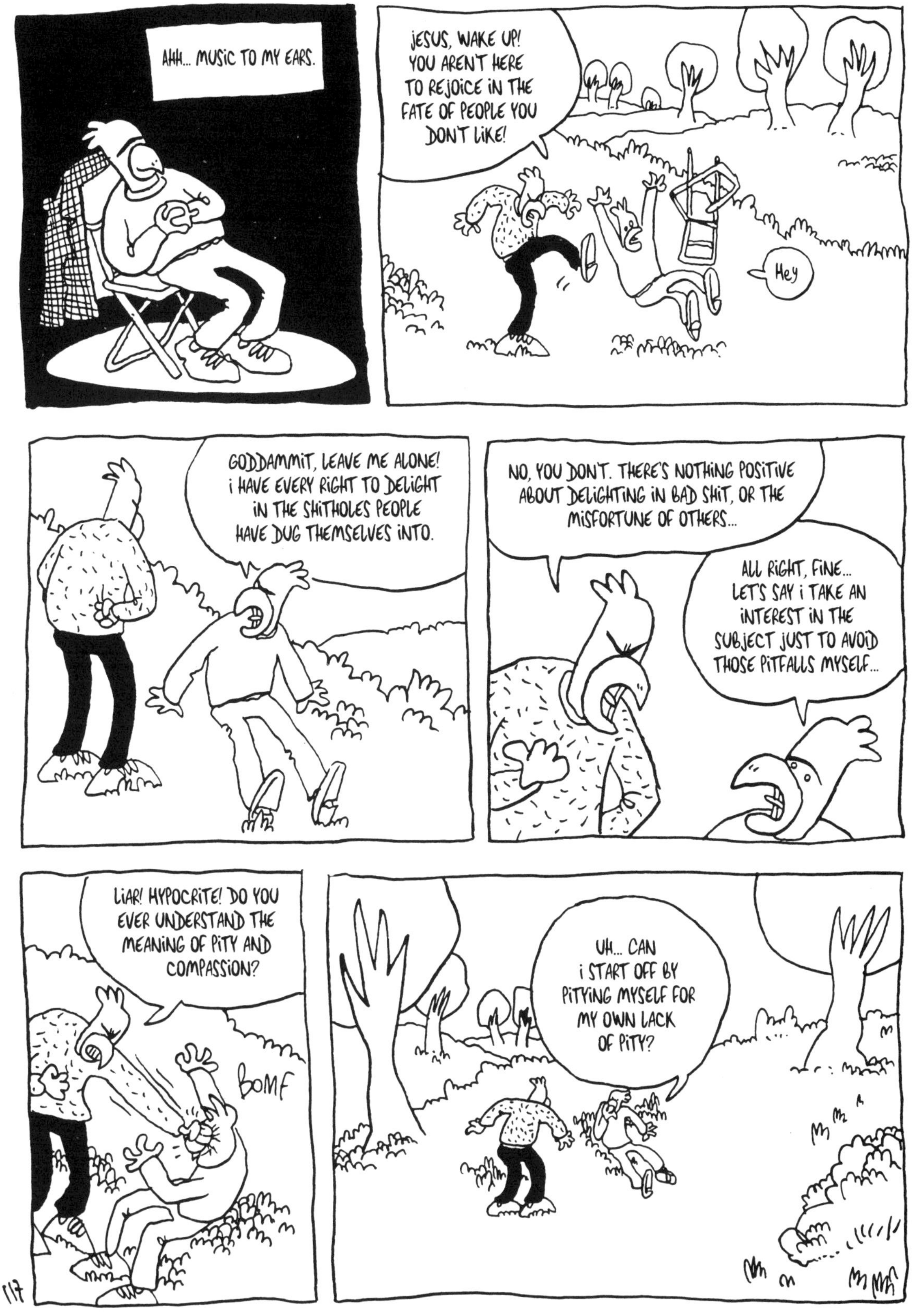
AHH... MUSIC TO MY EARS.
JESUS, WAKE UP! YOU AREN'T HERE TO REJOICE IN THE FATE OF PEOPLE YOU DON'T LIKE!
Hey
GODDAMMIT, LEAVE ME ALONE! I HAVE EVERY RIGHT TO DELIGHT IN THE SHITHOLES PEOPLE HAVE DUG THEMSELVES INTO.
NO, YOU DON'T. THERE'S NOTHING POSITIVE ABOUT DELIGHTING IN BAD SHIT, OR THE MISFORTUNE OF OTHERS...
ALL RIGHT, FINE... LET'S SAY I TAKE AN INTEREST IN THE SUBJECT JUST TO AVOID THOSE PITFALLS MYSELF...
LIAR! HYPOCRITE! DO YOU EVER UNDERSTAND THE MEANING OF PITY AND COMPASSION?
BOMF
UH... CAN I START OFF BY PITYING MYSELF FOR MY OWN LACK OF PITY?

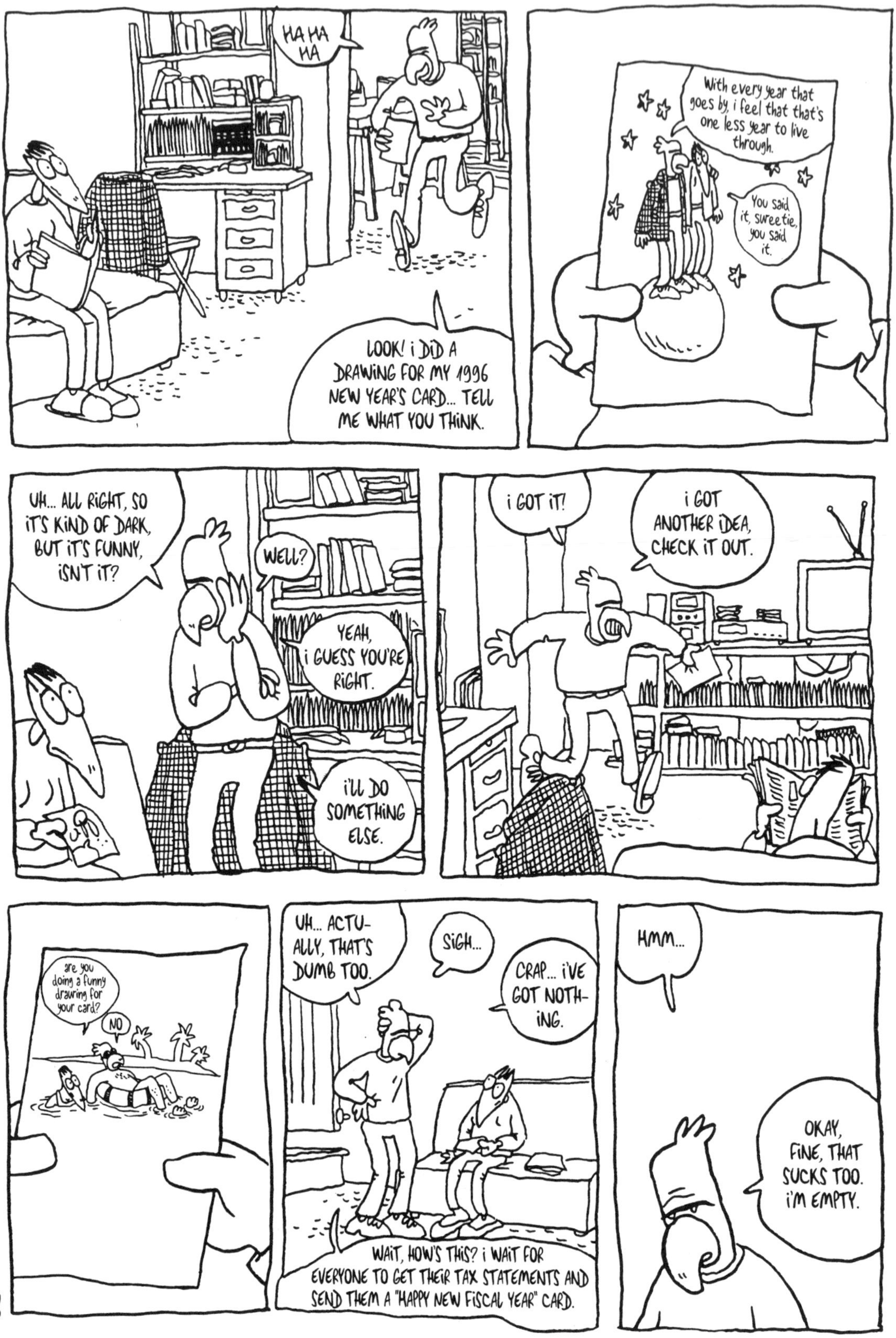
HA HA HA
LOOK! i DiD A DRAWiNG FOR MY 1996 NEW YEAR'S CARD... TELL ME WHAT YOU THiNK.
With every year that goes by, i feel that that's one less year to live through.
You said it, sweetie, you said it.
UH... ALL RiGHT, SO iT'S KiND OF DARK, BUT iT'S FUNNY, iSN'T iT?
WELL?
YEAH, i GUESS YOU'RE RiGHT.
i'LL DO SOMETHiNG ELSE.
i GOT iT!
i GOT ANOTHER iDEA, CHECK iT OUT.
are you doing a funny drawing for your card?
NO
UH... ACTU-ALLY, THAT'S DUMB TOO.
SiGH...
CRAP... i'VE GOT NOTH-iNG.
WAiT, HOW'S THiS? i WAiT FOR EVERYONE TO GET THEiR TAX STATEMENTS AND SEND THEM A "HAPPY NEW FiSCAL YEAR" CARD.
HMM...
OKAY, FiNE, THAT SUCKS TOO. i'M EMPTY.

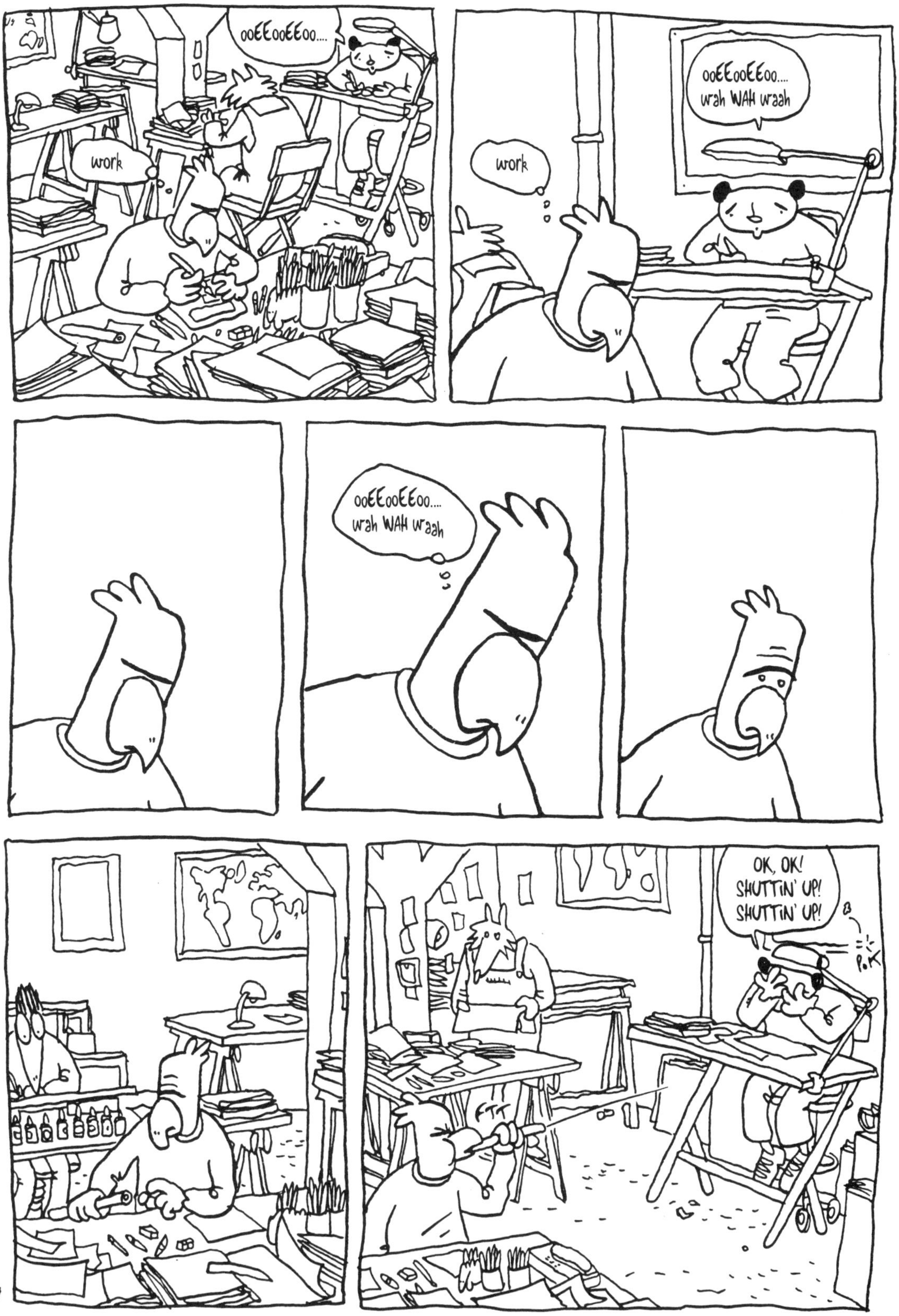
ooEEooEEoo....
work
ooEEooEEoo.... wrah WAH wraah
work
ooEEooEEoo.... wrah WAH wraah
FTT
OK, OK! SHUTTIN' UP! SHUTTIN' UP!
PoK

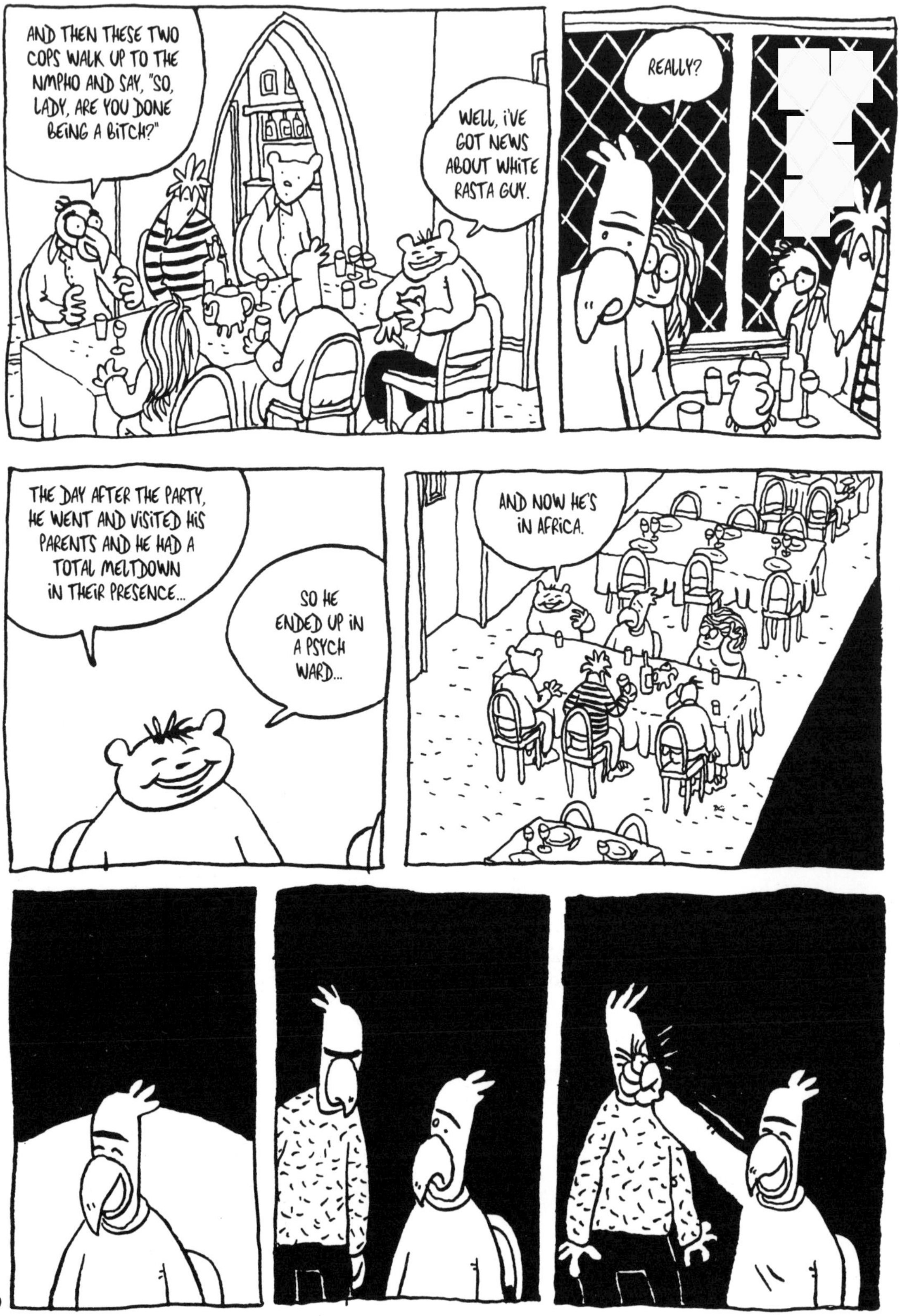
AND THEN THESE TWO COPS WALK UP TO THE NMPHO AND SAY, "SO, LADY, ARE YOU DONE BEING A BITCH?"
WELL, i'VE GOT NEWS ABOUT WHITE RASTA GUY.
REALLY?
THE DAY AFTER THE PARTY, HE WENT AND VISITED HIS PARENTS AND HE HAD A TOTAL MELTDOWN IN THEIR PRESENCE...
SO HE ENDED UP IN A PSYCH WARD...
AND NOW HE'S IN AFRICA.

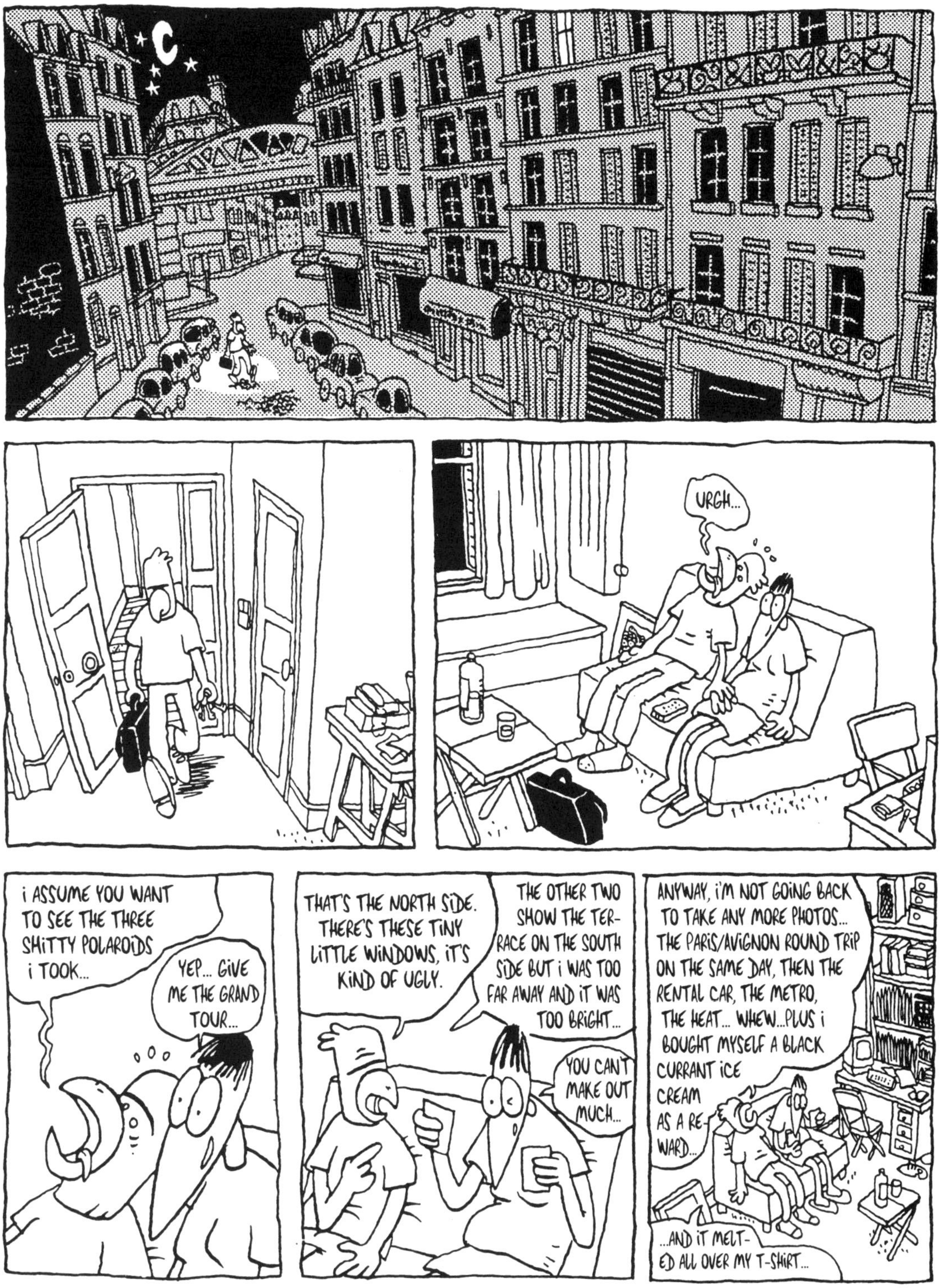
URGH...
i ASSUME YOU WANT TO SEE THE THREE SHITTY POLAROIDS i TOOK...
YEP... GIVE ME THE GRAND TOUR...
THAT'S THE NORTH SiDE. THERE'S THESE TINY LiTTLE WiNDOWS, iT'S KiND OF UGLY.
THE OTHER TWO SHOW THE TER-RACE ON THE SOUTH SiDE BUT i WAS TOO FAR AWAY AND iT WAS TOO BRiGHT...
YOU CAN'T MAKE OUT MUCH...
ANYWAY, i'M NOT GOiNG BACK TO TAKE ANY MORE PHOTOS... THE PARiS/AViGNON ROUND TRiP ON THE SAME DAY, THEN THE RENTAL CAR, THE METRO, THE HEAT... WHEW...PLUS i BOUGHT MYSELF A BLACK CURRANT iCE CREAM AS A RE-WARD...
...AND iT MELT-ED ALL OVER MY T-SHiRT...

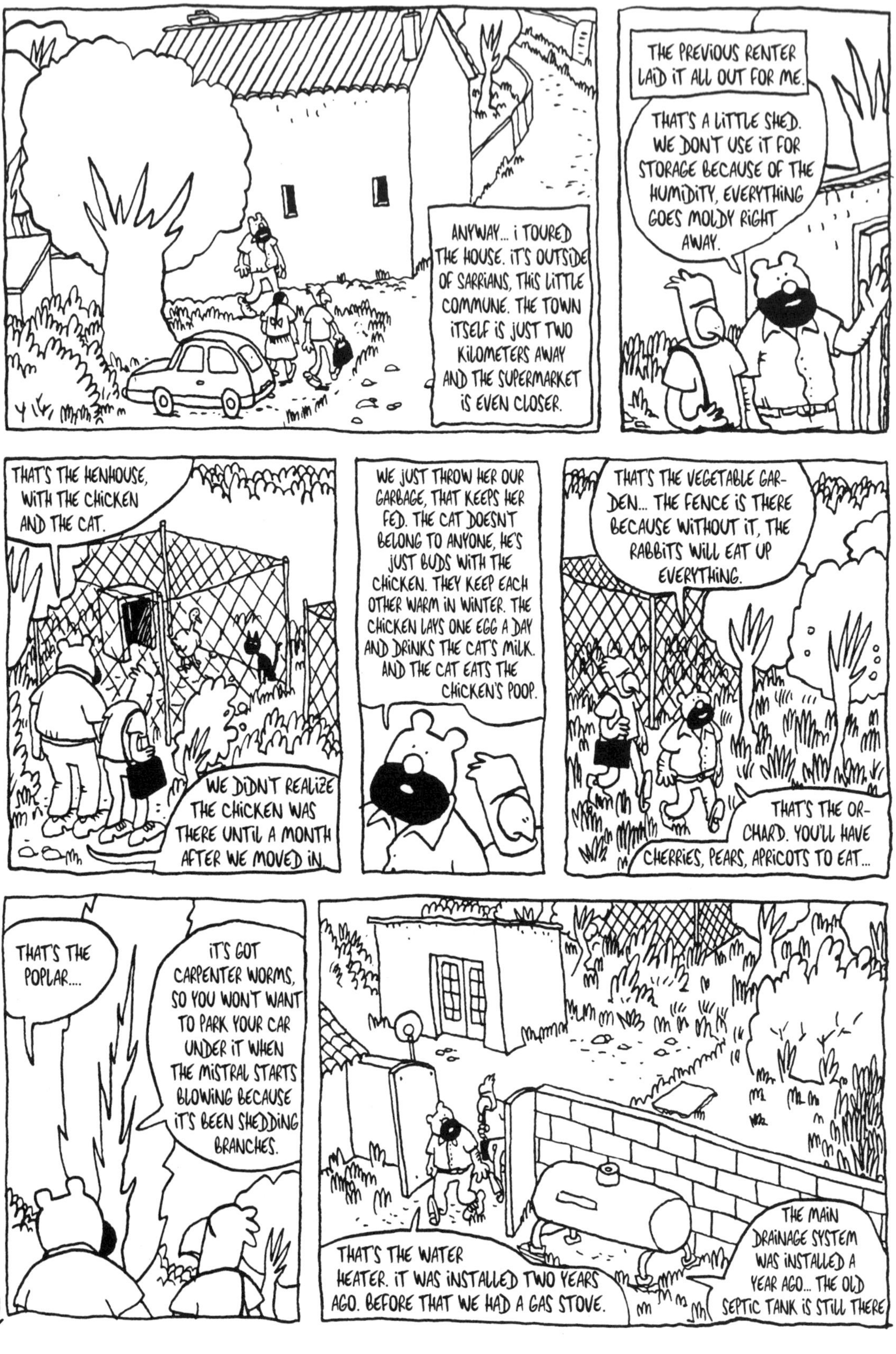
ANYWAY... i TOURED THE HOUSE. iT'S OUTSIDE OF SARRiANS, THIS LiTTLE COMMUNE. THE TOWN iTSELF iS JUST TWO KiLOMETERS AWAY AND THE SUPERMARKET iS EVEN CLOSER.
THE PREViOUS RENTER LAiD iT ALL OUT FOR ME.
THAT'S A LiTTLE SHED. WE DON'T USE iT FOR STORAGE BECAUSE OF THE HUMiDiTY, EVERYTHiNG GOES MOLDY RiGHT AWAY.
THAT'S THE HENHOUSE, WiTH THE CHiCKEN AND THE CAT.
WE DiDN'T REALiZE THE CHiCKEN WAS THERE UNTiL A MONTH AFTER WE MOVED iN.
WE JUST THROW HER OUR GARBAGE, THAT KEEPS HER FED. THE CAT DOESN'T BELONG TO ANYONE, HE'S JUST BUDS WiTH THE CHiCKEN. THEY KEEP EACH OTHER WARM iN WiNTER. THE CHiCKEN LAYS ONE EGG A DAY AND DRiNKS THE CAT'S MiLK. AND THE CAT EATS THE CHiCKEN'S POOP.
THAT'S THE VEGETABLE GAR-DEN... THE FENCE iS THERE BECAUSE WiTHOUT iT, THE RABBiTS WiLL EAT UP EVERYTHiNG.
THAT'S THE OR-CHARD. YOU'LL HAVE CHERRiES, PEARS, APRiCOTS TO EAT...
THAT'S THE POPLAR....
iT'S GOT CARPENTER WORMS, SO YOU WON'T WANT TO PARK YOUR CAR UNDER iT WHEN THE MiSTRAL STARTS BLOWiNG BECAUSE iT'S BEEN SHEDDiNG BRANCHES.
THAT'S THE WATER HEATER. iT WAS iNSTALLED TWO YEARS AGO. BEFORE THAT WE HAD A GAS STOVE.
THE MAiN DRAiNAGE SYSTEM WAS iNSTALLED A YEAR AGO... THE OLD SEPTiC TANK iS STiLL THERE

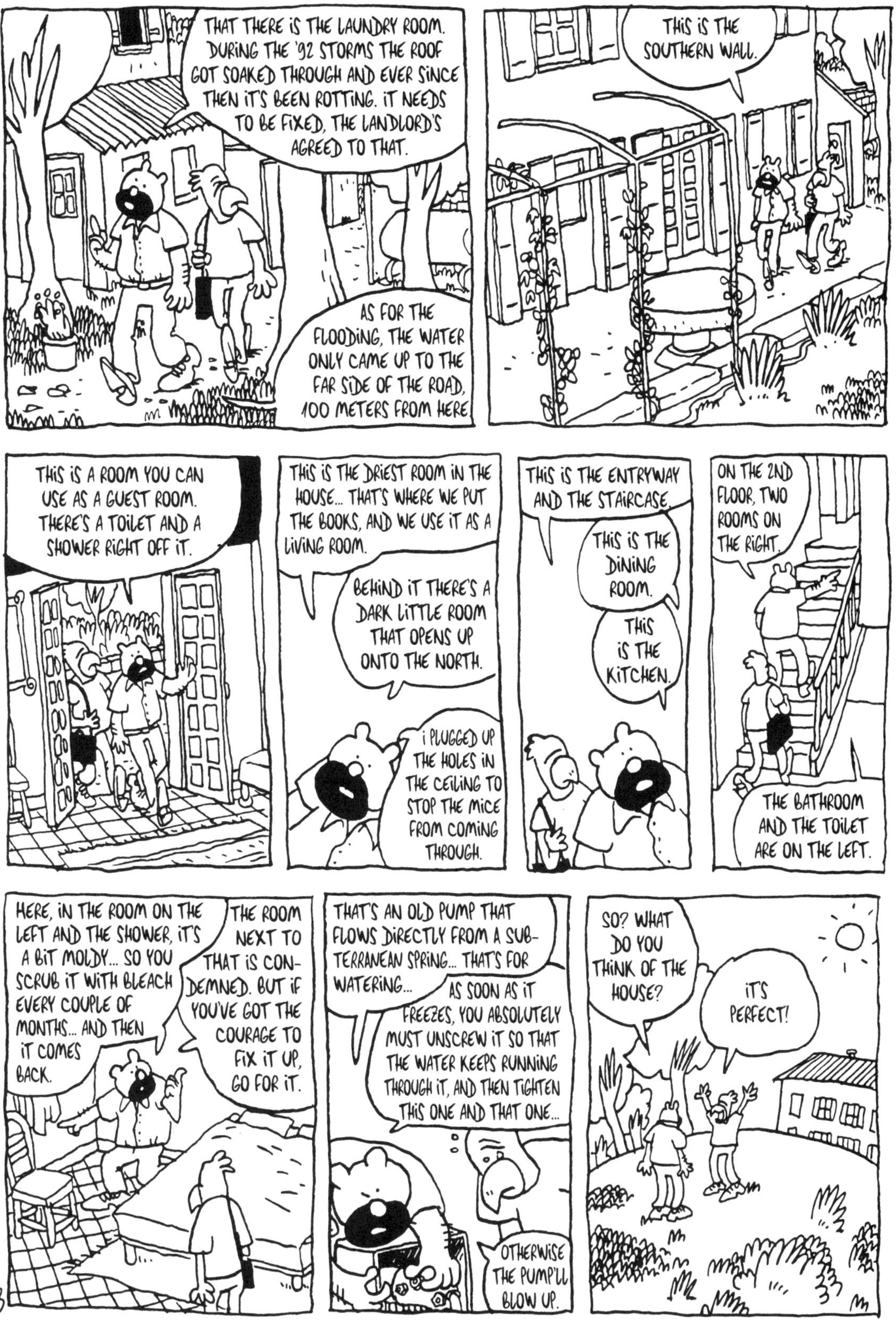
THAT THERE IS THE LAUNDRY ROOM. DURING THE '92 STORMS THE ROOF GOT SOAKED THROUGH AND EVER SINCE THEN IT'S BEEN ROTTING. IT NEEDS TO BE FIXED, THE LANDLORD'S AGREED TO THAT.
AS FOR THE FLOODING, THE WATER ONLY CAME UP TO THE FAR SIDE OF THE ROAD, 100 METERS FROM HERE
THIS IS THE SOUTHERN WALL.
THIS IS A ROOM YOU CAN USE AS A GUEST ROOM. THERE'S A TOILET AND A SHOWER RIGHT OFF IT.
THIS IS THE DRIEST ROOM IN THE HOUSE... THAT'S WHERE WE PUT THE BOOKS, AND WE USE IT AS A LIVING ROOM.
BEHIND IT THERE'S A DARK LITTLE ROOM THAT OPENS UP ONTO THE NORTH.
I PLUGGED UP THE HOLES IN THE CEILING TO STOP THE MICE FROM COMING THROUGH.
THIS IS THE ENTRYWAY AND THE STAIRCASE.
THIS IS THE DINING ROOM.
THIS IS THE KITCHEN.
ON THE 2ND FLOOR, TWO ROOMS ON THE RIGHT.
THE BATHROOM AND THE TOILET ARE ON THE LEFT.
HERE, IN THE ROOM ON THE LEFT AND THE SHOWER, IT'S A BIT MOLDY... SO YOU SCRUB IT WITH BLEACH EVERY COUPLE OF MONTHS... AND THEN IT COMES BACK.
THE ROOM NEXT TO THAT IS CONDEMNED. BUT IF YOU'VE GOT THE COURAGE TO FIX IT UP, GO FOR IT.
THAT'S AN OLD PUMP THAT FLOWS DIRECTLY FROM A SUBTERRANEAN SPRING... THAT'S FOR WATERING...
AS SOON AS IT FREEZES, YOU ABSOLUTELY MUST UNSCREW IT SO THAT THE WATER KEEPS RUNNING THROUGH IT, AND THEN TIGHTEN THIS ONE AND THAT ONE...
OTHERWISE THE PUMP'LL BLOW UP.
SO? WHAT DO YOU THINK OF THE HOUSE?
IT'S PERFECT!

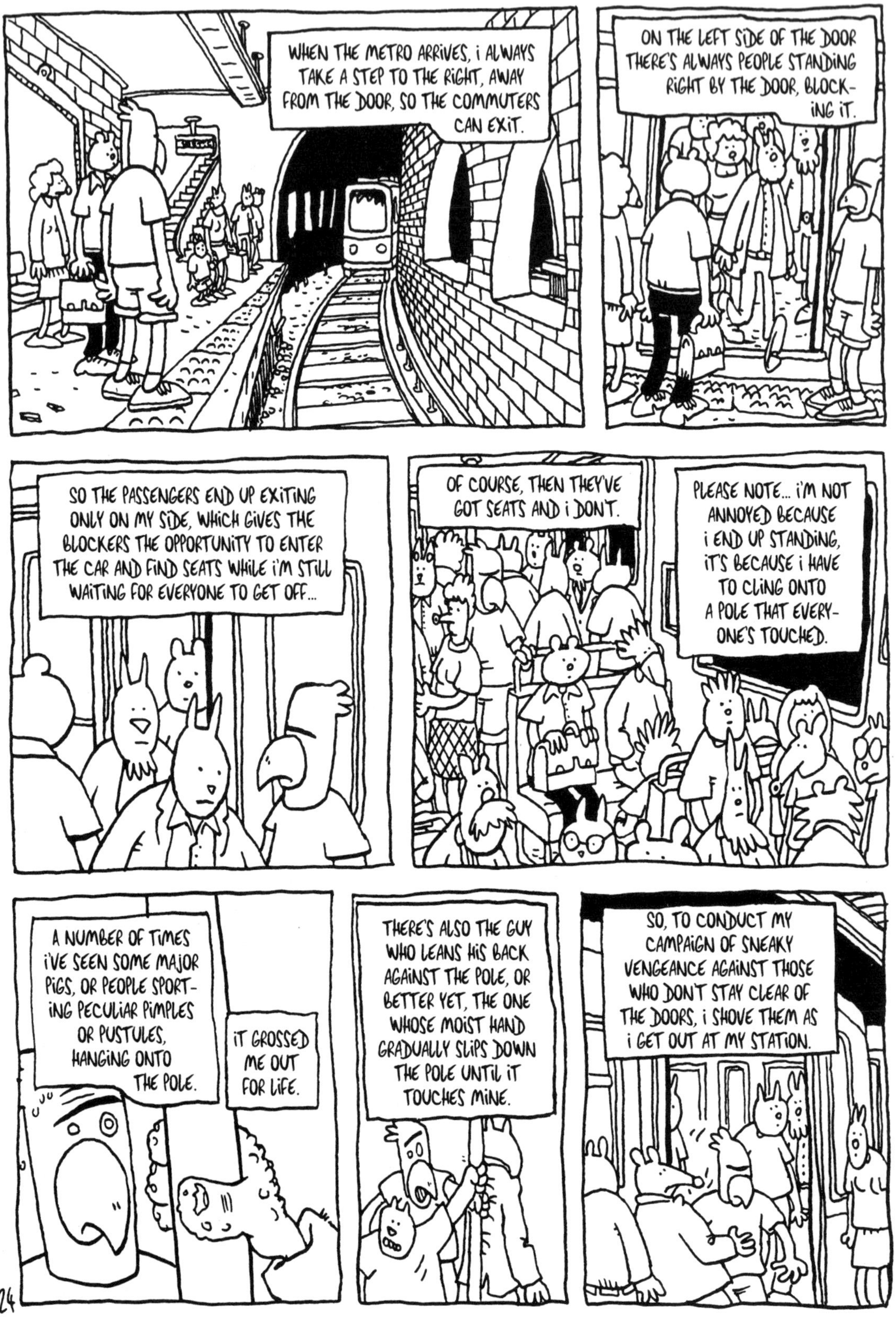
WHEN THE METRO ARRIVES, I ALWAYS TAKE A STEP TO THE RIGHT, AWAY FROM THE DOOR, SO THE COMMUTERS CAN EXIT.
ON THE LEFT SIDE OF THE DOOR THERE'S ALWAYS PEOPLE STANDING RIGHT BY THE DOOR, BLOCKING IT.
SO THE PASSENGERS END UP EXITING ONLY ON MY SIDE, WHICH GIVES THE BLOCKERS THE OPPORTUNITY TO ENTER THE CAR AND FIND SEATS WHILE I'M STILL WAITING FOR EVERYONE TO GET OFF...
OF COURSE, THEN THEY'VE GOT SEATS AND I DON'T.
PLEASE NOTE... I'M NOT ANNOYED BECAUSE I END UP STANDING, IT'S BECAUSE I HAVE TO CLING ONTO A POLE THAT EVERYONE'S TOUCHED.
A NUMBER OF TIMES I'VE SEEN SOME MAJOR PIGS, OR PEOPLE SPORTING PECULIAR PIMPLES OR PUSTULES, HANGING ONTO THE POLE.
IT GROSSED ME OUT FOR LIFE.
THERE'S ALSO THE GUY WHO LEANS HIS BACK AGAINST THE POLE, OR BETTER YET, THE ONE WHOSE MOIST HAND GRADUALLY SLIPS DOWN THE POLE UNTIL IT TOUCHES MINE.
SO, TO CONDUCT MY CAMPAIGN OF SNEAKY VENGEANCE AGAINST THOSE WHO DON'T STAY CLEAR OF THE DOORS, I SHOVE THEM AS I GET OUT AT MY STATION.

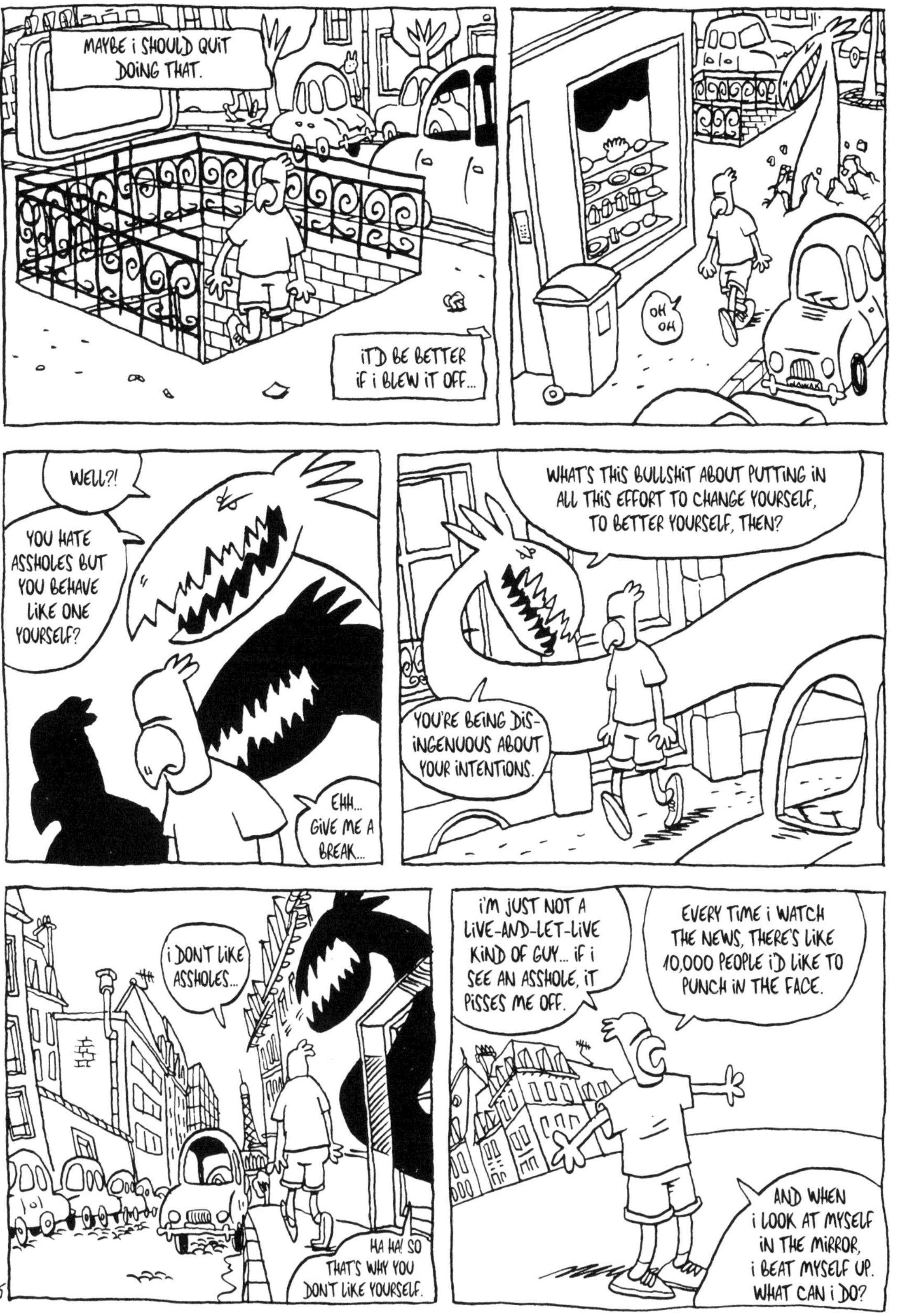
MAYBE i SHOULD QUIT DOING THAT.
iT'D BE BETTER iF i BLEW iT OFF...
OH OH
WELL?!
YOU HATE ASSHOLES BUT YOU BEHAVE LIKE ONE YOURSELF?
EHH... GIVE ME A BREAK...
WHAT'S THIS BULLSHIT ABOUT PUTTING iN ALL THIS EFFORT TO CHANGE YOURSELF, TO BETTER YOURSELF, THEN?
YOU'RE BEING DIS-iNGENUOUS ABOUT YOUR iNTENTIONS.
i DON'T LIKE ASSHOLES...
HA HA! SO THAT'S WHY YOU DON'T LIKE YOURSELF.
i'M JUST NOT A LIVE-AND-LET-LIVE KIND OF GUY... iF i SEE AN ASSHOLE, iT PISSES ME OFF.
EVERY TIME i WATCH THE NEWS, THERE'S LIKE 10,000 PEOPLE i'D LIKE TO PUNCH iN THE FACE.
AND WHEN i LOOK AT MYSELF iN THE MIRROR, i BEAT MYSELF UP. WHAT CAN i DO?

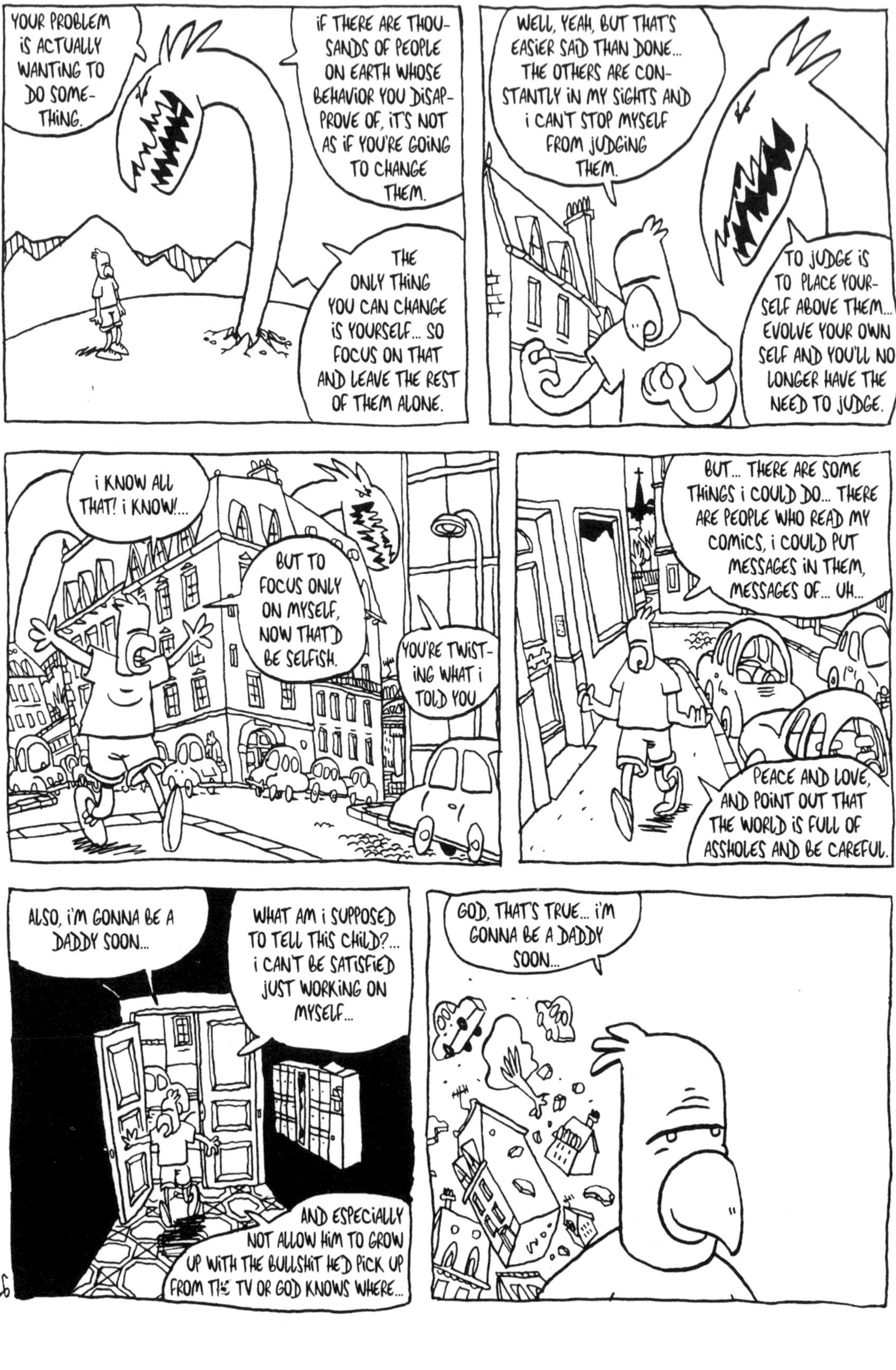
YOUR PROBLEM IS ACTUALLY WANTING TO DO SOME-THING.
IF THERE ARE THOUSANDS OF PEOPLE ON EARTH WHOSE BEHAVIOR YOU DISAPPROVE OF, IT'S NOT AS IF YOU'RE GOING TO CHANGE THEM.
THE ONLY THING YOU CAN CHANGE IS YOURSELF... SO FOCUS ON THAT AND LEAVE THE REST OF THEM ALONE.
WELL, YEAH, BUT THAT'S EASIER SAID THAN DONE... THE OTHERS ARE CONSTANTLY IN MY SIGHTS AND I CAN'T STOP MYSELF FROM JUDGING THEM.
TO JUDGE IS TO PLACE YOURSELF ABOVE THEM... EVOLVE YOUR OWN SELF AND YOU'LL NO LONGER HAVE THE NEED TO JUDGE.
I KNOW ALL THAT! I KNOW!...
BUT TO FOCUS ONLY ON MYSELF, NOW THAT'D BE SELFISH.
YOU'RE TWISTING WHAT I TOLD YOU
BUT... THERE ARE SOME THINGS I COULD DO... THERE ARE PEOPLE WHO READ MY COMICS, I COULD PUT MESSAGES IN THEM, MESSAGES OF... UH...
PEACE AND LOVE, AND POINT OUT THAT THE WORLD IS FULL OF ASSHOLES AND BE CAREFUL.
ALSO, I'M GONNA BE A DADDY SOON...
WHAT AM I SUPPOSED TO TELL THIS CHILD?... I CAN'T BE SATISFIED JUST WORKING ON MYSELF...
AND ESPECIALLY NOT ALLOW HIM TO GROW UP WITH THE BULLSHIT HE'D PICK UP FROM THE TV OR GOD KNOWS WHERE...
GOD, THAT'S TRUE... I'M GONNA BE A DADDY SOON...

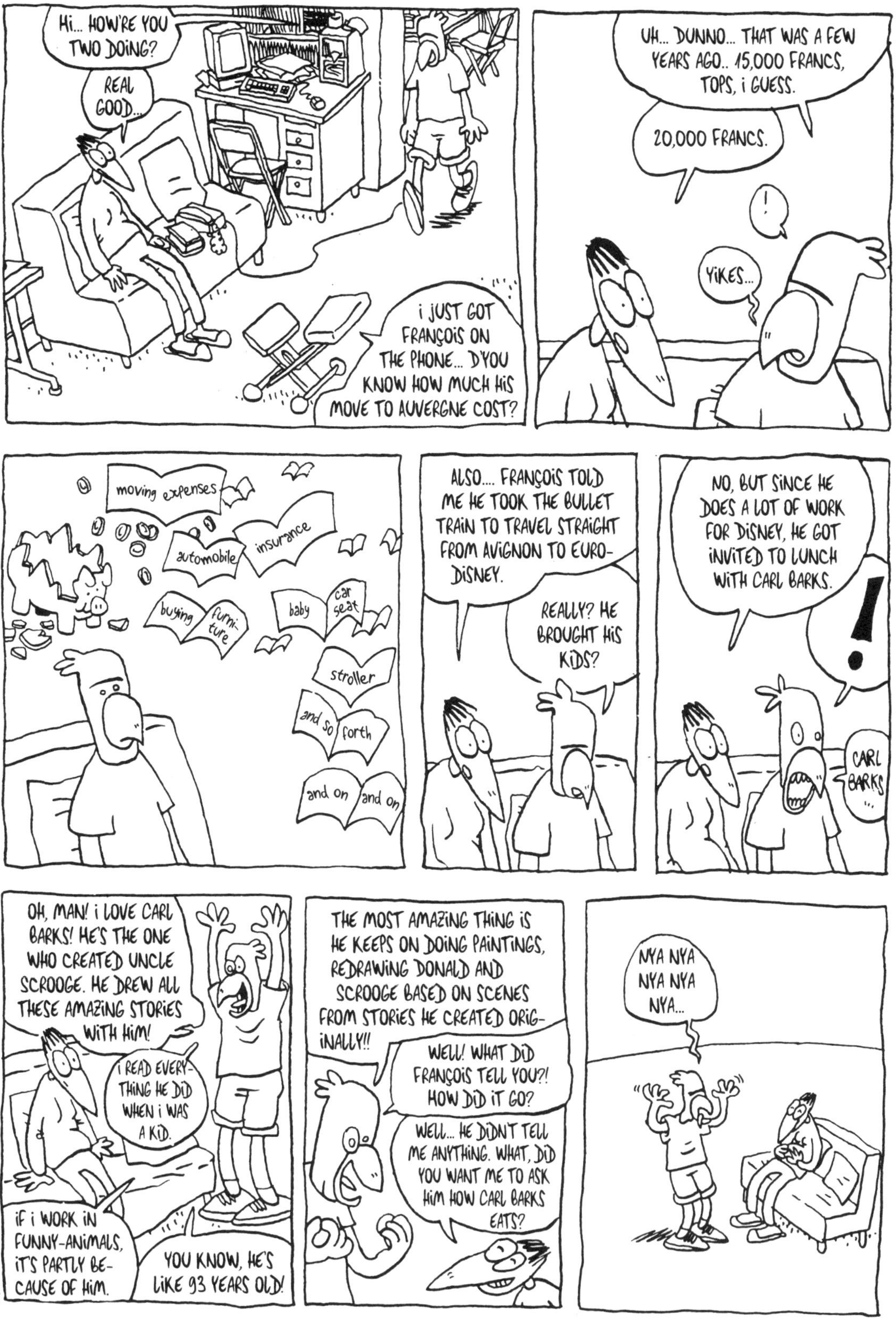

Hi... HOW'RE YOU TWO DOING?
REAL GOOD...
i JUST GOT FRANÇOIS ON THE PHONE... D'YOU KNOW HOW MUCH HIS MOVE TO AUVERGNE COST?
UH... DUNNO... THAT WAS A FEW YEARS AGO.. 15,000 FRANCS, TOPS, i GUESS.
20,000 FRANCS.
!
YIKES...
moving expenses
automobile
insurance
buying furniture
baby car seat
stroller
and so forth
and on and on
ALSO.... FRANÇOIS TOLD ME HE TOOK THE BULLET TRAIN TO TRAVEL STRAIGHT FROM AVIGNON TO EURO-DISNEY.
REALLY? HE BROUGHT HIS KIDS?
NO, BUT SINCE HE DOES A LOT OF WORK FOR DISNEY, HE GOT INVITED TO LUNCH WITH CARL BARKS.
!
CARL BARKS...
OH, MAN! i LOVE CARL BARKS! HE'S THE ONE WHO CREATED UNCLE SCROOGE. HE DREW ALL THESE AMAZING STORIES WITH HIM!
i READ EVERYTHING HE DID WHEN i WAS A KID.
iF i WORK IN FUNNY-ANIMALS, iT'S PARTLY BECAUSE OF HIM.
YOU KNOW, HE'S LIKE 93 YEARS OLD!
THE MOST AMAZING THING IS HE KEEPS ON DOING PAINTINGS, REDRAWING DONALD AND SCROOGE BASED ON SCENES FROM STORIES HE CREATED ORIGINALLY!!
WELL! WHAT DID FRANÇOIS TELL YOU?! HOW DID IT GO?
WELL... HE DIDN'T TELL ME ANYTHING. WHAT, DID YOU WANT ME TO ASK HIM HOW CARL BARKS EATS?
NYA NYA NYA NYA NYA...

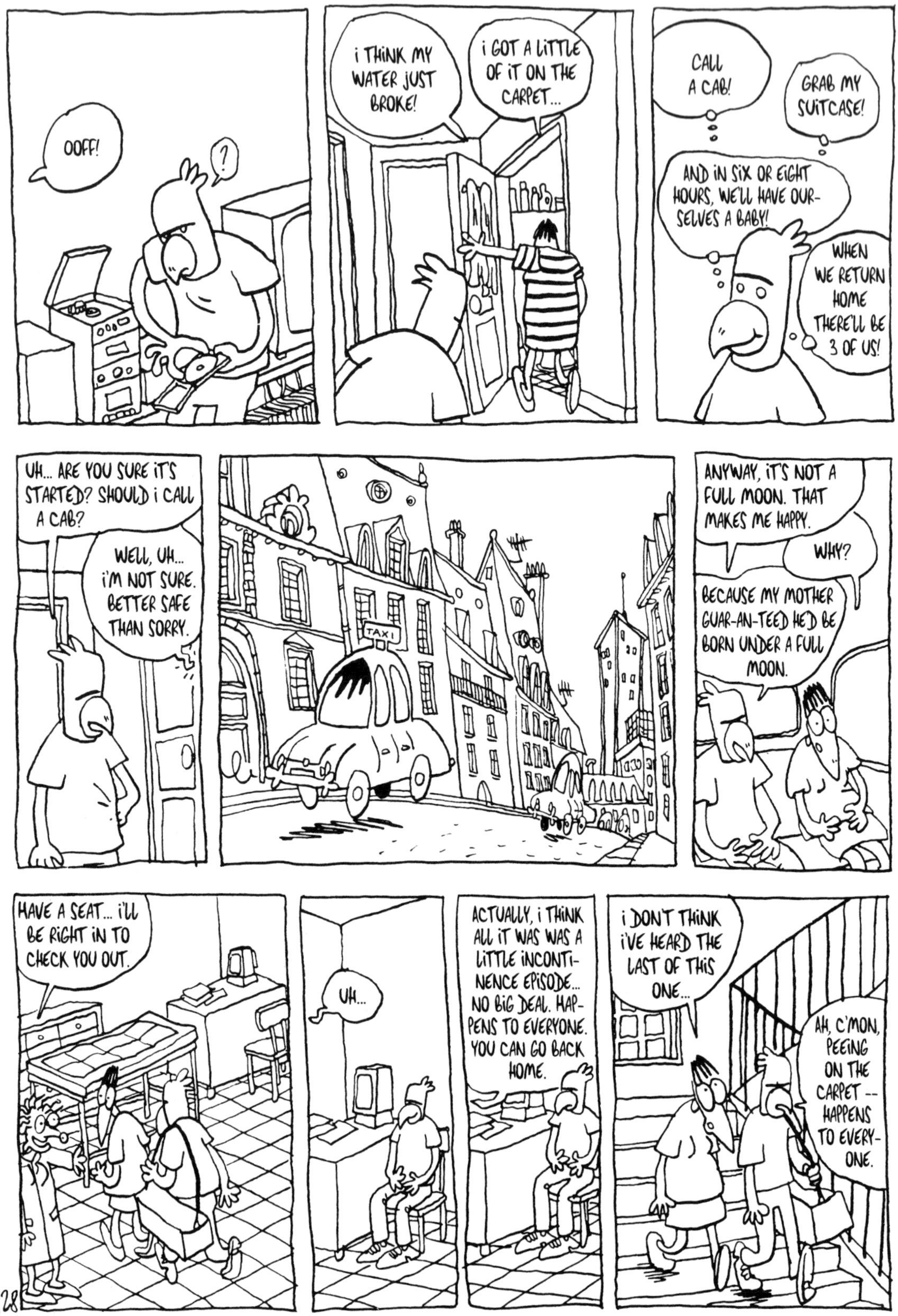
OOFF!
?
I THINK MY WATER JUST BROKE!
I GOT A LITTLE OF IT ON THE CARPET...
CALL A CAB!
GRAB MY SUITCASE!
AND IN SIX OR EIGHT HOURS, WE'LL HAVE OURSELVES A BABY!
WHEN WE RETURN HOME THERE'LL BE 3 OF US!
UH... ARE YOU SURE IT'S STARTED? SHOULD I CALL A CAB?
WELL, UH... I'M NOT SURE. BETTER SAFE THAN SORRY.
TAXI
ANYWAY, IT'S NOT A FULL MOON. THAT MAKES ME HAPPY.
WHY?
BECAUSE MY MOTHER GUAR-AN-TEED HE'D BE BORN UNDER A FULL MOON.
HAVE A SEAT... I'LL BE RIGHT IN TO CHECK YOU OUT.
UH...
ACTUALLY, I THINK ALL IT WAS WAS A LITTLE INCONTINENCE EPISODE... NO BIG DEAL. HAPPENS TO EVERYONE. YOU CAN GO BACK HOME.
I DON'T THINK I'VE HEARD THE LAST OF THIS ONE...
AH, C'MON, PEEING ON THE CARPET -- HAPPENS TO EVERYONE.

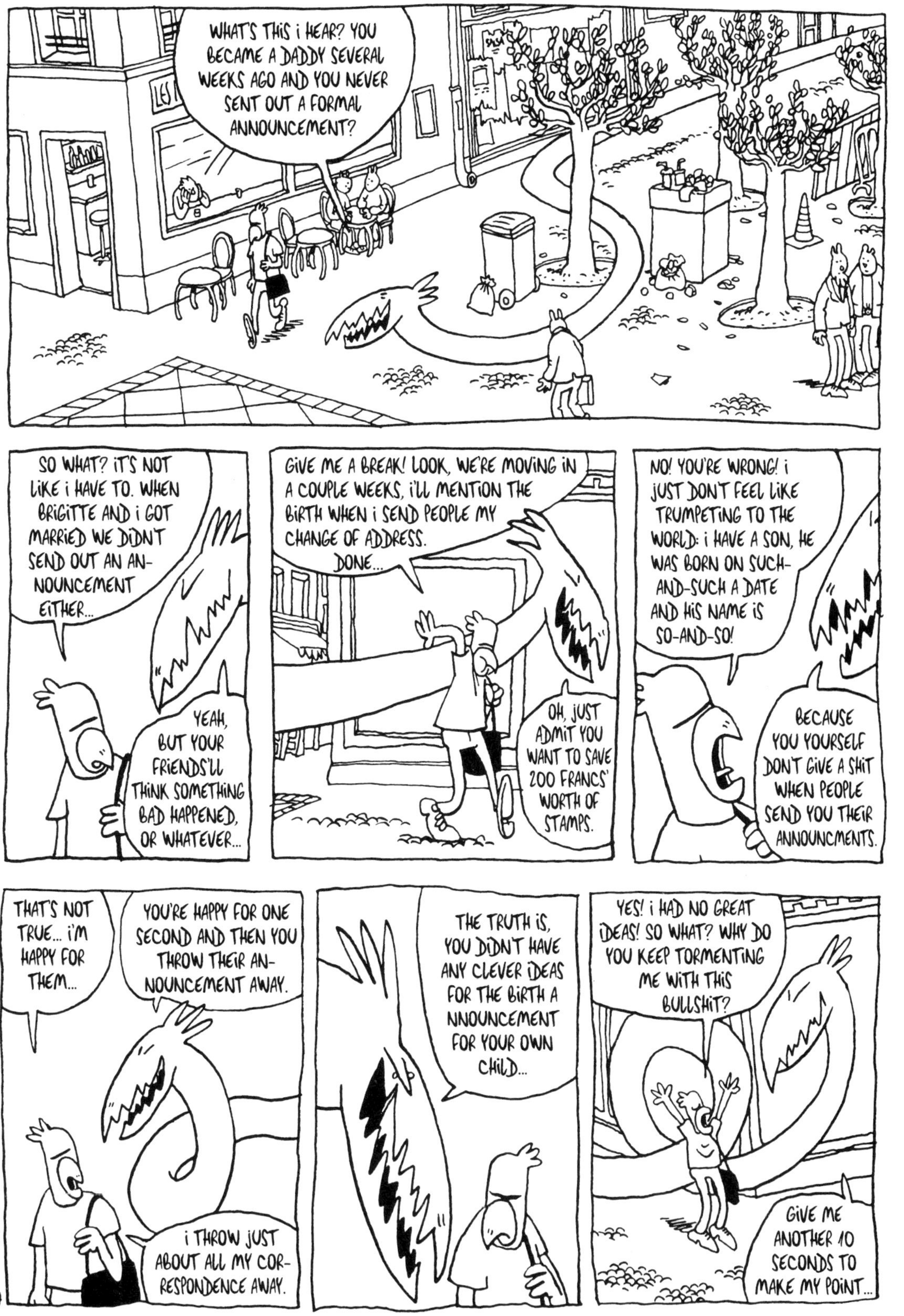
WHAT'S THIS i HEAR? YOU BECAME A DADDY SEVERAL WEEKS AGO AND YOU NEVER SENT OUT A FORMAL ANNOUNCEMENT?
SO WHAT? iT'S NOT LiKE i HAVE TO. WHEN BRiGiTTE AND i GOT MARRiED WE DiDN'T SEND OUT AN AN-NOUNCEMENT EiTHER...
YEAH, BUT YOUR FRiENDS'LL THiNK SOMETHiNG BAD HAPPENED, OR WHATEVER...
GiVE ME A BREAK! LOOK, WE'RE MOViNG iN A COUPLE WEEKS, i'LL MENTiON THE BiRTH WHEN i SEND PEOPLE MY CHANGE OF ADDRESS. DONE...
OH, JUST ADMiT YOU WANT TO SAVE 200 FRANCS' WORTH OF STAMPS.
NO! YOU'RE WRONG! i JUST DON'T FEEL LiKE TRUMPETiNG TO THE WORLD: i HAVE A SON, HE WAS BORN ON SUCH-AND-SUCH A DATE AND HiS NAME iS SO-AND-SO!
BECAUSE YOU YOURSELF DON'T GiVE A SHiT WHEN PEOPLE SEND YOU THEiR ANNOUNCMENTS.
THAT'S NOT TRUE... i'M HAPPY FOR THEM...
YOU'RE HAPPY FOR ONE SECOND AND THEN YOU THROW THEiR AN-NOUNCEMENT AWAY.
i THROW JUST ABOUT ALL MY COR-RESPONDENCE AWAY.
THE TRUTH iS, YOU DiDN'T HAVE ANY CLEVER iDEAS FOR THE BiRTH A NNOUNCEMENT FOR YOUR OWN CHiLD...
YES! i HAD NO GREAT iDEAS! SO WHAT? WHY DO YOU KEEP TORMENTiNG ME WiTH THiS BULLSHiT?
GiVE ME ANOTHER 10 SECONDS TO MAKE MY POiNT...

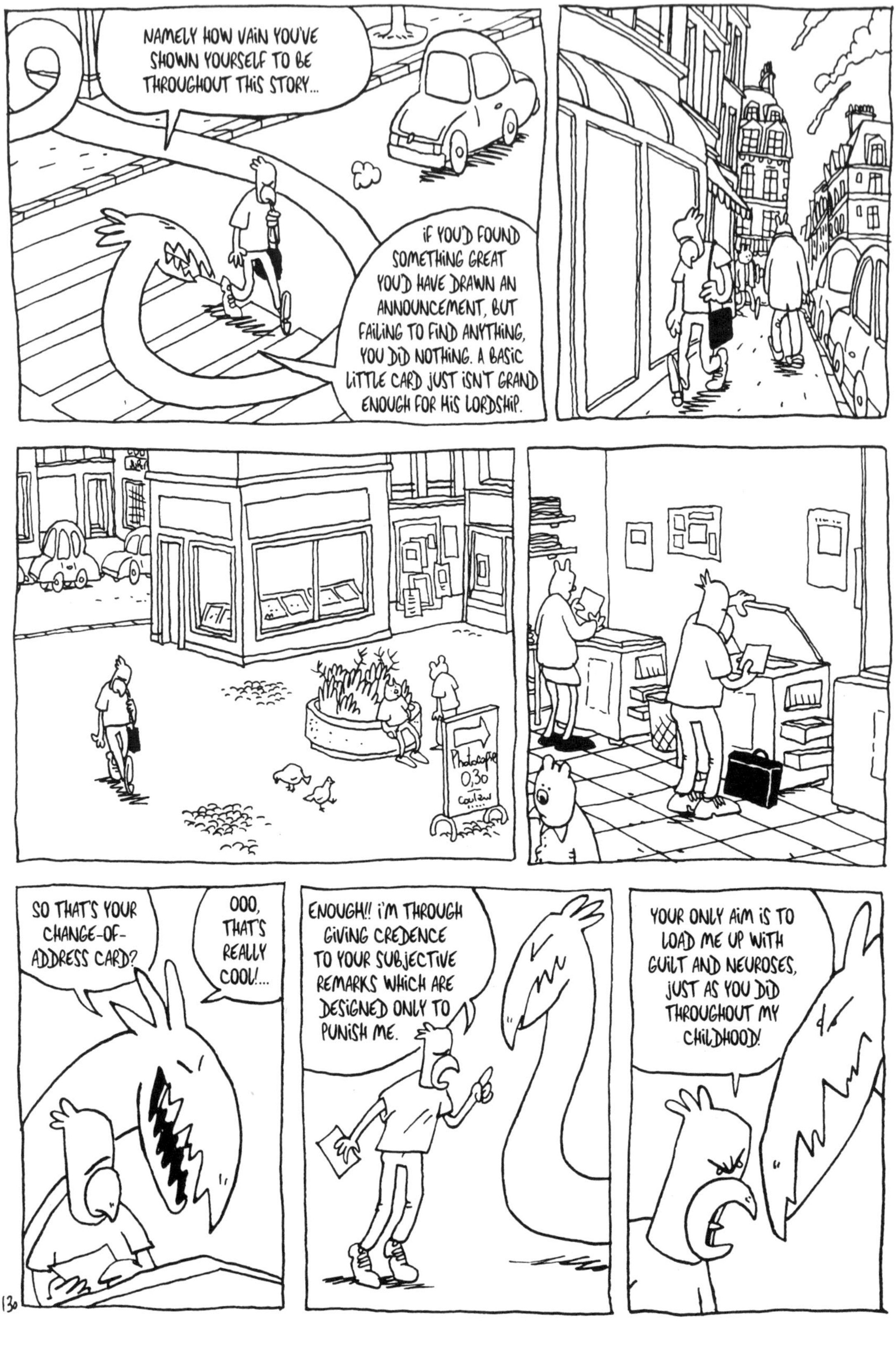
NAMELY HOW VAIN YOU'VE SHOWN YOURSELF TO BE THROUGHOUT THIS STORY...
IF YOU'D FOUND SOMETHING GREAT YOU'D HAVE DRAWN AN ANNOUNCEMENT, BUT FAILING TO FIND ANYTHING, YOU DID NOTHING. A BASIC LITTLE CARD JUST ISN'T GRAND ENOUGH FOR HIS LORDSHIP.
Photocopie
0,30
Couleur
SO THAT'S YOUR CHANGE-OF-ADDRESS CARD?
OOO, THAT'S REALLY COOL!...
ENOUGH!! I'M THROUGH GIVING CREDENCE TO YOUR SUBJECTIVE REMARKS WHICH ARE DESIGNED ONLY TO PUNISH ME.
YOUR ONLY AIM IS TO LOAD ME UP WITH GUILT AND NEUROSES, JUST AS YOU DID THROUGHOUT MY CHILDHOOD!

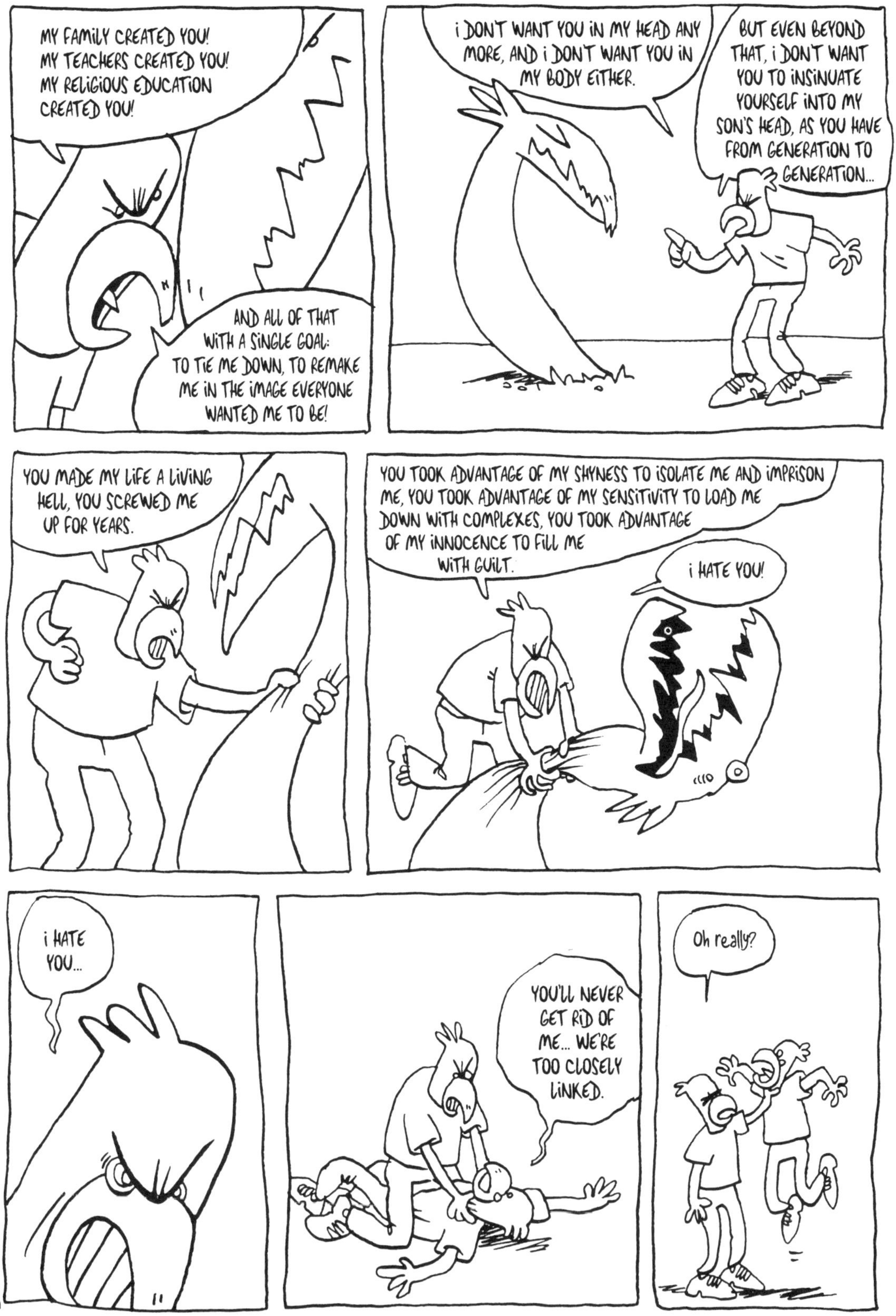
MY FAMILY CREATED YOU! MY TEACHERS CREATED YOU! MY RELIGIOUS EDUCATION CREATED YOU!
AND ALL OF THAT WITH A SINGLE GOAL: TO TIE ME DOWN, TO REMAKE ME IN THE IMAGE EVERYONE WANTED ME TO BE!
I DON'T WANT YOU IN MY HEAD ANY MORE, AND I DON'T WANT YOU IN MY BODY EITHER.
BUT EVEN BEYOND THAT, I DON'T WANT YOU TO INSINUATE YOURSELF INTO MY SON'S HEAD, AS YOU HAVE FROM GENERATION TO GENERATION...
YOU MADE MY LIFE A LIVING HELL, YOU SCREWED ME UP FOR YEARS.
YOU TOOK ADVANTAGE OF MY SHYNESS TO ISOLATE ME AND IMPRISON ME, YOU TOOK ADVANTAGE OF MY SENSITIVITY TO LOAD ME DOWN WITH COMPLEXES, YOU TOOK ADVANTAGE OF MY INNOCENCE TO FILL ME WITH GUILT.
I HATE YOU!
I HATE YOU...
YOU'LL NEVER GET RID OF ME... WE'RE TOO CLOSELY LINKED.
Oh really?

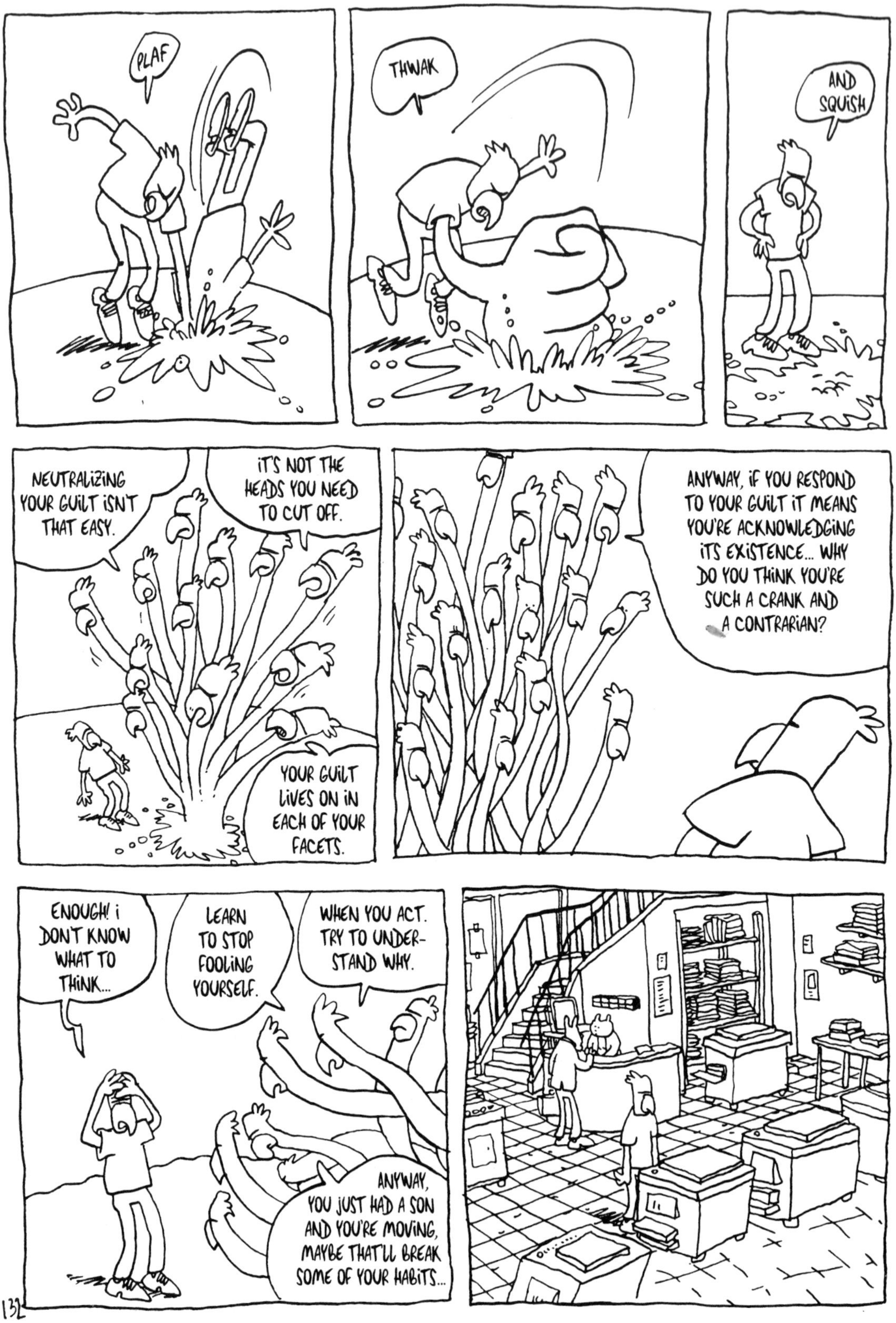
PLAF
THWAK
AND SQUISH
NEUTRALIZING YOUR GUILT ISN'T THAT EASY.
IT'S NOT THE HEADS YOU NEED TO CUT OFF.
YOUR GUILT LIVES ON IN EACH OF YOUR FACETS.
ANYWAY, IF YOU RESPOND TO YOUR GUILT IT MEANS YOU'RE ACKNOWLEDGING ITS EXISTENCE... WHY DO YOU THINK YOU'RE SUCH A CRANK AND A CONTRARIAN?
ENOUGH! I DON'T KNOW WHAT TO THINK...
LEARN TO STOP FOOLING YOURSELF.
WHEN YOU ACT. TRY TO UNDERSTAND WHY.
ANYWAY, YOU JUST HAD A SON AND YOU'RE MOVING, MAYBE THAT'LL BREAK SOME OF YOUR HABITS...

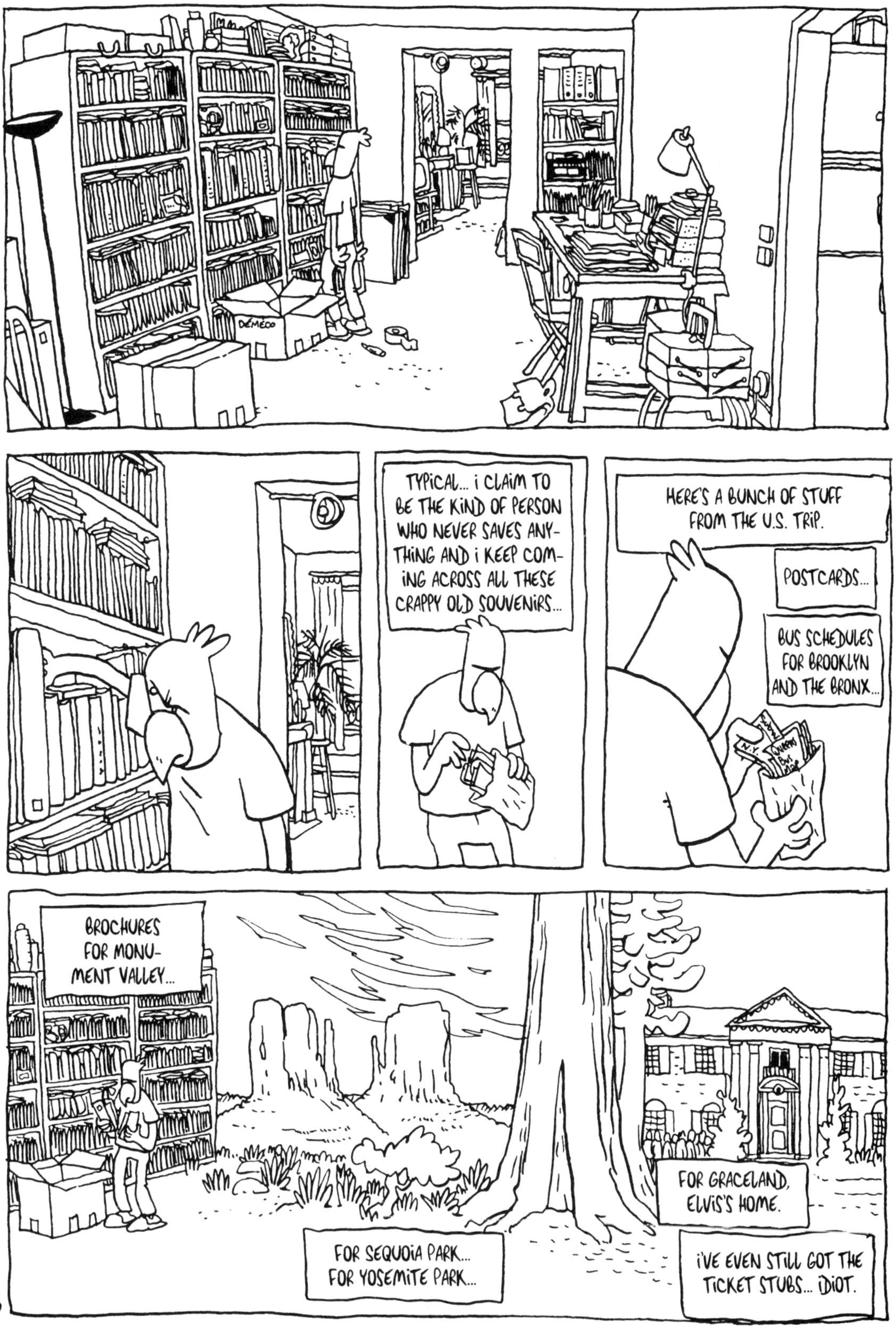
DÉMÉCO
TYPICAL... I CLAIM TO BE THE KIND OF PERSON WHO NEVER SAVES ANYTHING AND I KEEP COMING ACROSS ALL THESE CRAPPY OLD SOUVENIRS...
HERE'S A BUNCH OF STUFF FROM THE U.S. TRIP.
POSTCARDS...
BUS SCHEDULES FOR BROOKLYN AND THE BRONX...
BROCHURES FOR MONUMENT VALLEY...
FOR SEQUOIA PARK... FOR YOSEMITE PARK...
FOR GRACELAND, ELVIS'S HOME.
I'VE EVEN STILL GOT THE TICKET STUBS... IDIOT.

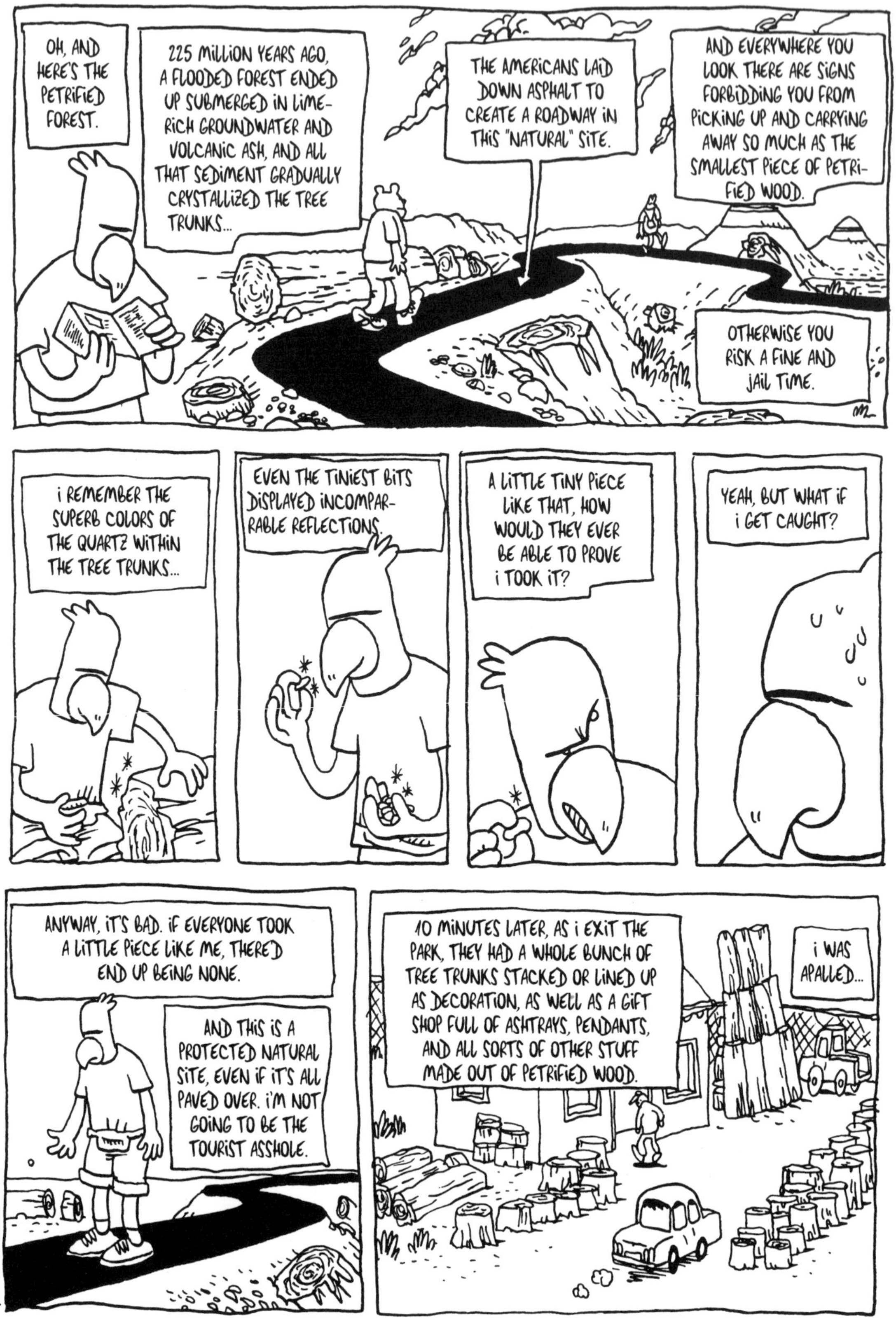
OH, AND HERE'S THE PETRIFIED FOREST.
225 MILLION YEARS AGO, A FLOODED FOREST ENDED UP SUBMERGED IN LIME-RICH GROUNDWATER AND VOLCANIC ASH, AND ALL THAT SEDIMENT GRADUALLY CRYSTALLIZED THE TREE TRUNKS...
THE AMERICANS LAID DOWN ASPHALT TO CREATE A ROADWAY IN THIS "NATURAL" SITE.
AND EVERYWHERE YOU LOOK THERE ARE SIGNS FORBIDDING YOU FROM PICKING UP AND CARRYING AWAY SO MUCH AS THE SMALLEST PIECE OF PETRIFIED WOOD.
OTHERWISE YOU RISK A FINE AND JAIL TIME.
I REMEMBER THE SUPERB COLORS OF THE QUARTZ WITHIN THE TREE TRUNKS...
EVEN THE TINIEST BITS DISPLAYED INCOMPARABLE REFLECTIONS.
A LITTLE TINY PIECE LIKE THAT, HOW WOULD THEY EVER BE ABLE TO PROVE I TOOK IT?
YEAH, BUT WHAT IF I GET CAUGHT?
ANYWAY, IT'S BAD. IF EVERYONE TOOK A LITTLE PIECE LIKE ME, THERE'D END UP BEING NONE.
AND THIS IS A PROTECTED NATURAL SITE, EVEN IF IT'S ALL PAVED OVER. I'M NOT GOING TO BE THE TOURIST ASSHOLE.
10 MINUTES LATER, AS I EXIT THE PARK, THEY HAD A WHOLE BUNCH OF TREE TRUNKS STACKED OR LINED UP AS DECORATION, AS WELL AS A GIFT SHOP FULL OF ASHTRAYS, PENDANTS, AND ALL SORTS OF OTHER STUFF MADE OUT OF PETRIFIED WOOD.
I WAS APALLED...

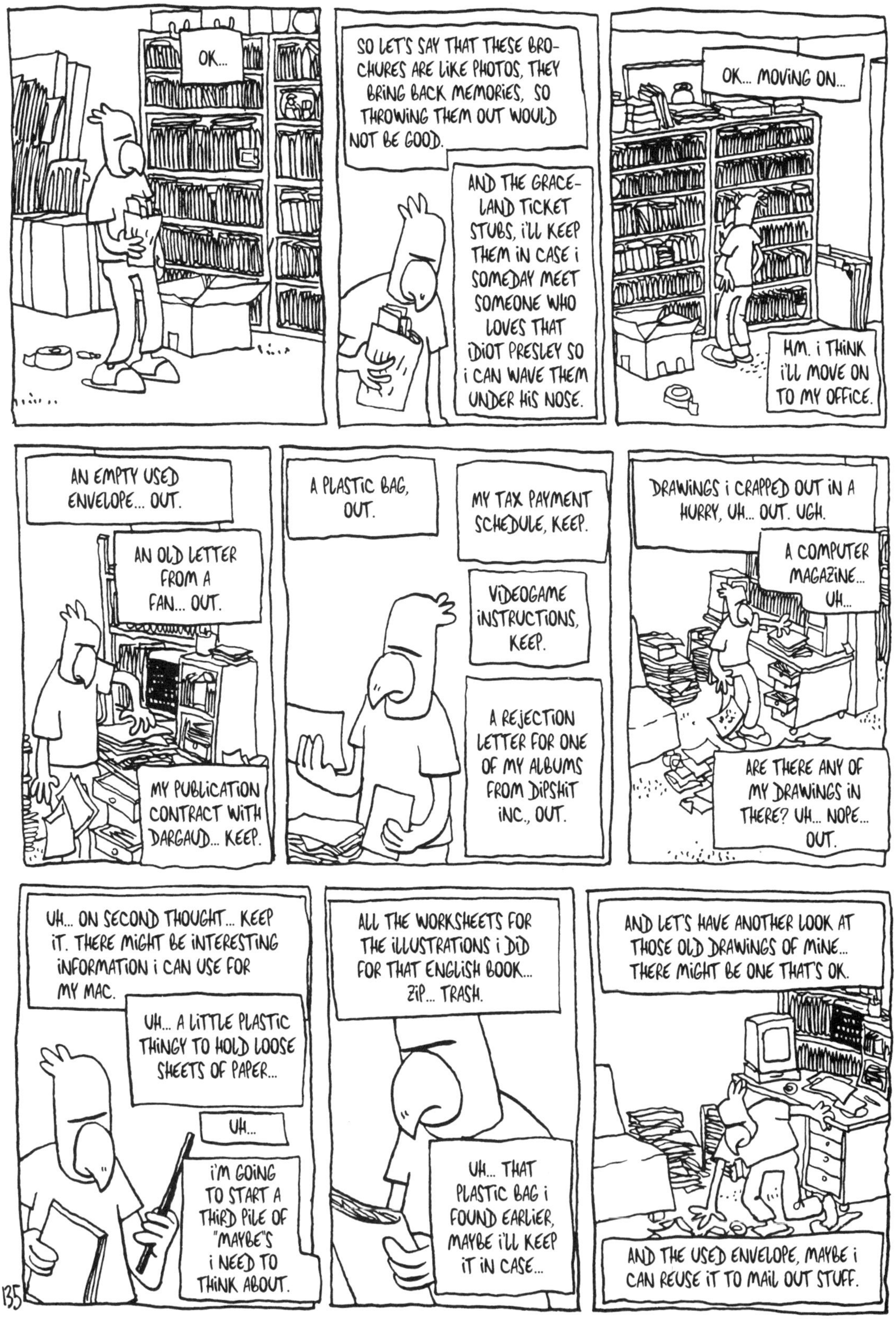
OK...
SO LET'S SAY THAT THESE BROCHURES ARE LIKE PHOTOS, THEY BRING BACK MEMORIES, SO THROWING THEM OUT WOULD NOT BE GOOD.
AND THE GRACELAND TICKET STUBS, I'LL KEEP THEM IN CASE I SOMEDAY MEET SOMEONE WHO LOVES THAT IDIOT PRESLEY SO I CAN WAVE THEM UNDER HIS NOSE.
OK... MOVING ON...
HM. I THINK I'LL MOVE ON TO MY OFFICE.
AN EMPTY USED ENVELOPE... OUT.
AN OLD LETTER FROM A FAN... OUT.
MY PUBLICATION CONTRACT WITH DARGAUD... KEEP.
A PLASTIC BAG, OUT.
MY TAX PAYMENT SCHEDULE, KEEP.
VIDEOGAME INSTRUCTIONS, KEEP.
A REJECTION LETTER FOR ONE OF MY ALBUMS FROM DIPSHIT INC., OUT.
DRAWINGS I CRAPPED OUT IN A HURRY, UH... OUT. UGH.
A COMPUTER MAGAZINE... UH...
ARE THERE ANY OF MY DRAWINGS IN THERE? UH... NOPE... OUT.
UH... ON SECOND THOUGHT... KEEP IT. THERE MIGHT BE INTERESTING INFORMATION I CAN USE FOR MY MAC.
UH... A LITTLE PLASTIC THINGY TO HOLD LOOSE SHEETS OF PAPER...
UH...
I'M GOING TO START A THIRD PILE OF "MAYBE"S I NEED TO THINK ABOUT.
ALL THE WORKSHEETS FOR THE ILLUSTRATIONS I DID FOR THAT ENGLISH BOOK... ZIP... TRASH.
UH... THAT PLASTIC BAG I FOUND EARLIER, MAYBE I'LL KEEP IT IN CASE...
AND LET'S HAVE ANOTHER LOOK AT THOSE OLD DRAWINGS OF MINE... THERE MIGHT BE ONE THAT'S OK.
AND THE USED ENVELOPE, MAYBE I CAN REUSE IT TO MAIL OUT STUFF.

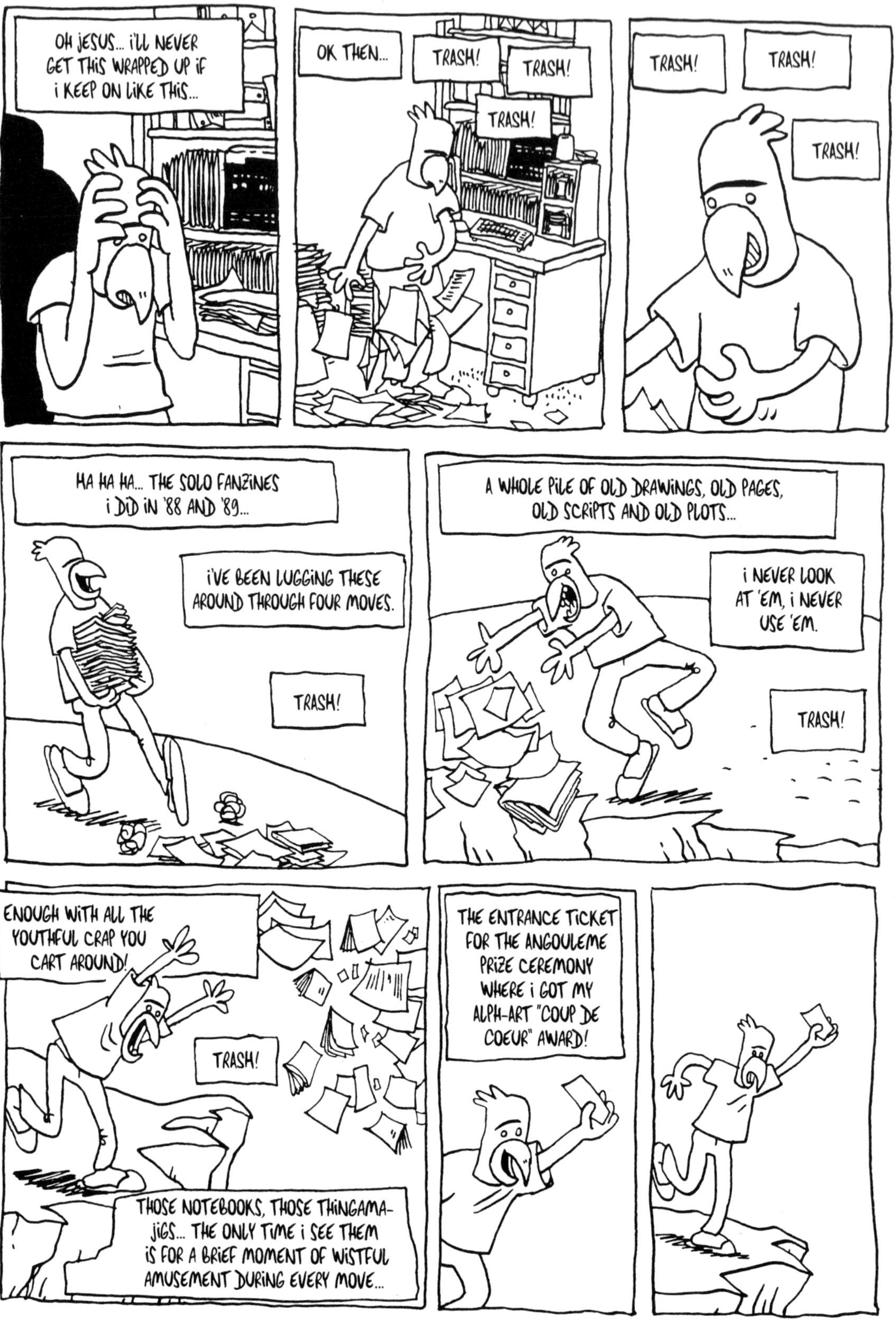
OH JESUS... i'LL NEVER GET THIS WRAPPED UP iF i KEEP ON LiKE THIS...
OK THEN...
TRASH!
TRASH!
TRASH!
TRASH!
TRASH!
TRASH!
HA HA HA... THE SOLO FANZiNES i DiD iN '88 AND '89...
i'VE BEEN LUGGiNG THESE AROUND THROUGH FOUR MOVES.
TRASH!
A WHOLE PiLE OF OLD DRAWiNGS, OLD PAGES, OLD SCRiPTS AND OLD PLOTS...
i NEVER LOOK AT 'EM, i NEVER USE 'EM.
TRASH!
ENOUGH WiTH ALL THE YOUTHFUL CRAP YOU CART AROUND!
TRASH!
THOSE NOTEBOOKS, THOSE THiNGAMA-JiGS... THE ONLY TiME i SEE THEM iS FOR A BRiEF MOMENT OF WiSTFUL AMUSEMENT DURiNG EVERY MOVE...
THE ENTRANCE TiCKET FOR THE ANGOULEME PRiZE CEREMONY WHERE i GOT MY ALPH-ART "COUP DE COEUR" AWARD!

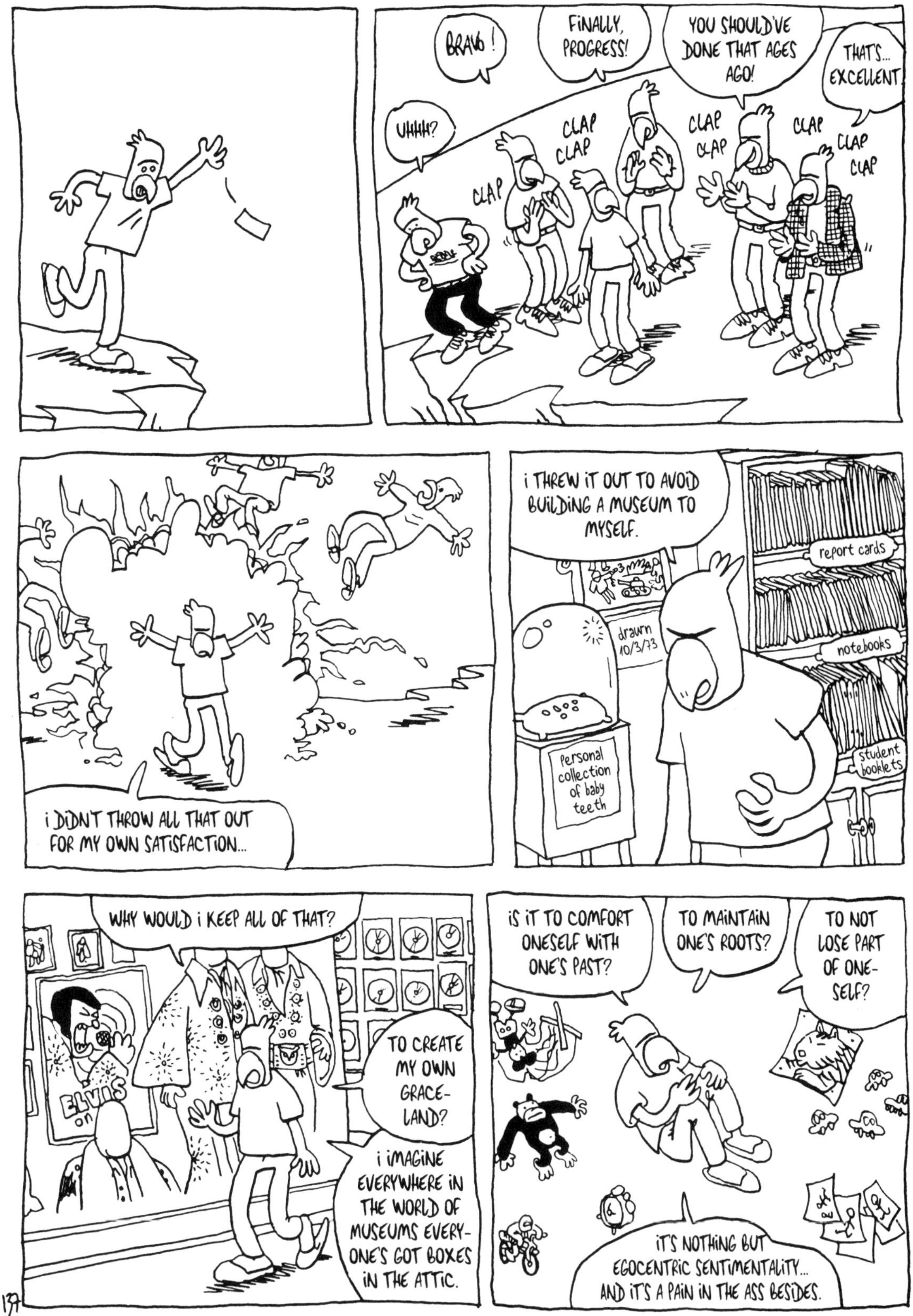
BRAVO!
FINALLY, PROGRESS!
YOU SHOULD'VE DONE THAT AGES AGO!
THAT'S... EXCELLENT.
UHHH?
CLAP
CLAP CLAP
CLAP CLAP
CLAP
CLAP CLAP
i DIDN'T THROW ALL THAT OUT FOR MY OWN SATISFACTION...
i THREW iT OUT TO AVOiD BUILDiNG A MUSEUM TO MYSELF.
report cards
notebooks
student booklets
drawn 10/3/73
personal collection of baby teeth
WHY WOULD i KEEP ALL OF THAT?
ELVIS on
TO CREATE MY OWN GRACE-LAND?
i iMAGINE EVERYWHERE iN THE WORLD OF MUSEUMS EVERY-ONE'S GOT BOXES iN THE ATTiC.
iS iT TO COMFORT ONESELF WiTH ONE'S PAST?
TO MAiNTAiN ONE'S ROOTS?
TO NOT LOSE PART OF ONE-SELF?
iT'S NOTHiNG BUT EGOCENTRiC SENTiMENTALiTY... AND iT'S A PAiN iN THE ASS BESiDES.

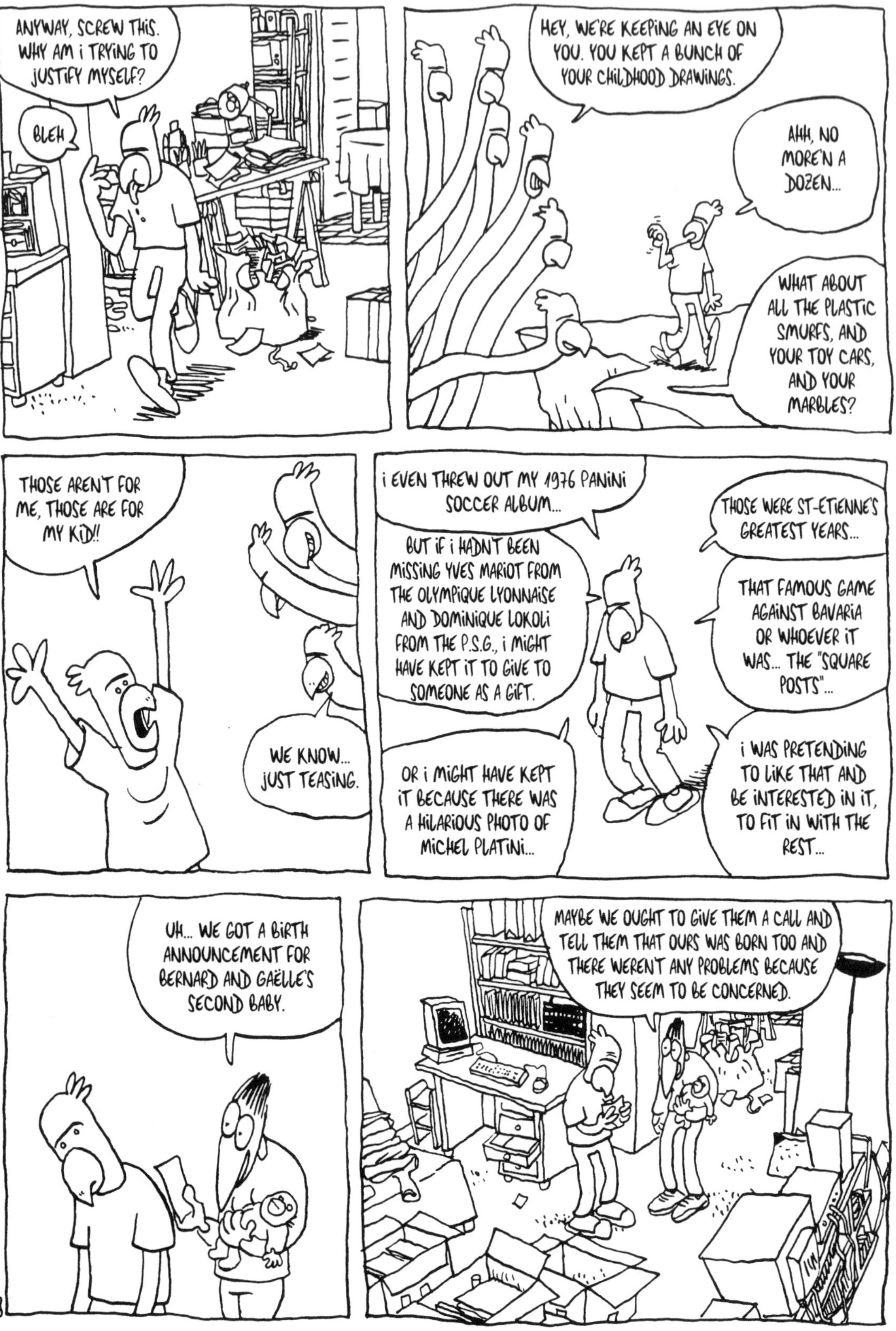
ANYWAY, SCREW THIS. WHY AM I TRYING TO JUSTIFY MYSELF?
BLEH
HEY, WE'RE KEEPING AN EYE ON YOU. YOU KEPT A BUNCH OF YOUR CHILDHOOD DRAWINGS.
AHH, NO MORE'N A DOZEN...
WHAT ABOUT ALL THE PLASTIC SMURFS, AND YOUR TOY CARS, AND YOUR MARBLES?
THOSE AREN'T FOR ME, THOSE ARE FOR MY KID!!
WE KNOW... JUST TEASING.
I EVEN THREW OUT MY 1976 PANINI SOCCER ALBUM...
BUT IF I HADN'T BEEN MISSING YVES MARIOT FROM THE OLYMPIQUE LYONNAISE AND DOMINIQUE LOKOLI FROM THE P.S.G., I MIGHT HAVE KEPT IT TO GIVE TO SOMEONE AS A GIFT.
THOSE WERE ST-ETIENNE'S GREATEST YEARS...
THAT FAMOUS GAME AGAINST BAVARIA OR WHOEVER IT WAS... THE "SQUARE POSTS"...
OR I MIGHT HAVE KEPT IT BECAUSE THERE WAS A HILARIOUS PHOTO OF MICHEL PLATINI...
I WAS PRETENDING TO LIKE THAT AND BE INTERESTED IN IT, TO FIT IN WITH THE REST...
UH... WE GOT A BIRTH ANNOUNCEMENT FOR BERNARD AND GAËLLE'S SECOND BABY.
MAYBE WE OUGHT TO GIVE THEM A CALL AND TELL THEM THAT OURS WAS BORN TOO AND THERE WEREN'T ANY PROBLEMS BECAUSE THEY SEEM TO BE CONCERNED.

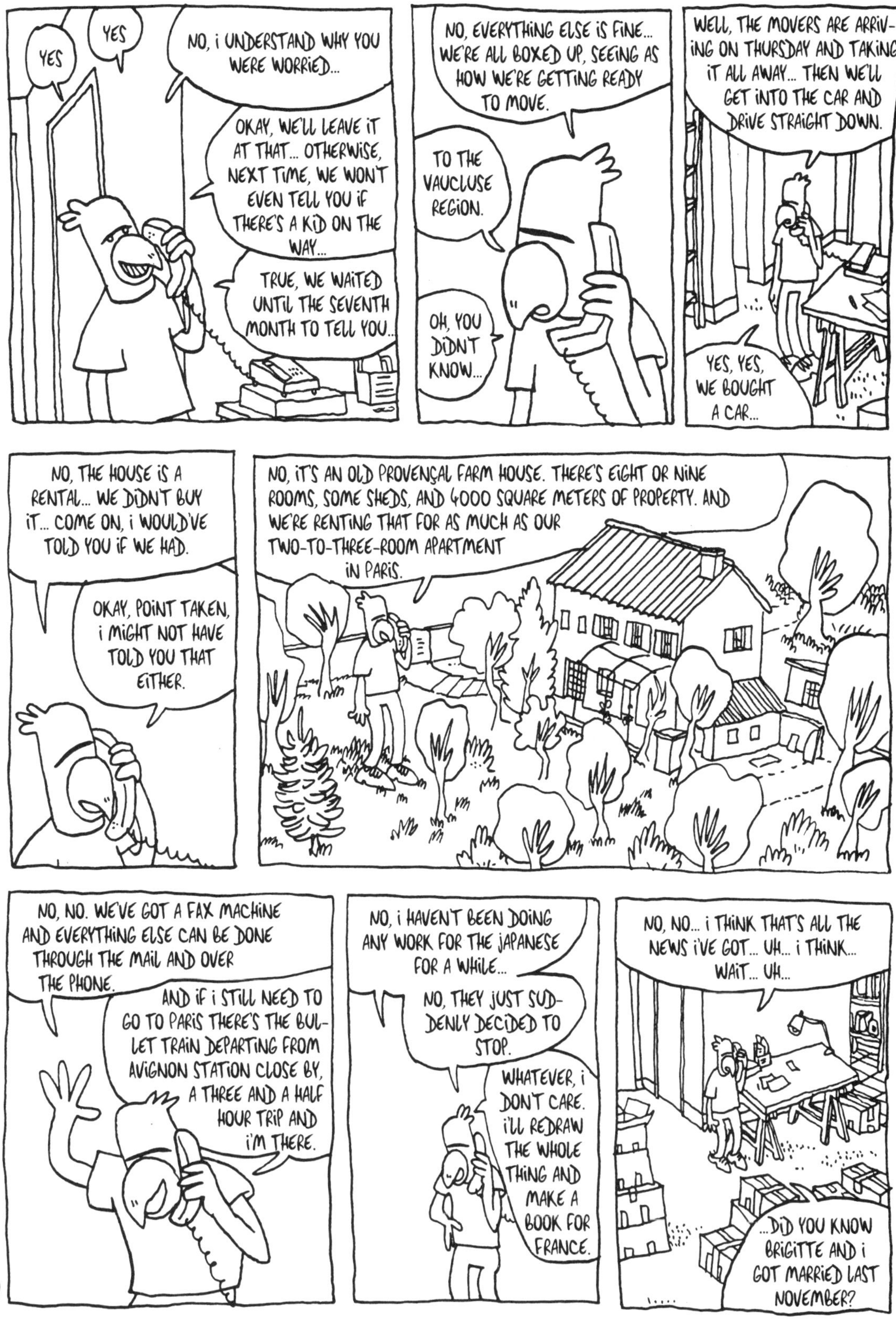
YES
YES
NO, i UNDERSTAND WHY YOU WERE WORRiED...
OKAY, WE'LL LEAVE iT AT THAT... OTHERWiSE, NEXT TiME, WE WON'T EVEN TELL YOU iF THERE'S A KiD ON THE WAY...
TRUE, WE WAiTED UNTiL THE SEVENTH MONTH TO TELL YOU...
NO, EVERYTHiNG ELSE iS FiNE... WE'RE ALL BOXED UP, SEEiNG AS HOW WE'RE GETTiNG READY TO MOVE.
TO THE VAUCLUSE REGiON.
OH, YOU DiDN'T KNOW...
WELL, THE MOVERS ARE ARRiV-iNG ON THURSDAY AND TAKiNG iT ALL AWAY... THEN WE'LL GET iNTO THE CAR AND DRiVE STRAiGHT DOWN.
YES, YES, WE BOUGHT A CAR...
NO, THE HOUSE iS A RENTAL... WE DiDN'T BUY iT... COME ON, i WOULD'VE TOLD YOU iF WE HAD.
OKAY, POiNT TAKEN, i MiGHT NOT HAVE TOLD YOU THAT EiTHER.
NO, iT'S AN OLD PROVENÇAL FARM HOUSE. THERE'S EiGHT OR NiNE ROOMS, SOME SHEDS, AND 4000 SQUARE METERS OF PROPERTY. AND WE'RE RENTiNG THAT FOR AS MUCH AS OUR TWO-TO-THREE-ROOM APARTMENT iN PARiS.
NO, NO. WE'VE GOT A FAX MACHiNE AND EVERYTHiNG ELSE CAN BE DONE THROUGH THE MAiL AND OVER THE PHONE.
AND iF i STiLL NEED TO GO TO PARiS THERE'S THE BUL-LET TRAiN DEPARTiNG FROM AViGNON STATiON CLOSE BY, A THREE AND A HALF HOUR TRiP AND i'M THERE.
NO, i HAVEN'T BEEN DOiNG ANY WORK FOR THE JAPANESE FOR A WHiLE...
NO, THEY JUST SUD-DENLY DECiDED TO STOP.
WHATEVER, i DON'T CARE. i'LL REDRAW THE WHOLE THiNG AND MAKE A BOOK FOR FRANCE.
NO, NO... i THiNK THAT'S ALL THE NEWS i'VE GOT... UH... i THiNK... WAiT... UH...
...DiD YOU KNOW BRiGiTTE AND i GOT MARRiED LAST NOVEMBER?

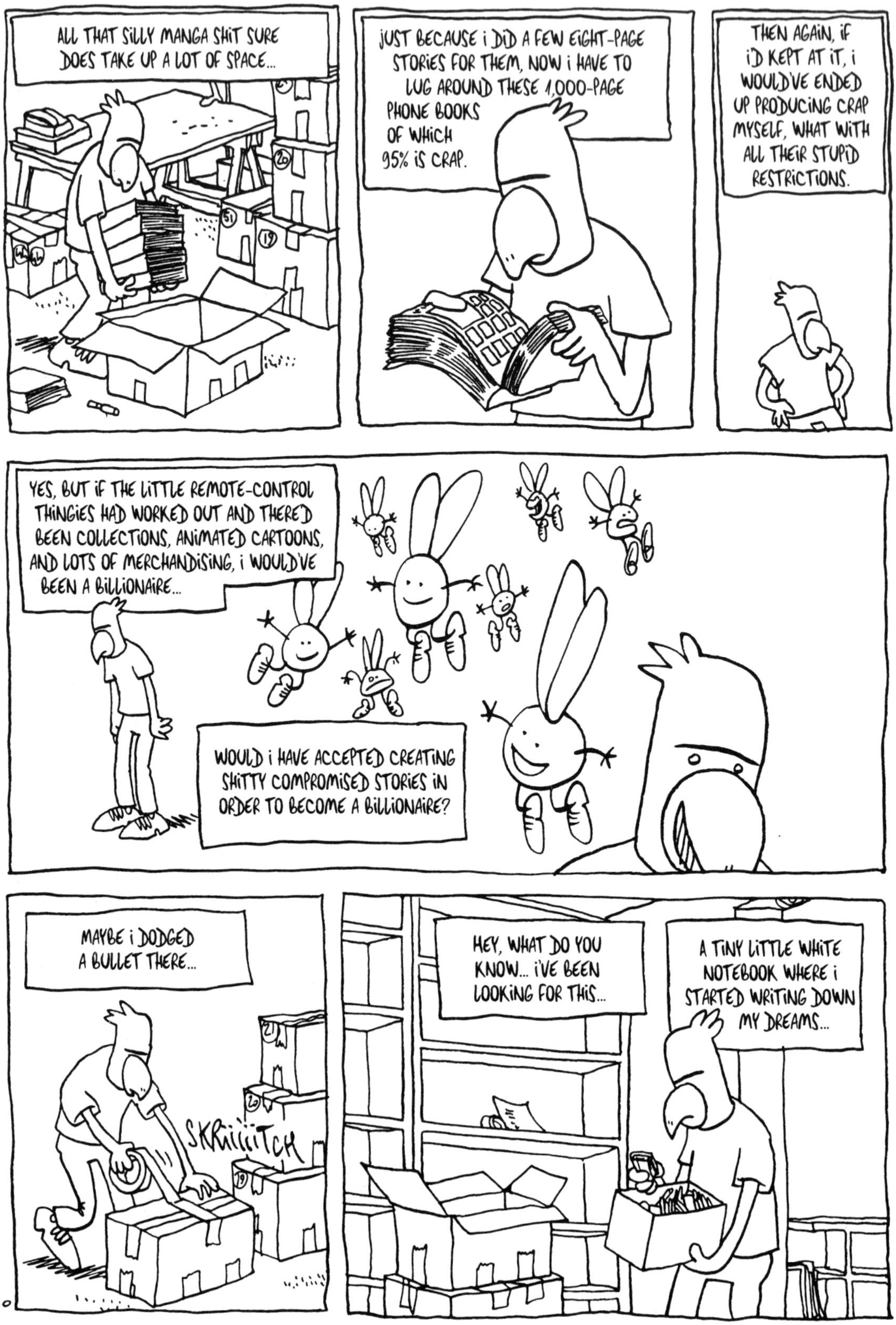
ALL THAT SILLY MANGA SHIT SURE DOES TAKE UP A LOT OF SPACE...
JUST BECAUSE I DID A FEW EIGHT-PAGE STORIES FOR THEM, NOW I HAVE TO LUG AROUND THESE 1,000-PAGE PHONE BOOKS OF WHICH 95% IS CRAP.
THEN AGAIN, IF I'D KEPT AT IT, I WOULD'VE ENDED UP PRODUCING CRAP MYSELF, WHAT WITH ALL THEIR STUPID RESTRICTIONS.
YES, BUT IF THE LITTLE REMOTE-CONTROL THINGIES HAD WORKED OUT AND THERE'D BEEN COLLECTIONS, ANIMATED CARTOONS, AND LOTS OF MERCHANDISING, I WOULD'VE BEEN A BILLIONAIRE...
WOULD I HAVE ACCEPTED CREATING SHITTY COMPROMISED STORIES IN ORDER TO BECOME A BILLIONAIRE?
MAYBE I DODGED A BULLET THERE...
SKRIIIIITCH
HEY, WHAT DO YOU KNOW... I'VE BEEN LOOKING FOR THIS...
A TINY LITTLE WHITE NOTEBOOK WHERE I STARTED WRITING DOWN MY DREAMS...

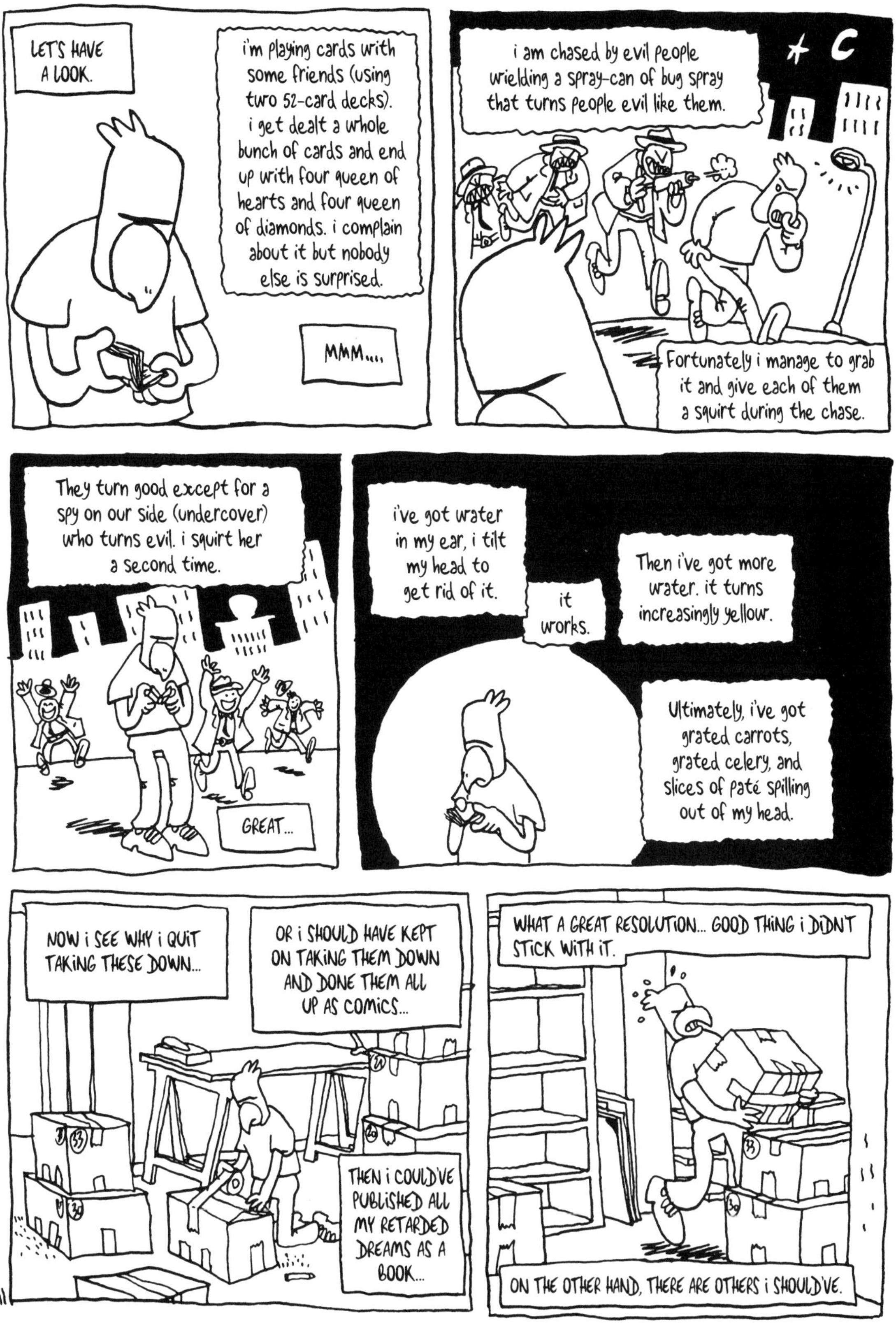
LET'S HAVE A LOOK.
i'm playing cards with some friends (using two 52-card decks). i get dealt a whole bunch of cards and end up with four queen of hearts and four queen of diamonds. i complain about it but nobody else is surprised.
MMM....
i am chased by evil people wielding a spray-can of bug spray that turns people evil like them.
Fortunately i manage to grab it and give each of them a squirt during the chase.
They turn good except for a spy on our side (undercover) who turns evil. i squirt her a second time.
GREAT...
i've got water in my ear, i tilt my head to get rid of it.
it works.
Then i've got more water. it turns increasingly yellow.
Ultimately, i've got grated carrots, grated celery, and slices of paté spilling out of my head.
NOW i SEE WHY i QUIT TAKING THESE DOWN...
OR i SHOULD HAVE KEPT ON TAKING THEM DOWN AND DONE THEM ALL UP AS COMICS...
THEN i COULD'VE PUBLISHED ALL MY RETARDED DREAMS AS A BOOK...
WHAT A GREAT RESOLUTION... GOOD THING i DIDN'T STICK WITH iT.
ON THE OTHER HAND, THERE ARE OTHERS i SHOULD'VE.

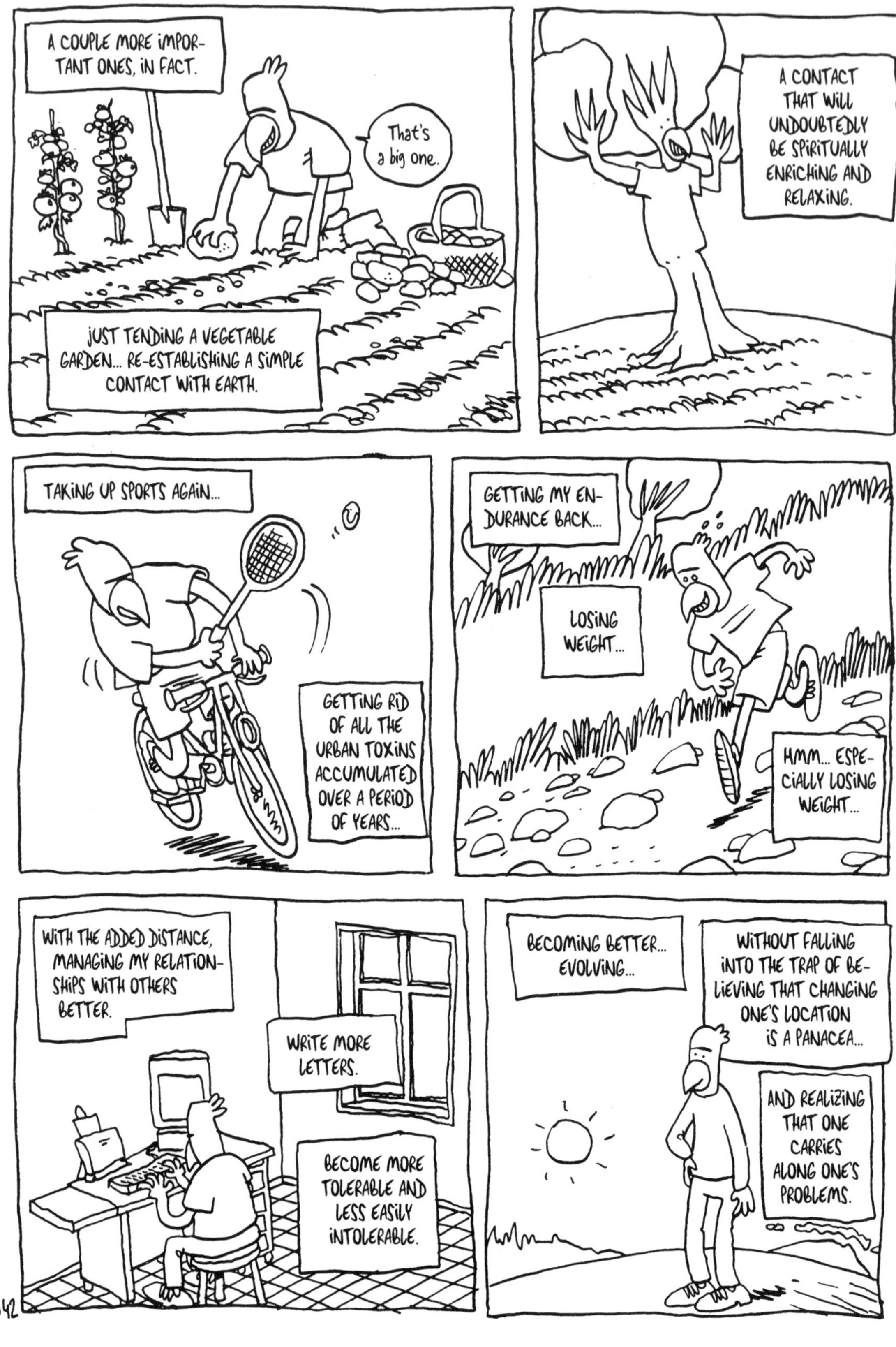
A COUPLE MORE IMPORTANT ONES, IN FACT.
That's a big one.
JUST TENDING A VEGETABLE GARDEN... RE-ESTABLISHING A SIMPLE CONTACT WITH EARTH.
A CONTACT THAT WILL UNDOUBTEDLY BE SPIRITUALLY ENRICHING AND RELAXING.
TAKING UP SPORTS AGAIN...
GETTING RID OF ALL THE URBAN TOXINS ACCUMULATED OVER A PERIOD OF YEARS...
GETTING MY ENDURANCE BACK...
LOSING WEIGHT...
HMM... ESPECIALLY LOSING WEIGHT...
WITH THE ADDED DISTANCE, MANAGING MY RELATIONSHIPS WITH OTHERS BETTER.
WRITE MORE LETTERS.
BECOME MORE TOLERABLE AND LESS EASILY INTOLERABLE.
BECOMING BETTER... EVOLVING...
WITHOUT FALLING INTO THE TRAP OF BELIEVING THAT CHANGING ONE'S LOCATION IS A PANACEA...
AND REALIZING THAT ONE CARRIES ALONG ONE'S PROBLEMS.

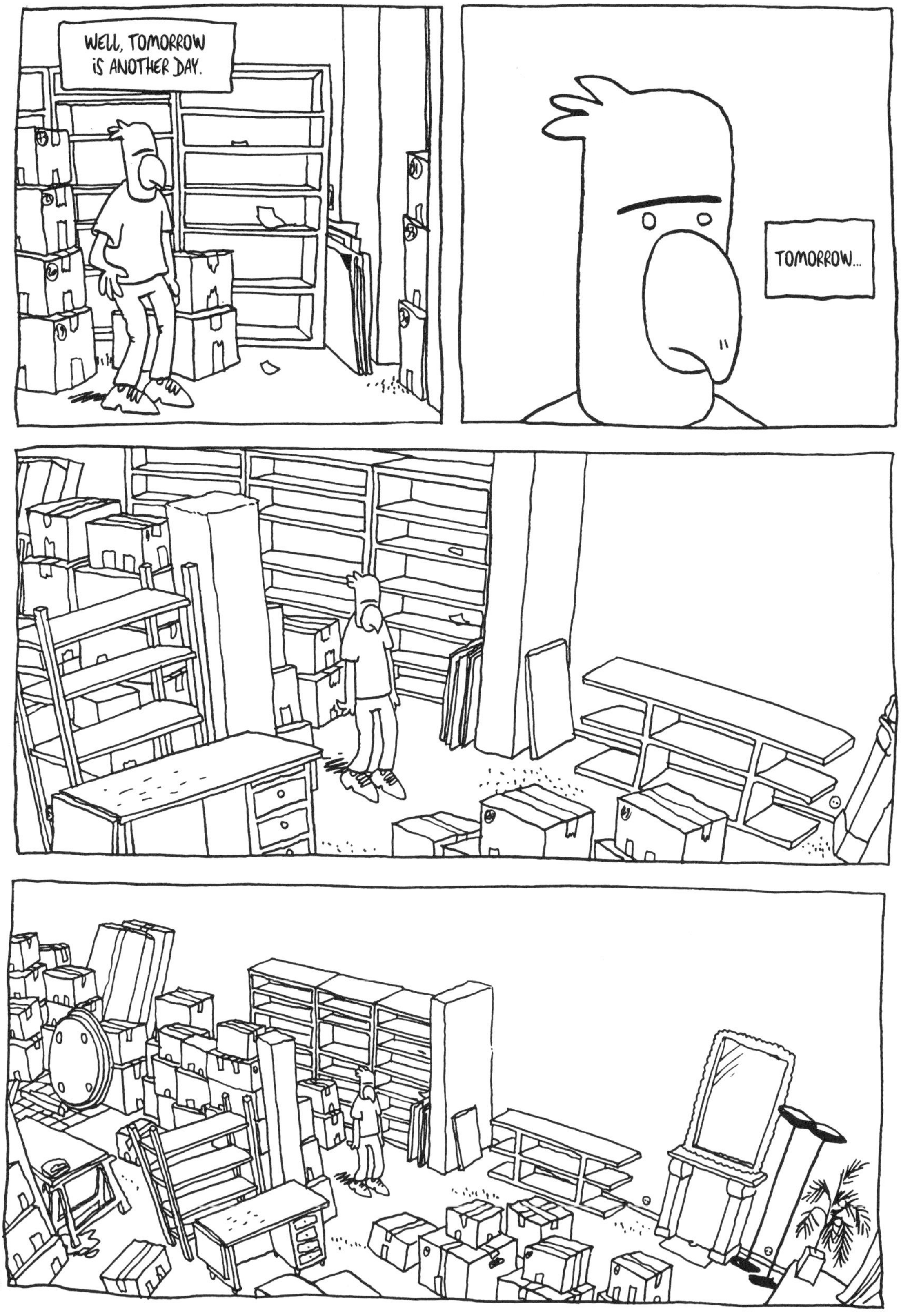
WELL, TOMORROW IS ANOTHER DAY.
TOMORROW...

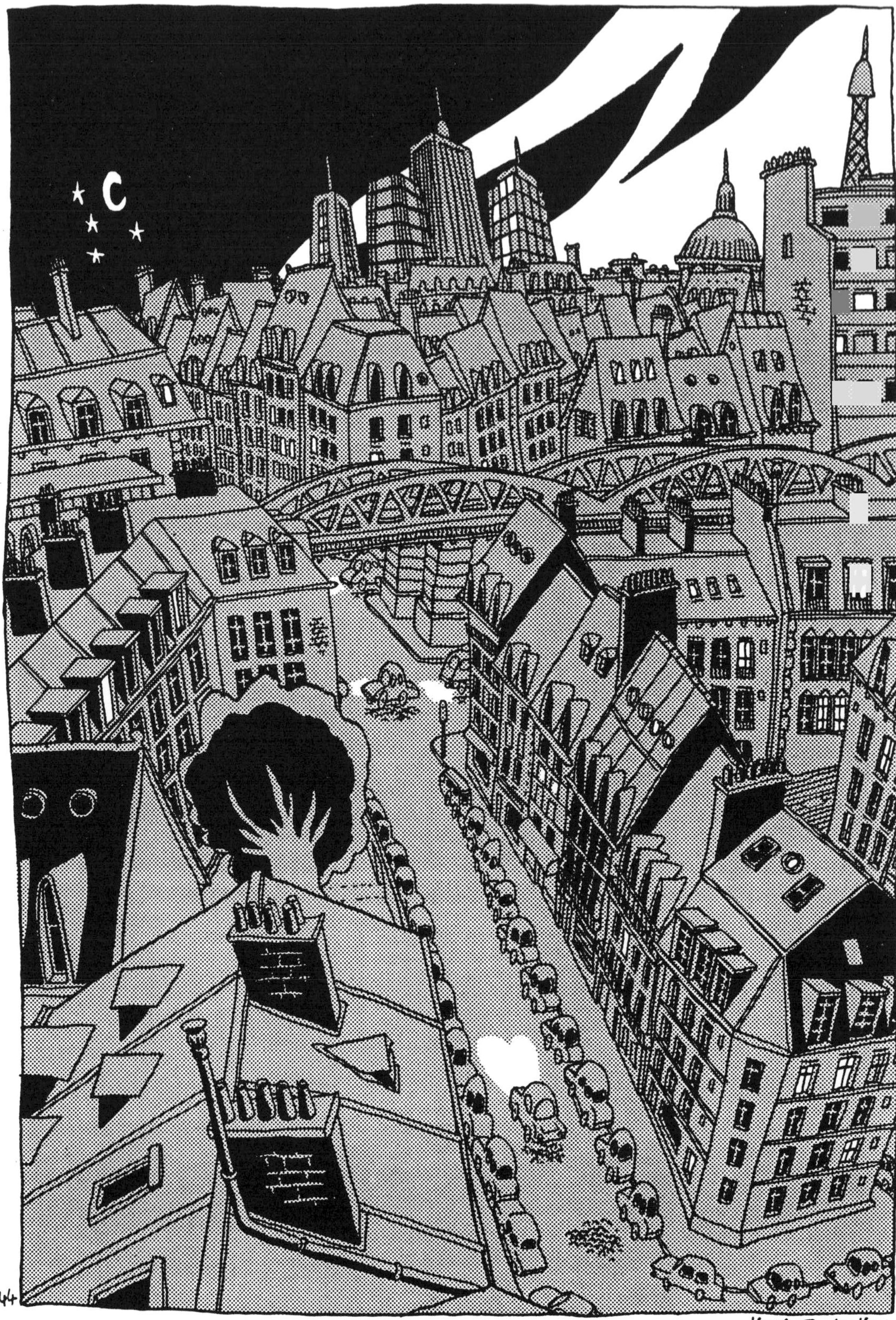
LEWIS TRONDHEIM

During the period when Lewis was working on his comic book, its quarterly schedule, despite its exhausting nature, also brought a stimulating aspect to the enterprise: The short amount of time between Lewis's finishing his pages and their being made available to the public. Consequently, the people close to him and more generally the people depicted in his comics were made aware of how Lewis perceived them, and which events and which thoughts he had chosen to highlight.

We thought it would be amusing to ask them for their reactions, and tell us in turn their feelings about Lewis and how he depicted them...

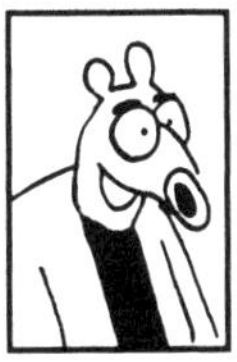

CHARLES BERBERIAN (cartoonist): Lewis turned me into a badger in this book. That's not really how I see myself, of course. But no big deal. I don't see Lewis as a... although, actually... Yes. He's perfect in that guise, the slight grumpiness, the stern gaze, and at the same time a touch of a stuffed animal you'd hand to a baby... Lewis has a good eye. I must have something of a badger in me. I'm fucked.

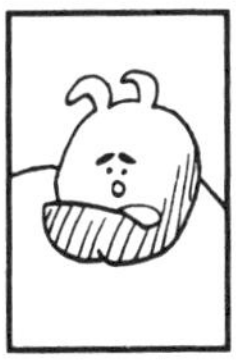

PHILIPPE DUPUY (cartoonist): Allow me to clear something up here! If I told these stories of proctology and severed fingers, it was not done out of mean-spiritedness, or with the intent of making Lewis sick. Killo egged me on. If not for him, I never would have talked about hemorrhoids the size of olives or anuses turned inside out like trumpets which, admittedly, must be awfully inconvenient if you want to sit down.

Nor would I have told the story of the broken glass that sliced off part of two of my fingers, the cool sensation that immediately followed, and my astonishment at the sight of these missing pieces of flesh... shortly thereafter the gush of blood, then the pain. And what pain! I should mention that the glass was razor sharp and went straight through. I should also mention that the tips of your fingers are dense with tiny, hypersensitive nerve endings... for the purpose of touching, of course... so you can imagine, once you slice into that...

Ah! And then there was the anesthesia, when they had to sow me back up again. One shot in each finger, right into the open wound!

All right, enough... Lewis is going to say I'm doing it on purpose. Not at all: It was Killo who pushed me into telling all this, I swear.

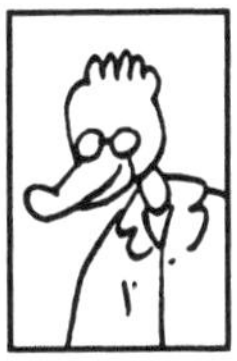

ROBERT (friend): In the real-life story Lewis relates, there is talk of the Bible and of gods. The discussion, initially quite inoffensive, is quick to degenerate. Instead of speaking of *Love*, the basic message of any god, a wall of incomprehension rose between us. One might give it the name *Religion*. The wall that motivates religious fanatics of every stripe: It blinds the weak and vulnerable spirit who, feeling invested with a divine mission, blindly strikes out against those who hadn't asked to get involved. At the end of the road: hate, death — appalling. Under such circumstances, how is one to believe... And yet life persists in believing. In believing in men and women so that — one day — we might focus on that which is essential.

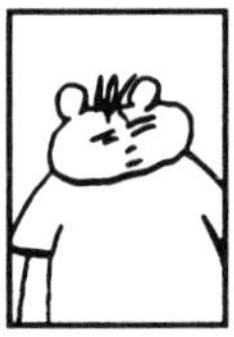

KILLOFFER (cartoonist): The stuff I tell Lewis in real life bears no relation to the stuff he puts in my mouth in this book. Among all the things I've said to him, Lewis deliberately chose to record only the least significant. Why? Because he is completely uninterested in the truth! Much less the hard truths that I inevitably lay on him.

For make no mistake, it is not through this book that the reader can hope to learn anything about Lewis. He may feel flattered, if he is so inclined, to be taken as a confidante in these faux confessions, so good for the publisher, but that's about it.

More than ever, Lewis remains an enigma.

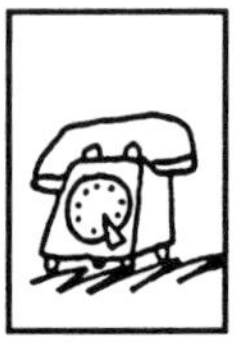

MY MOTHER: I recognized my telephone advice and I was amused to see the reactions on the other end (a valuable lesson for me).

Thank you for allowing me to learn about a big part of your hidden life and your inner demon. I have one of those too, a quite embarrassing one in fact.

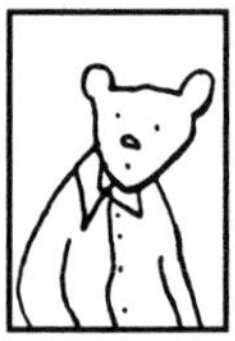

STANISLAS (cartoonist): One day, I confided a secret to Lewis:

"On the first Wednesday of every month, at noon, I'm always surprised by the song of the sirens, because I would really like to be expecting them, just before they're turned on."

Some time after that, Lewis called me on the phone:

"Hi, how're you doing? Bla bla bla... Hey, Stan! Listen to the sirens!"

It was shortly after 11:59, on the first Wednesday of the month. Ever since then, once a month when the sirens sing, I think of Lewis and he thinks of me.

In his comics, Lewis draws me as a speechless bear, and yet I do have stories to tell, as I just proved. Why? Maybe because everyday reality does not interest me. Anyway, Lewis chronicles that splendidly.

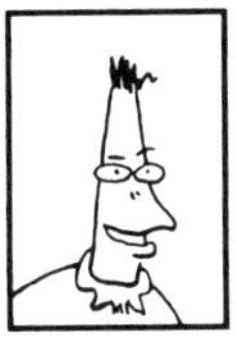

JEAN-LOUIS GAUTHEY (original publisher): My use as a character within this book allows me to specify a few details pertaining to the image Lewis has chosen to paint of me.

First of all, it will interest the reader to learn that the anecdote on page 49 was in no way related under the circumstances described herein by the author... My propensity toward telling horrific stories is indulged only within a small group and definitely never within the earsplitting promiscuity of an inexpensive restaurant. The truth is that I had told Lewis and Brigitte this story two or three days earlier, when they had very kindly asked me to break bread with them. The food was excellent and the company pleasant, and so I deemed it necessary to apply the brakes to this burgeoning friendship by unveiling one of those anecdotes that, for many years now, has enabled me to avoid the rigors of Parisian social life. Lewis and Brigitte laughed heartily, we parted ways in delight, and they never again invited me to their home. To this day I have not been allowed to meet their two children.

But allow me to focus on the main correction I need to bring to this episode. Let us render justice to History: This pee balloon was merely the final blow in a long row of insults and injuries this little girl and I had inflicted upon each other on a quotidian basis. On that very same day she had spat in my face, after I clocked her with my shoe, because she'd busted my skateboard, because I'd yanked out a fistful of her hair, because I was in love with her: An exemplary illustration of the sentimental confusion upon which childish romances run aground, and only the most trivial aspect of which Lewis sought to retain. How regrettable. For you see, dear reader, in order to make you laugh and enlist you onto his side, Lewis has reworked or occulted certain facts... E.g., the fact that it was David and I who "helped" the loathsome Rasta by pulling his underwear back up as he was standing, a task that was neither pleasant nor gratifying insofar as we had to engage in a tactile manner with his member, whose scale was on the pretentious side.

I realize, dear reader, my recriminations when measured against the quality of this book are but crabs and cavils. And moreover I realize that you will have found me pedantic and vain. But know that this assumed frown is what allows me to admit that I really like Lewis and I consider this book to be his greatest triumph. For which I am eternally grateful.

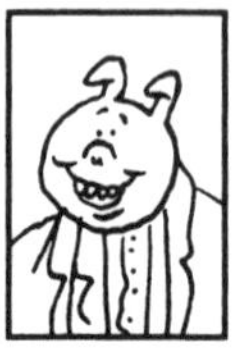

LAURENT (friend): Dear Lewis, when I had to move to Belgium for professional reasons, I thought I would be able to start from scratch, live as a stranger in a strange land, and enhance my own reputation by presenting a more positive facade. Alas, at the very first dinner to which I was invited, I met eight rabid fans of your work who soon realized that I was, and I quote, "the bonehead who fell asleep at the wheel." Thanks a lot! Due to your efforts, I have been classified as a stuntman with somnambulistic tendencies and my car insurance has mysteriously skyrocketed. Again — thanks, and kudos!

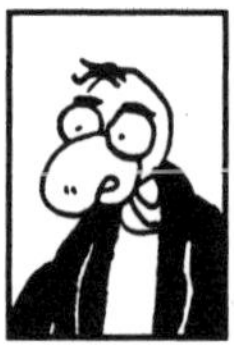

DAVID B. (cartoonist): So I'm a *Sarcorhamphus Condovae*? Physically I do see a certain resemblance, but depicting me as a carrion-eater, I who survive entirely on a diet of whole rice... The same sort of fantasy runs rampant in the depiction of the other characters... Were you not aware, Mister Trondheim, that the *Ailuropoda Melanolenca* (Giant Panda) lives exclusively on bamboo shoots? And yet, whom do you depict as a panda? Emile Bravo, one of the most appalling boozers to haunt the cartooning milieu. I will draw a discreet veil over Jean-Louis Gauthey, in whom one recognizes an *Ophiophagus Hannah* (King Cobra), with hands and feet!

Through this handful of examples one begins to get a sense of the ravages inflicted by this plague of today's comics: A failure to secure proper documentation.

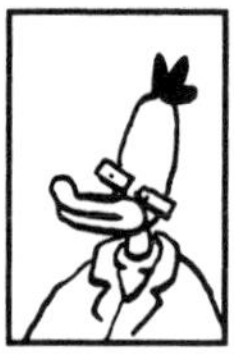

JEAN-YVES DUHOO: Out of the 973 panels that comprise the totality of *Approximate Continuum Comics*, depictions of Lewis Trondheim appear on 839, which is to say 86% of its acreage. Only the single displays have been inventoried here, as I have voluntarily omitted the 27 images showing the hero in duplicate, conversing with another incarnation of himself, sometimes stupider, sometimes tougher and meaner than the real Lewis Trondheim, or at least the real life he has revealed here, or that he revealed to his studio mates during the creation of this autobiography; I have also omitted the 4 panels where the hero splits into four, no doubt in his quest for self-improvement, which is praiseworthy when one knows that, even split into 18 pieces, taking the form of a multicephalic monster, he doesn't appear to succeed, at least by the end of his Parisian life, which by the way is depicted quite well, with a richness of detail that will always delight me. One thing is striking: In the totality of Lewis's appearances in adult form, one can see his eyes open in only 14% of the panels, whereas the frequency climbs to 66% in the scenes where he is a child, an eloquent image of the seriousness of adulthood that Lewis Trondheim introspects with such verve and irony that one almost forgets the furrowed brow of this odd bird whose adventures, I hope, do not end here.

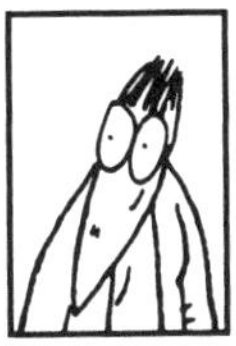

BRIGITTE FINDAKLY (colorist, spouse): Pursuant to page 127, I can inform you that on that day Carl Barks was wearing an Uncle Scrooge tie. He had lunch at the "Cinderella Inn" where he partook in some Chablis, and he found it so delicious that he drank a lot of it: Hence his good mood throughout the meal. He was accompanied by a couple of Americans who kept on pestering him, with the goal of having Carl Barks adopt them so that they might be his sole inheritors (Carl Barks having no heirs of his own), apparently a very common practice in the U.S. Shortly thereafter, he ran into Ray Bradbury, who was exiting from the "Chez Walt" restaurant.

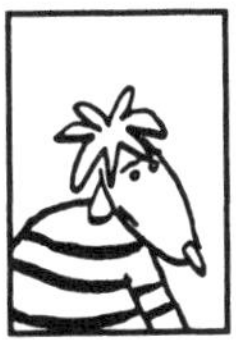

JEAN-CHRISTOPHE MENU (cartoonist):

Page 23: It's true: I've always got a runny nose, even when eating. I'll have to bear this in mind when I go to Japan.

Page 36: It's true that I'd started a story about my snow trip for Annestay's mythical project. All of us ultimately waited to see what the first issue would look like, wisely as it turned out.

Page 49: True. I also knew how to pee really high, bend my fingers every which way, and draw: in one word, a celebrity.

Page 67-72: It's true that I was a little bit drunk, but it's not true that I stuck the toilet brush in everyone's face, just David's and Lewis's, because I'd already punished Killo with a loogie, and Stanislas and Brigitte hadn't helped to shove me into the shower. Also, I don't think I still had the brush when David sent me careening head first into the microwave, but I don't remember that part very well. I was young.

Page 97: It's true that the homemade andouille from the Saint-

Vaast market is quite tasty. But it's not true that I ate it all myself. I shared a couple of slices. Well, at least one slice: with Joëlle Jolivet.

Page 101: Lewis does not know how to draw me engaged in one of my legendary dances. It looks like I'm endeavoring to take flight. But I never endeavor to take flight indoors.

Page 137: It's true.

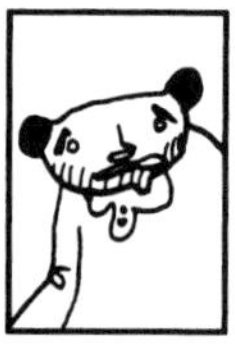

EMILE BRAVO (cartoonist): "No, Jean-Louis, I won't let you include that! It totally undermines me! Besides which, I want to be the only person to draw in my book!" That is how Lewis responded upon seeing my rebuttal, illustrated with very biting drawings. "Emile, what you did is great, but I just can't publish it. Lewis... You understand... Look, you can write some copy explaining that in exchange for an SASE and five francs, the readers can be sent this page in Xerox form. It's well worth that... We'll make a ton of dough!" That is what the original publisher of the piece of fiction you now hold in your hands told me... I'll let you imagine the reality of the milieu... Miles away from the friendly workspace described in... in this patchwork of lies! I have no further comment... Emile Bravo (professional artist.)

U.S. publisher's note: Go to the fantagraphics.com website (under the listing for *Approximate Continuum Comics*) to see Emile's rebuttal.

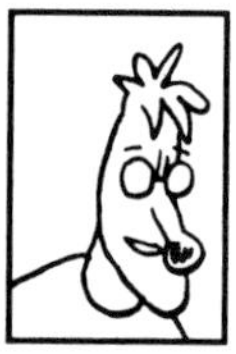

DIDIER TRONCHET (cartoonist): Lewis, please do not forget: I am that sensitive creature who, behind and to the left of you in the studio, was creating a work full of passion for future generations: A tall young man in love with literature who delighted in the oratorical jousts from which would inevitably flow witticisms and billingsgate.

What have you done, what have you made of me in this opuscule? A grotesque, long-nosed goofball whose, and I quote, "bicycle was stolen." There. That's it. What of the wounded man remains in this parody of accuracy?

Since your departure I have been feverishly awaiting your footstep in the hallway, burning with an interior flame (like all great betrayed romantics) so that I might inflict upon you the ass-kicking you so richly deserve.

PS: On the other hand, you sure nailed all those other jerks in the studio! Ha ha! Well done!

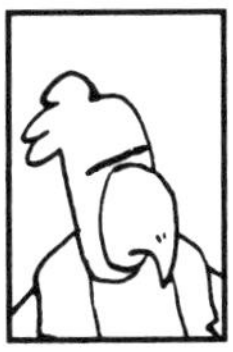

LEWIS: Originally, when Jean-Louis suggested that I create a quarterly comic book, I did not for a second think I would end up drawing the 144 pages that comprise this collection. My idea was to alternate fictional stories and gags with bits of dreams or true-life stories, and ultimately what I ended up with was almost exclusively autobiography. Once again, improvisation caused me to wander off in a direction different from the intended one. Ah well, so it goes. Oh, I called up Jean-Louis to ask him if my memory is accurate and he said it was seeing the first pages of "The Fly" that made him suggest I make a comic book out of it, and I was fine with this, but since it was wordless, it would've been a rather quick read, so he said I could interpolate bits of real-life stories to flesh it out, and then we agreed we'd call it *Bzz* but I became aware there already was something called *Bzzz* in Italy but fine, we'd do it anyway, and then ultimately, when I brought Jean-Louis my pages it was something totally different. And then fifteen years later, when Kim Thompson suggested that as a follow-up to the U.S. edition of this book Fantagraphics put out its edition of *The Fly* (which I eventually drew as a separate book anyway) under the title *Buzz Buzz*, I said, "Sure, why not?"

OTHER COMICS BY LEWIS TRONDHEIM IN ENGLISH:

Edited and translated by Kim Thompson. Design by Lewis Trondheim and Alexa Koenings. Production by Paul Baresh. Lettering by Stephanie Noell and Priscilla Miller. Special thanks to Kristy Valenti. Associate Editor: Eric Reynolds. Published by Gary Groth and Kim Thompson. *Approximate Continuum Comics (Approximativement)* © 2001 Lewis Trondheim and Cornélius. This edition © 2011 Fantagraphics Books. All rights reserved, permission to quote or reproduce material for reviews or notices must be obtained from Fantagraphics Books, in writing, at 7563 Lake City Way NE, Seattle, WA 98115. Visit the Fantagraphics website at www. fantagraphics.com. Distributed to bookstores in the U.S. by W.W. Norton and Company, Inc. (800-233-4830). Distributed to comics shops in the U.S. by Diamond Comic Distributors (800-452-6642 ex862). Distributed in Canada by Canadian Manda Group (800-452-6642 ex215). First edition April, 2011. Printed in Hong Kong ISBN 978-1-60699-410-8.